ASPEN PUBLISHERS

REAL ESTATE

Second Edition

Robin Paul Malloy

E.I. White Chair and Distinguished Professor of Law

Director, Center on Property, Citizenship, and Social Entrepreneurism

College of Law

Affiliated Professor of Economics
(by Courtesy Appointment)

Syracuse University

James Charles Smith

John Byrd Martin Professor of Law

University of Georgia

The *Emanuel Law Outlines* Series

Wolters Kluwer
Law & Business

AUSTIN   BOSTON   CHICAGO   NEW YORK   THE NETHERLANDS

www.AspenLaw.com

No part of this publication may be reproduced or transmitted in any form or by
any means, electronic or mechanical, including photocopy, recording, or any information storage
and retrieval system, without permission in writing from the publisher. Requests for permission
to make copies of any part of this publication should be mailed to:

Aspen Publishers
Attn: Permissions Department
76 Ninth Avenue, 7th Floor
New York, NY 10011-5201

To contact Customer Care, e-mail customer.service@aspenpublishers.com,
call 1-800-234-1660, fax 1-800-901-9075, or mail correspondence to:

Aspen Publishers
Attn: Order Department
PO Box 990
Frederick, MD 21705

Printed in the United States of America.

1 2 3 4 5 6 7 8 9 0

ISBN 978-0-7355-9010-6

Malloy, Robin Paul, 1956-
      Real estate / Robin Paul Malloy, James Charles Smith.—2nd ed.
            p. cm.—(The Emanuel law outlines series)
      Includes indexes.

      ISBN 978-0-7355-9010-6

   1. Vendors and purchasers—United States—Outlines, syllabi, etc. 2. Real estate business—Law and legislation--United
States—Outlines, syllabi, etc. 3. Real property—United States—Outlines, syllabi, etc. I. Smith, James Charles, 1952- II. Title.

   KF665.Z9M343 2010
   346.7304'37—dc22

                                                                                          2010028345

This book is intended as a general review of a legal subject. It is not intended as a source for
advice for the solution of legal matters or problems. For advice on legal matters, the reader
should consult an attorney.

About Wolters Kluwer Law & Business

Wolters Kluwer Law & Business is a leading provider of research information and workflow solutions in key specialty areas. The strengths of the individual brands of Aspen Publishers, CCH, Kluwer Law International and Loislaw are aligned within Wolters Kluwer Law & Business to provide comprehensive, in-depth solutions and expert-authored content for the legal, professional and education markets.

CCH was founded in 1913 and has served more than four generations of business professionals and their clients. The CCH products in the Wolters Kluwer Law & Business group are highly regarded electronic and print resources for legal, securities, antitrust and trade regulation, government contracting, banking, pension, payroll, employment and labor, and healthcare reimbursement and compliance professionals.

Aspen Publishers is a leading information provider for attorneys, business professionals and law students. Written by preeminent authorities, Aspen products offer analytical and practical information in a range of specialty practice areas from securities law and intellectual property to mergers and acquisitions and pension/benefits. Aspen's trusted legal education resources provide professors and students with high-quality, up-to-date and effective resources for successful instruction and study in all areas of the law.

Kluwer Law International supplies the global business community with comprehensive English-language international legal information. Legal practitioners, corporate counsel and business executives around the world rely on the Kluwer Law International journals, loose-leafs, books and electronic products for authoritative information in many areas of international legal practice.

Loislaw is a premier provider of digitized legal content to small law firm practitioners of various specializations. Loislaw provides attorneys with the ability to quickly and efficiently find the necessary legal information they need, when and where they need it, by facilitating access to primary law as well as state-specific law, records, forms and treatises.

Wolters Kluwer Law & Business, a unit of Wolters Kluwer, is headquartered in New York and Riverwoods, Illinois. Wolters Kluwer is a leading multinational publisher and information services company.

Dedication

For Gina and Giovanni

RPM

To my parents, Charles Tero Smith and Joyce Clara Poenisch Smith

JCS

Summary of Contents

Table of Contents

CHAPTER 1

MARKET CONTEXT FOR REAL ESTATE TRANSACTIONS

CHAPTER 2

REAL ESTATE BROKERS

CHAPTER 3

PREPARING TO CONTRACT

CHAPTER 4

THE EXECUTORY CONTRACT

CHAPTER 5

CONDITION OF THE PROPERTY

CHAPTER 6

CLOSING THE CONTRACT

CHAPTER 7

CONTRACT REMEDIES

CHAPTER 8

ALLOCATING TITLE RISK BY CONTRACT AND BY DEED

LAND DESCRIPTIONS

CHAPTER 10

THE PUBLIC LAND RECORDS

CHAPTER 11

TITLE PRODUCTS

CHAPTER 12

IMPROVING THE EFFICIENCY OF THE TITLE SYSTEM

CHAPTER **13**

HOUSING MARKETS AND PRODUCTS

CHAPTER 14

POSSESSION AND USE OF MORTGAGED PROPERTY

CHAPTER 15

RESIDENTIAL MORTGAGE MARKETS AND PRODUCTS

CHAPTER 16

MORTGAGE OBLIGATIONS

CHAPTER 17

TRANSFERS BY BORROWERS AND LENDERS

CHAPTER 18

DEFAULT AND ACCELERATION

CHAPTER 19

FORECLOSURE

CHAPTER 20

MORTGAGE SUBSTITUTES

CHAPTER 21
JUNIOR MORTGAGES

CHAPTER 22
THE COMMERCIAL REAL ESTATE MARKET

CHAPTER 23

COMMERCIAL REAL ESTATE FINANCING

Preface

Real Estate covers a lot of ground. Your course may include a range of different topics, depending upon your teacher, your law school, and the state or region where you attend school. Many schools offer a course called "Real Estate" or "Real Estate Transactions" that surveys all major areas. Other schools have more discrete offerings, sometimes called "Land Finance," "Mortgages," or "Real Estate Contracts." Whatever the nature of your course, we address all topics that you are likely to encounter. Most courses consider both residential and commercial transactions, with varying degrees of emphasis, and we give ample coverage to both sectors.

We have written this Emanuel Law Outline with two primary objectives in mind. First, we provide clear, concise statements of the relevant legal rules and principles. Real estate law has a special vocabulary of its own that you must master. The chapters and the glossary in your Emanuel Law Outline will supply you with definitions of all the key concepts. It will also give you a framework that will make it easier to understand the substantive law of real estate.

Our second objective relates to the lawyering process. In addition to laying out the basic substantive law, we describe the market context for real estate transactions. We explain what the buyer, seller, lender, borrower, and other participants are hoping to achieve as they enter into deals. We indicate the types of problems that parties to real estate transactions and their lawyers regularly confront. We also tell you about the lawyer's role in the real world as a planner, drafter, negotiator, risk manager, and problem solver.

We expect that this dual approach, highlighting both substantive legal rules and practical considerations, will prove especially useful to you. Your teacher may put primary importance on learning substantive law through traditional exam questions that lead you through issue spotting and legal analysis. Alternatively, your teacher's exam may expect you to demonstrate a knowledge of the problems encountered in the real world and the applications of real estate law to those problems. Virtually all teachers will want you to display some understanding of both types of expertise.

Please remember that your Emanuel Law Outline is intended to supplement your casebook and other assigned materials, not to replace them. It is a tool designed to reinforce your learning of the rules and the underlying principles contained in your course book.

Best of luck, and we hope you enjoy Real Estate!

Robin Paul Malloy
E.I. White Chair and Distinguished Professor of Law
Director, Center on Property, Citizenship,
   and Social Entrepreneurism
College of Law
Affiliated Professor Economics (by Courtesy
   Appointment)
Syracuse University

James Charles Smith
John Byrd Martin Professor of Law
School of Law
University of Georgia

Casebook Correlation Chart

(Note: General sections of the outline are omitted for this chart. NC = not directly covered by this casebook.)

Malloy/Smith: Real Estate Emanuel Law Outline (*by chapter and section heading*)	Bender, Hammond, Madison & Zinman: *Modern Real Estate Finance and Land Transfer* (4th Ed. 2008)	Korngold & Goldstein: *Real Estate Transactions: Cases and Materials on Land Transfer, Development and Finance* (5th Ed. 2009)	Nelson & Whitman: *Real Estate Transfer, Finance, and Development: Cases and Materials* (8th Ed. 2009)	Malloy & Smith: *Real Estate Transactions: Problems, Cases, and Materials* (3rd Ed. 2007)	Lefcoe: *Real Estate Transactions* (6th Ed. 2009)
CHAPTER 1 MARKET CONTEXT FOR REAL ESTATE TRANSACTIONS					
I. **Market Context for Real Estate Transactions**	NC	NC	NC	1-24	17-28
II. **Measuring Value**	NC	NC	NC	2-3, 4-5	22-23
III. **Categories of Costs**	19-29	13-15, 30-33	2	6-7	85-90
IV. **Market-Related Conduct**	NC	NC	NC	8-9	NC
V. **Categories of Market Risks**	NC	NC	NC	9-13	NC
VI. **Role of the Lawyer**	1-13	15-30	NC	13-24	7-16
CHAPTER 2 REAL ESTATE BROKERS					
I. **Types of Brokers**	NC	30-32	18-19	26-27	29-30
II. **Regulation of Brokers**	25-26	35, 50-51	8,18	25	34-38
III. **Brokers' Duties to Clients**	23-25, 26	30-31	18-21	28-32	47-57
IV. **Types of Brokers' Listing Contracts**	19-22	30-32	2-9, 16-17	26-27	38-47
V. **Whom Does the Broker Represent?**	NC	51-63	2-7, 18-19	28-32	47-57
VI. **When is the Commission Earned?**	19-22	43-49	4-5, 12-17	33-40	43-44
VII. **Brokers' Duties to Non-Client Buyers**	NC	50-53	19-21	NC	NC
VIII. **Brokers and Lawyers**	25-26	26-29	NC	41-60	37-38
CHAPTER 3 PREPARING TO CONTRACT					
I. **Real Estate Transaction Time Line**	NC	NC	NC	62-65	NC
II. **Precontract Activities**	27-35	2-7	NC	NC	22-27
III. **Contract Formation**	NC	85-92	21-42	66, 83-84	66-74
IV. **Letters of Intent**	NC	NC	NC	66-80	65-66
V. **Options**	NC	NC	NC	67-75	3-4

Malloy/Smith: Real Estate Emanuel Law Outline (*by chapter and section heading*)	Bender, Hammond, Madison & Zinman: *Modern Real Estate Finance and Land Transfer* (4th Ed. 2008)	Korngold & Goldstein: *Real Estate Transactions: Cases and Materials on Land Transfer, Development and Finance* (5th Ed. 2009)	Nelson & Whitman: *Real Estate Transfer, Finance, and Development: Cases and Materials* (8th Ed. 2009)	Malloy & Smith: *Real Estate Transactions: Problems, Cases, and Materials* (3rd Ed. 2007)	Lefcoe: *Real Estate Transactions* (6th Ed. 2009)
CHAPTER 4 **THE EXECUTORY CONTRACT**					
I. **Contract as Risk Management Device**	29-30, 33	99-109, 117-121	116-126	89-96, 97-102	97-103, 108-109, 115-118, 120-124
II. **Contract Modifications**	NC	NC	NC	NC	NC
III. **Equitable Conversion**	33	76, 81, 82-83	86-96	64, 90-96	120-124
IV. **Major Contract Conditions**	31-35	94-126	116-126	97-102	97-103, 108-109
CHAPTER 5 **CONDITION OF THE PROPERTY**					
I. **Quantity**	203-206	183-203	142-151	205-219	129, 361-371
II. **Quality**	120	211-235	168-187	111-136	105-118
III. **Lender Liability**	NC	235-246	NC	NC	NC
CHAPTER 6 **CLOSING THE CONTRACT**					
I. **The Closing Process**	86-90	167-178, 183	151-163	139, 141-144	314-323, 335-340, 342-344, 346
II. **Attorney's Role at Closing**	86-90	165-167	165, 259-260	NC	NC
III. **Doctrine of Merger**	34, 58-60	204-209, 210-211	574-581	145-150	146-149
IV. **Escrow**	271-273	178-183	163-168	152-155	314-323
CHAPTER 7 **CONTRACT REMEDIES**					
I. **Damages at Law**	NC	141-152, 161-163	43-52	157-158	NC
II. **Equitable Remedies**	70	127-141, 152-157, 159-161, 164	49, 51, 52-58	164-169	157-158
III. **Liquidated Damages**	64-73	164	59-65	159-163	159-164
IV. **Tort Remedies**	NC	NC	NC	175-178	NC
V. **Slander of Title and Lis Pendens**	NC	257-267	NC	170-175	158-159
VI. **Other Remedies**	NC	NC	NC	NC	NC
CHAPTER 8 **ALLOCATING TITLE RISK BY TITLE AND BY DEED**					
I. **Title Under the Real Estate Contract**	44-49	99-109	NC	181-191, 201-202	127-132, 135-137
II. **Formal Requirements for Deeds**	NC	167-173, 176-179, 183-203	127-136, 137-164	139	335-348
III. **Deed Constructional Rules**	NC	173-176	NC	NC	NC
IV. **Defective Deeds**	NC	171	NC	245, 293	338-339

Malloy/Smith: Real Estate Emanuel Law Outline (*by chapter and section heading*)	**Bender, Hammond, Madison & Zinman:** *Modern Real Estate Finance and Land Transfer* (4th Ed. 2008)	**Korngold & Goldstein:** *Real Estate Transactions: Cases and Materials on Land Transfer, Development and Finance* (5th Ed. 2009)	**Nelson & Whitman:** *Real Estate Transfer, Finance, and Development: Cases and Materials* (8th Ed. 2009)	**Malloy & Smith:** *Real Estate Transactions: Problems, Cases, and Materials* (3rd Ed. 2007)	**Lefcoe:** *Real Estate Transactions* (6th Ed. 2009)
CHAPTER 8 (cont'd) V. **Deed Covenants of Title**	51-53	NC	191-197	192-196, 197-200	348-356
VI. **Relationship Between Title Under Contract and Deed Covenants**	NC	NC	NC	157	NC
CHAPTER 9 **LAND DESCRIPTIONS** I. **Types of Descriptions**	204-206	183-195	142-150	205-210	361-71
II. **The Surveyor**	NC	196, 203-204	NC	210-217	371-377
III. **Legal Adequacy of Description**	NC	183, 197-203	139	217-229	344
CHAPTER 10 **THE PUBLIC LAND RECORDS** I. **Common Law Priority Rules**	NC	256	NC	231	258-261
II. **Functions of Recording System**	NC	256-257, 271-274, 311-312	201-204	231	244-245
III. **Title Search Process**	NC	282, 296-301, 306-311	219-233	231-237	246-256
IV. **Types of Recording Acts**	NC	257, 267-271	204-210	237-238	261-262
V. **Bona Fide Purchaser Status**	NC	281-282, 283-285, 286-292	213-217	238, 239-252	264-265
VI. **Off-Record Risks**	NC	NC	210-211, 217-218	252-257	NC
VII. **BFP Shelter Rule**	NC	NC	NC	257-261	265-271
VIII. **Recorded Interests That Are Difficult or Impossible to Find**	NC	299, 308-312	203	263-268	274-282
CHAPTER 11 **TITLE PRODUCTS** I. **Title Abstracts**	NC	314, 315-316, 316-321	238-239	269-270	291, 292
II. **Attorneys' Title Opinions and Certificates**	NC	314, 316, 316-321, 322, 323	238-239	271-276	292-293
III. **Title Insurance: Owners' and Lenders' Policies**	74-85	314, 324-334	238-253	277-281, 282-285, 289-290	287-289, 291, 294-308
CHAPTER 12 **IMPROVING THE EFFICIENCY OF THE TITLE SYSTEM** I. **Title Standards**	NC	339-340	NC	294-298	NC
II. **Adverse Possession**	NC	339-340	NC	293-294	NC
III. **Title Curative Acts**	NC	339-340, 342-344	NC	298-290	NC

Malloy/Smith: Real Estate Emanuel Law Outline (*by chapter and section heading*)	Bender, Hammond, Madison & Zinman: *Modern Real Estate Finance and Land Transfer* (4th Ed. 2008)	Korngold & Goldstein: *Real Estate Transactions: Cases and Materials on Land Transfer, Development and Finance* (5th Ed. 2009)	Nelson & Whitman: *Real Estate Transfer, Finance, and Development: Cases and Materials* (8th Ed. 2009)	Malloy & Smith: *Real Estate Transactions: Problems, Cases, and Materials* (3rd Ed. 2007)	Lefcoe: *Real Estate Transactions* (6th Ed. 2009)
CHAPTER 16 MORTGAGE OBLIGATIONS					
I. Form of Obligation	NC	NC	573	407	6, 175-176
II. Usury	241-243	414-416, 714-722	908-909, 958	407-414	NC
III. Late Payment	243-245	NC	561-568	414-416, 417-423	NC
IV. Prepayment	259-271	474-475, 711-712	546-560	416-423	209-222
V. Nondebt obligations	NC	NC	573-574	424-427	NC
CHAPTER 17 TRANSFERS BY BORROWERS AND LENDERS					
I. Transfers of Mortgaged Property	286-293	465-472, 472-475	447-455, 460-483	427-433, 438-440	225-230, 232-237
II. Transfers of Mortgage Debt	NC	479-485, 492-494	483-490, 492-507	433-438	NC
CHAPTER 18 DEFAULT AND ACCELERATION					
I. Setting for Default	389-390	497-498, 504	NC	NC	430
II. Default Clauses	NC	NC	NC	441	NC
III. Acceleration	401-06	504-507	586-595, 606	443-445	438-440
CHAPTER 19 FORECLOSURE					
I. The Nature of Foreclosure	418-419	509-510	612-614	447-448	430-432
II. Strict Foreclosure	97, 418-419, 475	509-512	627-640	449	433-434
III. Key Concepts	NC	546-555	NC	447-448	463-477
IV. Judicial Foreclosure	419-420, 425-427	512-519	614-627	449-452	440-445
V. Power of Sale Foreclosure	421-425	519-535	641-673	453-454	440-445
VI. Priority of Mortgage That Refinances Prior Mortgage	NC	NC	NC	455-461	NC
VII. Deed in Lieu of Foreclosure	394-397, 399-400	535-537, 872, 873-874, 875	581-585	471-472	481-482, 484
VIII. Economics of Foreclosure	451	NC	NC	461-464	454-456
IX. Statutory Mortgagor Protections	NC	537-545, 547-559	692-699	464-470	443-445
CHAPTER 20 MORTGAGE SUBSTITUTES					
I. The Use of Mortgage Substitutes	114-117	NC	272-277	473-474	NC

Malloy/Smith: Real Estate Emanuel Law Outline (by chapter and section heading)	Bender, Hammond, Madison & Zinman: Modern Real Estate Finance and Land Transfer (4th Ed. 2008)	Korngold & Goldstein: Real Estate Transactions: Cases and Materials on Land Transfer, Development and Finance (5th Ed. 2009)	Nelson & Whitman: Real Estate Transfer, Finance, and Development: Cases and Materials (8th Ed. 2009)	Malloy & Smith: Real Estate Transactions: Problems, Cases, and Materials (3rd Ed. 2007)	Lefcoe: Real Estate Transactions (6th Ed. 2009)
CHAPTER 20 (cont'd)					
II. Disguised Mortgage	112-113	NC	277-284	474-475	NC
III. Absolute Deed Intended as Security	112-113	NC	284-286, 291-292	474-475	NC
IV. Negative Pledge	113	369, 374-376	348-356	477-482	NC
V. Installment Land Contract	119-120	376, 559-572	294-307, 311-317, 326-327, 330-332, 342-345	483-494	711-713
CHAPTER 21 JUNIOR MORTGAGES					
I. Leveraging a Deal	351-353	NC	1200-1201	495-496	NC
II. The Market for Secondary Financing	351-353	NC	488	496-497	NC
III. Protecting the Junior Mortgage	353-356	455	NC	498-503	NC
IV. The Mortgage Subordination	361-369	777-787	NC	503-506	NC
V. The Wrap-Around Mortgage	352	NC	893-910	508-510	705-710
CHAPTER 22 THE COMMERCIAL REAL ESTATE MARKET					
I. Financing Arrangements by and Between Lenders	295-306	728-736, 740-777	NC	519-527, 539-563	502-513
II. Selecting a Development Entity	333-336	NC	NC	511-512	NC
III. Commercial Lending and Article 9 of the UCC	360-361	NC	NC	513-514	NC
IV. The Lawyer's Role in Commercial Transactions	210-215, 217, 218-223, 740	777	NC	NC	NC
CHAPTER 23 COMMERCIAL REAL ESTATE FINANCING					
I. Market Coordination of Commercial Development	NC	777-87	843-49	522-531	499-500
II. Common Devices for Structuring Loans	NC	NC	NC	511-512	501-502, 504-505
III. Gap Financing	179-184	NC	NC	NC	NC
IV. Loan Participations	494-495	NC	NC	529	NC
V. Leasing Considerations in Commercial Transactions	592-630	812-858	370-372, 1209-1225	519-522	741-742

Capsule Summary

CHAPTER 1
MARKET CONTEXT FOR REAL ESTATE TRANSACTIONS

I. MARKET CONTEXT FOR REAL ESTATE TRANSACTIONS

   A. **Creating and capturing value:** The primary objective in every real estate transaction is to create or capture value. [1–2]

   B. **Market choice:** Markets are all about choice and the opportunity for choice making. [2]

II. MEASURING VALUE

   A. **Accounting profits:** Accounting profits are returns from an activity compared to its costs. [2]

   B. **Economic profits:** Economic profits are the returns compared to alternative market choices. [2]

   C. **Risk and return:** Risk and return are related. The more risk a transaction has, the more return one expects. [2–3]

   D. **Value and utility:** Market choice and the measure of success are discussed in terms of value, utility, and comparative advantage. [3]

   1. **Marginal utility:** A measure of incremental value.

   E. **Comparative advantage:** When one party can perform a function more efficiently than another she has a comparative advantage. [3]

III. CATEGORIES OF COSTS

   A. **Out-of-pocket costs:** These are the actual expenses paid to participate in a transaction. [3]

   B. **Opportunity costs:** These costs are comparative in nature because they relate to the cost of forgone market opportunities. [3]

   C. **Sunk costs:** These are costs that cannot be recovered when a party abandons a course of action. [3]

IV. MARKET-RELATED CONDUCT

   A. **Transactional misbehavior:** Transactional misbehavior is a party's attempt to change the dynamics of a deal after it is made. [3–4]

   B. **Rent-seeking behavior:** Rent-seeking involves extracting value from favorable laws and regulations. [4]

V. CATEGORIES OF MARKET RISKS

A. Temporal risk: Temporal risk is usually due to incomplete knowledge or information. [4]

B. Transactional risk: The four types of transactional risk are investor or ownership risk, credit risk, marketplace risk, and transfer risk. [4–5]

   1. Investor or ownership risk: Entrepreneurial risk.

   2. Credit risk: Debtor's willingness and ability to pay.

   3. Marketplace risk: Risk from market forces.

   4 Transfer risk: Risk of error in the process of doing and documenting the transaction.

VI. ROLE OF THE LAWYER

A. Lawyer as risk manager: The lawyer who understands market context can use law to control, reduce, and spread risk for the client's benefit. [5]

B. Professional responsibility in a market context: The lawyer's duty to advance the client's interest in real estate transactions is limited by her ethical obligations. [5]

C. Types of real estate law practice: The two major divisions of law practice relate to residential and commercial activities. [5–6]

   1. Residential practice: Generally focused on housing products.

   2. Commercial practice: Generally focused on real estate development and financing.

D. Lawyer's fee arrangement: Under the Model Rules of Professional Conduct, the lawyer is to charge a reasonable fee based on a variety of factors. [6]

   1. Residential: Generally involves a fixed fee.

   2. Loans: Generally, a fixed fee or percentage of the loan amount.

   3. Commercial: Generally, fees are billed at an hourly rate.

CHAPTER 2

REAL ESTATE BROKERS

I. TYPES OF BROKERS

A. Market role: Brokers have expertise in locating parties who wish to enter into real estate transactions. [9]

B. Market segmentation: Most brokers specialize geographically and by type of transaction. [9–10]

   1. Residential brokers: Residential brokers mainly sell homes and condominiums.

   2. Commercial brokers: Commercial brokers sell office buildings, apartment houses, and other commercial properties.

3. **Leasing brokers:** Leasing brokers represent landlords who own residential or commercial properties.

4. **Mortgage brokers:** Commercial mortgage brokers help developers and other owners locate project financing at favorable terms. Residential mortgage brokerage began as a major activity in the United States in the 1980s.

II. REGULATION OF BROKERS

A. Licensing and state regulation: Each state licenses and regulates brokers and salespersons. [10–11]

    1. **Levels of licenses:** A broker has a "full" license. A real estate salesperson has a license to act only under the supervision of a licensed broker.

    2. **Effect of lack of license:** If an unlicensed person renders broker's services, he generally cannot collect a commission.

B. Antitrust law and price fixing: Brokers associations often set commission rates until 1950, when the Supreme Court held that this practice is illegal. [11]

III. BROKERS' DUTIES TO CLIENTS

A. Agency law: The broker's duties stem from the law of agency. They are fiduciary duties. [11]

B. Duty of loyalty: The broker owes the client the duty of loyalty. The broker may not disclose the owner's lowest acceptable offer or "bottom line" and may not engage in self-dealing. [11–12]

C. Duty of full disclosure: A broker must promptly give the client all material information. [12]

D. Duty of confidentiality: The broker must keep the confidences of the client. [12]

IV. TYPES OF BROKERS' LISTING CONTRACTS

A. Open listing (Nonexclusive): The broker earns his commission by procuring a *ready, willing, and able* buyer. [12–13]

    1. **Sale by owner:** The owner can sell the property by himself without paying a commission.

    2. **Procuring cause:** To earn the commission the broker must be the procuring cause of the sale.

B. Exclusive agency: The broker is the exclusive agent for the listed property. The owner can sell without paying a commission. [13]

C. Exclusive right to sell (Exclusive listing): The seller must pay the commission even if he sells the property on his own. [13]

D. Net listing: The seller agrees to pay the broker all amounts received in excess of a set price. [13]

E. Constructional preference for seller: Courts construe an ambiguous contract in favor of the client. [13]

F. Duration of listing contract: Listing contracts normally have fixed expiration dates. [13–14]

   1. Protective periods: A term requires the owner to pay a commission for a sale to a person who had contact with the broker within a set period of time after expiration of the listing contract.

V. WHOM DOES THE BROKER REPRESENT?

A. Listing broker as seller's agent: The broker represents the seller. [14]

B. Cooperating or selling broker: In many sales, two brokers are involved—not only a listing broker, but also a cooperating or selling broker. Within the Multiple Listing Service (MLS) system, most sales involve two brokers. The cooperating or selling broker is an agent of the listing broker and thus a subagent of the seller. [14]

   1. Multiple Listing Service: For residential sales within the Multiple Listing Service (MLS) system, most sales involve two brokers.

   2. Rule of subagency: Traditionally, the cooperating or selling broker is an agent of the listing broker and thus a subagent of the seller.

C. Buyer's broker: The buyer's broker represents the buyer. [14]

   1. Representation of multiple prospective buyers: A conflict of interest may arise when a broker represents two people who both seek to buy the same property.

D. Dual representation: A broker may, with full disclosure and consent, lawfully represent both seller and buyer in the same transaction. [14–15]

   1. Implied dual agency: A dual agency may arise by implication when both seller and buyer are led to believe the broker is representing them.

E. Transaction broker: A transaction broker has an arms'-length relationship with all parties. [15]

VI. WHEN IS THE COMMISSION EARNED?

A. Brokers' claims against sellers [15–16]

   1. Traditional rule: When customer is found: The broker earns his commission when he procures a ready, willing, and able buyer at terms acceptable to the seller.

   2. Different terms: The agreed terms of the sale may differ from those set forth in the listing agreement.

   3. Seller's acceptance of buyer: By signing the contract of sale, the broker agrees that the buyer located by the broker is acceptable.

   4. New rule: Implied condition that sale must close: A growing trend is to imply the condition that the sale must close in order for the broker to earn the commission.

   5. Express conditions in the contract of sale: If the transaction fails to close because a condition in the contract of sale is not satisfied, no commission is payable.

B. Brokers' claims against buyers [16]

    1. Lack of privity: The seller's broker may seek damages against a buyer who defaults after signing a contract, but generally this fails for lack of privity.

    2. Implied contract theory: Sometimes a broker succeeds in suing a defaulting buyer based on an implied contract.

    3. Tort theory: The seller's broker may also try to recover from a defaulting buyer for tortious interference with contract.

C. Requirement of a written listing agreement: Common law permits an oral listing agreement, but many states have statutes that require a written listing agreement. [16–17]

VII. BROKERS' DUTIES TO NONCLIENT BUYERS

A. Traditional tort duties: Traditionally brokers owe nonclient buyers the same duties that sellers owe nonclient buyers—not to commit fraud, not to make intentional or negligent misrepresentations of fact, and, in many states, to disclose material latent defects. [17]

    1. Broker liability for innocent misrepresentations: Some courts impose liability for innocent (nonnegligent) misrepresentations.

B. Trend: Enlarging broker disclosure duties: In some states, the broker may have a duty to investigate the property and disclose defects. [17]

VIII. BROKERS AND LAWYERS

A. Unauthorized practice of law: Most states now permit brokers to prepare standard-form contracts of sale. Several tests are used to determine when a broker's activities constitute unauthorized practice. [17–18]

    1. Contracts versus conveyances test: A broker can prepare contracts of sale but not deeds.

    2. Simple-complex test: A broker can complete simple forms.

    3. Incidental test: A broker can draft related documents without charge.

    4. Public interest test: A court can allow a broker to do what is in the public interest.

B. Lawyers acting as brokers: Statutes that provide for the regulation of brokers typically have an exemption for attorneys. [18]

    1. Incidental test: Some states exempt brokers' services incidental to the attorney's law practice.

    2. Total exemption: Some states totally exempt attorneys.

CHAPTER 3
PREPARING TO CONTRACT

I. REAL ESTATE TRANSACTION TIME LINE

A. Four stages [23–24]

1. **Precontract:** Parties gather information to reduce risk and negotiate. Information is valuable and often costly. Parties should consider disclosure issues and the potential interests of third parties.

2. **Executory contract:** After entering into the contract, the parties investigate and resolve conditions and get ready to perform their obligations.

3. **Closing:** At closing, the parties complete their transaction, performing their obligations and checking the other side's performance.

4. **Post-closing:** After closing, the parties and their lawyers record documents and handle other matters.

B. Legal capacity—consequences of simple rules: Simple rules have practical consequences for the practice of law. The requirement of a grantor and a grantee for every deed means that evidence of legal capacity is essential for an entity to serve as grantor. [24]

II. PRECONTRACT ACTIVITIES

A. Information: The process of gathering precontract information raises issues concerning the duties to investigate and to disclose. [24]

1. **Typical situation:** Generally, a seller/owner should have better information about the property than the buyer.

B. Cost of information: To encourage investment in information, we should limit the scope and content of the duty to disclose. [25]

C. Third-party factors: Interests of third parties or public regulation may limit the scope and content of a contract. [25]

III. CONTRACT FORMATION

A. Statute of frauds: Requires a memorandum with essential terms. [25–27]

1. **Elements of the writing:** To satisfy the statute of frauds, a writing must:

   ■ Name the parties

   ■ Describe the property

   ■ Show an intent to sell and buy

   ■ Be signed by the party to be charged

   ■ State the price (in many states)

2. **Distinction between writing and contract:** Parties may have a contract without a writing.

3. **Defendant's admission of contract:** Generally, admitting a contract without a writing does not bar operation of the statute.

4. **Part performance:** An oral contract is enforceable if a party can show part performance or equitable estoppel.

    a. **Evidentiary theory:** Possession and building improvements may be evidence of a contract.

    b. **Hardship theory:** Reliance on an oral contract may result in hardship.

5. **Equitable estoppel:** Equity may prevent the operation of the statute.

B. **Parol evidence rule:** Parol evidence cannot be used to contradict clear terms of a writing. [27]

1. **Four corners of the document:** Limits interpretation to the document.

2. **Ambiguity:** If there is ambiguity parol evidence can be used.

3. **Contradiction:** Parol evidence is not permitted to contradict the document.

4. **Timing:** The rule applies to action prior to the writing.

C. **Integration clauses:** An integration clause merges all the terms of negotiation and any other understandings into the written contract. [28]

IV. LETTERS OF INTENT

A letter of intent is used to outline essential terms while the parties are working toward a formal contract. [28]

A. **Legal effect:** A letter of intent, as a type of "agreement to agree," is usually unenforceable. In some cases, however, a letter of intent with enough terms may create a binding contract. [28]

V. OPTIONS

An option gives its holder an enforceable right to purchase on stated terms at a later date, upon exercise of the option. [28–29]

CHAPTER 4

THE EXECUTORY CONTRACT

I. CONTRACT AS RISK MANAGEMENT DEVICE

A. **Approaches to allocate executory period risk:** A well-drafted contract manages risk through a combination of five approaches: [33–34]

1. **Conditions**

2. **Warranties**

3. **Representations**

4. **Affirmative covenants and negative covenants**

5. **Remedies**

B. **Lawyer's role in explaining contract:** The lawyer makes sure that the contract is enforceable and has essential terms to protect the client's expectations. The lawyer's primary duty is to the client, but he may also owe duties to a nonclient. [34]

1. **Duty to nonclients:** A lawyer may have a duty to nonclients.

II. CONTRACT MODIFICATIONS

A. **Subsequent agreement:** Contract modifications are not usually subject to the parol evidence rule, but the statute of frauds may require a written modification. [35]

B. **Waiver:** Once a party waives a contract term, it is gone forever and cannot be reinstated. [35]

C. **Estoppel:** A party is estopped from enforcing a contract term if his actions have reasonably caused the other party to act to her detriment. Generally, the estopped party can reinforce the term with proper notice. [35]

III. EQUITABLE CONVERSION

A. **Split of title:** The doctrine of equitable conversion splits the title at the moment of contract. The buyer gets equitable title to the property, and the seller retains legal title. [35]

1. **Legal title:** Is in the seller.

2. **Equitable title:** Is in the buyer.

B. **Traditional risk of loss rule:** Risk of loss, under the traditional rule, goes to the buyer as equitable owner. [36]

C. **Other risk of loss rules** [36]

1. **Control:** Sometimes risk of loss is placed on the party with physical control over the property.

2. **Uniform Vendor and Purchaser Risk Act:** The seller has the risk of loss until he transfers possession or legal title to the buyer.

3. **Implied condition:** Some states put the risk on the seller, implying that improvements must continue to exist without material damages until closing.

D. **Contract allocation of risk of loss:** The parties may expressly allocate risk of loss between the parties. [36]

E. **Insurance:** Each party has an insurable interest. The benefit of insurance generally runs only to the party who is named as insured. [36–37]

IV. MAJOR CONTRACT CONDITIONS

A. Categories of conditions: Real estate contracts have express conditions, implied conditions, conditions precedent, conditions subsequent, and simultaneous conditions. A duty to act in good faith is generally implied. Identifying the proper nature of a condition is important because it can have different consequences for the parties. [37–38]

B. Inspection condition: The contract often conditions some elements of performance on the completion of a variety of building and property inspections. [38]

C. Mortgage financing: Since most real estate is not purchased in an all-cash deal, there is generally a provision making the purchase conditioned on obtaining suitable mortgage financing. [38–37]

    1. Seller financing: Seller takes a purchase-money mortgage.

CHAPTER 5

CONDITION OF THE PROPERTY

I. QUANTITY

Issues of quantity involve ensuring that the buyer gets and the seller gives nothing more or less than the amount of real estate bargained for in the contract. [43]

A. Sale by the acre: In such a sale, the price is calculated by the exact acreage or area. [43]

B. Sale in gross: In such a sale, the price is for property as a whole regardless of its exact quantity. A land description referring to acres followed by the term "more or less" denotes a sale in gross. [43–44]

C. Survey: The survey confirms the quantity of land or area of improvements. [44]

II. QUALITY

A. Caveat emptor: This traditional rule, "buyer beware," puts the burden of inspection on buyer unless expressly assumed by seller under the contract. [44]

B. Pro-buyer doctrines [44–45]

    1. Intentional or negligent misrepresentation: If seller intentionally or negligently misrepresents property quality, buyer can rescind or recover damages.

    2. Concealment: If seller takes action to conceal a defect, buyer can recover. Seller has made the defect latent.

    3. Latent dangerous defects: Seller must disclose a known latent defect that is dangerous to possessors or users of the property.

    4. Attorney liability: An attorney has a duty not to give false or misleading information to nonclients.

C. **Implied duty to disclose material defects:** In many states, a seller must disclose material latent defects known to her. There may also be a duty to disclose information when a buyer asks a direct question about an issue that is material and about which the seller has special knowledge. [45]

1. **Materiality:** A defect is material if it significantly affects value, or if it goes to an express contract representation.

2. **Knowledge:** Seller may have a duty to disclose known defects.

3. **Residential versus commercial transactions:** Generally, disclosure requirements are greater in a residential transaction.

D. **Stigma and nondisclosure statutes:** The seller may have a duty to disclose a stigma defect that affects the value of a property. Some state statutes shield sellers and brokers from failure to reveal certain stigma-related information, such as a horrible crime having been committed on the property or a possessor's disease. [46]

E. **Statutory duty to disclose:** Statutes require the disclosure of some information, such as the presence of radon gas or lead-based paints or lead pipes in a home. [46]

1. **Interstate Land Sales Full Disclosure Act:** A federal act applicable to certain land sales.

F. **Implied warranties for sale of new housing:** The seller of a new home by implication warrants the habitability of the property. Other implied warranties include fitness for a particular purpose. [46–47]

G. **Express allocations of risk of quality** [47–48]

1. **Right of inspection:** The buyer should contract for a right of inspection, and the contract should set a specific time for inspections and standards for confirming quality.

2. **"As Is" clause:** The "As Is" sale allocates all responsibility to the buyer. The seller makes no representations or warranties as to quality.

3. **Express warranties:** Express warranties should be in the contract to avoid problems with the parol evidence rule. Buyers of new homes often get a homeowner's warranty (H.O.W.) insurance policy. Sometimes similar policies are used for the sale of used homes to cover major defects.

   a. **Homeowner's Warranty (H.O.W.) programs:** Provide limited insurance to buyers for defects.

III. LENDER LIABILITY

A lender may be liable for defects in a property if it has exercised managerial control over the property or taken a proprietary interest in the property or if it knows or should know that the seller is likely to commit fraud. [48]

A. **Lender acting like developer:** There may be liability if lender exercises managerial control and has a proprietary interest in the project. [48]

B. **Lender's knowledge of seller's fraud:** There may be liability if lender participates in the seller's fraud. [48]

CHAPTER 6

CLOSING THE CONTRACT

I. THE CLOSING PROCESS

A. The exchange: At the closing, the buyer exchanges money for the seller's delivery of the documents of conveyance. [53]

B. Effective conveyance: An effective conveyance must be written, it must identify both parties, it must describe the property, it must show an intent to convey, there must be actual or constructive delivery, and the grantee must accept the grant. [54]

    1. Relationship to recording statutes: Recording is not required to create the interest.

II. ATTORNEY'S ROLE AT CLOSING

A. Multiple representation: An attorney should not represent multiple clients where doing so will impair her ability to represent the best interest of each. Multiple representation is allowed upon full disclosure to all clients and obtaining their consent. A lawyer must withdraw from multiple representation if a conflict becomes acute. [54–55]

    1. Conflict and removal: A lawyer must withdraw in the event of litigation.

    2. Seller and buyer: A lawyer may represent both with proper disclosure and consent.

    3. Payment of fees: A lawyer can accept a payment from a third party.

        a. The attorney as adverse party: The attorney must avoid being in an adverse position to the client.

B. Duty to nonclients: A duty to a nonclient may arise if the nonclient reasonably believes that the attorney is representing her, and the attorney understands or should understand that this misconception is operating. [55–56]

    1. Implied or informal representation: Dual representation may arise informally or by implication.

    2. Duty not to further client's wrongful conduct: Attorney must not further a client's wrongful actions.

III. DOCTRINE OF MERGER

Merger means that everything that came before the closing is merged into the documents exchanged at closing. Prior warranties and representations are extinguished. [56]

A. Exceptions to the doctrine of merger [56–57]

    1. Collateral matters: Collateral matters are generally ones that do not affect title. Parties can express an intent to have collateral agreements survive closing and operation of merger.

    2. Fraud: A party who commits fraud cannot benefit from merger.

3. **Mutual mistake:** Reformation avoids the doctrine of merger when both parties proceeded under a mutual mistake.

IV. ESCROW

A. **Loan escrow:** Each month the borrower pays the lender an amount to be placed in escrow for paying property taxes, insurance premiums, and other charges. [57]

B. **Closing escrow:** In some states, like California, third-party agents close transactions in escrow. Documents and funds are delivered in escrow, with the agent completing the closing when all contract requirements are satisfied. [57]

C. **Contingency escrow:** This type of escrow is used to permit the parties to close despite their discovery of a problem, such as needed property repairs or a title flaw. Funds are paid to an escrow agent, who releases them when the problem is resolved pursuant to the provisions of the escrow agreement. [57–58]

CHAPTER 7

CONTRACT REMEDIES

I. DAMAGES AT LAW

The basic idea behind damages is *fungibility*—that a person can be made whole by a payment in cash. [63]

A. **Expectancy damages:** Either party may recover expectancy damages for loss of bargain. [63–64]

1. **Resale by seller after buyer's breach:** The time of resale is not generally the same as the time of the breach.

B. **Reliance damages:** Either party may recover reliance damages, including out-of-pocket costs and lost profits, if proven and foreseeable. [64]

C. **Fair market value** [64–65]

1. **Fair:** Fairness depends on the method of calculating the loss.

2. **Market:** The appropriate market for calculating the loss depends on geographical proximity and the type of property.

3. **Value:** The three primary ways to calculate value are comparable sales, replacement cost, and income flow.

   a. **Comparable sales:** Value relative to similar properties.

   b. **Replacement cost:** Cost to rebuild.

   c. **Income flow:** Value of income generated by rents.

4. **Time value of money:** Money paid today is worth more than the same amount paid in the future. Future payments must be discounted to present value.

5. **Time of the breach:** The measure of damages is the difference between the contract price and the fair market value at the time of breach.

D. **Lost profits:** An injured party may recover lost profits, provided there is proof of damage in fact and a reasonable estimate of the amount. [65]

II. EQUITABLE REMEDIES

A. **Reformation:** When, due to mutual mistake, the documents do not reflect the parties' intentions, the court may correct the documents through reformation. [66]

B. **Rescission:** This releases a party from a contract due to the other party's default, misrepresentation, or an unfulfilled condition. [66]

C. **Specific performance:** Traditionally the buyer or the seller is entitled to cause a breaching party to perform through specific performance. Uniqueness and mutuality of remedy are the usual explanations. The trend is to require that each party show an independent basis for this relief. [66]

1. **Specific performance with abatement:** If the breaching party cannot fully perform, the court may grant specific performance with a reduction in the purchase price.

D. **Equitable liens:** The vendor's lien secures the unpaid price. The vendee's lien secures return of the deposit and any out-of-pocket costs that are recoverable. [66–67]

1. **Vendor's lien:** Secures unpaid price.

2. **Vendee's lien:** Secures deposit.

III. LIQUIDATED DAMAGES

The parties may agree to quantify damages from a breach that may take place in the future. Such liquidated damages must not operate as a penalty or forfeiture. They must be reasonable, and actual damages must be difficult to ascertain at the time of the contract. [67]

A. **Actual damages not easy to ascertain:** As determined at the time of contracting. [67]

B. **Reasonable amount:** The amount cannot operate as a penalty. [67]

IV. TORT REMEDIES

Tort law, unlike contract law, allows for recovery of punitive damages. Tort law allows damages unrelated to economic loss. It also eliminates the need for contract privity. Instead, one must show a duty, a breach of that duty, and the foreseeability of the loss. Tort based recoveries include: [67]

A. **Negligence** [67]

B. **Strict liability** [68]

C. **Emotional distress** [68]

D. **Punitive damages** [68]

V. SLANDER OF TITLE AND LIS PENDENS

    A. Slander of title: Slander of title is a tort that allows the owner of property to sue a person who wrongfully records documents that cloud title. This action protects the "good name" of title to property. [68]

    B. Lis pendens: Lis pendens is a procedure that puts notice of pending judicial action on the public record. To be proper, the subject matter of the action must relate to the status of title to the property. [68–69]

VI. OTHER REMEDIES

There are other remedies available including injunction, declaratory judgment, and ejectment. [69]

CHAPTER 8

ALLOCATING TITLE RISK BY CONTRACT AND BY DEED

I. TITLE UNDER THE REAL ESTATE CONTRACT

    A. Implied term of marketable title: Marketable title is both an implied condition and an implied promise. [73–75]

        1. Definition: Marketable title is title that is (1) good in fact, (2) subject to no encumbrances except those agreed to by the parties, and (3) free from reasonable doubt.

        2. Title-related matter: A valid title objection must identify a defect in the seller's title rather than some other problem.

        3. Timing: Seller's title must be marketable at closing. Buyer must object and give seller a reasonable period of time to cure title.

        4. Buyer's knowledge: Buyer's knowledge of a title defect usually does not preclude buyer from objecting to the defect.

    B. Record title compared to marketable title: Generally, the seller must have record title for title to be marketable. [75]

        1. Problem of adverse possession: A seller with adverse possession title lacks record title.

    C. Encumbrances: An encumbrance is a nonpossessory right or interest in the property that reduces the property's market value, restricts its use, or imposes an obligation. Marketable title means the property must be free of all encumbrances, with four exceptions. [75–76]

        1. De minimis encumbrances: A de minimis encumbrance has no appreciable effect on the value of the property or its use. A lien, even if small, is never de minimis.

        2. Visible encumbrances: Improvements or other property features may disclose a visible encumbrance.

        3. Superfluous encumbrances: A superfluous encumbrance is one that does not impose any obligations on the landowner in addition to those otherwise required by law.

4. Obsolete encumbrances: These are covenants and other encumbrances that are no longer enforceable.

D. Encroachments: Two types of encroachments render title unmarketable. [76]

    1. Seller's improvements encroach: In this case, improvements on the land being purchased encroach across a boundary line or across a setback line.

    2. Seller's neighbor's improvements encroach: Here improvements on neighboring land encroach on the land being purchased.

E. Zoning and other public regulation: Zoning or other land use regulations may raise marketable title questions. [76–77]

    1. Narrow view of title: Zoning laws and other types of public regulation of use do not render title unmarketable.

    2. Broad view of title: Some courts protect buyers whose expectations concerning property use and value are frustrated when zoning problems are encountered.

    3. Non-title approaches: Other claims such as mutual mistake of fact may protect the buyer when zoning does not conform to the buyer's expectations.

F. Express contract provisions: Three main types of contract provisions address title. [77]

    1. Contract title: The parties may replace the judicial definition of marketability with their own standard.

    2. Record title: The parties may contract for record title, which requires proof of the status of title gathered solely from deeds and other instruments that are recorded in the public records.

    3. Insurable title: The contract may provide that buyer will obtain a title insurance policy.

G. Buyer's remedies for title defects [77–78]

    1. English rule: Buyer usually recovers only out-of-pocket costs. Buyer can recover expectancy damages only if seller has acted in bad faith.

    2. American rule: Buyer can select among the full range of damage awards, including expectancy damages whenever the property value exceeds the contract price at the time of breach.

II. FORMAL REQUIREMENTS FOR DEEDS

A. Statute of frauds: The statute of frauds requires a writing that (1) identifies the parties, (2) identifies the land, and (3) shows an intent to convey. [78]

B. Execution: The grantor must sign the deed. [78]

C. Delivery: The grantor must deliver the deed to the grantee. [78]

D. Acceptance: The grantee must accept delivery of the deed. [79]

E. Acknowledgment and recordation: In almost all states, a deed is effective upon delivery even if it is not acknowledged (usually by a notary public) or recorded. [79]

III. DEED CONSTRUCTIONAL RULES

There are a number of rules of interpretation. [79]

A. **Intent of the parties:** The goal is to arrive at the parties' intent by looking at the whole deed. [79]

B. **Conflict between parts of deed:** When different parts of a deed conflict, the deed may be construed against the grantor. Another rule accords priority to certain clauses: The granting clause and the habendum clause take precedence over conflicting language found elsewhere. [79]

C. **Extrinsic evidence of the parties' real intent:** Extrinsic evidence is admissible to explain the parties' intent only if the deed has an ambiguity. [79]

   1. **Presumption against ambiguity:** Some courts keep extrinsic evidence out by calling a deed not ambiguous in debatable cases.

   2. **Latent and patent ambiguity:** Extrinsic evidence is admissible to resolve a latent ambiguity, but not a patent ambiguity.

D. **Reformation:** A party may reform an error in a deed. Reformation cannot affect any bona fide Purchaser (BFP) who has relied on the deed. [79]

IV. DEFECTIVE DEEDS

A. **Void deeds:** A void deed, such as a forgery or an undelivered deed, has no legal effect. [79–80]

   1. **Forgery:** A grantee or successor who relies on a forged deed has no right or title whatsoever.

   2. **Lack of delivery:** An undelivered deed is void, even if signed by the proper person.

B. **Voidable deeds:** Some other types of defects, which are less serious, make the deed voidable. The rescission right cannot be asserted against subsequent BFPs. [80]

V. DEED COVENANTS OF TITLE

A. **Warranty deeds** [80]

   1. **General warranties:** These protect the grantee against any and all defects that may have arisen anytime during the entire chain of title up to the time of delivery.

   2. **Special or limited warranties:** These protect the grantee only against defects arising while the grantor owned the property.

B. **Quitclaim deeds:** A quitclaim deed has no covenants of title. The grantee bears all risk. [80]

C. **Types of covenants:** At common law, all title covenants in deeds must be express. Many states today use a statutory form for a deed, which implies certain covenants. [80–82]

   1. **Present covenants:** Present title covenants do not run with the land. They are breached, if at all, at the time of delivery of the deed.

      a. **Covenant of seisin:** The grantor promises he is seized of the estate.

    b. Right to convey: The grantor promises that he has the legal right to convey the estate the deed purports to convey.

    c. Covenant against encumbrances: The grantor promises that there are no encumbrances on the land.

  2. Future covenants: These covenants run to subsequent grantees. A future covenant is breached by actual or constructive eviction of the grantee.

    a. Covenant of quiet enjoyment: The grantor promises that the grantee may possess and quietly enjoy the land.

    b. Covenant of warrant: The grantor warrants the title to the grantee.

    c. Covenant of further assurances: The grantor promises to give whatever "further assurances" may be required in the future to vest the grantee with the title the deed purports to convey.

  3. Remedies for breach of deed covenants: Damages are the remedy for the first five covenants listed above. Most states limit the grantor's liability for damages to the purchase price. Under the covenant of further assurances, the remedy of specific performance is available as an alternative to damages.

VI. RELATIONSHIP BETWEEN TITLE UNDER CONTRACT AND DEED COVENANTS

At delivery of the deed, merger extinguishes the title provisions of the executory contract. The deed covenants then control. [82]

A. Quitclaim deed and marketable title: If a contract calls for the delivery of a quitclaim deed and is otherwise silent, the purchaser may raise a title objection prior to closing based on the implied right to marketable title. [82]

CHAPTER 9

LAND DESCRIPTIONS

I. TYPES OF DESCRIPTIONS

Three types of land descriptions are in common use in real estate transactions. [87]

A. Metes and bounds: This method describes every boundary line by length and direction. Length is usually given in feet. The description for each line is known as a *call*. Direction, also called the *course*, is given in degrees east or west of north or south. [87–88]

B. Government survey system: The basic units are *sections* and *townships*, which were laid out using squares and rectangular grids. Each section has approximately 640 acres and is a square with sides of 1 mile each. Each township has 36 sections. [88]

C. Subdivision plats: The plat or map shows lots and is filed as part of the public land records. [88]

II. THE SURVEYOR

The "title survey" or "boundary survey" locates all the boundary lines of a tract on the ground. [88]

A. **Discretion:** Often the surveyor must weigh conflicting evidence and exercise judgment in locating boundaries. [89]

B. **Reasons for a survey:** There are a number of reasons for obtaining a survey. [89]

1. **Existence of the property:** The survey confirms that the tract exists, that it has a certain quantity of acres or square feet, and that the legal description is sufficient.

2. **Relationship of the property to adjoining properties:** The survey may disclose whether the boundary lines are consistent with the descriptions of adjoining properties.

3. **Relationship of occupied lines to record lines:** The survey shows any discrepancy between deed record lines and evidence of possession and occupation.

4. **Location of physical improvements:** A survey shows the location of all physical improvements.

5. **Unrecorded easements and other facts not of record:** The survey shows unrecorded physical features that may evidence unrecorded property rights.

C. **Types of surveys** [89–90]

1. **Instructions:** The client or attorney should specify the type of survey desired.

2. **ALTA/ACSM standards:** The American Land Title Association (ALTA) and the American Congress on Surveying and Mapping (ACSM) have adopted uniform national standards for surveys.

D. **Surveyor liability** [90–91]

1. **Certificate:** The surveyor's certificate may promise that the survey has a particular degree of accuracy.

2. **Negligence:** The surveyor is held to a standard of professional competence based on the norms and customs of the surveying profession.

3. **Persons who may recover**

   a. **Those in contract privity:** The owner or lender who purchases a survey may recover for loss caused by the surveyor's breach of duty.

   b. **Third parties:** Most courts permit some third parties to recover from the surveyor.

4. **Statute of limitations:** A cause of action for breach of duty may be barred by the statute of limitations.

III. LEGAL ADEQUACY OF DESCRIPTION

A. **Descriptions in contract of sale:** The major goal is to ascertain the parties' intent, yet the statute of frauds requires a written description of the land. [91]

1. **Formalism:** Under formalism, the court requires that the writing completely describe the tract with no ambiguity and no resort to extrinsic evidence.

2. **Effectuating intent:** Many courts are more lenient, allowing any written description if extrinsic evidence is able to explain what the parties meant by their writing.

B. **Descriptions in deeds and other recorded instruments:** Courts have developed a number of rules to resolve apparent conflicts in deed language. [91–92]

1. **Policy approach:** Courts tend to be stricter concerning the quality of the land descriptions in deeds and other recorded instruments than those in land contracts. Courts often craft rules that minimize or eliminate the use of extrinsic evidence.

2. **Major rules of deed interpretation**

   a. **Prefer the grantee in cases of doubt or ambiguity:** The intent is to give the grantee the most land and the greatest estate possible.

   b. **Interpret deed so that it conveys some land:** If one interpretation would result in the grantee receiving no land, the court will seek an interpretation that conveys some land.

   c. **Deeds may expressly incorporate other writings in order to show what land is granted:** The deed may refer to a prior deed in the chain of title, to a survey, or to another instrument.

   d. **Specific language controls over general language:** If general language and specific language conflict, give effect to the specific language.

   e. **Natural monuments control over artificial monuments:** Natural monuments, such as rivers, trees, and rocks, take precedence over artificial monuments.

   f. **Monuments control over calls (distances and courses):** If there is a conflict between a monument and a call, the monument prevails.

CHAPTER 10

THE PUBLIC LAND RECORDS

I. COMMON LAW PRIORITY RULES

The basic common law rule for priorities is "first in time, first in right." [97]

A. **Delivery:** The deed that is delivered first is "first in time." [97]

B. **Exception for prior equitable interest:** At common law, an equitable claim is cut off by a subsequent purchaser who acquires legal title without notice of the prior equity. [97]

C. **Significance of common law rules:** The recording acts only partially displace the common law rules. Any subsequent purchaser who is not entitled to statutory protection is subject to the common law rules preferring interests that are prior in time. [97]

II. FUNCTIONS OF RECORDING SYSTEM

A. Title assurance: The recording system provides a method for determining who owns any tract of land. [98]

B. Priority ranking: The recording system establishes relative priorities among successive transfers that do not directly conflict. [98]

III. TITLE SEARCH PROCESS

A. Construct chain of title: The searcher's first step is to construct the record chain of title. [98]

B. Check for adverse recorded transfers: The second step is to check the records for adverse transfers. [98]

C. Study recorded instruments: The third step is to read all instruments found in steps 1 and 2. [98]

D. Check other records: The last step is to check other records that may reflect adverse transfers, such as judgment liens, tax liens, and bankruptcy filings. [98]

IV. TYPES OF RECORDING ACTS

There are three types of recording acts. [98]

A. Race statute: A subsequent purchaser who records first wins. [98]

B. Notice statute: A subsequent purchaser who takes without notice wins. [99]

C. Race-notice statute: A subsequent purchaser who takes without notice and who records first wins. [99]

D. Jurisdictions: Roughly half the states have notice statutes and the other half have race-notice statutes. Only several states have race statutes. [99]

V. BONA FIDE PURCHASER STATUS

A subsequent grantee or taker of an interest prevails against a prior-in-time interest if he is a bona fide purchaser (BFP). [99]

A. "Purchaser": The taker must pay more than nominal value. [99]

    1. Mortgagee as purchaser: A loan made by a mortgagee counts as value.

B. "Without notice" [99–100]

    1. Actual notice: A purchaser with actual knowledge of a prior interest is disqualified.

    2. Constructive notice: The purchaser is charged with notice of all recorded interests.

    3. Inquiry notice: When the purchaser has knowledge of facts that suggest that someone may have an unrecorded interest, he has the duty to inquire. The purchaser has a duty to inspect the property to spot parties in possession.

VI. OFF-RECORD RISKS

A. Inquiry notice: The purchaser takes the risk of all unrecorded interests that he should have discovered. [100]

B. Unrecordable interests: Recording acts protect BFPs only against an off-the-record interest that is capable of being recorded. There are two types of nonrecordable interests. [100–101]

    1. Interests that cannot be created by instrument: Examples are claims of adverse possession, prescriptive easements, and marital property rights.

    2. Instruments that are not eligible for recording: Many states have a statutory exception making short-term leases nonrecordable.

VII. BFP SHELTER RULE

Once a BFP cuts off a prior unrecorded interest, the BFP can transfer good title to any grantee. [101]

A. Rationale: The rule serves to protect the BFP by making her title alienable. [101]

B. Exception for reacquisition by creator of prior interest: The BFP shelter rule does not apply when the BFP transfers title to the person who earlier created the prior unrecorded interest. [101]

VIII. RECORDED INTERESTS THAT ARE DIFFICULT OR IMPOSSIBLE TO FIND

A. Name indexes: Most states have name indexes, also called grantor-grantee indexes. Some recorded documents are difficult or impossible to find using name indexes. [101–102]

    1. Wild deed: A wild deed is both recorded and properly indexed in the name indexes, but cannot be found because the deed into the grantor is a missing link that was never recorded. Courts treat the wild deed as unrecorded.

    2. Late-recorded deed: A deed is late recorded if there is a substantial time gap between delivery and recordation and in the meantime the record owner has transferred ownership to someone else.

    3. Early-recorded deed: With an early-recorded deed, a grantor conveys land he does not own and subsequently acquires an estate in that land. Upon acquisition, the doctrine of estoppel by deed transfers that title to the prior grantee.

    4. Effect of late-recorded and early-recorded deeds: Courts split on whether late- and early-recorded deeds impart constructive notice.

B. Tract indexes: Tract indexes are set up by legal description and reduce search problems. [102]

C. Defective recorded instruments [102–103]

    1. Nondelivered deed: This deed is void.

    2. Forged deed: This deed is void.

3. **Improper acknowledgment:** Generally, a defectively acknowledged deed that is recorded does not impart constructive notice.

   a. **Latent versus patent defect:** Many courts hold that all improperly acknowledged deeds fail to impart constructive notice, but some courts distinguish between latent and patent defects.

4. **Misindexed deed:** In most states, a misindexed deed gives constructive notice. But, a growing number of states mandate proper indexing for a deed to be legally recorded.

CHAPTER 11

TITLE PRODUCTS

I. TITLE ABSTRACTS

The abstract is a summary of all instruments for a tract of land found by searching the public records. [107]

A. **Types of abstracts:** Three types of abstracts are in common use. [107]

   1. **Complete abstract:** This takes the chain of title back to the sovereign.

   2. **Partial abstract:** This goes back only a customary period, such as 50 or 60 years.

   3. **Updated abstract:** Rather than order a new abstract, a purchaser may order an updated abstract from the date of the original abstract to the present.

B. **Standard for liability:** An abstractor's liability for an erroneous title abstract generally is based on negligence. [108]

C. **Who may rely on abstract** [108]

   1. **Those in privity rule:** Only the client who purchased the abstract has an action against the abstract company.

   2. **Third-party beneficiaries:** Many courts expand liability to protect a third party when, at the time the abstract is ordered, it is clear the abstract will be given to a third party who can be expected to rely on it.

   3. **Subsequent buyers of land:** Under a tort theory of negligent misrepresentation, some courts may extend liability to protect subsequent buyers of the land.

II. ATTORNEYS' TITLE OPINIONS AND CERTIFICATES

The attorney's title opinion or title certificate states a professional opinion that title appears marketable. [108]

A. **Standard for liability:** The attorney's liability depends on proof of negligence. [108]

   1. **Marketable title standard:** The attorney should disclose each item of record that is a *cloud* on title even if there is some basis for arguing that the possible adverse claim is not legitimate.

2. **Attorney's representation of scope of work:** The opinion or certificate should disclose the work the attorney performed in order to prepare the opinion.

B. **Who may rely on attorney's title opinion** [109]

1. **Those in privity:** Many courts limit recovery to the client.

2. **Third-party beneficiaries:** A third party may recover for negligence if the attorney knew the client intended to give the opinion to that party.

3. **Subsequent buyers of land:** Under the tort of negligent misrepresentation, an attorney may conceivably be liable to subsequent buyers who receive the title opinion and rely on it to their detriment.

III. TITLE INSURANCE: OWNERS' AND LENDERS' POLICIES

Title insurance is the dominant product in the title assurance market. [109]

A. **Primary functions:** Title insurance serves two primary functions. [109]

1. **Search and disclosure:** The title insurer searches the records and discloses its findings.

2. **Risk spreading:** The title policy insures undisclosed risks. This is risk spreading among the pool of insured policyholders.

B. **Process of issuing title insurance policy** [109–110]

1. **Title search:** The company either conducts or obtains a title search on the parcel.

2. **Title commitment:** Based on the title search, the company issues its written commitment. This is delivered prior to issuing a final policy.

3. **Title policy:** Issued after closing to replace the commitment.

   a. **Specific exceptions:** Outstanding interests in the property are listed on the commitment as specific exceptions to coverage.

   b. **Closing requirements:** The commitment usually lists the documents needed at closing to establish the title the parties expect to be insured.

C. **Absolute liability:** The title insurer is absolutely liable to pay claims for insured defects. [110]

D. **Policy exclusions and exceptions:** All title insurance policies have preprinted exclusions and exceptions. [110]

E. **Off-record risks:** Title risks that are not reflected by the public records are often not insured. [110]

1. **Survey exceptions:** Policies generally except "matters which would be disclosed by an accurate survey."

F. **Who may rely on title insurance:** The policy insures only the person or persons defined as the "insured." Each new owner must obtain a new policy. [110]

    1. **Warrantor's coverage:** An insured owner who conveys the property has warrantor's coverage if a title defect results in a claim against the grantor based on the deed covenants of title.

G. Recovery on title insurance: Recovery is limited to an actual loss up to the amount of the policy. [111]

H. Tort liability: A few courts hold that a title insurer has an implied duty to conduct a reasonable search before issuing a policy. This benefits plaintiffs because recovery in tort has no dollar limits, policy exclusions and exceptions do not apply, and punitive damages are available in tort. [111]

    1. **Significance of tort theory:** It extends the scope and the extent of potential liability relative to contract theory.

I. Ethical problems [111]

    1. **Conflicts of interest:** An attorney who serves as *agent* or as *examining counsel* for a title company typically earns a share of the insurance premium. This may create a conflict of interest with the client.

    2. **Confidentiality:** A confidentiality problem may arise if the attorney learns of a title problem that is unknown to the title company.

    3. **Good faith and fair dealing:** An insurance company owes its insured the duty of good faith and fair dealing.

CHAPTER 12
IMPROVING THE EFFICIENCY OF THE TITLE SYSTEM

I. TITLE STANDARDS

Many states have bar-approved standards for reviewing and approving titles. [115]

A. Minor variations in names: Standards provide that certain minor variations are not likely to present risk and should not be the basis of title objections. [115]

B. Period of search: Bar standards often prescribe a recommended period of search, such as 50 years. [115]

C. Legal effect: Bar title standards are not statutory and do not bind courts, but courts often defer to them. [115]

D. Parties' incorporation of bar standards: Many contracts explicitly define marketable title by reference to specified bar title standards. [116]

II. ADVERSE POSSESSION

The law of adverse possession both improves record titles and diminishes record titles. [116]

A. Title-clearing function: Adverse possession bars potential claims of persons who have been out of possession for a long time. [116]

B. Modification of boundary lines: Adverse possession of an area often changes the record boundary line. [116]

III. TITLE CURATIVE ACTS

Title curative acts provide that instruments of record that bear certain defects are valid after a specified number of years. [117]

A. Types of defects: Curative acts often resolve a missing or defective acknowledgment, the failure to pay the recording fee or a transfer tax, and lack of delivery. [117]

B. Period of time: The time to cure a defect varies, but typically ranges from 3 to 21 years. [117]

C. Legal effect: Unlike title standards, a title curative act is state legislation and binds the courts. [117]

IV. MARKETABLE TITLE ACTS

The basic concept is to extinguish interests that are older than the root of title. Twenty states presently have marketable title acts. [117]

A. Goals: These acts shorten the period of search and render more titles marketable by eliminating stale interests. [117–118]

B. Root of title: The marketable title act operates to extinguish interests and defects that are older than the "root of title." [118]

C. Function: An interest created prior to the root of title is cut off unless it is referred to in a post-root instrument, or re-recorded, or reflected by possession after the root of title. [118]

D. Exceptions: All marketable title acts have exceptions. [118]

V. TORRENS SYSTEM: TITLE REGISTRATION

The government issues a certificate of title for each tract of land. This certificate is intended to be conclusive as to ownership and the existence of all outstanding interests and encumbrances. [118]

A. History: Sir Robert Richard Torrens developed a land registration system for Australia in the 1850s. [118]

B. U.S. experience: Many states passed Torrens statutes in the 20th century, but only a handful of states use Torrens today. [118]

C. Weaknesses of Torrens in the United States: Indemnity funds are often insufficient to pay claims for losses incurred in connection with the system. Because registration is voluntary, most owners choose not to register their land. A Torrens certificate is not conclusive as to title because certain interests are valid, even though they are not referenced on the certificate. [118-119]

CHAPTER 13

HOUSING MARKETS AND PRODUCTS

I. BASIC REAL ESTATE MARKET PROFILE

A. Rate of home ownership: The current rate of home ownership in the United States is approximately 70 percent. [123]

B. Median cost of housing: Over the years, the median cost of the typical home has increased dramatically in constant dollar terms. In part this is because the typical home is now bigger and much better equipped than it was years ago. [123–124]

C. Product changes: Housing products today have more space, plumbing, electrical devices, and other amenities than those of earlier generations. [124]

D. Variations in ownership rate: Home ownership rates vary based on a number of factors, including race, age, gender, level of education, income, and family composition. [124]

E. Access to housing: The law prevents discrimination in housing. [124]

F. Housing products: There is wide diversity in housing products. The various products are designed and priced to appeal to a variety of consumer markets and life styles. [124]

II. THE SINGLE-FAMILY HOME

The single-family home is still the mainstay product in the home ownership market. [124]

A. Land use controls: The three primary sources of regulation affecting many single-family homes are zoning, covenants and restrictions, and planned unit developments (PUDs). [124–125]

1. Zoning: Land regulations passed and enforced by local government.

2. Covenants and restrictions: Private regulations affecting the land.

3. Planned unit developments: A special public zoning control for large residential projects.

B. Owners associations: Homeowners are often automatically made members of a homeowners association in modern subdivisions and PUDs. The association functions like a quasi-governmental body. [125]

III. CONDOMINIUM HOUSING

A condominium is a single unit in a multiunit project, together with an undivided interest in the common elements. [126]

A. Creatures of statute: Each state has a statute to govern condominiums. The primary legal documents are the Declaration of Condominium, the bylaws for the owners association, and the rules and regulations. [126]

B. Ownership interests [126–127]

    1. The unit: Generally, the unit is owned in fee and consists of the interior space of a unit along with its interior surfaces.

    2. Common elements: The unit owners hold the common elements (internal building structures, electrical and plumbing systems, stairwells, elevators, and various amenities) as tenants in common.

    3. Limited common elements: Sometimes the Declaration designates certain common elements (parking space or balcony) for the exclusive use of a particular unit.

C. Owners association: Condominiums have homeowners associations so that unit owners can participate in the governance of the property in which they all have a common interest. [127–128]

D. Right of first refusal: The homeowners association sometimes has a right of first refusal on any unit sale. [128]

IV. COOPERATIVE HOUSING

A. Corporate form: In the cooperative, a corporation holds title to the entire project and buyers acquire stock in the corporation. Each stockholder has a proprietary lease for her dwelling unit. [128]

B. Ownership interest: Owners in a cooperative become stock shareholders and have a right to a proprietary lease of their unit. [128]

    1. Stock certificate: Owners are shareholders.

    2. Proprietary lease: Stock ownership entitles one to a lease for a particular unit.

    3. Real or personal property: In some states this is a split property transaction (part real property, the lease, and part personal property, the stock), and in other states it is completely personal property.

C. Corporate governance: Owners of the cooperative work through an owners association to govern the project and their shared interests therein. [129]

D. Right of approval: The cooperative has a right to approve or disapprove any sale of stock and its related unit. [129]

E. Financing [129–130]

    1. Cooperative mortgage: The entire cooperative property is usually subject to a blanket mortgage. All unit owners share in the financial obligation to pay this underlying mortgage debt.

    2. Individual unit mortgage: An owner can finance his own unit by giving a leasehold mortgage on the proprietary lease and a UCC Article 9 security interest on his shares. In some states the entire transaction is governed by the stock and there is no real property interest.

V. TIME-SHARE HOUSING

Time-share ownership divides a dwelling unit into intervals of time. [130]

A. **Creatures of statute:** The time-share project exists by virtue of enabling statutes. [130]

B. **Ownership interests:** The time-share project has an owners association for group governance. Time-share projects are arranged one of three ways: a real property interest (fee or leasehold), a license, or a club membership. [130]

   1. **Real property interest:** Buying a unit in fee.

   2. **License:** Buying a contract right for use.

   3. **Club membership:** Buying club membership points for use.

C. **Exchange features and swaps:** Owners can generally participate in exchange or swap programs. [130]

D. **Financing:** A time-share interest can be mortgaged. [130]

CHAPTER 14

POSSESSION AND USE OF MORTGAGED PROPERTY

I. NATURE AND PURPOSE OF MORTGAGE

A. **Mortgage defined:** A mortgage is a grant of an interest in real property to secure an obligation. [135]

B. **Parties to the mortgage:** The owner who grants the mortgage is the "mortgagor." The holder of the secured obligation is the "mortgagee." The real property is the "collateral." [135]

C. **Written instrument:** A mortgage must comply with the statute of frauds. [135–136]

D. **Importance of possession and use in mortgage transactions:** The mortgagee's ability to gain the rights of possession and use upon the mortgagor's default is what makes the collateral economically valuable. [136]

II. MORTGAGE THEORIES

The mortgage theories deal with the title and the right to possession. [136]

A. **Title theory:** Under the title theory, the lender takes title for the entire duration of the mortgage. [136–137]

   1. **English common law mortgage:** The mortgagor conveyed a defeasible or indefeasible freehold estate to the mortgagee.

   2. **Title theory in the United States:** A number of states, all of them in the eastern United States, have retained the title theory.

   3. **Effect on possession:** The mortgagee has the right to possession from the moment the mortgage is granted, unless otherwise agreed.

  B. Lien theory: Most states follow the lien theory, which says that the mortgagee has only a lien prior to foreclosure. [137]

    1. Rationale: Title is not necessary to protect the mortgagee's legitimate interests. A lien is sufficient.

    2. Effect of mortgage language: The lien theory applies as a matter of status, regardless of the language used in the mortgage instrument.

    3. Effect on possession: The mortgagor has the right to possess the property at all times prior to foreclosure.

  C. Intermediate theory: A few states follow the intermediate theory or hybrid theory. Title is in the mortgagor until he defaults, and then title automatically passes to the mortgagee. [137]

    1. Effect on possession: The mortgagor has the right to possession until default; the mortgagee has the right to possession after default.

    2. Creditor protection: The intermediate theory helps a mortgagee gain possession during the interval between default and foreclosure.

III. EQUITY OF REDEMPTION

  A. Hardship at law: Under the English common law mortgage, a borrower's failure to pay on time (by law day) made the mortgagee's title absolute. [137]

  B. Intervention of court of equity: The English Chancellor (court of equity) intervened, giving the borrower the right to pay late. This is known as the *equity of redemption*. [138]

  C. Anti-clogging rule: The court struck down mortgage clauses that waived or restricted the mortgagor's equity of redemption. [138]

  D. Late payment and foreclosure: The equity of redemption clouded the mortgagee's title whenever the mortgagor failed to pay on time. [138]

    1. Strict foreclosure: Lenders began to file bills asking for a decree ordering the borrower to pay by a fixed date. The Chancellor responded by recognizing an action that became known as *foreclosure*.

  E. Relationship to mortgage theories: The equity of redemption applies in title-theory, lien-theory, and intermediate-theory states. The interest redeemed by the borrower is either title or a release of the lien. [138]

IV. DEED OF TRUST

In some states, the deed of trust is used to secure real estate loans. The deed of trust and the mortgage both serve the same purpose. [138]

  A. Power of sale: The deed of trust adds a third party, the trustee, to the transaction. The trustee has a power of sale. [138]

    B. Trustee's role: In principle, the trustee is neutral, but the lender selects a trustee who is likely to serve its interest. [138]

V. POSSESSION BY MORTGAGOR

    A. Doctrine of waste: The law of waste protects the mortgagee when the mortgagor has possession. [139]

      1. Balance: The goal is to preserve the economic value of the mortgagee's collateral.

      2. Voluntary waste: Voluntary waste is intentional conduct that substantially diminishes the value of the property.

      3. Permissive waste: The mortgagor has affirmative duties to protect the property value. He must make repairs and pay real estate taxes.

    B. Relationship of waste to underlying debt: The doctrine of waste comes from tort law and thus does not depend on a clause in the mortgage. [139-140]

      1. Discharge in bankruptcy: If a mortgagor gets a bankruptcy discharge from personal liability on the debt and remains in possession, he has the duty not to commit waste.

      2. Nonrecourse loans: Under a nonrecourse loan, the lender is limited to proceeding against the collateral if the mortgagor defaults. Personal liability for waste is unclear in nonrecourse loans.

        a. Permissive waste: A nonrecourse provision in the mortgage may insulate the mortgagee from liability for permissive waste.

        b. Bad faith waste: Under California anti-deficiency judgment legislation, the mortgagor is personally liable for "bad faith" waste.

VI. POSSESSION BY MORTGAGEE

    A. Mortgagee in possession: A "mortgagee in possession" obtains possession of the property with the mortgagor's consent. [140]

    B. Fiduciary duties: The mortgagee in possession owes fiduciary duties to the mortgagor. [140–141]

      1. Standard of care: The mortgagee must manage the property prudently.

      2. Duty to account: The mortgagee must collect rents and profits to reduce the debt.

      3. Third parties: Ordinarily, the mortgagee's fiduciary duties run only to the mortgagor.

VII. ASSIGNMENT OF RENTS

    A mortgagor may assign rents from the property to the mortgagee. [141]

    A. Express assignment of specific leases: Instead of a general assignment of rents, a mortgagor may assign a specific named lease. [141]

B. Types of assignments of rents: An assignment of rents, whether general or specific, may be collateral or absolute. [141–142]

   1. Collateral assignment: A collateral assignment creates a lien on the rents, with the mortgagor still owning the rents and the right to collect them.

   2. Absolute assignment: An absolute assignment passes title to the rents to the lender.

   3. Presumption of collateral assignment: In cases of ambiguity, courts presume the assignment is collateral.

C. Effect on leases of mortgagee taking possession: A lease is either senior or junior to a mortgage. This depends on recording act principles. [142]

   1. Senior lease, junior mortgage: A senior tenant's rights are not affected when the lender takes possession, invokes an assignment of rents, or forecloses.

   2. Junior lease, senior mortgage: A junior tenant's rights may turn in part on the mortgage theory followed by the state.

   a. Title and intermediate theories: Under both theories, upon default the lender has the right to possession and may evict the junior tenant.

   b. Lien theory: Under the lien theory, the lender cannot affect the junior tenant's right to possession prior to foreclosure. The lender may seek judicial appointment of a receiver to collect rents.

D. Drafting consideration: The lender's counsel must pay attention to the particular state laws governing absolute and collateral assignments, and should consider obtaining express agreements from tenants, such as subordination agreements and estoppel certificates, and consider whether the assignment will cover senior leases or only junior leases. [142]

VIII. RECEIVERS

A receiver takes possession of mortgaged property at the instance of the lender. [143]

A. Judicial appointment: The mortgagee may ask a court to appoint a receiver. [143]

   1. Procedure: Many states allow the ex parte appointment of a receiver after a judicial foreclosure begins.

B. Scope of receiver's powers: The court may grant the receiver broad powers, including the right to enter into new leases and contracts. [143]

C. Advantages of receiver for lender [143]

   1. Getting possession fast: A receiver can get speedy possession to protect the lender from borrower misbehavior.

   2. Getting income from nonrental property: A receiver may generate income from property that is not presently rented.

CAPSULE SUMMARY

3. **Getting preforeclosure protection in lien-theory states:** In some lien-theory states, a lender cannot get possession before foreclosure. A receiver can stop waste and apply rents or income to the debt prior to foreclosure.

4. **Avoiding fiduciary duties:** A receiver spares the lender from the fiduciary duties of a mortgagee in possession.

D. **Disadvantages of receiver for lender** [143]

1. **Paying receiver's fee:** The receiver charges a fee.

2. **Going to court:** Judicial action is necessary to appoint a receiver.

3. **Losing control:** The lender loses control over the property while the receiver has possession.

E. **Standards for appointment** [144]

1. **Proceeding in equity:** The petition to appoint a receiver is in equity.

2. **Default and other factors:** Proof of material default is essential, and most states require proof of additional facts demonstrating the need for a receiver.

3. **Receivership clause:** A mortgage clause may give a lender the right to the appointment of a receiver if the borrower defaults.

4. **Relationship of appointment standard to receiver's functions:** Some states use a more lenient standard of proof if the receiver will have a limited role, such as only the collection of rents from existing tenants.

CHAPTER 15

RESIDENTIAL MORTGAGE MARKETS AND PRODUCTS

I. ACCESS TO MORTGAGE MARKETS

A. **Security for the loan** [149–150]

1. **Unsecured credit:** Gives the lender the right to levy against available assets of the defaulting debtor.

2. **Secured credit:** Gives the lender the right to proceed against specific assets described in the mortgage or security agreement.

B. **Evaluating the loan applicant:** Loan applicants are evaluated based on ***ability*** and ***willingness*** to pay the loan. [150]

1. **Debt ratios:** Ability to pay is measured by two formulas. Monthly mortgage payments should not exceed 28 percent of the debtor's gross monthly income. Nor should monthly payments plus all other debts exceed 36 percent of the gross monthly income.

2. **Willingness to pay:** This is a subjective evaluation of the debtor.

3. **Race:** Mortgage access can vary by race although it is illegal to use race as a factor in qualifying for a loan.

C. **Market definition:** Access to mortgage financing varies according to race. [150–152]

    1. **Redlining:** An illegal practice that identifies geographic areas where a lender will not make loans.

    2. **Fair Housing Act:** Prohibits redlining.

    3. **Greenlining:** This is an illegal activity that defines a wealthy market where the lender will make loans to the exclusion of other areas.

    4. **Exploitation and predatory pricing:** Lenders cannot price discriminate based on race.

    5. **Higher credit risk loans:** Alt-A form mortgages and subprime mortgages are made to people and in situations where risk is higher than permitted for prime rate lending.

    6. **Market reform:** The collapse of the mortgage markets during 2007-2009 has given rise to efforts to reform the lending process.

II. PRIMARY MORTGAGE MARKET

The primary mortgage market involves loan originations, in which lenders make loans to home buyers. The lender views loans as investments, charging fees for processing the paperwork needed to approve and fund the loan. [152]

A. **Savings:** Lenders take in money from savers. [152]

B. **Intermediaries:** Financial institutions act as mortgage market intermediaries. [152]

C. **Borrowing:** Mortgages represent borrowing to the debtor and investments for the lender. [152]

D. **Alternative markets:** Financial intermediaries have alternatives to the real estate mortgage markets. [153]

III. SECONDARY MORTGAGE MARKET

In the secondary mortgage market, loan originators sell their mortgages. This way the primary lenders get new cash to make additional loans. In return, the secondary market investors acquire the mortgages and the income flow they represent. [153]

A. **Diversity of mortgage investments:** Lenders use the secondary mortgage market to reduce their investment risk by diversifying their holdings. [153]

B. **New investment capital:** The secondary mortgage market attracts new investors to realestate-related activities by offering investment opportunities that compete with stocks and bonds. [153]

C. **Intermediaries:** Intermediaries buy mortgages in the primary market and sell them in pools to investors in the secondary market. Often they prepare mortgage-backed securities for sale to investors. [153–154]

D. **Direct sales to investors:** In a few situations, a primary mortgage lender may have the ability to locate and directly sell large loan originations to investors. [154]

E. **Changing market dynamics:** Prior to the 1980s, most local lenders originated loans and held them as long-term investments. Now most lenders sell on the secondary mortgage market, specializing in origination work and making profits from fees for service rather than from the long-term holding of mortgages. [154]

F. **Secondary mortgage market financial products:** Mortgage-related securities are based on the value and quality of underlying mortgages. [154]

G. **Derivatives and swaps:** Financial markets also include derivatives and swaps related to real estate mortgage activities. [154–155]

H. **Secondary market provides funds for primary market:** The quality of the underlying real estate transaction is directly related to the value of securities issued against the underlying mortgages. As the mortgage moves up the market chain, cash is paid down. Thus, a pipeline for continuing loan originations is fed by ongoing sales of originated mortgages. [155]

IV. MORTGAGE PRODUCTS

A. **Preliminary matters** [155–156]

   1. **Points:** Points are charged as part of the origination fee for making a loan. One point equals 1 percent of the loan amount. One hundred "basis points" equal one point.

   2. **Annual percentage rate:** The APR is a federally required disclosure of the cost of a mortgage loan, designed to permit consumers to comparison shop for loans.

   3. **Mortgage insurance:** Mortgage insurance protects a lender from loss in the event of a foreclosure.

B. **Fixed-rate mortgages:** A fixed-rate mortgage has the same monthly payment throughout the life of the loan. It puts the risk of inflation on the lender. [156]

C. **Adjustable-rate mortgages:** The adjustable-rate mortgage or ARM has an interest rate that varies over the life of the loan. It puts some or all of the risk of inflation on the borrower. There are four key characteristics of the ARM. [156–157]

   1. **Index:** This is the reference for adjustments.

   2. **Adjustment period:** The timing and frequency of adjustments.

   3. **Caps:** Limits the change in rate adjustment over a stated period of time and the life of the loan.

   4. **Convertibles:** Ability to convert the adjustable-rate loan to a fixed-rate loan at a future date.

D. **Alternative mortgage instruments** [157–158]

   1. **Balloon mortgage:** The balloon mortgage is short term and has a large balance due at the maturity date.

   2. **Level payment adjustable-rate mortgage:** This ARM keeps payments constant during the life of the loan even though the actual interest rate changes.

   3. **Shared appreciation mortgage:** The lender takes an interest in equity appreciation on the property in exchange for a lower interest rate.

4. **Reverse annuity mortgage:** The RAM loan is designed for senior citizens who put up their equity as security to get annuity payments.

E. **Purchase money mortgage:** The purchase-money mortgage (PMM) is the most common way to structure seller financing extended to the buyer. In some contexts, a PMM also includes third-party financing that enables the buyer to purchase the property. [158]

F. **Deed of trust:** A mortgage that includes a third-party trustee. Typically used in a state permitting nonjudicial foreclosure. [158]

CHAPTER 16
MORTGAGE OBLIGATIONS

I. FORM OF OBLIGATION

Every mortgage secures the payment or performance of an obligation. [163]

II. USURY

A usury law limits the amount of interest a lender may charge a borrower. Most usury laws are state laws. [163]

A. **Traditional fixed limit:** Traditional usury laws set a fixed maximum interest rate for certain categories of loans. [163]

B. **Compounding of interest:** The term "compounding" refers to how often interest on the loan is calculated. Frequent compounding raises the effective interest rate. [163–164]

1. **Simple interest:** The term "simple interest" means that interest on the loan is compounded annually. A usury law with a fixed annual maximum rate is usually calculated based on simple interest.

2. **Market customs:** Simple interest is common for a loan with only a single payment, due at maturity. For installment loans, interest is usually compounded at the end of the period when an installment is due.

C. **Spreading interest over the loan term:** Generally, the borrower's interest payments are not distributed equally over the loan term. [164–165]

1. **Prepaid interest:** Prepaid interest, including points paid up front to get a mortgage loan, may cause a usury violation unless the spreading of interest is allowed.

2. **Adjustable interest rate:** An adjustable or variable interest rate may violate a usury law if an upward adjustment exceeds a fixed maximum rate.

   a. **Usury savings clauses:** A usury savings clause protects an adjustable-rate loan that is subject to a fixed usury limit.

D. **Time-price rule:** In some states, a purchase money mortgage loan must comply with any applicable usury laws, but many states immunize them under the *time-price* or *credit-sale* rule. [165]

   E. **Remedies for usury violations:** At a minimum, the lender forfeits the interest that exceeds the usury limit. [165–166]

      1. **Statutory damages:** Some states give the borrower statutory damages.

      2. **No interest:** Some states bar the lender from collecting interest.

      3. **No further payments:** A few states bar the lender from collecting any further payments, both interest and outstanding principal.

   F. **Lender defenses:** On occasion, a lender raises affirmative defenses, such as waiver and estoppel. These rarely succeed. [166]

   G. **Federal preemption: The Depository Institutions Deregulation and Monetary Control Act:** In 1980, Congress passed the Depository Institutions Deregulation and Monetary Control Act, which preempts state usury laws on almost all loans secured by first liens on residential real property. [166]

III. LATE PAYMENT

   When a mortgage borrower pays late, the lender is entitled to compensation. [166]

   A. **Interest on unpaid sum:** The primary remedy is interest from the due date until the borrower pays the principal. [167]

      1. **Higher default interest rate specified:** Some promissory notes require that the maker pay a higher interest rate upon the event of default.

      2. **No default interest rate specified:** When the promissory note does not specify the rate of interest after maturity, the borrower should pay the market rate at the time of default.

   B. **Late payment charge:** Many mortgage loans expressly provide for a late charge. [167–169]

      1. **State statutory limits:** Many states have statutes that limit the amount of late charges.

      2. **Federal regulations:** At the federal level, residential mortgage lenders are subject to various regulations concerning late charges.

      3. **Liquidated damages:** A late payment charge is a type of liquidated damages clause.

      4. **State usury laws:** In some states, a late payment charge is interest for purposes of usury laws.

      5. **Effect of statutes and regulations on common law liquidated damages rules and usury rules:** When a statute or regulation authorizes a late charge, it is generally held valid.

IV. PREPAYMENT

   Prepayment occurs when the borrower pays part or all of the principal before the due date specified in the promissory note. [169]

   A. **Total prepayment:** The borrower pays the entire loan balance before the due date. [169]

B. Partial prepayment: The borrower pays some, but not all, of the principal before the due date. [169]

C. Voluntary prepayment: Prepayment is voluntary when the borrower decides to pay early. [169]

D. Involuntary prepayment: Prepayment is involuntary when the lender compels prepayment due to the borrower's default or the occurrence of some other event. [169]

E. Borrower's right to prepay: There are two implied rules for promissory notes that lack a prepayment clause. [169–171]

　　1. Perfect tender in time: Under this implied rule, the borrower has no right to prepay.

　　2. Implied right to prepay: The trend is for states to reject the rule of perfect tender in time. They imply a borrower right to prepay.

　　3. Express prepayment provisions: Many loans expressly permit total and partial prepayments without penalty.

V. NONDEBT OBLIGATIONS

Most mortgages secure debts held by the mortgagee. But a mortgage can secure other legally enforceable obligations. [171]

A. Definition of debt: A "debt" is an obligation to pay a fixed amount of money with or without interest. [171]

　　1. Collateral promises: The mortgagor usually makes promises in addition to the promise to pay the debt. These are secured by the mortgage.

B. Primary obligation is not a debt: A property owner may grant a mortgage to secure an obligation that is not a debt. For the mortgage to be enforceable, there are several requirements commonly imposed by courts. [171–172]

　　1. Written description of obligation: The mortgage must expressly describe the obligation it secures.

　　2. Definitely ascertainable amount: The obligation must be capable of reduction to a definitely ascertainable amount.

C. Support mortgage: A purchaser of property promises to provide financial support for the seller for the remainder of his life and secures this promise by giving a support mortgage. [172]

CHAPTER 17

TRANSFERS BY BORROWERS AND LENDERS

I. TRANSFERS OF MORTGAGED PROPERTY

Upon the transfer of mortgaged property, the grantee may agree to *assume* the mortgage debt or to *take title subject to* that debt. [177]

A. Assumption of mortgage obligation: Assumption means the grantee promises the grantor to pay all of the debt in accordance with its terms. [177–179]

1. **Buyer's position:** The grantee becomes *personally liable* to pay the debt.

2. **Seller's position**

   a. **Primary liability of buyer:** The grantee is primarily liable to pay the debt.

   b. **Seller is surety:** The grantor's liability is now secondary: She becomes a surety with respect to the debt.

   c. **Surety's rights:** The grantor as surety may pay the debt and by subrogation obtain the mortgagee's rights to enforce the promissory note and to foreclose. In most states, the grantor instead may sue the grantee for breach of the promise to assume.

3. **Further transfer and assumption:** If the assuming buyer sells the property with her buyer assuming the existing debt, the original seller usually becomes a *subsurety*.

4. **Express release of liability:** The seller can avoid continuing liability as a surety by getting an express release of liability from the mortgagee.

5. **Mortgagee's position:** The mortgagee can collect the debt from the assuming grantee.

   a. **Direct contract between buyer and mortgagee:** If the grantee and the mortgagee sign an assumption agreement, the mortgagee can collect.

   b. **No contract between grantee and mortgagee:** When they do not sign an assumption agreement, the mortgagee can enforce the grantee's assumption promise made to the grantor as a third-party beneficiary or on the basis of derivative rights.

B. Taking subject to mortgage obligation: Taking subject to debt is permitted as an exception to good title. The buyer does not promise to pay the debt. [179]

1. **Nonrecourse financing:** Taking subject to debt means that the buyer has no personal liability for failing to pay.

2. **Relevance of amount of equity:** The distinction between assumption and taking subject to the mortgage is much more important when the buyer makes a very small or no down payment.

C. Modification and extension of mortgage debt: After an assumption or a transfer subject to debt, the mortgagee and the grantee may modify or extend the debt, but the mortgagor is generally discharged. [179–181]

1. **Assumption: Discharge of surety:** The extension of the maturity date for payment of the debt discharges the surety.

2. **Negotiable instruments and the UCC:** Some mortgage obligations are evidenced by negotiable instruments, subject to Article 3 of the UCC.

3. **Taking subject to debt:** Three alternative rules deal with extensions and modifications when the grantee takes subject to mortgage debt. The mortgagor may get a total discharge, a partial discharge to the extent of property value, or no discharge.

4. **Reservation of rights clause:** A clause stating that the mortgagee and a successor owner may extend or modify the debt is generally enforceable.

D. **Restrictions on transfer by mortgagor** [181–184]

1. **General rule of free alienability:** The mortgagor's property rights are freely alienable under all three theories of mortgage law (title, lien, and intermediate).

2. **Due-on-sale clause:** The parties may agree to restrict the mortgagor's right to transfer the mortgaged property. The "due-on-sale" clause restricts the borrower's right to sell.

3. **Federal rule on enforcement of due-on-sale clauses:** The Garn-St. Germain Depository Institutions Act (1982) makes due-on-sale clauses automatically enforceable under certain circumstances.

4. **Prior state law approaches:** Before the Act some state courts automatically enforced due-on-sale clauses and other states required that the lender demonstrate that the transfer would impair security.

5. **Garn-St. Germain Depository Institutions Act**

   a. **Automatic enforceability:** Generally, the Act makes due-on-sale clauses automatically enforceable.

   b. **Lender's conditions to transfers:** The lender can impose any condition it wishes on a proposed transfer.

   c. **Express standard in due-on-sale clause:** The parties may bargain for an express standard that governs the lender's criteria for approval of a transfer.

   d. **Act's scope:** The Act applies to every *real property loan*.

   e. **Office of Thrift Supervision (OTS) regulation:** The OTS regulations take a broad view of preemption, including leasehold mortgages and installment land contracts within the scope.

   f. **Act's definition of "due-on-sale" clause:** It is a clause that "authorizes a lender, at its option, to declare" the entire debt due "if all or any part of the property . . . is sold or transferred without the lender's prior written consent."

   g. **Act's exemption for nonsubstantive transfers:** The Act protects residential borrowers by prohibiting a lender from using a due-on-sale clause for certain transfers called "nonsubstantive transfers."

   h. **Effect of exemptions on state law:** The Act preempts any state law that permits acceleration based on events covered by the exemptions.

6. **Seller-buyer avoidance of due-on-sale clauses:** Mortgagors and buyers sometimes try to hide a transfer from a lender when the mortgage has a due on sale clause.

II. TRANSFERS OF MORTGAGE DEBT

Mortgage loans in both the residential and the commercial sectors are often sold and assigned. Many loans, especially residential loans, are transferred as part of a pool of loans. The bundling, marketing, and sale of mortgages is known as *securitization*. [184]

A. How mortgage loans are assigned: The transfer of an ownership interest in a mortgage loan is often called an *assignment*. A mortgagee's sale of her entire interest in a loan involves four steps: assignment, endorsement, delivery, and recordation. [184–185]

B. Mortgage Electronic Registration System (MERS): MERS, developed in the 1990s, facilitates transfers of ownership interests in residential mortgage loans. MERS acts as a nominee for loans and is the mortgagee of record, regardless of how many times the mortgage is sold. MERS eliminates the need to record assignments of mortgages in the public records. [185]

C. Mortgage follows obligation: The obligation is primary in importance. An attempt to transfer the mortgage apart from the obligation is invalid. A transfer of the promissory note alone automatically conveys the mortgage to the assignee. [185]

D. Failure to record assignment of mortgage: An assignee of the debt has priority from the date of recordation of the mortgage. [185]

E. Types of assignments of mortgage debts [185–186]

   1. Outright sale: The mortgagee transfers her whole interest in the note and other instruments.

   2. Security interest: The mortgagee can pledge the note, granting a security interest in the note and instruments.

      a. Perfection under the Uniform Commercial Code: UCC Article 9 governs the creation and perfection of the security interest.

F. Negotiable instruments: Some mortgage debts are evidenced by negotiable instruments under the Uniform Commercial Code. [186–188]

   1. Assignee of nonnegotiable debt: If a debt is not negotiable, the assignee takes subject to defenses the mortgagor has against the mortgagee.

   2. Assignee of negotiable instrument: A holder in due course of a negotiable instrument takes free of personal defenses, but remains subject to real defenses.

   3. Negotiation of mortgage: In most states a mortgage that secures a negotiable instrument is also negotiable (thus the mortgagor cannot assert personal defenses in foreclosure).

   4. When is an instrument negotiable? An instrument is negotiable when it contains an unconditional obligation to pay a fixed amount of money and no additional undertakings of the maker.

   5. Who is a holder in due course? To be a holder in due course, an assignee of a negotiable instrument must have possession of the instrument, the transfer must be by "negotiation," the assignee must pay value, and the assignee must take the instrument in good faith.

   6. Statutory and regulatory restrictions on rights of holder in due course: State and federal law sometimes protect the mortgagor from the normal consequences of assignments of negotiable instruments to holders in due course.

CHAPTER 18

DEFAULT AND ACCELERATION

I. SETTING FOR DEFAULT

A. Market role: Mortgages reduce risk for lenders by allowing the lender to reach the mortgaged property if the debtor fails to perform her obligation to pay. [193]

B. Importance for parties: Default threatens the lender's expectations that the loan will be profitable. Often the borrower's expectations about property value or available income have not been realized. [193–194]

II. DEFAULT CLAUSES

A. Purpose: The default clause allows the lender to exercise one or more of the remedies provided in the mortgage, including foreclosure. [194]

B. Lender's decision making: For minor defaults, lenders often forbear resorting to remedies. For major defaults, lenders usually take prompt action. [194]

   1. Foreclosure: The lender moves to get possession or foreclose if the borrower has intentionally defaulted, is threatening the value of the security, or has no realistic hope of being able to pay.

   2. Workout potential: If the borrower has suffered a short-term hardship and is willing to pay the debt, foreclosure may be avoided.

C. Interpretation of default clauses: Default clauses are interpreted in accordance with standard principles of contract law. [194]

   1. Place and manner of payment: Payment is made upon actual receipt by the lender. The "mailbox rule" does not apply.

III. ACCELERATION

Acceleration makes the principal balance, together with all accrued interest, immediately due and payable. [195]

A. Types of acceleration clauses [195]

   1. Automatic acceleration: The debt is due and payable upon the occurrence of a specified event, like a certain type of default.

   2. Optional acceleration: The lender has the option to accelerate the debt.

B. Lack of acceleration clause [195]

   1. No acceleration: If there is no express acceleration clause, the lender cannot accelerate the debt.

   2. **Anticipatory repudiation theory:** A few courts accept the lender's argument that failure to pay a series of installments amounts to anticipatory repudiation.

C. **Procedure for acceleration** [196]

   1. **Automatic acceleration clause:** With an automatic clause, the lender does not need to take any action to accelerate the loan.

   2. **Optional acceleration clause:** With an optional clause, the lender must take affirmative action to accelerate.

D. **Defenses to acceleration** [196–198]

   1. **History of late payments:** Waiver or estoppel may apply, even if the loan has an *anti-waiver* clause. If there is waiver or estoppel, to insist on timely payment, the lender must warn the borrower that from now on he must pay on time.

   2. **Materiality of default:** Most courts allow acceleration only for serious defaults.

   3. **Borrowers' statutory rights to cure default:** State statutes often require notice to the borrower prior to acceleration or authorize the borrower to pay arrearages after acceleration and reinstate the installment loan.

E. **Amount payable upon acceleration:** The entire principal balance, plus accrued interest, is due. [198–199]

   1. **Prepayment premiums:** Generally, the lender cannot both accelerate and receive a prepayment penalty.

   2. **Late payment charges:** The lender cannot impose late payment charges after acceleration because installments are no longer payable.

CHAPTER 19

FORECLOSURE

I. THE NATURE OF FORECLOSURE

A. **Purpose of foreclosure:** Foreclosure is the process by which the mortgagee gets the property and causes its value to be applied to the obligation. [203]

B. **Types of foreclosure:** The three main types of foreclosures are strict foreclosure, judicial foreclosure, and power of sale (nonjudicial) foreclosure. [203]

II. STRICT FORECLOSURE

Under strict foreclosure, if the mortgagor does not redeem by a date set by the court, the mortgagee retains the property. [204]

A. **Modern usage:** Only a few states make extensive use of strict foreclosure. [204]

B. Specialized applications: In many states, strict foreclosure is available to handle specialized problems. [204]

III. KEY CONCEPTS

A. Action on the debt: The mortgagee sues for a judgment equal to the unpaid principal, interest, and other charges. [204]

B. Foreclosure action: The mortgagee seeks to take ownership of the property away from the mortgagor and to cause a sale. [204]

C. Deficiency: If the value of the property is less than the debt, foreclosure results in a deficiency. The deficiency is the difference between the debt and the sales proceeds. [204]

D. Surplus: If the value of the property is more than the debt, the mortgagor has equity. There is a surplus if the sales proceeds exceed the debt. [204–205]

    1. Payment of surplus: The surplus goes to the mortgagor unless other parties have a better claim to it.

E. Election of remedies: Generally, the mortgagee brings an action on the debt or forecloses. [205]

    1. Action on debt first: The mortgagee may bring an action on the debt without trying to foreclose.

    2. Foreclosure first: The mortgagee may foreclose without bringing an action on the debt.

    3. Both remedies simultaneously: With judicial foreclosure, the mortgagee may seek foreclosure and an action for a deficiency judgment simultaneously.

IV. JUDICIAL FORECLOSURE

A. Goal in terms of title: The purchaser at foreclosure should get title in the condition it was when the mortgage was signed. [205]

B. Necessary parties: Persons with interests that are junior to the mortgage being foreclosed are necessary parties. [205–206]

    1. Omitted necessary parties: The owner of a junior interest who is not joined as a defendant in the foreclosure action is an omitted necessary party.

        a. Omitted party's rights: The omitted party retains property rights.

        b. Foreclose purchaser's rights: The purchaser at foreclosure has to deal with the rights of the omitted party.

        c. Intentionally omitted necessary party: Intentional failure to join a necessary party may result in no relief.

C. Proper parties: These are persons with senior rights. They can be joined as defendants without consent. [206]

D. **Foreclosure of mortgages held by Mortgage Electronic Registration System (MERS):** Many recent residential mortgages appoint MERS as the mortgagee of record as nominee for the originating lender, who then sells the mortgage in the secondary market. MERS continues as the mortgagee of record. In many cases, homeowners have challenged foreclosures based on the involvement of MERS. Usually, the foreclosure must be brought in the name of the real owner of the debt and cannot be brought by MERS as nominee. [206–207]

V. POWER OF SALE FORECLOSURE

A. **Goal in terms of title:** The goal is the same as for judicial foreclosure. [207]

B. **Cheap and fast:** Power of sale foreclosure is less costly and faster than judicial foreclosure. [207]

   1. **Notice to junior interests:** In many nonjudicial foreclosure states, junior interest owners are not entitled to notice of the foreclosure in the absence of contract.

C. **Statutory procedures:** State statutes specify notice provisions, sales procedures, and other formalities. A deviation from statutory requirements means the foreclosure sale is subject to invalidation. [207]

D. **Title risk** [207]

   1. **Judicial foreclosure:** Because a judicial decree is a final judgment, the foreclosure purchaser's title to the property is relatively safe.

   2. **Nonjudicial foreclosure:** Nonjudicial foreclosure results in weaker titles than those produced by judicial foreclosure.

VI. PRIORITY OF MORTGAGE THAT REFINANCES PRIOR MORTGAGE

A. **Equitable subrogation:** A lender who pays off a senior mortgage and takes a new mortgage is subrogated to the rights of the first mortgagee as against intervening lienholders. The lender must lack actual notice of the junior claims at the time of the refinancing. The refinancing mortgagee is protected only up to the amount of the senior mortgage debt. [208]

B. **Record priorities prevail:** A few states reject equitable subrogation. Normal recording act rules dictate the priority of a mortgage that refinances prior debt. [208]

VII. DEED IN LIEU OF FORECLOSURE

A borrower who has defaulted may agree to convey the property to the lender by deed in lieu of foreclosure. [209]

A. **Advantages for borrower:** The lender cancels part or all of the mortgage debt. [209]

B. **Risks for borrower:** The borrower loses her equity. [209]

C. **Advantages for lender:** The lender gets title quickly and avoids foreclosure proceedings. [209]

D. Risks for lender: The borrower may assert defenses such as a clog on the equity of redemption, inadequate consideration, or unconscionability. The deed in lieu of foreclosure does not cut off junior interests, and it is a preference for bankruptcy purposes. [209]

VIII. ECONOMICS OF FORECLOSURE

A. Problem of price adequacy: Foreclosure sale prices are usually low. [209]

B. Low price by itself does not invalidate sale: The borrower needs to prove additional grounds. [209]

C. Grossly inadequate price coupled with mistake: A court may refuse to confirm a foreclosure sale if the injured party made a good faith mistake. [210]

D. Inadequate price coupled with irregularity: Any irregularity, procedural or otherwise, creates risk that a court will set aside the foreclosure sale. [210]

IX. STATUTORY MORTGAGOR PROTECTIONS

A. One-action rule: A one-action rule limits the mortgagee to a single action, which must include foreclosure. [210]

B. Statutory redemption: Statutory redemption, in effect in 33 states, is the right to redeem the property after completion of the foreclosure sale. The price is the foreclosure sale price, plus interest and foreclosure costs. Generally, waiver of the right to redeem is invalid. [210–211]

C. Limits on deficiency judgments: Many states bar lenders from obtaining deficiency judgments under certain circumstances. [211]

D. Fair value rule: Fair value legislation permits a deficiency judgment only to the extent the debt exceeds the proven "fair value" of the property. [211]

CHAPTER 20

MORTGAGE SUBSTITUTES

I. THE USE OF MORTGAGE SUBSTITUTES

A. Market role: A mortgage substitute is a transaction that performs a credit function that is not documented by the execution of a standard mortgage instrument. [215]

B. Opting out of mortgage law: Often the reason for using a mortgage substitute is to avoid one or more of the following mortgage law principles: [215–216]

   1. Mortgage as status: Freedom of contract is limited.

      a. Anti-clogging rule: Terms that clog the mortgagor's equity of redemption are void.

      b. Foreclosure procedures: Statutory procedures cannot be waived because they protect mortgagors and third parties.

C. **Types of mortgage substitutes:** Common mortgage substitutes include the absolute deed, lease with option to purchase, sale-leaseback, negative pledge, and installment land contract. [216]

II. DISGUISED MORTGAGE

In a disguised mortgage, also called an "equitable mortgage," the substance of the transaction is a debt secured by real property. The court applies mortgage law. [216]

III. ABSOLUTE DEED INTENDED AS SECURITY

A regular warranty deed is a mortgage if it is intended to secure a debt owed to the grantee. [217]

A. **Written evidence of owner's right to regain title:** Written evidence that the grantor has a right to pay and reacquire the property points toward a disguised mortgage, but it is not dispositive. [217]

B. **Parol evidence:** Parol evidence is admissible to explain the intent of an absolute deed. [217]

C. **Factors:** Factors that point toward a deed intended as security include a prior loan, unequal bargaining positions, a low price, a fiduciary relationship, and the grantor's retention of possession. [217–219]

1. **Prior loan transaction between the parties:** The parties were borrower-lender prior to making the deed.

2. **Unequal bargaining positions:** The grantor's financing need and the parties' unequal bargaining positions.

3. **Price less than fair market value:** A low price compared to fair market value.

4. **Fiduciary relationship between the parties:** The grantee owes the grantor a fiduciary duty due to a special relationship such as attorney-client.

5. **Grantor retains possession:** The grantor retains possession after making the deed.

6. **Existence of debt:** Courts often say the existence of a debt is another important factor.

IV. NEGATIVE PLEDGE

A. **Definition:** With the negative pledge (negative covenant), the borrower promises the lender not to convey or encumber specified property before the loan is repaid. [219]

B. **Status as equitable mortgage:** Courts have split on whether the negative pledge is a mere contract promise or in substance a mortgage. [219]

V. INSTALLMENT LAND CONTRACT

A. Definition: Under an installment land contract (contract for deed), the purchaser takes possession and pays the price in installments over a lengthy period of time. The seller conveys title upon final payment. [220–221]

    1. Possession: The buyer goes into possession immediately upon signing the contract.

    2. Title retention and deed: The seller retains title until the purchaser makes the final payment. Sometimes the vendor signs the deed at the outset and puts it in escrow.

B. Market uses of installment land contract: Land contracts are primarily used for sales when purchasers do not qualify for standard mortgage financing and for sales of vacation property. [221]

C. Vendor's remedies for purchaser's default [221–222]

    1. Forfeiture clause: Under the traditional approach, forfeiture clauses are enforceable as written, absent contract defenses. The modern trend is to treat forfeiture clauses as a type of penalty.

    2. Expectancy damages: The vendor may terminate the contract and sue for expectancy damages.

    3. Restitution: The vendor collects damages equal to the value of possession since the date of the contract less the installment payments made by the purchaser.

    4. Purchaser's right of redemption: Some states give a redemption right.

    5. Foreclosure as a mortgage: The vendor forecloses the contract as an equitable mortgage. In a few states, every land contract is an equitable mortgage. In some states, after the purchaser has made substantial payments, the vendor must foreclose as an equitable mortgage.

D. Transfers by purchaser [222–223]

    1. General rule: The purchaser's rights under the land contract, including the right to possession, are freely alienable.

    2. Express restrictions: Land contracts may restrict transfers.

CHAPTER 21

JUNIOR MORTGAGES

I. LEVERAGING A DEAL

A. Sources of leverage: Leverage may come from junior mortgage loans, from refinancing with a larger mortgage, and from selling equity interests. [227–228]

B. Leverage, risk, and return [228]

    1. Rate of return: Higher leverage increases the rate of return to the borrower for a successful property.

2. **Effect of leverage:** The risk to the lenders is greater because they have more capital at stake. The risk to the owners is greater because high leverage reduces their equity and can raise the potential for default.

II. THE MARKET FOR SECONDARY FINANCING

A. **Rank of multiple mortgages:** Most junior mortgages are second mortgages, but they can be of even lower priority. [228]

B. **Other junior finance devices** [228–229]

1. **Assignment of lease:** For rental property.

2. **Pledge of ownership interest:** Using an interest in a legal entity as collateral.

3. **Negative pledge agreement:** A promise not to further encumber the property.

C. **Home equity loans:** Home equity loans are commonly used to finance home improvements and repairs, and for debt consolidation purposes. [229]

1. **Loan terms:** Many are secured by second mortgages and are amortized over a fixed term.

2. **Home equity line of credit:** The borrower can borrow from time to time, up to the credit limit.

3. **Income tax incentive:** For federal income tax purposes, a borrower may deduct interest paid on a home equity loan of up to $100,000.

4. **Bankruptcy impact:** Under the exception in Bankruptcy Code § 1322(b)(2), courts have refused to let borrowers modify home equity loans.

D. **Commercial market for junior mortgages:** Local banks and major financial institutions make such loans. [229]

E. **Relationship between markets for first and second mortgages:** As an alternative to secondary financing, the owner should consider refinancing or seeking a future advance from the existing lender. [229]

III. PROTECTING THE JUNIOR MORTGAGE

A. **Contract terms and practices that reduce risk:** The junior mortgagee charges more for her loan than for a first mortgage due to the greater risk. The junior mortgagee tries to reduce the risk of foreclosure in several ways. [229–230]

1. **Planning:** The junior lender should get an estoppel letter from the senior lender. The junior loan documents should contain both borrower representations and warranties about the first loan and a cross-default provision.

   a. **Drafting junior loan documents:** The documents should contain protective provisions.

2. **Monitoring:** The junior lender can monitor by requiring the borrower to submit proof of payment of all installments due under the senior loan.

3. **State law protection of junior lienors:** In judicial foreclosure states, the junior mortgagee is a necessary party, provided the senior mortgagee has notice of the junior mortgage.

B. **Marshalling of assets:** A senior creditor with multiple assets as security may be required to marshal assets when she forecloses. This means the senior creditor proceeds first against the asset that is not subject to a junior lien. [230]

IV. THE MORTGAGE SUBORDINATION

Owners of mortgages and other liens may contract to alter their priorities by entering into a subordination agreement. [230]

A. **Methods of subordination:** Subordination is achieved either by the sequence of recording (automatic subordination) or by express agreement, in which a party expressly subordinates her mortgage to a superior mortgage. [230–231]

B. **Other provisions besides priority rank:** The subordination agreement may address issues other than lien priority. When a subordination agreement fails to address future advances, courts tend to protect the junior lender. [231]

C. **Modification or extension of senior loan:** A modification or extension of the senior loan that prejudices the rights of a junior lienor may result in a novation. This promotes the junior lienor to the senior position. [231]

V. THE WRAP-AROUND MORTGAGE

A wrap-around mortgage is a junior mortgage in which the junior debt includes the senior debt. Both of the debts are installment obligations. The borrower pays the holder of the junior debt (the wrap-around loan), who in turn pays the holder of the senior debt (the wrapped loan). [231]

A. **Purpose:** To preserve the senior loan. [231]

B. **Risk to wrap-around lender:** Reduced because borrower pays all money to the junior and the junior forwards the amount to the senior lender. [231–232]

C. **Risk to wrap-around borrower:** Borrower has risk that junior will not properly forward funds to the senior lender. [232]

D. **Wrap-around note:** It is always overstated because it includes the wrapped debt with the new money. [232]

CHAPTER 22

THE COMMERCIAL REAL ESTATE MARKET

I. FINANCING ARRANGEMENTS BY AND BETWEEN LENDERS

A. **Construction loans:** The construction loan is used to finance development and construction of a real estate development project. [237–238]

C
A
P
S
U
L
E

S
U
M
M
A
R
Y

1. **Risk and term:** The construction loan is high risk, based on the potential value of the project if it is completed as planned. The loan is short term.

2. **Structure:** Usually recourse, with periodic draws, and payable when the project is completed.

3. **Supervision:** Requires supervision at the project location and of the funding and expenditure process.

B. **Permanent loans** [238–239]

1. **Risk and term:** The permanent loan pays off the construction loan. It is lower risk because the project is complete and generally long term and nonrecourse.

2. **Structure:** The owner pays the permanent loan out of the revenues from the finished project. It is lower risk because construction is complete and the lender can actually evaluate a finished project.

3. **Supervision:** Permanent lenders need expertise in property management and cash-flow controls.

C. **Loan coordination:** The commercial project requires coordination between the construction lender and the permanent lender. The construction lender wants a permanent lender committed to *take out* the construction loan. The permanent loan will then need to be paid by the developer/ borrower. This will be done by making monthly payments to the permanent lender over the life of the loan. [239–241]

1. **Promoting comparative advantage:** Construction lender and permanent lender work together to take advantage of the unique expertise of each.

2. **Three-party agreement or buy-sell agreement:** This agreement binds the construction lender to make its loan, the permanent lender to pay off that loan, and the developer to accept each loan on the agreed terms.

3. **The take-out:** The three standard types of take-outs are the lock-in, the stand-by, and the open-ended take-out.

   a. **Lock-in** requires permanent funding of the loan.

   b. **Stand-by** sets up a contingent obligation to fund.

   c. **Open-ended** funding is not prearranged.

II. SELECTING A DEVELOPMENT ENTITY

The developer of a commercial project usually selects a form of ownership that reduces the risk of personal liability. The developer needs to make a reasonable contribution to the capitalization of the entity. Typical entities include the corporation, the partnership or limited partnership, and the limited liability company. [241]

III. COMMERCIAL LENDING AND ARTICLE 9 OF THE UCC

Commercial real estate finance involves issues that extend beyond real property. A number of issues will involve personal property interests that are covered under Article 9 of the UCC. [241–242]

A. Nature of the Article 9 interest: Article 9 covers the process of getting a security interest in personal property and fixtures. These include goods and other property like accounts and general intangibles. [242]

B. Security and priority for three categories of property [242–243]

    1. Real property: Real property is covered under real property and mortgage law and is not subject to Article 9.

    2. Personal property: Is covered under Article 9 of the UCC.

    3. Fixtures: Fixtures are covered under both real property mortgage law and Article 9 of the UCC. The determination of what is a fixture is made by reference to state real property law.

C. Priority issues: A conflict can arise with respect to fixtures because they start out as personal property. They can be covered by a mortgage and an Article 9 security interest. Priority conflicts between a mortgage creditor and an Article 9 creditor are addressed in § 9-334. [243]

IV. THE LAWYER'S ROLE IN COMMERCIAL TRANSACTIONS

A. Opinion letters: The lawyer prepares or reviews opinion letters that cover the legal status or correctness of a number of elements of the transaction. Liability for errors is based on the standard of skill and care practiced by members of the legal community. [243]

B. Conflicts: The lawyer must avoid conflicts of interest with her client and must avoid dual representation unless each client consents to such after full disclosure. [243]

CHAPTER 23

COMMERCIAL REAL ESTATE FINANCING

I. MARKET COORDINATION OF COMMERCIAL DEVELOPMENT

Commercial projects emerge in five main phases.

A. Project phases [247–248]

    1. Planning: The developer comes up with an idea and does market studies.

    2. Acquisition: If the developer does not already own the property, he negotiates and contracts for its acquisition.

    3. Development: This phase involves basic land improvement and arrangements for utilities and service to the property.

    4. Construction: Buildings, structures, and related facilities are constructed.

   5. Completion: At project completion, the property becomes income producing.

B. **Loan relationship** [248–249]

   1. Investors: During the planning phase, the developer seeks contributions to capitalize the development entity and to provide the equity needed to get debt financing.

   2. Acquisition, development, and construction funding: Sometimes acquisition, development, and construction financing are combined in one package called an ADC loan.

   3. Permanent financing: After completion and the take-out of the construction loan, the project generates income that can be used to pay the permanent loan.

II. COMMON DEVICES FOR STRUCTURING LOANS

A. **Retainage and holdbacks:** A construction loan usually calls for retainage or holdback on each draw of between 10 to 15 percent. [249]

B. **Performance standards:** Both the construction lender and the permanent lender use performance standards, which set goals for marketing and completing different elements of the project. [249]

C. **Price maintenance:** For performance standards to work properly, they must include specific price guidelines. [249]

D. **Release schedules:** If the parties agree to *partial releases* of portions of the property from the mortgage lien, a schedule will specify the order, form, and cost of such releases. [249–250]

III. GAP FINANCING

   Gap financing can handle short-term needs arising from cost overruns or the nature of a take-out arrangement. [250]

A. **Future advance:** A future advance clause in the construction loan may facilitate gap financing. [250]

IV. LOAN PARTICIPATIONS

   Multiple lenders can make a large loan together with a loan participation agreement. [250]

A. **Spreading risk:** Some lenders do loan participations to reduce their risk by allocating some of the project risk to other participants. [251]

B. **Lending requirements:** Some lenders do loan participations because banking laws limit the amount they can lend to one borrower or to one project. [251]

V. LEASING CONSIDERATIONS IN COMMERCIAL TRANSACTIONS

A. Space leasing: When units are not for sale, they are held for lease to commercial or residential tenants. [251–252]

B. Ground lease: The landowner may lease the ground to the developer, who adds a building and other improvements. Ground leases are long term, and they provide a secured bundle of rights for both lessor and developer. [252]

C. Sale-leaseback: A sale-leaseback is an alternative to a mortgage loan. The owner sells the property and leases it back for a long term. The buyer pays cash, like making a loan of funds, and the seller pays back the cash by way of rent payments. [252]

D. Leasehold mortgage: A tenant can mortgage its leasehold to a lender. Upon foreclosure, the lender sells the leasehold to a new tenant. [252]

    1. Attornment and nondisturbance agreement: When there is a fee mortgage granted by the landlord, an attornment and nondisturbance agreement can reduce risk for both the lender and the tenants of the project. If the lender takes possession or forecloses, this agreement provides for the continuation of the leases.

CHAPTER 1

MARKET CONTEXT FOR REAL ESTATE TRANSACTIONS

ChapterScope ━━

This chapter explores the basic market context of real estate transactions. It introduces basic concepts concerning market motivation, risk, and transaction costs.

- ■ **Market motivations:** Parties to a real estate transaction are looking to capture and create value.

- ■ **Measures of success:** The two primary measures of success are accounting profits and economic profits.

- ■ **Market choice:** People have market choices among different types of real estate markets and between real estate markets in general and alternative market activities, including investing in other types of ventures, such as the computer industry or securities markets.

- ■ **Categories of costs:** The major categories of costs are out-of-pocket costs, opportunity costs, and sunk costs.

- ■ **Strategic behavior:** Lawyers need to think strategically in structuring transactions. They must also account for two types of strategic behavior: transactional misbehavior and rent-seeking behavior.

- ■ **Categories of market risks:** Two main categories of market risks are temporal risk and transactional risk.

- ■ **Risk and return:** The greater the risk the higher the return expected in order to induce a proper level of investment.

- ■ **Role of the lawyer:** The lawyer acts as a risk manager in the real estate transaction, assisting in the identification, reduction, and shifting of risk.

I. MARKET CONTEXT FOR REAL ESTATE TRANSACTIONS

A lawyer should understand the market context of real estate transactions in order to appreciate the motivations of the parties and to propose and evaluate potential courses of action that a party might take.

A. Creating and capturing value: Each party to a real estate transaction hopes to capture and create value. Typically parties look for value in the form of profits, equity appreciation, or cash flow. Sometimes the value is not directly economic in nature. For example, a home buyer may seek to gain control or autonomy by moving from an apartment to a home, or a buyer may seek tax benefits from a deal.

Example: Cidra represents Shawnda in purchasing a vacant tract of land that has commercial development potential. Shawnda needs financing, and the local bank offers her a variety of loan types from which to select. Each type of mortgage has different terms. Some are adjustable rate mortgages, some are fixed-rate mortgages, some have negative amortization, and various interest rates and fees are set for each. To counsel Shawnda, Cidra needs to know more than the legal rules related to each mortgage. She needs to know the market context: how each mortgage fits with different expectations of future market performance, cash flow, equity and tax objectives, and trade-offs among a wide range of market variables. She needs to know her client's income and financial expectations and goals. Likewise, to negotiate effectively on her client's behalf, Cidra needs to understand how the bank expects to realize profit from each type of mortgage. Knowing the market expectations of the parties will permit Cidra to provide intelligent advice about economic and legal differences in each type of mortgage.

B. Market choice: The parties to a transaction generally have a number of available market choices. They have a variety of ways to spend and invest their money. The available choices exist because of competition in the marketplace. A person's alternatives for spending or investing may consist of real estate opportunities. In real estate markets, choices involve selecting between residential or commercial properties. Competing investments outside of real estate might include stocks and bonds.

II. MEASURING VALUE

A transaction may be said to be profitable in one of two ways. It may create an accounting profit or an economic profit. Over the long run, market choices are generally motivated by economic profit, not accounting profit.

A. Accounting profits: Accounting profit is the financial return from a given activity relative to the costs of that activity.

B. Economic profits: Economic profit is measured by comparing market options. These profits are the excess returns available from an activity relative to the returns available from other similar market choices.

Example: Anthony can invest $1 million in a new pizza place or in a partnership interest in an upstart computer company. Both businesses have the same risk outlook but the pizza business has an expected payout of 5 percent in the first year while the computer investment has an expected return of 7 percent in the first year. Assuming everything else is equal, both businesses will have an accounting profit (each has a return over expenses). The pizza place, however, represents a 2 percent economic loss because Anthony could easily have made 2 percent more on his investment given the same risks. Economic profits account for opportunity loss with respect to other similar opportunities that could have been taken.

C. Risk and return: The degree of risk relates to the rate of return for an investment or transaction. The riskier investment choice must provide a higher rate of return to attract a proper level of investment. Persons who buy or invest must trade off aversion to risk and potential rates of return.

Example: Maurie, a cautious person, has saved $2,000. He can put this money in an insured bank account that will earn 2.5 percent interest or buy a real estate limited partnership investment that promises a 15-20 percent return if it is successful. If the real estate venture fails, Maurie will lose everything. He confronts the typical trade-off between risk and return. If he is risk averse, he may prefer the safer bank account with the low rate of return.

D. **Value and utility:** In economic terms, value is equated to utility. Utility is a measure of how much a person desires a particular good, service, or activity. In our markets, utility is generally set by money serving as a proxy. A person's utility is often said to be measured by her willingness to pay, but this can present problems. Willingness to pay and ability to pay sometimes diverge because wealth and bargaining power are not evenly distributed in our society.

1. **Marginal utility:** The amount of utility a person attaches to the prospect of purchasing a particular property or thing can vary according to what the person presently owns. Marginal utility measures the value a person places on purchasing an additional asset. When she already owns one or more of a particular type of asset, she may place a lower value on the acquisition of an additional asset of the same type.

E. **Comparative advantage:** Comparative advantages may make trades more likely. A person has a comparative advantage in performing a function if she can handle the task more efficiently or produce a better outcome due to such factors as education, experience, or information. A lawyer should have a comparative advantage over a lay person in being able to undertake and complete a legal task.

III. CATEGORIES OF COSTS

Real estate transactions involve a number of costs referred to in general terms as transaction costs. In economics transaction costs include a number of categories of costs including those related to the expense of gathering information and managing risk. Three key categories of costs are set out below.

A. **Out-of-pocket costs:** These costs are the actual expenses incurred to acquire or own property. They can include the costs of acquisition, survey, title examination, broker fee, lawyer fee, and other such expenses that have to be paid.

B. **Opportunity costs:** These costs are the market choices a person gives up in order to pursue a certain transaction. Opportunity costs vary from individual to individual because people do not have the same utility or preference for alternative market choices and they do not share the same comparative advantage.

C. **Sunk costs:** These are costs that cannot be recovered when a party abandons a course of action. For example, the cost of a property survey, initial title examination, and contract negotiation will generally be unrecoverable if the parties fail to enter into an enforceable purchase and sale agreement. High sunk costs may distort decision making, inducing a party to go forward on a deal or stay in an unfavorable transaction rather than seeking to exit from the transaction. If this happens, one can anticipate tension and difficulty between the parties as they move forward.

IV. MARKET-RELATED CONDUCT

A. **Transactional misbehavior:** Transactional misbehavior is a party's attempt to change the dynamics of a deal after it has been struck. Every agreement provides for a certain allocation or trade-off between price and risk. Transactional misbehavior occurs when a party tries to improve its position by changing the price and risk relationships that were previously agreed on.

Example: Clare asks Big Bank to lend her $20 million for a major construction project. As part of the deal, she explains how she has a large accounting staff on hand and how all funds will be closely monitored with continuous daily reporting to Big Bank on all expenditures. Any funds not currently being used will be kept in an insured account so as to preserve their availability for the construction project. Based on this, Big Bank agrees to a written deal that provides Clare with a very low and fixed rate of interest. Her business practices put her in the lowest risk group for business borrowers. After the deal is done, Clare experiences some cash flow problems because of some unanticipated changes in the market. She fires the accounting staff and takes all of the reserve construction funds and puts them into high-risk investments. Clare feels lucky, and she figures that she can cut costs by reducing the staff, plus with a couple of good investments, she figures that she won't have to worry about cash flow problems. Clare has changed a low-risk loan into a high-risk one, extracting extra value from her original deal. Her higher-risk operating structure would have required a higher rate of interest on her loan, but with a fixed-rate mortgage she gets to keep the lower cost loan and this is how she extracts extra value. Such misbehavior raises not only ethical problems, but also legal issues for structuring transactions. Since Big Bank can predict this kind of misbehavior, it will structure the transaction in ways to reduce the ability of Clare to change her conduct.

B. Rent-seeking behavior: A person engages in rent seeking when she tries to manipulate legal regulations or markets in order to create additional value. To the extent that law serves as a source of economic value, it can be thought of as a commodity.

Example: Erik has identified a piece of vacant property located on the edges of a commercial district that is currently zoned for residential use only. As residential property, its market value is $100,000, but Erik figures it is worth $1 million if zoned for commercial use like the nearby properties. Erik plans to spend time and money to get an option on the property and to get a change in the zoning. His attempt to create value by changing the legal rule is a form of rent seeking (sometimes referred to as ***opportunistic behavior***).

V. CATEGORIES OF MARKET RISKS

A. Temporal risk: Temporal risk consists of risk factors related to time, including past, present, or future information about a property or a transaction. ***Past historical information*** about a property being free of environmental contaminants may be wrong, for instance. ***Present soil samples*** of a property as part of an environmental audit may be inaccurate or incomplete, and ***future action or information*** may change the entire calculus on which an investment was made. Transactions that take place over a long time horizon, as compared to a simultaneous exchange, involve considerable risk because so many expectations can change during the course of the parties' relationship. Time also raises a problem with respect to value (the ***time value of money***) because we cannot be certain of the worth of a dollar in the future.

B. Transactional risk

1. Investor or ownership risk: This is the set of risks related to owning and investing in property and is sometimes called ***entrepreneurial risk***. It includes environmental and tort liabilities, contract liability in connection with the property, and the risk of loss from casualty, wear and tear, and physical and economic depreciation.

2. **Credit risk:** When a transaction involves financing, credit risk is presented due to the possibility that the debtor may turn out to be unwilling or unable to pay. Credit risk arises apart from financing transactions whenever parties to a transaction do not complete their performances simultaneously.

3. **Marketplace risk:** This risk stems from general market forces that can affect the profitability of any given transaction; for example, inflation, economic recession, changing interest rates, new technology, and population shifts may all affect the market for particular types of property. These risks may indirectly impact value by changing the liquidity of an investment. *Liquidity* is a measure of the ease with which one can sell property.

4. **Transfer risk:** When parties try to complete a transaction, transfer risk is present because of the possibility of errors, false or incomplete information, or mistaken assumptions. For example, documents may have errors in them or may get improperly recorded or lost.

VI. ROLE OF THE LAWYER

A. **Lawyer as risk manager:** A primary function of the lawyer in real estate transactions is to identify and manage the wide assortment of risks that may possibly arise. Many risks can be reduced or eliminated by engaging experts, such as building inspectors, environmental auditors, accountants, title companies, and surveyors. The lawyer should follow the rule of *IRS*, which means that the lawyer must work to **I**dentify, **R**educe, and **S**hift risk in structuring the transaction to benefit her client. The lawyer must draft documents and structure the transaction in a way that best reduces the risk of an unfavorable outcome while simultaneously achieving the client's legal and economic objectives. An important aspect of this process is authentication, which involves taking steps to confirm the validity and substance of the key elements of a deal. This includes the quality of title, the legal status of the parties, the enforceability of the documents, and the economic substance of any credit requirements.

B. **Professional responsibility in a market context:** Tension is inherent in the lawyer's role. She is a zealous advocate who properly seeks to reduce her client's risk and maximize her client's profit. The lawyer, however, is governed by a code of professional conduct that sets real limits on her behavior. This code incorporates values and obligations that may not always be consistent with the client's market objectives. The lawyer may also find that her obligations run to nonclients and third parties.

Example: In *Bohn v. Cody*, 832 P.2d 71 (Wash. 1992), an attorney, Cody, represents one party to the transaction (the borrower) but also works with the other party (the lender). In doing the transaction Cody repeats on several occasions that he only represents the borrower. When the transaction becomes problematic and the lender loses priority of its lien for repayment, Cody is sued by the lender. The court holds that there is no attorney-client relationship between the parties but finds a basis for requiring further investigation as to the third-party liability of Cody to the nonclient. An attorney must be careful to avoid liability to third parties who may assert reliance.

C. **Types of real estate law practice**

1. **Residential practice:** This typically involves home sales (including single-family homes, condominiums, and cooperatives), purchase financing, and sometimes includes loan refinancing and leasing work for such properties. The residential lawyer usually represents buyer, seller, or lender. In some cases, the lawyer represents more than one party, but this raises ethical

issues concerning dual representation. The residential practice has become increasingly competitive as a result of permitting nonlawyers to do much of the basic work. Typical nonlawyers in the residential transaction are real estate brokers and title companies.

2. **Commercial practice:** This goes beyond the basic contract, property, and mortgage law foundations of a residential transaction. The commercial lawyer deals regularly with other legal subjects, such as all areas of the Uniform Commercial Code (UCC), taxation, corporations and business associations, securities, bankruptcy, and environmental and land use law, as well as nonlegal matters concerning market and financial information.

D. **Lawyer's fee arrangement:** The lawyer is to charge a reasonable fee based on factors such as the complexity of the work, the amount of effort and expertise required, the likelihood that other employment opportunities will be forgone by taking the matter, the significance of or the amount involved in the matter, the time limitation imposed, and any special reputational skills or talents possessed by the lawyer.

1. **Residential:** In residential transactions, a lawyer for seller or buyer typically charges a fixed fee, which is disclosed to the client ahead of time.

2. **Loans:** In loan transactions, a lawyer representing the lender usually has her fee paid by the borrower as a cost of the loan. For residential loans, most attorneys charge a fixed amount. For commercial loans, an hourly rate is usually charged because many more things are open to negotiation and the nature of the transaction makes it subject to less standardization. For commercial loans, some lawyers charge on a percentage basis related to the loan amount. This practice, which is also occasionally used in some communities for residential loans, is declining due to competition and questions as to its legitimacy.

3. **Commercial:** In commercial transactions other than loans, most attorneys bill on an hourly basis. This market has become very competitive, with a growing trend to compete on hourly rates and on services offered to clients.

Quiz Yourself on
MARKET CONTEXT FOR REAL ESTATE TRANSACTIONS

1. Dora lists her house for sale at $450,000 on an "As Is" basis. Glen is interested in the house but is worried that perhaps the roof or plumbing may need work or repairs. Glen wants to buy the house but also wants Dora to warrant that the house has a good roof and a well-operating plumbing system. Without concern for the legal issues, will Glen's counteroffer impact the risk and pricing of the transaction? _____

2. Sharron has $1 million and she can invest it in a new office building project or buy herself a very nice sailboat. She believes that the sailboat will provide a lot of pleasure and will be a good investment. She is not sure what the sailboat resale market is like but she is confident that she can at least get her money back if she decides to sell it within 12 months. At the same time she feels that the office building project will be able to return about 20 percent on her investment. If Sharron decides to buy the sailboat, does she have an opportunity cost? _____

3. Rod runs a small service-oriented business. In order to please customers, he has been open 365 days a year and has hours from 7:00 A.M. to 11:30 P.M. He has been in business for 10 years and has always saved a great deal of his income. Rod goes to the local banker and seeks a loan, which he plans to secure against the equity in his business. He tells the banker not to worry about a loan repayment problem because Rod's secret to success is working long hours every day. The banker knows Rod is a hardworking and dependable guy with very conservative spending and investment tendencies. Based on this, the bank makes a loan to Rod at its lowest rate of interest. After getting the loan, Rod decides he has worked too hard in his life and needs to reward himself. He decides to cut back on his hours, having the business open only from 9 to 5 on Monday through Friday and closed for four weeks out of the year. As a consequence, business drops off, and Rod's cash flow falls to 40 percent of what it used to be prior to the loan. Should the local banker account for this type of behavior in setting up its loan with Rod? _____

4. Margaret is a solo practitioner and is hired by Beth to be the real estate lawyer on a $5 million purchase of vacant land to be used for development. In setting up the fee for services, Beth wants to know how she will be billed. Margaret says, "Don't worry about it; we will work it out later. It is all a matter of freedom of contract, so we can just do whatever we want after we see how much profit is in the deal for you." Is Margaret proceeding properly? _____

Answers

1. **Yes.** From our general knowledge of markets, we can expect that Dora will see the request for warranty protection as one that raises the cost of her performance. She will have to pay if there is a problem with the roof or the plumbing. Therefore, all things being equal, Dora will need to get a higher price if she wants to make the same return on the transaction. This is because risk and return are related, where risk is understood as a cost.

2. **Yes.** Sharron has an opportunity cost. Her next best option is her opportunity cost. Thus, not being able to invest in the office building is her opportunity cost of buying the sailboat.

3. **Yes.** The bank should anticipate such a potential problem. Transactions often start out with a set of expectations that can vary or change over the course of the relationship. In this case, Rod is displaying transactional misbehavior. He is doing things after the deal is set that change the risk dynamics of the transaction. If Rod had presented his new business plan to the bank, he might have been offered the loan at a higher rate of interest, since it would have been uncertain as to how the new approach would affect cash flow and the value of the enterprise. The bank should guard against this by providing some protection in its agreement with Rod. Perhaps the bank should expressly require that Rod maintain stated and established hours and days of business operation, and that failure to do so will result in an event of default on the loan. The bank might also require Rod to maintain a minimum cash flow or else be in default.

4. **No.** The fee arrangement between a lawyer and her client is not fully governed by the doctrine of freedom of contract. The fee arrangement is governed by rules of professional responsibility that provide for factors that must be considered in setting a fee. Furthermore, arrangements for contingency or bonus payments must be in writing. The lawyer must be careful to give a full and clear understanding of the fee arrangement to the client.

Exam Tips on
MARKET CONTEXT FOR REAL ESTATE TRANSACTIONS

☛ **Transaction time line:** You should be clear about the time horizon of a real estate transaction. The greater the time line for completing a transaction the more risk.

☞ Be sure to address the various temporal risks involved.

☛ **Be alert to costs and trade-offs:** Whenever a real estate transaction is identified be sure to look for and consider opportunities that will be forgone or given up by proceeding with the transaction. Remember that these are relevant to the cost of the transactions and the ability to measure its economic success.

☞ Make sure that you distinguish between accounting and economic profits.

☛ **Put costs into appropriate categories:** When considering facts related to the cost of a transaction be sure to categorize your analysis using key categories of cost such as those related to out-of-pocket costs, opportunity costs, and sunk costs.

☛ **Attorney and client relationship:** Be sure to pay close attention to the facts concerning the attorney and client relationship. Remember that the lawyer must comply with a code of professional responsibility, and the lawyer must be careful to avoid liability to third-party nonclients.

Chapter 2

CHAPTER 2

REAL ESTATE BROKERS

ChapterScope ───────────────────────

This chapter explores the roles played by real estate brokers in real estate transactions, along with the legal rules that govern their relationships with sellers and buyers. Brokers owe fiduciary duties to their clients, but they must also treat nonclients honestly and fairly. This chapter also covers unauthorized practice of law issues raised by brokers' activities and the right of attorneys to provide brokers' services.

- **Types of brokers:** For sales of properties, residential brokers concentrate on homes and commercial brokers concentrate on other properties. Leasing brokers and mortgage brokers also play prominent roles in many real estate transactions.

- **Licensing and codes of conduct:** Each state regulates real estate brokers through licensing. Brokers must follow professional codes of conduct.

- **Listing agreements:** There are four types of broker listing agreements:

  - Open listing (nonexclusive)

  - Exclusive agency

  - Exclusive right to sell (also commonly called an "exclusive listing")

  - Net listing

- **Who is the broker's client?** The broker usually represents the seller, but there are buyer's brokers. Dual agency also takes place.

- **Brokers and lawyers:** Brokers are prohibited from practicing law, yet they often assist the parties with contracting, financing, and other matters that have legal aspects. The line between a broker's legitimate activities and the ***unauthorized practice of law*** is often fuzzy. Most states now permit brokers to prepare standard-form contracts of sale for customers.

- **Lawyers acting as brokers:** Lawyers who are not separately licensed as brokers may legally perform real estate brokerage services. In most states, however, they do not have a ***total exemption*** from brokers' licensing laws. They have a ***partial exemption***: they may provide brokers' services only if they are incidental to their legal representation of a client.

I. TYPES OF BROKERS

A. Market role: Real estate brokers find parties who engage in real estate transactions. The broker's central role is that of an intermediary in the market for the sale and exchange of properties. The key to this role is the broker's possession of and access to ***market information***. Brokers have information about properties and the terms at which prospective participants are willing to deal, and this information is often highly valuable for parties.

B. Market segmentation: There are several types of brokers who work in different markets. Most brokers are hired to sell real estate, and some specialize in either residential or commercial brokerage.

1. **Residential brokers:** Residential brokers sell homes, condominiums, and sometimes vacant lots. Usually they concentrate on a limited geographical area, and sometimes they specialize in particular price ranges for the properties they market.

2. **Commercial brokers:** Commercial brokers handle office buildings, apartment houses, shopping centers, raw land, warehouses, and industrial facilities. Commercial brokers often also specialize by type of property in addition to geographical locality. Some commercial brokers, however, have regional or even national practices with respect to the property type in which they specialize.

3. **Leasing brokers:** Leasing brokers operate in both the residential and commercial sectors, typically representing landlords. They earn commissions based on rents payable by the tenants they find. Usually the commission is paid upon lease execution or occupancy; sometimes the commission is a percentage of continuing rents. For commercial leases, the broker may earn commissions later on if the tenant exercises renewal or expansion options.

4. **Mortgage brokers:** Mortgage brokerage is a major real estate activity, which just as for property sales is divided between commercial and residential activities. A mortgage broker does not make or fund a mortgage loan; instead, the broker matches a borrower with a lender. Commercial mortgage brokers have contacts with institutional lenders such as banks, savings and loans, insurance companies, and pension funds. Developers often engage commercial mortgage brokers for help in locating financing for a project. Residential mortgage brokerage did not begin as a major activity in the United States until the 1980s, when banking and lending law reform reconfigured the market. Many home buyers and owners who refinance their existing homes choose to deal with residential mortgage brokers. In 2006, mortgage brokers arranged for 45 percent of all U.S. residential mortgage loans. Residential mortgage brokers have thrived due to their low overhead compared to "bricks and mortar" lending institutions and their access to wholesale capital markets and pricing discounts.

II. REGULATION OF BROKERS

The occupation of real estate brokerage, like many other occupations in modern society, is subject to a number of different types of regulation. Those regulations consist of a mix of state and federal laws.

A. Licensing and state regulation: In every state, brokers are licensed professionals who are regulated by a state administrative agency, often called the real estate commission or the department of real estate. To be licensed, the broker must pass an examination demonstrating knowledge of business and legal principles involved in real estate transactions.

1. **Levels of licenses:** A broker has a "full" license, and he is qualified, just like an attorney, to "hang out his own shingle." In contrast, a ***real estate salesperson*** has a license that permits him to act as a broker only under the supervision of a licensed broker. Many states require that a broker first work as a salesperson before obtaining a broker's license. Typically, the salesperson must serve as an apprentice for a minimum of one or two years.

2. **Effect of lack of license:** If an unlicensed person renders brokers' services, the licensing laws generally prohibit that person from collecting a commission or other compensation.

   Example: Courtney asks Barry, a real estate salesperson, if he can find a buyer for her house. She agrees to pay him a 5 percent commission if he is successful. Barry finds a buyer at a price that is acceptable to Courtney. She sells to this buyer, but refuses to pay the commission to Barry. Barry sues to collect the commission. At trial, it is proven that, at the time Barry procured the buyer, he was not employed by or working under the supervision of a fully licensed broker. For this reason, Barry cannot collect the commission. This is true whether Barry sues on the express contract or uses an alternative theory, such as quantum meruit, unjust enrichment, or promissory estoppel.

B. **Antitrust law and price fixing:** Until 1950 it was a common practice for local brokers' associations to establish commission rates for their members to follow. In *United States v. National Association of Real Estate Boards*, 339 U.S. 485 (1950), the Supreme Court prohibited the fixing of commission rates because it violated the federal antitrust statute known as the Sherman Act.

   1. **Recommended commission rates:** Subsequent federal antitrust cases make it clear that the issuance of advisory or recommended prices by brokers' groups also constitutes illegal price-fixing.

   2. **Modern residential commission rate:** Today in most communities residential brokers tend to charge the same commission rate. In many cities, a homeowner who contacts a number of brokers' firms to ask about entering into a listing agreement will receive the same quoted rate (for example, 6 or 7 percent from each firm). This phenomenon, in which firms are aware of what their competitors charge and match that price, is known as ***conscious price parallelism***. This conduct is not illegal unless it is combined with evidence of conspiracy or other misconduct.

III. BROKERS' DUTIES TO CLIENTS

A. **Agency law:** The broker's duties to her client stem from the law of agency. The broker's client, whether seller, buyer, or both, is called the principal. Under agency principles, the broker owes fiduciary duties to her client. Breach of such a duty subjects the broker to liability to the client and to the risk of disciplinary action from the state agency that regulates brokers.

B. **Duty of loyalty:** The broker owes the client the duty of loyalty. This means the broker should do her utmost to protect the client and advance the client's interest. In selling property, the seller wants to sell at the ***highest price*** possible, so a broker who represents the seller is charged with the duty of obtaining a sufficient sales price. More generally, the broker is charged with the duty of obtaining the best terms for the client. See *Daubman v. CBS Real Estate Co.*, 580 N.W.2d 552 (Neb. 1998), holding that a seller's broker breached her fiduciary duties by putting her own interest in earning a commission above her clients' interests. The broker first represented incorrectly that the buyers were preapproved for financing, later advocated that the buyers get extra time to obtain financing from another lender, and finally contacted an apartment complex where the sellers hoped to rent a unit without the seller's permission, which resulted in the complex pressuring the sellers into signing a lease immediately.

   1. **Disclosure of client's bottom line:** For this reason, without the client's consent the broker may not disclose to potential purchasers the owner's lowest acceptable offer or "bottom line."

Example: A farm owner lists his property for sale for $9,500. The broker tells a prospective buyer that there is an outstanding offer at $8,250, which was too low, and that "in all probability he could get it for $8,500." The buyer turns in an offer for $8,500, which is accepted. The owner refuses to pay the commission. The jury is entitled to decide that the broker acted in bad faith, and thus cannot collect the commission. *Haymes v. Rogers*, 219 P.2d 339 (Ariz. 1950).

2. **Self-dealing:** The broker is prohibited from self-dealing. This occurs when a person engages in a transaction in which his self-interest is opposed to a fiduciary duty owed to another person. A broker representing a seller may not secretly purchase the property using a straw or a front person, hoping to make a profit.

   Example: A broker is hired by the owner of a gas station to sell the property for $300,000. The broker learns that adjoining land is being rezoned to permit high-density commercial development, and this will make the gas station property much more valuable. Without disclosing this fact to the owner, the broker advises his brother to turn in an offer to buy for $300,000, with the broker and brother agreeing to share the profit from a resale they hope to make in the near future. This constitutes self-dealing and thus is a breach of the broker's fiduciary duty to his client.

C. **Duty of full disclosure:** The broker must keep the client informed. When the broker learns facts or other information that is material to the client's position or interests, the broker should promptly tell the client. Thus, the broker must promptly communicate all offers to the client.

   1. **Duration of duty:** After the broker-client relationship terminates, the broker and the client may transact on an arms' length basis. This means that the broker may use new information to the broker's advantage without disclosing that information to the former client.

      Example: The owners of a cooperative apartment wanted to gain more space by purchasing their neighbor's unit and combining the spaces. After the neighbor refused to sell, the owners listed their apartment for sale. Later, the broker submitted an offer to buy the apartment for herself, which the owners accepted. Prior to closing, the broker contracted to buy the neighbor's unit—the neighbor had changed her mind. The broker had no fiduciary duty to inform the owners that the neighbor was now willing to sell her unit. That duty ended when the broker and the owners entered into the contract of sale. *Dubbs v. Stribling & Associates*, 752 N.E.2d 850 (N.Y. 2001).

D. **Duty of confidentiality:** The duty of confidentiality is the flip side of the disclosure duty. In the course of representing a client, the broker naturally gains information about the client's objectives and the property. Absent the client's consent, the broker should not disclose such information to third parties. Sometimes, the client interest is simply privacy, but often the information has economic value. The broker must keep the confidences of the client.

IV. TYPES OF BROKERS' LISTING CONTRACTS

A. **Open listing (Nonexclusive):** With an open listing (also called a nonexclusive listing), the broker earns his commission by procuring a ***ready, willing, and able buyer*** for the property. The seller is entitled to engage other brokers, in which event the first one to procure a buyer earns the commission.

1. **Sale by owner:** The seller can sell his property by himself, without a broker's help, in which event no commission is payable.

2. **Procuring cause:** To earn a commission the broker must demonstrate a causal connection between her actions and the ultimate sale.

   Example: A nonexclusive listing contract had an extension clause by which the seller agreed to pay the commission "in the event the property described herein is within one year after the termination of this Agreement, sold, traded or otherwise conveyed to anyone referred to Seller by the Broker or with whom Seller had negotiations during the term of this Agreement." Within the one year, the seller sold the property to a person who had previously told the broker that he was interested in buying a property like the one owned by the seller. The broker, however, was not entitled to a commission because the broker did nothing more, such as show the property to the buyer, participate in negotiations, or assist in closing the sale. *Business Consulting Services, Inc. v. Wicks*, 703 N.W.2d 427 (Iowa 2005).

B. **Exclusive agency:** With an exclusive agency, the broker is the exclusive agent with respect to the listed property. The seller promises not to engage another broker during the term of the agreement. If the owner sells using another agent, the exclusive agent is entitled to his commission. The owner, however, may sell by his own efforts and thereby avoid a commission.

C. **Exclusive right to sell (Exclusive listing):** With an exclusive right to sell (also called an exclusive listing), the broker gets the most protection with respect to earning a commission. The seller is obligated to pay the commission if any buyer purchases the property during the term of the agreement. It does not matter whether the broker procures the buyer, whether another broker finds the buyer, or whether the buyer and seller meet without the assistance of any broker.

D. **Net listing:** With a net listing, the commission is not specified as a percentage of the price, and the seller agrees to pay the broker all amounts received in excess of a set price established by the broker and seller. The word "net" means the seller is guaranteed a net amount of sales proceeds, but that's also the limit to what the seller can get from the sale. The net listing is less common than the other three types. The broker typically has discretion with respect to setting the listing price and will seek to sell at a higher price and pocket the difference.

E. **Constructional preference for seller:** When a broker's contract is ambiguous as to the type of listing it creates, courts tend to construe the contract in favor of the client because brokers generally control the contract language, either through standard forms or due to their expertise.

F. **Duration of listing contract:** Listing contracts normally have fixed expiration dates, with typical periods ranging from three or four months to one year. Under the terms of most listing contracts, if a contract of sale is signed before the expiration date, a commission is payable even though the sale closes after the expiration date.

   1. **Protective periods:** Listing contracts often contain a term that provides that a commission is payable if the owner sells the property to a person who had contact with the broker within a set period of time after expiration of the listing contract. This is designed to protect the broker from transactional misbehavior, in which the owner attempts to appropriate the value of the broker's services without paying for them by holding off on a possible sale until the listing contract expires. Protective period clauses are extremely common for exclusive right to sell agreements. They are used less frequently for other types of listing.

Example: The Johnstons list their property for sale with Galbraith, using an open listing. The listing includes a protective period, which calls for a commission to be paid if the owners sell within one year after expiration of the listing to anyone with whom the broker had negotiated prior to expiration. Galbraith shows the farm to Kenworthy. The Johnstons terminate the listing agreement, and several months later list the farm with another broker, Paterno. Prompted by Paterno's advertising, Kenworthy looks at the farm again and purchases it. The Johnstons pay a commission to Paterno, who is the procuring cause of the sale. Galbraith sues the Johnstons and also collects a commission under the protective period of the expired listing. *Galbraith v. Johnston*, 373 P.2d 587 (Ariz. 1962).

V. WHOM DOES THE BROKER REPRESENT?

A. **Listing broker as seller's agent:** In most sales, the broker represents the seller. She is known as the listing broker because she obtains a listing from the seller to sell the property. The seller and broker typically sign a listing agreement, which details their agency relationship, the commission arrangements, and other matters related to the undertaking.

B. **Cooperating or selling broker:** In many sales, two brokers are involved—not only a listing broker, but also a cooperating or selling broker. The buyer is found by the cooperating broker, who then splits the commission with the listing broker.

1. **Multiple Listing Service:** For residential sales within the Multiple Listing Service (MLS) system, a large percentage of transactions involve two brokers.

2. **Rule of subagency:** The traditional rule is that the cooperating or selling broker is an agent of the listing broker and thus a subagent of the seller. This means the cooperating broker has fiduciary duties to the seller, not the buyer. No one is representing the buyer. This legal doctrine is contrary to the expectations of most home buyers and the general public.

C. **Buyer's broker:** Buyers' brokers, who represent the buyer and not the seller as agent, are increasingly used by home buyers. The buyer's broker contracts with a prospective buyer, promising to represent the buyer in finding and purchasing property. Typically the buyer's broker is compensated by a split of the commission paid to the listing broker, with no payment due if the buyer does not find a house through the use of the broker's services.

1. **Representation of multiple prospective buyers:** Under some circumstances, a broker's representation of multiple bidders for the same property may violate the broker's duty to a buyer client. At least one of the clients will not succeed in the objective of buying the property. A brokerage firm with multiple agents, however, may succeed in defending an action brought by a disappointed prospective buyer. See *Rivkin v. Century 21 Teran Realty LLC*, 887 N.E.2d 1113 (N.Y. 2008), holding that a brokerage firm may represent multiple bidders for the same property without disclosure and consent when separate agents working for the brokerage firm independently represent prospective buyers.

D. **Dual representation:** A broker may lawfully represent both seller and buyer in the same transaction, as a dual agent. The broker must disclose the dual agency to both parties, who must then consent to the arrangement. Problems stemming from dual agency include the potential for conflicting duties of loyalty, disclosure, and confidentiality.

1. **Implied dual agency:** Dual agency may be express, and it is better for all the parties when it is express. Then both principals as well as the broker intend and understand the dual agency. However, a dual agency may arise by implication and may be proven by circumstantial evidence. See *Stefani v. Baird & Warner, Inc.*, 510 N.E.2d 167 (Ill. Ct. App. 1987), holding that a broker who was a subagent of the seller also became the buyer's agent by assisting the buyer in attempting to buy a house and by conducting negotiations.

   Example: Buyer contacts Broker to look at houses. They do not discuss whether Broker is representing Buyer or some other person. Buyer loves one of the houses shown to her by Broker. With Broker's assistance, Buyer turns in an offer to purchase this house. Seller, who had previously listed his house for sale with Listing Broker, accepts this offer. These facts do not clearly indicate whether Broker represents Seller alone, Buyer alone, or if Broker might represent both Buyer and Seller as a dual agent.

E. **Transaction broker:** A transaction broker sells services, but has no agency relationship with seller or buyer. This avoids fiduciary duties. Many states have passed statutes that authorize transaction brokerage. This practice is also called nonagency brokerage.

VI. WHEN IS THE COMMISSION EARNED?

A. **Brokers' claims against sellers**

1. **Traditional rule: When customer is found:** Under the traditional rule, the broker earns his commission when he procures a ready, willing, and able buyer at terms acceptable to the seller.

2. **Different terms:** The terms agreed to by the buyer and the seller need not be the same as those set forth in the listing agreement.

   Example: The seller lists her house for sale at $300,000 with closing no later than two months after the date of contract signing. The broker tenders a buyer's contract for $280,000 with closing deferred for four months. If the seller accepts this offer, the broker has earned the commission.

3. **Seller's acceptance of buyer:** By signing the contract of sale tendered by the buyer, the seller signifies her acceptance of the buyer procured by the broker. Under the traditional analysis, this means that if the buyer subsequently defaults, the seller cannot defeat the broker's claim to the commission by arguing the buyer was not ready, willing, and able.

4. **New rule: Implied condition that sale must close:** Some states have replaced the traditional rule with an implied condition that the sale must close in order for the broker to earn the commission. This is the minority approach, but a growing trend. The landmark case is *Ellsworth Dobbs, Inc. v. Johnson*, 236 A.2d 843 (N.J. 1967), which refers to the parties' probable expectations as the rationale for the new rule. Brokers generally wait until closing to collect their commissions, and sellers generally expect that no commission is payable if the sale fails to close.

   a. **Exception under new rule when seller defaults:** Even under the new closing condition rule, a seller may still be liable to the broker for the commission when the seller's default causes the failure of the transaction to close. Some courts may evaluate the reason for default, excusing the seller from liability for the commission if the default was not intentional. In *Hillis v. Lake*, 658 N.E.2d 30 (Mass. 1995), the sale failed to close because the land was contaminated by an underground gasoline leakage. Although the seller had failed to meet a contract term that required a clean environmental report, the seller was not liable for the commission because the default was unintentional.

  b. Relevance of express term in listing contract: Most listing agreements have an express term dealing with the issue when the broker earns the commission. In a state adopting the new closing condition rule, the broker's contract may attempt to alter this rule by contract. There is a split of authority as to whether such a term is valid. One view is that such a pro-broker term is per se unconscionable when there is unequal bargaining power. *Ellsworth Dobbs, Inc. v. Johnson*, 236 A.2d 843 (N.J. 1967). Another view preserves some freedom of contract but calls for judicial supervision on a case-by-case basis. See *Tristram's Landing, Inc. v. Wait*, 327 N.E.2d 727 (Mass. 1975), holding that no commission is payable when a sale fails to close due to the buyer's default. The Massachusetts court stated that an express agreement by the seller to pay a commission even though the buyer defaults is "to be scrutinized carefully" and "if not fairly made . . . may be unconscionable or against public policy."

 5. Express conditions in the contract of sale: If the transaction fails to close because a condition in the contract of sale is not satisfied, no commission is payable. This is true both under either the traditional approach or the new rule requiring closing as a condition to earning the commission. For example, no commission is payable when the buyer conditions his obligation on the ability to obtain a commitment for certain mortgage financing and he is unable to obtain the contemplated commitment.

B. Brokers' claims against buyers

 1. Lack of privity: The seller's broker may seek damages against a buyer who defaults after signing a contract on the theory that the buyer's wrongful conduct has deprived the broker of the commission. This theory has often failed due to the lack of privity—there is no express contract between the parties. Instead, under the traditional rule of when the commission is earned, the broker may recover the commission from the seller. Then the seller in turn should generally have an action against the defaulting buyer for consequential damages.

 2. Implied contract theory: Sometimes, a broker succeeds in suing a defaulting buyer for the commission based on the theory of implied contract. The buyer has impliedly promised the broker that she will complete the transaction. This theory is also explained in terms of third-party beneficiary. The broker is a third-party beneficiary of the purchase agreement between the buyer and seller.

 3. Tort theory: Another theory the seller's broker can use to recover from a defaulting buyer is tortious interference with contract. This is especially likely to succeed when the broker, such as a subagent who serves as cooperating broker, has a working relationship with the buyer. The rationale is that the buyer who defaults has tortiously interfered with the listing contract, pursuant to which the broker was to earn a commission. This deprives the broker of her prospective economic advantage.

C. Requirement of a written listing agreement: At common law, an oral listing agreement is valid. Thus, a broker may recover a commission if she meets the burden of proof that the parties entered into an oral contract, that the broker earned a commission, and that the principal failed to pay the commission. Many states today, however, have statutes that require a written listing agreement. See *Pargar, LLC v. Jackso*n, 670 S.E.2d 547 (Ga. Ct. App. 2008), where a buyer's broker could not recover a commission from a buyer who defaulted on a contract to buy property. Although there was a written listing agreement, the paragraph dealing with the commission was struck out, with a margin note "N/A" [not applicable].

VII. BROKERS' DUTIES TO NONCLIENT BUYERS

A. Traditional tort duties: Buyers often sue the seller and seller's broker when they find the property is less desirable than they had expected due to a physical defect or some other problem. Traditionally brokers owe nonclient buyers the same duties that sellers owe nonclient buyers—not to commit fraud, not to make intentional or negligent misrepresentations of fact, and, in many states, to disclose material latent defects.

Example: A buyer noticed metal bars on the windows of a house and inquired about safety. In the presence of the seller's brokers, the seller represented that there were currently no problems, even though there was a recent rape on the property and several other rapes in the neighborhood. In a damage action brought by the buyer against the seller and the brokers, the brokers (but not the seller) were entitled to summary judgment. Although the brokers as well as the seller knew of the rapes, they made no affirmative misrepresentation and were under no affirmative duty to disclose their knowledge of the recent crimes. *Van Camp v. Bradford*, 623 N.E.2d 731 (Ohio Ct. Common Pleas 1993).

  1. Broker liability for innocent misrepresentations: Although brokers are liable for intentional and negligent misrepresentations, just like sellers, there is a split of authority as to liability for innocent (nonnegligent) misrepresentations that are relied on by the buyer to his detriment. Some courts impose liability, reasoning that the broker should be held to determine the truth of her representations. Others hold the broker to a professional standard of reasonable care, which means the broker is not liable unless it is proven she negligently failed to check the truth of information. See *Hoffman v. Connall*, 736 P.2d 242 (Wash. 1987), holding a broker not liable for misrepresenting a boundary line to the buyers when it was subsequently discovered that a fence and improvements encroached on the neighbor's land.

B. Trend: Enlarging broker disclosure duties: In some states, court decisions or statutes create a greater duty for the broker to protect a nonclient buyer. The broker may have a duty to investigate the property and disclose defects that are reasonably ascertainable. This is an aspect of the broker's duty to treat all parties to the transaction fairly. Typically, this heightened disclosure duty runs only to home buyers, not buyers of commercial properties.

VIII. BROKERS AND LAWYERS

A. Unauthorized practice of law: Most states now permit brokers to prepare standard-form contracts of sale for customers who are not represented by an attorney. Several tests are used to determine when a broker's activities constitute unauthorized practice.

  1. Contracts versus conveyances test: The broker may prepare the contract of sale or earnest money contract between the parties, but may not prepare deeds and other closing instruments that convey interests in land.

  2. Simple-complex test: If the transaction is simple and straightforward, a broker is permitted to select standard-form instruments and assist the parties in filling in blanks.

3. **Incidental test:** Broker drafting of instruments is authorized if it is incidental to the broker's business and no separate compensation is paid therefor.

4. **Public interest test:** New Jersey has seen extensive litigation between brokers and the bar concerning unauthorized practice issues. The New Jersey Supreme Court has fashioned a "public interest" test to decide what tasks nonlawyer professionals may perform in connection with residential sales. See *In re Opinion No. 26 of the Committee on the Unauthorized Practice of Law*, 654 A.2d 1344 (N.J. 1995). The New Jersey court allows a broker to provide and fill in a standard-form contract for parties who do not have lawyers, provided that the contract has a three-day attorney review clause. Either party who retains counsel after signing the contract may revoke within three days. Brokers and title companies may close residential sales involving unrepresented sellers and buyers, but only if they receive a written notice informing them of the risks involved in proceeding without attorneys. A broker who acts without giving such notice commits the unauthorized practice of law. An attorney who knowingly facilitates a transaction in which no notice was given has engaged in unethical conduct. *Id.* Brokers may order title searches and title abstracts, and title companies may clear up minor title objections such as monetary liens and marital property rights. Only lawyers may draft deeds and handle serious title matters such as easements and restrictive covenants. *Id.*

B. **Lawyers acting as brokers:** Statutes that provide for the regulation of brokers typically have an exemption for attorneys. There is a split of authority as to the scope of the attorney exemption.

1. **Incidental test:** In some states, the exemption is limited to brokerage services that are incidental to the attorney's law practice. Thus, an attorney can sell or rent property only for clients for whom his primary work is the provision of legal services. See *In re Roth*, 577 A.2d 490 (N.J. 1990), in which an attorney represented an employee of his law firm, seeking to lower the purchase price by serving as the selling broker and remitting his commission to the buyer. The court called this unethical because the commission arrangement creates a conflict of interest that might affect the attorney's performance of legal services.

2. **Total exemption:** In some states, attorneys are totally exempt from the licensing requirements based on the reasoning that due to their professional education and training they are generally competent to provide real estate brokerage services and their conduct is independently regulated by the bar association.

Quiz Yourself on *REAL ESTATE BROKERS*

5. Patty hires broker Bruno to sell her house, agreeing to a listing price of $200,000. Bruno shows the house to Alex, who really likes the house. Alex asks Bruno, "200's a whole lot. I don't think I can pay that much. How much do I really need to offer to get this place?" Bruno responds, "The seller might very well take less than the listing price. Let's turn in any offer you're comfortable with, and we'll see what happens." Alex turns in an offer of $180,000, which Patty accepts. Two weeks later a very similar house down the street goes under contract of $192,000. When Patty learns this, she claims that Bruno had a duty to negotiate for a higher sales price and owes her $12,000. Must he pay? _____

6. Palazzo wants to sell his grocery store. In January he enters into an exclusive right-to-sell listing contract with Amanda, a broker. The contract names the selling price as $400,000 and has a term of six months. In May Palazzo's cousin, Vincent, asks Palazzo if he might buy the store. Vincent is aware that Palazzo has listed the store for sale with Amanda, but he does not contact Amanda or otherwise deal with her. Palazzo also fails to tell Amanda about Vincent's interest in the store. In May Palazzo and Vincent sign a contract of sale, calling for a price of $380,000 and a closing date in September. Amanda does not find a buyer for the store, and the listing contract expires in July. In September, Palazzo conveys the store to Vincent pursuant to the May contract.

(a) May Amanda collect a commission from Palazzo? _____

(b) May Amanda collect a commission from Vincent? _____

7. Julio and Linda, a young married couple, move to Bigtown and contact broker Bell in order to find a nice "starter" home to buy. They tell Bell exactly what they want in terms of price, location, school district, and house style. Bell spends three days showing them properties listed within the Bigtown Multiple Listing Service, and they turn in an offer on a house for $128,000, which the owner accepts. Before closing, they learn the roof will have to be replaced soon, and under their contract, this is their risk and expense. Has Bell breached any duty to Julio and Linda by failing to protect them from an old decaying roof? _____

8. Stacy, an attorney who also has a full real estate broker's license, is engaged by Henry to sell his 640-acre farm. May Stacy bargain for and collect both a broker's commission and a legal fee in this transaction? _____

Answers

5. **No.** While Bruno owes his client, Patty, the duty to obtain the highest sale price possible, these facts are not sufficient to show a breach of that duty. Most real estate sells at a price below the seller's listing price. For this reason, Bruno should not discourage offers at less than Patty's asking price of $200,000. A broker who told potential buyers you must or should offer full price would chill offers, and *that* conduct would harm the client and might well be considered incompetent behavior. Bruno may have had a duty to inform Patty that the offer was too low if he knew or should have known that it was substantially below market value.

6. (a) **Yes.** Palazzo and Amanda entered into an exclusive right to sell, which means that the seller is obligated to pay the commission on any sale made before the six-month term expires. It doesn't matter that the closing took place after the expiration of the term, or that Vincent paid less than the $400,000 asking price. The commission, however, is calculated based upon the $380,000 price that Vincent actually paid.

(b) **Yes, probably.** Vincent did not sign the exclusive right-to-sell contract or hire Amanda. Thus, he does not have an express contract duty to pay a commission to her. In many states, however, Amanda will have a cause of action against Vincent based upon implied contract or tortious interference with contract.

7. **No, probably.** Generally the outcome will turn on who Bell, the selling broker, represents in this transaction. Bell is a selling broker, and the general rule is that the selling broker is a subagent of the seller, and thus owes fiduciary duties of care to the seller, not to the buyer. Bell, as subagent for the

seller, does have a duty to treat Julio and Linda fairly and honestly, but there is no evidence of misrepresentation, deceit, or other forms of misconduct here. It should be emphasized that there is also no evidence that the roof is defective and that Bell knew the roof was defective.

Julio and Linda want to argue that Bell has acted as a buyer's broker, in which case Bell should have a duty to protect them. Bell should have either made sure their contract had an inspection clause with appropriate conditions or warranties or advised them to hire an attorney prior to entering into a binding contract. It is also possible that, based on Bell's interactions with the buyers, he is a dual agent—representing both the seller as subagent and the buyers. At the time of engaging the broker, the relationship should be clarified.

8. **No.** Because the commission is paid only if a sale of the farm results, there is a potential conflict of interest. In her role as Henry's attorney, situations may arise where her best legal advice would be to tell him not to go forward with a proposed sale. This advice would be contrary to her financial self-interest, and there is the risk that for this reason Stacy would be less likely to give such advice.

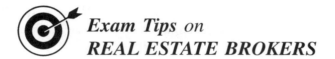

Exam Tips on REAL ESTATE BROKERS

It's not likely that you'll have a major essay question with brokers' issues as the primary focus. However, it's easy to add one or more brokers to a complicated fact pattern involving the sale of real property. In that event, you'll be called upon to assess the broker's role in the transaction to determine whether the broker can collect a commission or whether the broker is liable to another party.

☛ **Brokers' duties to clients:** Be prepared to discuss the duty of loyalty, the duty of full disclosure, and the duty of confidentiality. It will help to emphasize that these are fiduciary duties. Remember that these duties come from the law of agency, and thus are owed only to the broker's client (the broker's principal).

　　☞ **Transaction brokers:** Also, consider the possibility that the broker might be a transaction broker, in which event the broker does not owe fiduciary duties to anyone.

☛ **Types of listing contracts:** Whenever a broker appears in the fact pattern, consider whether you ought to classify the type of listing agreement. You need to know all four types of listing agreements. They will be relevant if there is an issue as to whether a broker's commission is payable.

☛ **Whom does the broker represent?** Whenever an essay question mentions one or more real estate brokers, you should start your analysis by exploring whom the broker or brokers represent. Brokers owe duties to clients and to nonclients, but these duties are very different in nature and scope. Too often students miss this step and just dive into an examination of whether the broker has behaved properly or committed some type of wrong.

☞ **Two brokers:** When there are two brokers, a listing broker and a selling broker, there may be a subagency, or the selling broker may be a buyer's broker. When there is more than one possibility as to the identity of the broker(s)' client(s), you should explain all possibilities and why it matters.

☞ **Broker's right to a commission:** A fact pattern may reveal a dispute over the earning of a broker's commission based upon a contract of sale that did not proceed to closing. Remember there is a split of authority on whether a broker earns a commission by finding a buyer who signs a contract, or whether closing is an implied condition. Be sure to fully discuss both lines of authority.

☞ **Unauthorized practice of law:** This is not often tested as an issue or subissue in a major essay. For this reason, you should not discuss unauthorized practice issues unless the question directly asks you to do so, or the facts unmistakably highlight such issues. If all the facts tell you is that a broker assisted a person in contracting to buy or sell land, or in making closing arrangements, the teacher probably doesn't want analysis of whether the broker is providing legal services and thus is subject to unauthorized practice sanctions.

CHAPTER 3

PREPARING TO CONTRACT

ChapterScope ―――――――――――――――――――――――――――――――――

This chapter discusses important issues and considerations for the precontract and negotiation phase of a proposed real estate transaction.

- ■ **Property and contract:** Preparing for a real estate contract involves a number of important considerations, particularly with respect to basic *property and contract* rules.

- ■ **Four key time periods:** During the *preparation stage* of contracting, one must consider four key time periods for the transaction: the *precontract, executory contract, closing, and post-closing stages*.

  - ■ The *precontract* period involves negotiation.

  - ■ The *executory* period is after contract signing but before completion ("closing") of the contract.

  - ■ The *closing* period is when the deed is exchanged for the money and other consideration.

  - ■ The *post-closing* period involves taking care of matters after closing such as recording documents in the public records.

- ■ **Statute of frauds:** Preparation of an enforceable contract depends on compliance with the statute of frauds.

- ■ **Parol evidence:** The parol evidence rule and the use of integration clauses regulate the content and scope of the parties' contract.

I. REAL ESTATE TRANSACTION TIME LINE

   A. **Four stages:** In preparing to contract, the parties must have a clear understanding of contract law and property law as they relate to the sequence of events or stages through which their transaction will pass. The big picture is critical because at the preparation stage one must negotiate and contract about all the issues that may come up later. The *four key stages* of the real estate transaction are:

   1. **Precontract:** The time when initial investigative and negotiating work is undertaken. Offers and counteroffers are entertained. Legal issues may arise with respect to identifying the point when negotiation ends and an agreement becomes binding. There may also be disagreement as to the terms that become part of an enforceable contract.

   2. **Executory contract:** The time, after signing the contract, when the parties work toward the completion and satisfaction of all of the elements of their contract undertaking. At the moment both parties have signed the contract certain rules and risks are triggered as a consequence of the *doctrine of equitable conversion*.

3. **Closing:** The time when the parties finalize their contract by acknowledging the completion and satisfaction of all obligations and conditions. It is when the money is exchanged for the deed or instrument of conveyance. At closing the **doctrine of merger** operates and eliminates a number of potential claims under the terms of the contract.

4. **Post-closing:** The time when the parties finish the paperwork and details of the transaction, which has closed. Documents get recorded in the public records, final title policies are issued, and the lawyers complete the file with a final transmittal letter.

This chapter examines the first stage, including issues of contract formation. The executory contract stage is discussed in Chapters 4 and 5, and the closing and post-closing stages are discussed in Chapter 6.

B. **Legal capacity—consequences of simple rules:** In preparing to contract, one must consider basic legal rules and how they may impact your job as a lawyer. A key rule in a contract to convey an interest in real estate is that you need **a grantor and a grantee**. This means that the parties must have the **legal capacity** to engage in the transaction. You will need evidence to support a conclusion of legal capacity. The contract must provide for the right to see and review such evidence, or else there will be no right to demand it at a later date.

Example: If a corporation is to convey real property to a buyer, it must be a validly formed corporation in good standing and authorized to make the transfer. The question for the buyer is how to check into the seller's legal capacity. The lawyer must think about the kinds of things that make a corporation and corporate action valid. In drafting a contract, you want to include requirements that the seller produce evidence of the elements necessary to prove capacity. This may include articles of incorporation, a certificate of good standing from the state, a current listing of the officers and board of directors, evidence of the person or persons authorized to bind the corporation by signing documents, and a resolution of the board of directors approving of the sale.

II. PRECONTRACT ACTIVITIES

A. **Information:** Prior to contracting, the parties gather information about possible market choices. Information is valuable. It helps to clarify the risk and the value of a proposed exchange. Each party seeks to discover as much valuable information as possible. Each party often has an incentive to withhold information from the other party. Generally, a seller must reveal information about latent defects, and in all cases, a court may sanction nondisclosure if the facts reveal fraud, misrepresentation, or undue advantage. Disclosure duties are discussed in more detail in Chapter 5. Information problems are a type of transaction cost that the lawyer helps to reduce and manage for the client.

1. **Typical situation:** Each party generally has access to different information. A seller, for example, may have lived on the property and, through experience, learned something about the problems with the house, or the way the rainwater settles in the yard after a downpour, or the way snow drifts around the house in the winter. A buyer that has not lived through a season or two with the property may not know as much about it. Traffic patterns around a property may vary with the time of day and the season, and a broker may show a buyer the property only during the most favorable times. A seller should also have some knowledge about the status of title and taxes for the property, as well as the expected costs of utilities.

B. Cost of information: One important factor to consider is the cost of information. If the gaining of information has come at a cost, then perhaps it should be protected information because we want to encourage people to invest in information that may reveal a better assessment of value for a particular activity.

C. Third-party factors: In preparing to contract, the parties should consider the interests of existing and prospective third parties. For example, a seller may already have obligations to a real estate broker, which will have an impact on a proposed sale contract. A buyer who anticipates getting mortgage financing needs to consider the potential demands of a lender with respect to matters such as the title and the quality of the land and improvements. Similarly, government regulation may constrain the parties' freedom of contract.

III. CONTRACT FORMATION

The line between the precontract and the executory contract stages can be blurry. *Formation* issues concern the matter of when arrangements become so concrete and complete that they are no longer considered mere preliminary negotiations, but rather *legally enforceable promises*. Standard contract rules resolve most questions of formation. Thus, the contract must meet the basic tests requiring *consideration, an offer, an acceptance,* and *a legal purpose*. Parties often talk and exchange written information during negotiation. A point may be reached when one party asserts that a binding contract has come into existence, while the other party is not willing to proceed and asserts that the exchanges between them have never left the precontract negotiation stage.

Example: Deb and Sean have had several meetings and have exchanged notes relating to aspects of a proposed deal. Deb anticipates that a favorable (profitable) contract is forthcoming, but Sean refuses to go forward. Deb then alleges that the deal has already been consummated. She claims that, based on the extent of information already exchanged, a detailed written contract would merely formalize an agreement already struck by the parties. Sean responds by asserting the lack of a formal agreement and the unenforceability of any alleged understanding. Thus, formation issues arise.

A. Statute of frauds: The statute of frauds prohibits the enforcement of an oral contract unless there is a writing signed by the party to be charged. The parties' entire contract need not be in writing; parts of it may be oral. This writing need not be a long and integrated contract; it can be a short memorandum. It may also consist of multiple writings so long as it can be established that they are tied together to the same transaction.

1. Elements of the writing: Under the statute, a "memorandum" is sufficient, provided it sets out the key elements:

- Identifies the parties.

- Describes the property.

- Indicates the intent to buy and sell.

- Is signed by the party to be charged. In most states, both parties do not have to sign the contract or writing for an underlying oral contract to be enforceable. It suffices if the party resisting enforcement (generally the defendant) has signed the writing.

■ **Electronic signature:** Congress passed the Electronic Signature in Global and National Commerce Act, 15 U.S.C. §§ 7001-7031, in 2000. This permits signature by electronic means and may include e-mail- and voice mail-related signatures as electronic communications.

■ Names the price or other consideration. States are divided as to whether this is a necessary element that must be written. Many states insist on a written price term, but others are willing to imply a reasonable price if the evidence shows that the parties failed to agree on a price.

Example: Husband signs a contract for the sale of property. Wife participated in the negotiations and was fully aware of the transaction, even though she did not sign the contract. Later the buyer learned that Wife owns an interest in the property as tenant by the entirety. Husband refuses to perform the contract on the basis that the contract is not signed by the party to be charged. The general rule is that the statute of frauds requires both spouses to sign the writing, but here Husband is estopped from raising the defense due to Wife's participation and knowledge. *Jill Real Estate, Inc. v. Smyles*, 541 N.Y.S.2d 515 (App. Div. 1989).

2. **Distinction between writing and contract:** The idea of a contract for the sale of property and an enforceable contract for sale are two different concepts. Parties may have an oral contract for the sale of land, but such a contract is unenforceable under the statute of frauds.

3. **Defendant's admission of contract:** The traditional rule, still followed in most states, is that a party may admit in judicial proceedings (e.g., pleadings, testimony) that she has entered into an oral contact and still raise the statute of frauds as a defense. A growing minority of states hold that no writing is necessary when a person admits she agreed to an oral contract. Thus, defendant's admission bars the statute of frauds defense. This rule is similar to that for the sale of personal property under UCC § 2-201(7).

Example: Amy and Bill orally agree to the sale of Bill's property to Amy for $100,000, with the closing date set for three weeks from the date of their agreement. On the appointed date, Amy brings the money to Bill and expects to receive a conveyance of the property. Bill refuses to convey the property, even though he freely admits that he had orally agreed to all of the terms asserted by Amy. Under traditional real estate law, Bill can admit the contract, yet escape it by virtue of the statute of frauds. But some states reject this approach and would hold for Amy.

4. **Part performance:** Under the doctrine of part performance, an oral contract to purchase real property is enforceable when a party can demonstrate substantial reliance on that contract. Possession by the buyer under the oral contract is generally required, and most states also require an additional act that shows a change of position: (1) The buyer has made repairs or improvements to the property, or (2) the buyer has paid all or part of the purchase price.

   a. **Evidentiary theory:** Some courts explain the doctrine by reasoning that the performance itself gives evidence to the contract between the parties. Thus, the function of the doctrine is to excuse a writing only when there is alternative solid proof that the contract exists and is not the buyer's fabrication.

   b. **Hardship theory:** Some courts apply the hardship theory, which excuses a writing when there is proof that a party who relied on the oral contract will suffer irreparable injury unless the contract is enforced. Most states have not firmly adopted either the evidentiary theory or the hardship theory. Their case law displays strains of each theory.

5. Equitable estoppel: Both the evidentiary and the hardship theories relate to the doctrine of equitable estoppel. This is because the part performance by the buyer under circumstances where her reliance on a contract is reasonable estops the seller from denying the enforceability of the contract for lack of a writing. Under an equitable estoppel approach, the focus is on the affirmative actions of the seller that may have misled the buyer or made the buyer's part performance reasonable under the circumstances. The partial performance approach places a slightly different focus on the analysis by giving more attention to what the buyer did.

Example: Kayto and Sandra agree that he will buy a lot from her for $30,000. Kayto wishes to construct a small cottage on the lot. Kayto pays $10,000 of the price and moves onto the lot and commences construction. Sandra passes by the lot every day on her way into work, and she observes Kayto building his cottage. After the cottage is complete, Sandra asserts the statute of frauds and demands that Kayto leave the property. Equity may step in to help Kayto because he has made substantial improvements. Sandra may also be estopped from denying the contract because she drove by the property every day and could have told Kayto he had no right to build on the property. Moreover, if the court fails to enforce the contract, it may order Sandra to pay Kayto for the value of the improvements if he has to leave them on the property.

B. Parol evidence rule: This rule often works in tandem with the statute of frauds. It prohibits the admission of prior written or contemporaneous oral evidence that adds to or is inconsistent with the parties' final written agreement.

1. Four corners of the document: As a general rule, courts will not favor the admission of parol evidence if there is a writing that appears to address the basic elements of the transaction. This approach is often called the *four corners* approach because the courts speak in terms of limiting their inquiry to the meaning of the terms within the four corners of the contract.

2. Ambiguity: Courts allow parol evidence to clarify a contract term that is *ambiguous* on its face. Conversely, if the writing is not ambiguous as to the matter in question, parol evidence is excluded.

Example: John and Sally have a writing that does not specifically address many of the fine points of their agreement to buy and sell a piece of real property. The agreement does say, however, that "Sally will pay the price of $30,000 on March 17 of this year for said described property." When March 17 arrives, Sally pays only $1,000, claiming that there was an oral understanding that she would pay only $1,000 per month toward the total payment of $30,000. Sally is prevented from making this argument based on parol evidence because the term of the writing is not ambiguous on its face.

3. Contradiction: Parol evidence is generally not permitted to contradict a written term that is not, on its face, ambiguous.

Example: Continuing with the above example, Sally's assertion of the extended time payment at $1,000 per month is a contradiction of the written term, and it is a contradiction that results in a very different transaction. Based on the time value of money, this is a very different price for John. Given that the credit sale contradicts the written term, which seems clear on its face, the parol evidence rule should block Sally's attempt to prove a credit sale.

4. Timing: Parol evidence offered to prove a term or an understanding *reached after a writing was entered into* may be admitted, since it would be a new term and not some point of negotiation that could be assumed to have been resolved by the writing itself.

C. **Integration clauses:** Many contracts have an integration clause, which says that all terms of negotiation are merged into the document, which is the parties' full and complete agreement. This is meant to raise the parol evidence bar.

IV. LETTERS OF INTENT

Parties sometimes sign a letter of intent, letter of commitment, or memorandum of understanding before entering into a formal detailed contract. Such writings are a major category of ***agreements to agree***. They can be used to outline the essential terms of a deal. The purpose is to give a purchaser or borrower some degree of assurance that a deal is likely before expending additional time and money on the transaction. The seller or lender agrees to the letter of intent in order to retain the other party's interest in the transaction. Sometimes it is very difficult to determine if a contract has been formed, and this can become increasingly complex if one party assures the other that the property is off the market during the time allocated for further negotiation. *GMH Associates, Inc. v. Prudential Realty Group*, 752 A.2d 889 (Pa. Super. Ct. 2000).

A. **Legal effect:** Often, the preliminary writing is not legally binding. Sometimes, the writing states that it is not intended to bind or commit the parties and that they will be bound only when and if a formal contract is executed. In many cases, however, a letter of intent does bind the parties in the sense that they are obligated to go forward in good faith and agree to each other's proposals of reasonable terms for the final agreement. Consequently, one must be careful in using a letter of intent or other such preliminary document in the negotiation process.

Example: A partnership negotiates to buy land for a small residential subdivision from Lisenby. They draft and sign a letter of intent to purchase, which includes some specific terms and an option to purchase. The partnership attempts to exercise the option, but Lisenby refuses to sell. Lisenby says the letter was not a binding contract and was unenforceable because it fails to satisfy the statute of frauds. The trial court agrees and grants a directed verdict for Lisenby, but the appellate court reverses. Because the letter named the parties, described the property, and stated the price, the statute of frauds is satisfied. Thus, the partnership is permitted to present further evidence that the parties had reached an agreement in fact. *Beller & Gould v. Lisenby*, 268 S.E.2d 611 (Ga. 1980).

Example: Ashford wants to build an office and warehouse complex. It applies for a loan from USLife, filling out a letter of financing intent and paying an $11,000 fee. Its proposed development plan, submitted with the letter, shows a main road of access. Later, USLife adds a condition requiring the completion of an additional road for access to the property. Ashford says the condition is a counteroffer and demands a refund of his $11,000 fee. USLife refuses, stating that the letter is a binding agreement with a provision for additional terms. The court holds for Ashford because the new road condition "did not naturally flow from the terms of the letter of intent." *Ashford Development, Inc. v. USLife Real Estate Services Corporation*, 661 S.W.2d 933 (Tex. 1983).

V. OPTIONS

Option contracts are widely used in real estate. The purchaser or optionee pays a negotiated amount to obtain the option, getting a solid right to buy at specified terms, but with no obligation to buy. The purchaser desires an option rather than a normal contract when she is not yet certain she wants the property and needs to acquire further information about the property, market choices, potential financing, or similar matters. The writing describes the option price, when and how the option is to be exercised, the closing date, and other specific terms and conditions. Usually the duration is short term. Depending on the option contract, the amount paid for the option may or may not be credited to the purchase price. An option contract is usually as detailed as a regular contract of sale and purchase.

Example: Benito pays $3,000 in order to get a one-month option to purchase a small strip shopping center for $900,000. The option contract sets forth all appropriate terms and conditions. The seller has taken the property off the market, and Benito has an absolute right to purchase the center if he complies with the terms of the option.

Quiz Yourself on
PREPARING TO CONTRACT

9. Mary has listed an office building for sale. Frank is interested in buying the building. He looks at the property and then has a discussion with Mary. At the end of the conversation, Frank tells Mary he would like to have her draft a contract for sale and purchase of the property at a price of $3 million, with provisions for an 80 percent mortgage loan not to exceed an interest rate of 12 percent, with closing to be set for 60 days from now, and including contract terms for assorted standard inspections of the property. They shake hands on it and Frank leaves. The next day Mary drafts a contract based on the conversation and she calls Frank to arrange for signing the contract. Frank says he changed his mind and is not interested in the property any longer. Mary asserts that Frank is bound, but Frank claims he was only making an inquiry. Is Frank bound on the deal? _____

10. The day after Frank and Mary met, as stated in the question above, Frank comes to Mary's office with a form contract completed and signed by him with the terms discussed with her. Mary says, "This looks great, I will take the property off the market today." Later that night she gets a call from a friend, Anna, and Anna indicates that she is interested in buying that same property for $3.2 million. Mary asks Anna to come by the office early in the morning to sign a contract for that price. The next day Mary and Anna each sign a contract to convey the property for $3.2 million. When Frank discovers the sale to Anna he threatens to sue Mary on the grounds that he and she already had a deal at $3 million. Mary responds that she did not have a deal with Frank. Is Mary obligated to sell to Frank for $3 million? _____

11. Assume that, based on the signed contract delivered by Frank, as stated in the question above, Mary permits Frank to move into the property. Frank makes some improvements to the space and looks forward to getting his financing and closing on the deal. About a month later Anna contacts Mary and offers her $3.2 million. Mary and Anna sign a deal (Mary still not having actually signed the contract presented by Frank). Frank sues Mary, asserting that he has a contract to purchase the property. Does Frank have an enforceable agreement? _____

12. Betty is interested in buying Jack's house. During the course of negotiation, Jack shows Betty plans for a pool he was once going to put in the backyard. Betty indicates that she might consider such a project herself after she buys the property. The two sign a detailed contract that says nothing about the pool. The contract includes a statement that "this written contract expresses the entire agreement and understanding between the parties." During the executory contract period, Betty learns that the zoning has changed and no pool can be built. Can Betty lower the purchase price or get out of the deal? _____

13.   Shannon and Gerry, husband and wife, own land as joint tenants with rights of survivorship. Gerry enters into a contract to sell the land to Barney for $100,000. When the time comes for closing, Shannon discovers the deal and refuses to sell. Can Barney force the sale? _____

Answers

9.   **No.** The statute of frauds requires a writing, and we have none here. Also, in a contract of this nature Frank will want to review and negotiate more details. Frank is really taking steps toward further preliminary negotiations. At this point Mary has not taken the property off the market nor really changed her position in any detrimental way in reliance on thinking she has made a sale.

10.   **No.** Mary did not sign the written contract with Frank. Thus, there is no written contract between the parties. If Frank seeks to enforce the writing he has, he will have to overcome the statute of frauds, which requires that the writing be signed by the party to be charged. If Frank sues Mary, she is the party to be charged and she has not signed the contract.

11.   **Maybe.** The problem is failure to comply with the statute of frauds. Mary still has not signed the contract presented by Frank. Many courts, using the doctrine of part performance and their equity power, will get around this problem if a buyer has taken possession of the property and made substantial improvements. This case will turn on an assessment of the reasonableness of concluding that an agreement has been fully reached between the parties, and on an assessment of whether or not Frank's improvements are substantial.

12.   **No.** The contract has an integration clause that excludes earlier discussions from the terms of the agreement between the parties. Betty would have to overcome the parol evidence rule, which keeps out such matters. Betty has taken the risk on this point. If the pool was important to Betty, she should have added a written condition to the contract.

13.   **No.** Both Shannon and Gerry must transfer the property, but only Gerry is on the contract. Barney needed to determine who owned the property and whether Gerry had the power to convey. In the absence of any special circumstances, the contract will be unenforceable against Shannon. It is quite possible that Barney can hold Gerry liable for damages, but this will not give him the property for which he bargained.

 *Exam Tips on*
PREPARING TO CONTRACT

☛ **Duty to disclose:** Remember that it is not always required that each party share all information with everyone else. There must be a *duty to disclose* to the particular party in question. Consider the nature of the information, how it was obtained, and who had a right to this information, as well as who was under a duty to disclose, and disclose to whom.

☛ **In written and oral contracts the sequence of events is important:** When an examination question includes a lot of information about the contract negotiation process, be sure to keep track of which exchanges between the parties were written and which were oral. Students frequently make mistakes by not keeping track of the sequence and nature of events that transpire between the parties.

☛ **Statute of frauds:** Remember that part performance and equitable estoppel relate to ways to enforce an oral contract for the sale of land in spite of noncompliance with the statute of frauds. You must find a contract. This is not the same thing as arguing that, in the absence of a contract, the court should take action based on contract substitutes, such as detrimental reliance or theories of quasi-contract.

☛ **Paying attention to the statute of frauds and parol evidence:** Don't be too quick to use equity to help a party. Courts are likely to override the statute of frauds and the parol evidence rule only when confronted with strong facts and well-reasoned arguments. Also be careful when dealing with contract negotiation issues. If one party asserts a contract based on the exchange of information and informal writings, there may be no foundation for dealing with integration clause concerns because the parties would have had little reason to think in such terms.

☛ **The agreement to agree (the letter of intent):** Remember that parties can enter into a letter of intent that is meant to be nonbinding but certain facts may permit one to argue that such a letter is in fact an enforceable option contract or a sufficient writing to be enforced as a contract.

☞ **Contract alternatives:** Remember that promissory estoppel or equitable estoppel may come into play as methods of imposing an obligation in the absence of finding an enforceable contract between the parties.

CHAPTER 4

THE EXECUTORY CONTRACT

ChapterScope ─────────────────────────────────────

This chapter examines issues raised after entering into a contract for purchase and sale.

■ **Risk:** During the executory contract period, parties encounter a multitude of risks. These include a variety of temporal and transactional risks as discussed in Chapter 1.

■ **Lawyer's role:** The lawyer's role is to manage activities and risks related to completion of the contract, including issues related to satisfaction of conditions, and contract modifications.

■ **Doctrine of equitable conversion:** The *doctrine of equitable conversion* applies throughout the executory period. In many cases, it transfers risk of loss to the buyer.

■ **Contract conditions:** Major contract *conditions* include those providing for financing, inspections, title, zoning, and other matters.

I. CONTRACT AS RISK MANAGEMENT DEVICE

The executory period lasts from the moment the contract becomes binding and enforceable up to closing. During this period, a party's expectations may be upset by changes in market conditions, intervening government regulations, the discovery of new information, or the occurrence of a natural or personal disaster. The parties generally enjoy freedom to contract, meaning they have great latitude in specifying the details and elements of their transaction. A well-drafted contract manages many of the risks that are present during the executory stage of a transaction. The parties cannot eliminate all risk, but they can do their best to identify risks and assign them to the party who can reduce or prevent loss at the *least cost.*

A. Approaches to allocate executory period risk

    1. Conditions: Conditions serve to allocate risk by excusing one or both parties from completing the exchange when a described event fails to occur. See part IV of this chapter.

    2. Warranties: A party who warrants the quality of a particular element of the transaction takes on the risk of that quality not being true. Simultaneously the other party has a reduced risk.

        Example: In the sale of Greenacre, Seller warrants that the property is free of any environmental contamination that violates any local, state, or federal regulation. Soil testing reveals environmental contamination in violation of the law. Seller has the risk (cost) of having to correct this problem, or in the alternative of reducing the price by an amount equal to the difference between the value of the property with the contamination and the value of the property without the contamination. If environmental quality was also made a condition of Buyer's obligation to close on the contract, Buyer would be free of any further duty under the contract. Breach of warranty, in other words, does not generally excuse performance.

3. **Representations:** These are *express disclosures* or statements about important elements of the transaction. They are stated in the contract to show the *materiality and relevance* of the information. The party making the representation takes on the risk of its falsehood.

   Example: In the sale of Greenacre, Buyer informs Seller of his desire to use the property as a business location for the sale of erotic and adult art and literature. Seller represents that the property can be used for that purpose when in fact the property is not zoned to allow such a use. By including the specific representation in the contract the term can be identified as a material term and this shifts some of the risk as to use to Seller, allowing Buyer to assert a failure of a material term. Depending upon the drafting, the failure of a material term may affect damages as a remedy but might not excuse performance unless also written in the form of a proper condition.

4. **Covenants and negative covenants:** These are promises allocating the responsibility between the parties. Covenants (generally understood as affirmative covenants) express the actions and risks that a party agrees to take on. Negative covenants are promises with respect to actions that a party agrees not to take during the executory contract period.

   Example: In the sale of Greenacre, Buyer promises to apply for a $90,000 bank loan within 24 hours of signing the contract (*an affirmative covenant*). Seller agrees not to remove any of the improvements from the property or to commit undue waste or deterioration during the executory contract period (*a negative covenant*).

5. **Remedies:** In the contract, the parties should state the consequences of particular events in advance, including the failure of conditions, warranties, representations, and covenants. Courts often defer to the parties' clarification of the nature and scope of remedies.

B. **Lawyer's role in explaining contract:** The lawyer must assure the client that the contract is enforceable and that all of the essential terms are included in the writing. The lawyer must be sure the contract reflects the client's expectations and interests. He should fully explain to the client all documents prepared in connection with the contract.

1. **Duty to nonclients:** The lawyer also has a duty to a party who is not his client. This duty generally involves notifying the nonclient that the lawyer does not represent her and is not protecting her interests in the transaction. If the lawyer offers any explanation to the nonclient of the documents he has prepared, he must take extreme care to explain the basic terms accurately so the nonclient understands each document's nature and scope.

   Example: A buyer of real estate hires a lawyer to represent him in a purchase from Cowan, an elderly person who is not represented by counsel. The contract and related financing documents are very one-sided in the buyer's favor. The lawyer closes the purchase on the buyer's behalf without any interaction with Cowan. After closing, Cowan complains about several of the terms. The lawyer breached a duty to explain to Cowan that he represented the buyer, whose interests are different from those of Cowan. Also, he had a duty to explain the material terms of the documents to Cowan. *Florida Bar v. Belleville*, 591 So. 2d 170 (Fla. 1991).

II. CONTRACT MODIFICATIONS

A. Subsequent agreement: Parties often agree to changes in the nature or scope of their agreement after the date of the original contract. Since a modification comes after the original contract, it is possible to avoid the operation of the parol evidence rule. An issue under the statute of frauds, however, is whether the modification must also be written because the original contract was written. Some courts require a writing, but others allow proof of a later parol modification on the basis that the original writing establishes the foundation of a real agreement between the parties.

B. Waiver: A contract may be modified by a party's waiver of a term or condition. A party can waive a term or requirement of a contract by word, writing, or action. A term or requirement, once waived, is said to be gone forever. This means it cannot later be reinstated.

C. Estoppel: A party can be estopped from enforcing a contract term or requirement if the other side has reasonably and detrimentally relied on the party's action or inaction. The party subject to estoppel may usually reinstate the term or requirement by giving the other side ample notice of the intention to do so.

Example: John sells real property to Sally, who agrees in writing to pay $1,000 on the first day of each month until the full price is paid. The contract says that, for any late payment, Sally must pay $75 per day and is subject to eviction from the property and foreclosure. Sally makes the first two payments on time. On the third payment, she is two days late, and the next four payments are each two weeks late. In each case, John accepts the late payment without assessing a penalty and without comment. John's actions may amount to a waiver of the strict need for Sally to pay on the first of the month. This means John must accept payment at any reasonable time. Estoppel also may prevent John from enforcing the due date. Under an estoppel approach, however, John may reinstate this requirement if he gives notice to Sally that he can no longer tolerate the late payments and, beginning next month, she must adhere to the original terms.

III. EQUITABLE CONVERSION

A. Split of title: The doctrine of equitable conversion splits title to the property between the seller and the buyer when the contract is signed. The seller retains legal title, while the buyer acquires equitable title. Both parties own property rights and have the ability to deal with and transfer their respective interests.

    1. Legal title: The seller has legal title only as a trustee, as security for the forthcoming payment of the purchase price. Legal title is considered personal property. For example, if the seller dies and devises his personal property to a named person, that person takes the seller's interest in the contract.

    2. Equitable title: The buyer, as equitable owner, is the real owner of the property prior to closing, just as if an express trust were created. This does not mean, however, that the buyer has the right of possession prior to closing. The general rule is that the seller retains possession until closing unless the contract expressly provides otherwise. Equitable title is considered real property.

B. Traditional risk of loss rule: Under equitable conversion, the traditional rule is that the buyer has the risk of loss from fire and other casualty from the time the contract becomes enforceable. This rule can apply to a broad range of risks, including earthquake, hurricane, sinkholes, drought, and even unexpected zoning problems.

Example: Chen contracts to sell one acre of land with a large home to Junko for $500,000. Closing is to take place 60 days after the date of contract. Ten days after the contract is signed, the house burns to the ground from a fire that was not caused by either party. Junko says that the house alone was worth $400,000, and she refuses to go forward. But under the traditional rule, risk of loss goes to Junko, who has equitable title. She must go through with the contract.

C. Other risk of loss rules

  1. Control: Some courts look to see which party controlled the property at the time of loss and whether or not the ability to control would have in any way made it possible to prevent or reduce the risk of loss.

  Example: If the seller keeps possession and could have prevented a loss, a court may decide that risk of loss stayed with the seller. Assume that Chen's house burns down as a result of an electrical problem related to the fact that Chen improperly overloaded his circuit box capability by using excessive extension cords and running too many electrical devices at one time. Here a court might look at possession and control and find that the risk of loss stayed with the seller even though the seller did no intentional wrong.

  2. Uniform Vendor and Purchaser Risk Act: Adopted by a dozen states, the act places the risk of loss on the seller until the buyer receives possession or legal title to the property.

  3. Implied condition: The courts in Massachusetts and several states have rejected the traditional equitable conversion rule, instead placing the risk of loss on the seller. The explanation is that there is an implied condition that the improvements will continue to exist without material damage up to the time of closing. This is based on the parties' probable expectations.

  Example: Buyer contracts to buy land for an ice cream and frozen fruit plant. When the contract is signed, zoning allows this use, but the local government rezones to prohibit this use while the contract is executory. Seller sues for specific performance. Under the traditional risk of loss rule, Seller prevails. But if Buyer shows that the parties made a mutual mistake of fact—both believed the property could be used for the buyer's intended purpose—the court in equity may deny specific performance. This reasoning is similar to that in *Clay v. Landreth*, 45 S.E.2d 875 (Va. 1948). In essence, the court implies the condition that the zoning will remain unchanged until closing based on the parties' mutual expectations.

D. Contract allocation of risk of loss: The parties can alter the doctrine of equitable conversion by express contract and allocate some or all of the risk of loss to either party. Most written contracts specifically address risk of loss. Typically parties will place the risk of loss on the person to retain control and possession of the property, which is usually the seller. The real importance of clarifying the risk of loss is that it identifies who should account for this risk by retaining insurance to cover the risk of loss.

E. Insurance: Both seller and buyer have an insurable interest and may obtain a policy of fire and casualty insurance. Often, the seller is already carrying insurance and just continues with that coverage until the closing. A buyer can get insurance at the same time. Generally, a person is not held to have taken on the risk of loss simply because he happens to have insurance. Usually, insurance is only for the benefit of the person who purchases the policy.

Example: Chen's house burns down while it is under a contract to be sold to Junko. Chen has insurance on the home, but Junko does not. Under the traditional risk of loss rule, Junko has to go forward with the contract and pay the full contract price. Chen can collect on the insurance and also get the contract price. But in many states the buyer receives the benefit of the seller's insurance proceeds to prevent a windfall to the seller. The buyer receives a price abatement equal to the proceeds less the premium paid by the seller.

Example: In another instance, a contract provides that Buyer may rescind if the improvements are materially damaged during the executory period. Buyer obtains an insurance policy that also lists Seller as having an interest in the property and a beneficial interest in insurance. Fire destroys a cabin on the property, and Buyer rescinds. Seller can collect under Buyer's insurance policy under the doctrine of third-party beneficiary because he was listed in the policy. *Holscher v. James*, 860 P.2d 646 (Idaho 1993).

IV. MAJOR CONTRACT CONDITIONS

Contract conditions are used pervasively to allocate risk between the parties. They address the timing of performance and the consequences of certain events happening or not happening in the future. They permit a buyer to evaluate the suitability of the sale with respect to items such as the title, land survey, physical defects, financing, and legal status. If a party's conduct may influence whether a condition is met, that party has an implied obligation to act in good faith by taking steps to satisfy that condition.

A. **Categories of conditions:** The general categories of conditions of importance to the real estate contract are express conditions, implied conditions, conditions precedent, conditions subsequent, and simultaneous conditions. With a *condition precedent*, a party avoids certain risks or duties under the contract if a certain condition is not met. With a *condition subsequent*, a party is relieved of a risk or duty that was undertaken when an expected event does not happen. *Simultaneous conditions* require both parties to perform at the same time. Precise drafting is highly important. How conditions are cast can have dramatic consequences.

Example: Carlos negotiates to buy land from Margaret for $200,000. The land is currently zoned for commercial use, which is what Carlos needs. Local news discloses that some community leaders want to rethink the county land use plan. Carlos drafts his contract to include this term: "Buyer agrees to purchase the property provided that the current zoning, allowing for commercial uses, continues in full force and effect during the executory contract period." This language creates a *condition subsequent* because, if rezoning occurs, Carlos is relieved of his obligation to go forward. Margaret takes the risk of a zoning change prior to closing. If the property was currently zoned for residential purposes, Carlos might have used a *condition precedent*, such as "Buyer agrees to purchase the property provided that the current zoning can be changed within the executory contract period to allow for commercial uses." In both cases, the parties are under an implied obligation to act in good faith: in the first case, to do nothing to increase the chances of undesirable rezoning; in the latter, to use good-faith efforts to get rezoning.

Example: Conditions can function much like strategies in a poker game. Carlos and Margaret agree that he will pay $200,000 for her property and she will produce evidence of good fee simple title. Before closing, Margaret discovers a problem with title, which she does not want to reveal to Carlos or, if she must, she wants to delay revealing as long as possible. If the contract language makes displaying evidence of good title a **condition precedent** to Carlos's duty to pay, Carlos can hold onto his money until he sees proof of good title. If the evidence shows a defect, Carlos can refuse to pay, and Margaret will have to sue Carlos if she thinks the contract is still enforceable. What is important here is that Carlos never has to show his hand. It may be that Carlos was unable to get the money together for the purchase, but was able to show up at closing without ever revealing his own inability to perform. In the alternative, if the contract language sets up evidence of good title as a **condition subsequent** to the payment by Carlos, we get a different result. In this situation, Margaret does not need to reveal her hand until after Carlos pays the full amount. If Carlos is unable to pay, Margaret will never have to show that she had a title problem. Also, the dynamics change, as Carlos must pay first, so that if he pays and then objects to the evidence of title presented by Margaret, he will have to sue to get his money back. Finally, if we can construe the contract language as creating a **simultaneous condition**, then both parties must reveal their "hands" at the same time. Payment and evidence of title must both be shown.

B. Inspection condition: Buyers often bargain for a condition to inspect the building, fixtures, and other improvements. The condition should clearly specify what is to be inspected, by whom, and at whose expense, and what the consequences of the information revealed by the inspections are to be. Inspections typically cover such items as the structural soundness of a building, water quality, soil testing, and other environmental factors.

C. Mortgage financing: This condition protects the buyer from the risk that he may not be able to obtain the financing he needs in order to buy the property. If the contract does not have a mortgage financing condition, the buyer has agreed to engage in an "all-cash" exchange. The financing condition should state the amount of financing needed, along with financing constraints, such as the interest rate, monthly payment, loan term, points, and nature of the loan.

Example: Carlos agrees to buy a home from Margaret for $200,000. Carlos does not have enough cash for the purchase. He drafts the contract so that it says, "Buyer's obligation to go forward with this contract is conditioned upon his being approved for a $190,000 fixed rate mortgage loan from Big Bank at a rate of interest not to exceed 12 percent." This language makes obtaining a loan from Big Bank a condition precedent. If it does not occur, Carlos has no further obligations to Margaret.

Example: Crocker owned a home and entered into a contract with Butler as buyer. Butler agreed to purchase the home for $770,000 and put down a deposit of $12,500. The financing condition required that Butler be able to secure financing at an interest rate not to exceed 8.5 percent. Butler did not get the type of loan he wanted at that interest rate and sought to get out of the contract. Because other types of loans could be available at the stated rate of interest Butler was not excused from performance under the contract condition, and Crocker got to keep the deposit. The problem for Butler was a failure to be more specific in the condition by limiting the type of mortgage he was willing to accept at the stated interest rate. *Louisiana Real Estate Commission v. Butler*, 899 So. 2d 1512 (La. App. 2005).

1. Seller financing: When the buyer is denied a mortgage loan from an institutional lender, occasionally the seller offers to finance the sale at the terms specified in the condition. There is a split of authority as to whether the buyer must accept this offer. On the one hand, the cost of financing to the buyer is no greater regardless of who provides the financing. On the other hand, the buyer may have desired an institutional loan in order to build a better credit rating or out of confidence that it would administer the loan in a commercially reasonable manner.

Proctor v. Holden, 540 A.2d 133 (Md. Ct. Spec. App. 1988) (buyer not obligated to accept seller financing when, prior to signing the contract, seller said that she would not finance the sale).

Quiz Yourself on *THE EXECUTORY CONTRACT*

14. Carlos contracts to buy a home from Tomeka. The home is serviced by well water. The contract states, "Buyer shall close on the purchase contract provided that the well water on the property meets all health code requirements and is suitable for human consumption and use." The contract also provides for an inspection. Carlos has an independent lab test the water. The lab reports levels of bacteria and iron that exceed the current health code restrictions. Carlos tells Tomeka he is rescinding the contract and asking for a return of his deposit. Tomeka counters that Carlos must go forward under the contract, although she is willing to reduce the contract price by $2,000, from $105,000 to $103,000. Tomeka asserts that the contract language simply provides for a warranty and representation as to water quality. When such a promise or warranty is broken the remedy is damages or a contract offset, and not release from the contract itself. Is Tomeka correct? _____

15. On January 1, Fred contracts to buy a nice single-family home from Rick. The home is located in Syracuse, NY. The home has air conditioning, which usually operates for about one month each summer. Closing is scheduled for March 10. In January and all the way through to the closing date it is too cold to test the air conditioning system in Syracuse without risking major damage. The contract contains a provision wherein Rick warrants the air conditioning is in good working order as of the date of the contract. Fred closes on the contract and is unable to test the air conditioning system prior to closing. In July, Fred tries to use the air conditioning system and it does not work. When he contacts a repair company, Fred is told that the coils are rusted and he is advised to buy a new unit. Fred wants to sue Rick for the cost of a new unit. Should Fred win on this claim? _____

16. Roger contracts to sell certain property to Aja. After signing the contract, which sets a closing date for 120 days later, Roger takes out a business loan and puts up a mortgage on the property. Can Roger do this? _____

17. Rebecca contracts to sell her house and quarter-acre lot to Sue. The contract price is $350,000, and everyone agrees the house is worth $275,000 and the lot accounts for the remaining cost. Rebecca has carried $200,000 worth of homeowner's insurance on the home for the past 10 years. Sue expects that Rebecca will maintain her insurance until closing, but she decides to get some extra coverage just in case. She orders $150,000 of insurance to cover her interest up to closing, when she will talk to her agent about additional coverage. During the executory contract period, the home is struck by lightning and burns to the ground. Under the traditional approach who has the risk of loss? _____

18. Zack contracts to buy a house from Melissa for $300,000. The contract has a financing condition requiring Zack to get loan approval for borrowing $250,000 at 7 percent interest for 30 years. Closing is scheduled for 60 days after the date of the contract. After signing the contract bad economic news is announced and the economy weakens, including a softening of housing prices. Zack becomes less interested in buying the house from Melissa. Zack comes up with a plan to legally get out of his contract. Since the contract does not have any express language requiring Zack to apply for a mortgage loan he decides not to do so. This means he will not have mortgage financing and will then not have to close on the contract. When the closing date arrives Zack says that the condition precedent to closing has failed (he did not end up getting a mortgage approved). Melissa objects and Zack responds that she should have protected herself by simply adding express language to the contract requiring Zack to actually apply for the loan. Should Zack prevail?   _____

Answers

14. **No.** Carlos will characterize the language as a condition precedent by arguing that his obligation to close is conditioned upon getting the passing report. The language itself seems to support that it is a condition placed upon the obligation to go forward. If it is a condition precedent, this would free him of further obligation and allow his recovery of the deposit. On the other hand, Tomeka is trying to characterize the language as a warranty, representation, or affirmative covenant. As a warranty, the failure of this warranty does not allow Carlos out of the transaction. Instead, Carlos must go forward with the transaction, and Carlos should be made whole by getting an abatement in the price. Assuming that the problem can be fixed for $2,000, it probably is not material, and Tomeka can either correct the problem or reduce the price. Carlos has a good chance to prevail here, but the outcome is not certain. The total cost to fix the problem is small and thus a court might be willing to see this as more of a damage or setoff claim.

15. **Maybe.** On the basic idea of the contract terms Fred probably has a good claim that the promise concerning the good working order was false at the time of the contract because it is unlikely that a coil would rust in a few months' time. However, it is possible that the unit had been working fine the last time Rick had used it, even if it was already rusting. This will be a fact determination. While it may seem like a fairly simple dispute there is another issue here. This issue involves the doctrine of merger, which is discussed in Chapter 6. Under the doctrine of merger promises made in the contract are often made unactionable after the closing of the contract, unless specifically preserved in a new agreement made at closing. Fred will be able to get to the merits of his claim only if he is able to get an exception to the doctrine of merger. This kind of promise, as to the working condition of an air conditioner, is probably considered an ancillary or collateral matter and may remain actionable after closing, particularly if there is evidence that the parties intended such a result.

16. **Yes.** When the contract is signed, equitable conversion takes place. Roger continues to hold legal title, and Aja takes equitable title. Each party has an interest that can be bought, sold, devised, mortgaged, and insured. Depending on the terms of the contract, however, Roger must still deliver good title at closing. This will require him to remove the lien of the mortgage unless Aja has accepted this or failed to protect herself from this possibility in the contract.

17. **Sue has the risk of loss.** Both parties have an insurable interest. Under the traditional rule related to the doctrine of equitable conversion, Sue has the risk of loss. Given that she has the risk of loss, she can collect $150,000 from her insurance company, and she is not entitled to any insurance proceeds from Rebecca's policy. Similarly, if the traditional rule is rejected in favor of holding Rebecca liable for the risk of loss, then Rebecca collects $200,000 from her insurance company and is not able to benefit from Sue's insurance. Whichever party ends up with the risk may assert that she was a third-party beneficiary of the extra insurance taken out by the other party. This is a long shot, but worth exploring.

18. **No.** It is true that Melissa could have provided for this event in the contract by having an express term such as "Buyer to apply for a mortgage loan within three business days from the date of this contract." At the same time the case law has implied a duty on the part of the buyer to make reasonable efforts to satisfy conditions included in a contract for his benefit. The financing condition benefits the buyer here, and reasonable and good faith effort is required to satisfy that condition. This means that even without an express term, Zack has an obligation to take reasonable steps to apply for and secure mortgage financing.

Exam Tips on ## THE EXECUTORY CONTRACT

☛ **Understand and address the full context of the contract:** A common mistake in analyzing an exam fact pattern is failing to see how different approaches to allocating contract risk (covenants, conditions, warranties, and representations) work together. In addition, don't forget that activity during the precontract stage, including negotiation and information exchanges, may impact the nature or scope of a condition, warranty, representation, or covenant.

☛ **Be sure to connect changes in the contract with concepts such as waiver and estoppel:** Amendment, waiver, and estoppel issues are often ambiguous. Show your understanding of the relationship between modification problems, and the statute of frauds and parol evidence. Also be ready to explain the difference between waiver and estoppel with respect to the ability to reinstate a contract term.

☛ **Identify the party with risk of loss:** Usually, it is best to start your analysis with the traditional rule, which puts risk of loss on the buyer as a consequence of equitable conversion. Then deal with exceptions and modifications, given the facts before you. Look to see if the parties have any language in their contract that might bear on risk of loss. Don't forget to consider insurance. Even if the facts do not indicate that either party has coverage, it may be useful to discuss who could and should have insured.

☛ **The language of conditions:** Conditions are very fact specific. Be sure to focus on specific wording and language in an agreement, and remember to consider alternative interpretations before drawing a conclusion as to the best interpretation.

CHAPTER 5

CONDITION OF THE PROPERTY

ChapterScope ━━━━━━━━━━━━━━━━━━━━━━━━━━━━━━━━━━

This chapter examines the condition of property in a real estate transaction. This involves concerns as to the quality and quantity of the property and relates to physical and nonphysical attributes of the property.

- ■ **Property condition:** Each parcel of real property has a certain quantity (physical size and shape) and quality. Together, characteristics relating to quantity and quality make up the property's condition.

- ■ **Transfer terms respecting quantity:** Two contract terms that allocate risk as to quantity are a per acre or unit transfer, and a transfer "in gross." A specific acre transfer might be stated as "100 acres," compared to a transfer in gross stated as "100 acres, more or less." A transfer in gross may also be based on a visual inspection of the property where the understanding is that one gets what one sees, without any specific statement as to acreage.

- ■ **Quality concerns:** Quality issues concern the physical, environmental, and psychological characteristics of the land and improvements.

- ■ **Allocating risk related to quality:** Risk related to property quality is allocated by the caveat emptor doctrine, implied and statutory disclosure duties, implied warranties, and contract provisions such as express warranties, conditions, inspection clauses, and "As Is" clauses.

- ■ **Caveat emptor:** A traditional doctrine in real estate transactions, now in decline, meaning "let the buyer beware." The effect of the doctrine is that buyer has the risk as to the quality of the property and must take appropriate steps to manage this risk. The doctrine, while an important reference point for modern risk allocation rules, has been substantially eroded under modern real estate law.

━━━

I. QUANTITY

Quantity issues concern the amount of land to be transferred, the legal description, the certainty of boundary lines, and encroachments.

A. Sale by the acre: The parties may bargain for a price to be determined on the basis of a certain amount per acre or per square foot. In this event, a price adjustment is to be made if it is determined that the acreage is more or less than the parties expected. When exact area is ***material*** to the transaction, the contract should provide for a survey to determine the exact quantity and to confirm the legal description.

B. Sale in gross: If the parties specify a total purchase price for the property with no breakdown into a per acre unit price, the presumption is a sale in gross. This means the buyer is usually not entitled to a price adjustment when a shortage is discovered. Most shortages are considered minor even though the buyer's expectations may be defeated. If the property description states the quantity, but adds the phrase ***"more or less,"*** this strengthens the presumption of a sale in gross. If the shortage is extreme, approaching 50 percent or more, the court may grant relief to the buyer under the doctrine of mutual mistake, even though the sale is in gross.

C. **Survey:** An accurate survey is necessary to confirm the quantity of land. The buyer should obtain a survey prior to closing. If a mortgage is involved, a lender will typically require an updated survey. (The survey is discussed further in Chapter 9.) If the buyer discovers the shortage in quantity only after closing, the doctrine of merger (discussed in Chapter 6) may be an additional bar to relief.

   Example: Ferrin contracts to sell a ranch to Turner. The contract describes the land as "96 acres more or less." Turner inspects the property three times, looking at the boundaries of the ranch. After taking possession, Turner orders a survey of the ranch and learns it has only about 90 acres. Turner is not entitled to rescind the contract or recover damages for the shortage in acreage because the sale is in gross. He got what he bargained for. *Turner v. Ferrin*, 757 P.2d 335 (Mont. 1988).

   Example: At closing, a home builder gives the buyer a survey, which shows that the home complies with a 20-foot setback requirement. Later the buyer finds the survey is in error and the home lies two feet rather than twenty feet from the boundary. The buyer brings a damage action against the seller. Although merger might often bar recovery under such circumstances, the buyer may prevail by characterizing the erroneous survey as a misrepresentation of material information. *Richard v. Waldman & Sons*, 232 A.2d 307 (Conn. 1967).

   Example: The Perfects contract to sell 81.1 acres of land to McAndrew for $252,500. After contracting, a survey was done and it revealed that the property was really 96.2815 acres. The Perfects did not want to perform on the terms of the contract, given the new information indicating that the property contained much more acreage than previously expected. The court enforced the contract by specific performance, holding that the sale was "in gross" and that there was no mutual mistake as to the land intended to be the subject of the contract. *Perfect v. McAndrew*, 798 N.E.2d 470 (Ind. Ct. App. 2003).

II. QUALITY

A. **Caveat emptor:** The traditional baseline rule governing physical quality of the land and improvements is caveat emptor. This means ***buyer beware***; the buyer has no implied rights with respect to quality. As a consequence of the caveat emptor doctrine, the buyer has the duty to inspect the property to determine whether its quality is satisfactory and suitable for the buyer's purposes prior to entering into the contract. The seller has no duty to reveal information to the buyer. If the buyer fails to inspect or inspects carelessly, the loss is the buyer's, not the seller's. This doctrine is in disfavor and decline.

B. **Pro-buyer doctrines:** The caveat emptor doctrine has substantially eroded over the years. Buyers often prevail on claims relating to property quality by using a number of doctrines or rules. Depending on how they are viewed, these doctrines and rules are either exceptions to caveat emptor, or not within the scope of the doctrine because the defect cannot be detected by a reasonable inspection by the buyer. The defect issues can relate to physical, environmental, or psychological conditions of the property.

   1. **Intentional or negligent misrepresentation:** If the seller or her agent intentionally or negligently misrepresents the quality of the property, the buyer may be entitled to rescind the

contract or recover damages. The buyer must show that the represented fact was material and that she detrimentally and reasonably relied on the representation. Many courts use the term "fraudulent misrepresentation" instead of intentional misrepresentation. To some extent, the defect must be latent (not easily observable), not patent (reasonably observable), for the buyer's reliance on the representation to be reasonable. However, a buyer who bargains for a representation is permitted to rely on the representation and thus may be excused from making an inspection of the item in question. Once a party discloses information, a partial selective disclosure may be misleading. Generally, the disclosing party should fully disclose relevant information related to the subject matter in order to avoid potential liability.

2. **Concealment:** The buyer may recover if the seller takes affirmative action to hide a material defect or prevent the purchaser or her inspector from discovering the defect. By definition, the seller's act has made the defect latent rather than patent.

3. **Latent dangerous defects:** If the seller knows of a latent defect that makes the property dangerous to possessors or users, the seller has an affirmative duty to disclose the defect. The policy is to reduce the risk of personal injury to the buyer and third parties. Some states require that the duty to disclose latent defects only applies to those latent defects that pose a danger, rather than to all latent defects.

4. **Attorney liability:** An attorney who provides false information or misleading partial information (even if done without intent to mislead or cause harm) may be liable to a nonclient for negligence if the nonclient proves reliance and damages. *Petrillo v. Bachenberg*, 655 A.2d 1354 (N.J. 1995) (attorney edited soil percolation tests, giving positive tests to buyer and withholding negative tests and thereby creating a false impression as to soil quality). An attorney may also be liable for malpractice or breach of a professional obligation under appropriate circumstances.

C. **Implied duty to disclose material defects:** Some states go beyond the duty of the seller to disclose known dangerous defects and hold that the seller has an implied affirmative duty to disclose all material defects known to the seller.

1. **Materiality:** A defect is material if it has a significant effect on market value. An alternative measure is whether the defect would be a concern to most buyers in terms of their willingness to buy the property or the price they would pay. A matter can also be made material if a party has extracted a contract representation covering the issue. For example, a buyer extracts the following from a seller in the terms of the contract: "Seller represents that the roof is sound and does not leak." If it turns out that the roof is defective and does leak, this would be material because the buyer cared enough to have extracted a specific representation as to this particular matter.

2. **Knowledge:** Some courts impose an affirmative duty to disclose only when the seller actually knows of the defect. This is a subjective intent standard. A few courts go further, imposing a disclosure duty when the seller knows or should know, in the exercise of reasonable care, of the defect.

3. **Residential versus commercial transactions:** Almost all the cases that require a seller to disclose material latent defects that are not dangerous involve home sales. Many courts that protect home buyers as consumers in these situations tend to retain some form of caveat emptor for buyers of commercial properties.

D. **Stigma and nondisclosure statutes:** Occasionally, buyers of used homes have recovered for defects that are not physical, but relate to the property's reputation in the community or its negative history. Stigma may have either a *material impact on value or* an *emotional impact* on the buyer. Stigma has nothing to do with the structural soundness or physical attributes of a property, but relates to a *psychological defect*. Two theories have succeeded for buyers: misrepresentation of the status of the property and an affirmative duty to disclose. In response to such cases, over 20 states have statutes providing that the seller or broker is not liable for failing to disclose potential stigmas, such as the site of a murder or suicide or the residency of persons with certain diseases such as AIDS or tuberculosis.

Example: Van Camp is looking to buy a house. She notices a home that has metal bars on the windows and inquires about the crime rate in the neighborhood and the safety of the residence. Seller says there was a break-in 16 years earlier, but there are currently no problems. In fact, seller knows of a variety of recent crimes in the community, plus a recent rape on the property and another rape nearby. Van Camp learns the truth after moving in. She is entitled to relief because the property is stigmatized and seller misrepresented its status. *Van Camp v. Bradford*, 623 N.E.2d 731 (Ohio Ct. Common Pleas 1993).

Example: For years, the owner of a house publicizes that it is haunted. A person from out of town who is not aware of the reputation enters into a contract to buy the house. The buyer is entitled to rescission because the seller created the stigma, it materially impairs value, and a prudent buyer exercising due care is not likely to discover this defect. *Stambovsky v. Ackley*, 572 N.Y.S.2d 672 (App. Div. 1991).

E. **Statutory duty to disclose:** Some information about the condition of real property must be disclosed as the result of local, state, or federal statutes. A seller may have to disclose whether the premises have ever been flooded or whether the property contains lead paint or lead pipes. Statutory requirements eliminate uncertainty about who needs to disclose information relevant to a particular subject matter. A growing number of states have statutes that require home sellers to disclose known latent defects to purchasers. They apply not only to merchant sellers, but also to individuals who sell their used homes.

1. **Interstate Land Sales Full Disclosure Act:** This federal act, adopted in 1968, applies to the sale of unimproved lots in subdivisions with 25 or more lots. The Act requires the developer to file a registration known as a "Statement of Record" for approval by the government before offering any lots for sale. As part of marketing, the developer must give each prospective purchaser a detailed "Property Report," which contains required disclosures about the lots and the overall real estate development. *Hester v. Hidden Valley Lakes, Inc.*, 495 F. Supp. 48 (N.D. Miss. 1980) (seller is strictly liable for delivery of property report that contains untrue statement of material fact or omits to state a material fact required to be given; buyer does not have to prove that seller had intent to mislead or that buyer relied on untrue statements).

F. **Implied warranties for sale of new housing:** In most states, a buyer of a new home receives an implied warranty of habitability from her merchant seller. The implied warranty rests on the expectations of buyers. Builders generally hold themselves out as having the expertise necessary to construct a habitable dwelling. In many states, the scope of the implied warranty of habitability is not clearly defined. One approach is merchantability. By analogy to the UCC, the warranty of habitability means the house must be merchantable; that is, it must be reasonably fit to live in according to the community standards for housing of the type involved. This covers all latent material defects and excludes only minor defects, such as cosmetic flaws. The second approach is habitability. The defect breaches the warranty of habitability only if it is serious enough that the house is not fit to live in if the defect is not repaired. This tends to limit the warranty to major defects that relate to health and safety. In a number of states, a builder who sells a new house makes a statutory warranty that the house complies with the building code. The buyer may insist that the builder repair material code violations. In many states, the scope of the warranty goes beyond improvements constructed by the seller and includes problems relating to the natural condition of the site, such as groundwater and soil stability.

Example: Developer builds an adequate house, but due to soil conditions is unable to produce potable water from a well. Thus, buyers are stuck with a house that does not have access to potable water. Therefore, buyers are entitled to the protection of the implied warranty of habitability because they are in a situation in which it would be extremely difficult for them to protect themselves. *McDonald v. Mianecki*, 398 A.2d 1283 (N.J. 1979).

G. Express allocations of risk of quality: The parties may specify by contract their agreement as to property quality. Promises, representations, warranties, and conditions may all be used, singly or in combination, to allocate the risk of quality.

    1. Right of inspection: The buyer should have the contract provide for ample rights to inspect by qualified people selected by the buyer. These provisions should establish standards for assessing quality, time frames for objections, and guidelines for repairs, price reductions, and contract termination.

    Example: Seller contracts to sell a house to Buyer with an "As Is" term. Buyer includes in the contract a provision giving her the right to inspect the property. Part of the conversation leading up to the contract involved the question of whether the basement had ever had water damage. Later it was discovered by Buyer that there had been water in the basement even though Seller had indicated that such was not the case. The court held against the buyer in this case because the buyer had a contract right of inspection, in which the prior water problem would have been discovered, but failed to actually do an inspection. *Aires v. McGehee*, 85 P.3d 1191 (Kan. 2004). The lesson here is that the buyer should get a right-to-inspect provision in the contract and then actually do the inspection. Otherwise anything that would have been discovered in an inspection may be held against the buyer.

    2. "As Is" clause: Under an "As Is" clause, the buyer agrees that the property quality in its present condition, when the contract is signed, is acceptable. This places all the risk on the buyer and should be coupled with providing the buyer an opportunity to inspect. An "As Is" clause often helps to persuade a court to apply the doctrine of caveat emptor.

    Example: The buyer of a 140-year-old house signs a contract with an "As Is" clause. The contract also lets the buyer inspect and states that neither party has relied on any statement or representation not embodied in the contract. The buyer hires an inspector whose large body size prevents him from looking at the crawl spaces. It is also impossible to check behind all of the walls without actually ripping them apart. After moving in, the buyer begins remodeling and finds major structural damage. The buyer is not entitled to damages or other relief. The "As Is" clause is enforceable, and the court properly applies the doctrine of caveat emptor. It does not matter whether the seller had actual knowledge of the structural damages at the time of contracting. *Pitre v. Twelve Oak Trust*, 818 F. Supp. 949 (S.D. Miss. 1993).

    3. Express warranties: Express warranties are ones that are made as part of the agreement between the parties. They should be set forth in the formal contract to avoid problems with the parol evidence rule. The doctrine of merger usually extinguishes an express warranty as to the physical condition of the property at the closing unless the warranty is expressly extended beyond closing.

    a. H.O.W. programs: Homeowner's warranty (H.O.W.) programs provide one form of express warranty. They are warranty contracts that can be purchased with new homes and in a variety of forms for used homes. The idea is that you get a warranty protection plan that provides repair services in the event of problems with the home.

III. LENDER LIABILITY

    A. Lender acting like developer: Mortgage lenders are generally not liable to buyers for defects in new or used housing. A buyer has no legal right to rely on the lender's appraisals or inspections. If the lender functions as a partner or joint venturer with the housing developer, the lender may become liable to buyers for defects created by the developer. Such a lender exercises managerial control over a project or shares in a proprietary interest. When a lender is found liable, it is because it had a duty to the buyer/borrower and failed to fully perform up to the level of that duty.

    Example: Bank, the lender for a large residential subdivision, went far beyond normal lending activities for construction lenders. It engaged in supervision, exercised control, and due to Bank's extensive rights, the project was determined to be a cooperative work effort between Bank and the developer. Bank was in a position to exercise supervision of the project and should have known the developer was undercapitalized, inexperienced, and prone to cutting corners in its construction projects. For this reason, lot buyers who were injured by poorly constructed foundations had a damage action against Bank. *Connor v. Great Western Savings & Loan Association*, 447 P.2d 609 (Cal. 1968).

    B. Lender's knowledge of seller's fraud: If the lender knows or should know that the seller is committing fraud on the buyer, the buyer who gets a mortgage loan from the lender may assert fraud as a defense to the lender's action to enforce the debt.

Quiz Yourself on
CONDITION OF THE PROPERTY

19. Jamie contracts to buy a home from Sandra. The contract requires Sandra to convey the two-acre property with improvements in fee simple absolute by warranty deed. At closing the deed is delivered and it says that the property is conveyed by general warranty deed in fee simple so long as liquor is never sold on the property. The property history indicates that the property has never been used as a place for selling liquor and Jamie does not intend to sell any. Jamie is buying the property to enjoy the house and space it provides in a nice suburban area. Zoning regulations also prevent use of the property for any purpose other than single-family residential. Nonetheless, Jamie wonders if Sandra has complied with the contract terms. Has Sandra delivered the quality of estate that the contract requires? _____

20. Bill contracts to purchase a subdivision lot from Mary that fronts along a lake. This lot and neighboring lakefront lots are all 150 feet deep, but they vary as to lake frontage. The lots are valued and priced at $10,000 per frontage foot. Bill contracts to buy Mary's lot based on 42 feet of lake frontage. The price is $420,000. As part of the inspection process, Bill gets a survey, which reveals that the lot is only 40 feet and 6 inches. Is Bill entitled to a contract price reduction of $15,000? _____

21. In the above problem, what if the survey reveals that the property is actually 44 feet with respect to lake frontage? Should Mary be entitled to an extra $20,000? _____

22. Referring back to the contract between Jamie and Sandra in Question 19 above, assume that Jamie has 10 days from the date of the contract to "inspect all structures and electrical systems for soundness and compliance with building codes." While checking out the electrical system, Jamie's electrician observes that some parts of the house plumbing system are made out of old lead pipes. Jamie objects to the lead pipe in the home because it poses a health problem, and subsequent water tests indicate lead residue in the tap water. Can Jamie recover anything from Sandra? _____

23. Ahmed recently built a new home in West Palm Beach, Florida. After living in it for only three months, he took a new job in New York and put the house up for sale. Ahmed contracted to sell the home to Chen Lee for $600,000. In the contract Ahmed provides the following: "The home is newly constructed, I am the original and only owner of the property, I have occupied it for three months, and as such I provide no warranty expressed or implied with respect to the property. Buyer shall look directly to the builder in the event of discovering any defects." Chen Lee provides the following provision: "Buyer has a right to inspect the structure and property within 15 days of contract, and if a major defect is discovered shall present a report as to the defect to seller and upon doing so shall be excused from the contract." Chen is busy with other matters and does not get an inspector out to the property for 18 days. The inspector determines that the sheetrock/plasterboard used in the house is from China and is defective. Chen has read about such defects in the newspaper and is concerned. Chen presents the report to Ahmed and elects to be excused from the contract. Should Ahmed be able to hold Chen to the contract? _____

Answers

19. **No.** The contract calls for an estate interest that is a fee simple absolute. The actual language in the deed presented at closing is that of a fee simple determinable ("so long as liquor is never sold on the property"). In terms of quality of estate, these are two very different estate interests. Note that the facts of liquor never being sold on the property, not intended to be sold in the future, and being prohibited by current zoning law do not negate the fact that the fee simple determinable is of a lesser quality than that which was bargained for in the contract. Sandra has not performed under the contract. Note: You do not want to make the common mistake of thinking that the "so long as" language is some kind of a restrictive covenant running with the fee simple absolute. It is actually the language defining the estate interest to be conveyed.

20. **Probably.** Bill says that the exact footage was material to his price and contract expectations. Bill should recover if he can show the parties used the formula to calculate their price. It would be best if the contract were specific about the reliance on the 42 feet of lake frontage. Mary argues caveat emptor—Bill should have checked the frontage out before signing the contract, or he should have

bargained for the contract to include an express warranty of frontage or a price clause that expressly incorporates the formula (a price adjustment based on survey results).

21. **Probably not.** This is probably going to be more difficult for Mary to win than it would be for Bill to win in the above problem. Mary is the owner and is expected to have the best information concerning the property; therefore, the law may not be so helpful. On the other hand, Mary might argue that they contracted under a mutual mistake as to the frontage or that the price formula indicates the intent to have the price specifically reflect the actual measure of frontage.

22. **Maybe.** If the lead pipe violates the building code or if Jamie can argue that a home comes with an implied warranty of fitness that extends to healthy water. Sandra can object that water and plumbing were not within the language of the inspection clause that Jamie bargained for in the contract. As a result, Jamie has no grounds to object, but rather took the risk as to property conditions that he did not specifically address in the contract.

23. **Probably not.** The defective sheetrock is a latent defect. It is unclear if it poses a danger but some news stories do indicate that it might cause bad health effects. This could be an ample danger. Ahmed tried to set up an "As Is" contract even though he did not use that term. It would have been better if he did use these words. Instead, he basically said that Chen had to look to the builder for any problems or complaints. Nonetheless, both parties agreed to an inspection provision and a means for Chen to object and be released from the contract. Chen did an inspection, but it was done beyond the time provided for in the contract. If time is of the essence in the contract, then the dates will be strictly enforced and Chen will not be excused. If time is not of the essence, then Chen may be given a reasonable time to inspect if there is a good faith basis for his inability to get the inspection done on time. Note that even if Chen can be said to have objected within a reasonable time, it is still unclear as to what is meant by a major defect that excuses performance. How do we distinguish a major from a lesser defect if the contract does not define the meaning of "major"? Should major mean a defect costing more than some specifically stated amount that should be expressed in the contract?

Exam Tips on CONDITION OF THE PROPERTY

☛ **Pay attention to contract language on quality and condition:** You need to be clear as to the exact subject matter of the contract in terms of the condition of the property and the "quality" of the condition that is within the expectation of the parties.

☛ **Caveat emptor:** Caveat emptor and the doctrines related to it are fact-specific. You must be careful to evaluate facts thoughtfully and to refer to them specifically when addressing issues of quality in an answer.

☛ **Distinguish patent and latent defects:** Pay close attention to the distinction between latent and patent defects, because this is often the basis of confusion for students and is an area of testing on examinations. Be careful to remember that the general default rule is that the latent defect must be one that is also dangerous. Note that not all states require this element.

☛ **Determine the quantity term in the contract:** Look first to the language of any written contract to determine if the parties intended a sale per acre (or foot) or a sale in gross. If it is the former, decide how to adjust the price for the shortage or surplus. If it is the latter, decide whether the shortage or surplus is minor or extreme enough to be considered material. Also remember that issues of merger and privity of contract (who bought the survey) are often intertwined with quantity issues.

☛ **Address materiality:** Materiality of information goes to two distinct matters. First, how important is the information to the particular party in reaching a contract decision? Second, how does the information impact the market determination of property value? Generally, the parties can make a matter material to the contract by including a specific representation as to the matter.

☛ **Clarify the type of risk involved:** In most fact patterns dealing with property condition, you will have an opportunity to address each of the ways to allocate risk (covenant, representation, warranty, condition). Map out all of the possibilities before jumping to a conclusion as to the best approach or outcome.

☛ **Identify the source of a duty to disclose:** Be careful to identify the source of law used when describing a duty to disclose. There are a number of issues related to duty to disclose and a good analysis requires clarity on the source of the duty. This includes reference to common law and statutory law.

☛ **Consider third parties:** Be sure to consider the potential for any third-party claims such as those that might be actionable against a lender in a transaction.

CHAPTER 6

CLOSING THE CONTRACT

ChapterScope ━━━

This chapter discusses the closing of the contract. At closing, a number of activities take place and the legal status of the property changes hands.

- **Closing the contract:** At closing, the parties complete the transaction, exchanging the instrument of conveyance (typically the deed) for the consideration (the purchase price). When this process is completed, the buyer has both the equitable and legal title to the property and the seller has the proceeds of sale.

- **Satisfaction of conditions:** At closing, the parties confirm that all conditions have been satisfied or waived. Evidence of satisfaction or waiver may be presented at closing, if not required in advance.

- **Six elements of conveyance:** An effective conveyance must meet six requirements involving (1) a writing to satisfy the statute of frauds, (2) a proper grantor and a grantee, (3) a legal description, (4) an intent to convey, (5) a delivery, and (6) an acceptance.

- **Role of an attorney:** An attorney is advised to represent only one party in a transaction but may represent more than one party, provided their interests are not adverse, the attorney makes full disclosure, and all clients consent. In the event of a dispute where the attorney represents more than one party, the attorney cannot represent either party in litigation.

- **Doctrine of merger:** The *doctrine of merger* operates at closing to extinguish prior representations and promises. Thus, all causes of action after closing must be on documents taken at closing and not on the prior contract.

- **Exceptions to doctrine of merger:** There are three general exceptions to the operation of the doctrine of merger, allowing an action on the contract even after closing. The exceptions are for (1) fraud, (2) collateral matters, and (3) certain mutual mistakes.

- **Escrows and closing:** There are three common escrows related to closing activities. These are loan escrows, closing escrows, and contingency escrows.

I. THE CLOSING PROCESS

At closing, each party should review performance under the contract and object to any shortcomings. Each side wants to get everything it bargained for and not give up more than it promised.

A. The exchange: At the closing, the instrument of conveyance is exchanged for the consideration. Usually, the instrument is a warranty deed, but it may be another instrument, such as a lease, depending upon the interest to be conveyed.

B. Effective conveyance: To be effective, the instrument of conveyance must satisfy six elements: (1) The instrument must *be in writing*, (2) the instrument must *identify the grantor and the grantee*, (3) the instrument must *adequately describe the property*, (4) there must *be an intent to convey*, (5) there must *be actual or constructive delivery of the instrument to the grantee*, and (6) the grantee must *accept the grant*.

    1. Relationship to recording statutes: Recording the instrument is not necessary to create the interest in the grantee. The conveyance is complete when the six elements are met. Recording is a *voluntary act* that puts third parties on notice and establishes the priority of the interest with respect to potential competing interests in the same property.

    Example: Sam contracts to sell a home to Phil for $300,000. The contract provides for closing in 60 days and requires Sam to convey by general warranty deed. Sam agrees to furnish evidence of good fee simple title to the property at closing. In addition, Sam agrees to convey a stove, an oven, a clothes washer, and a clothes dryer by *bill of sale* with warranties of fitness, merchantability, and good title. At the closing, Sam delivers a commitment of title insurance, indicating that Sam is currently the fee simple owner and identifying Phil as the prospective insured. Sam also delivers a special warranty deed to Phil, which includes a statement transferring the specifically identified personal property items.

    We have several problems. Sam has delivered a special warranty deed, which is of lesser quality than the general warranty deed that he promised. Thus, Phil has accepted less than he bargained for. Also, Sam's transfer of the personal property in the deed lacks the proper warranties, is not what the contract requires, and is not the proper way to transfer personal property. Real property is transferred by deed, and personal property is transferred by bill of sale. At closing, Phil should inspect the documents carefully and reject Sam's performance.

II. ATTORNEY'S ROLE AT CLOSING

The attorney's role is to assist the client in completing performance of the executory contract, to confirm that the client is getting all that he bargained for, and to make sure the client is not giving up more than he previously agreed to.

A. Multiple representation: A lawyer has a duty of *loyalty* to his client, which may be compromised when he represents multiple clients who have different or competing interests in a real estate transaction. Nevertheless, the Model Rules of Professional Conduct (Rule 1.7) authorize multiple representation, subject to:

- Full disclosure to all parties, including the risks of multiple representation.

- Informed consent by all parties.

    1. Conflict and removal: The lawyer must withdraw from all representation in the event of *litigation*. The attorney has *confidential information* from both sides and cannot participate in an *adversarial proceeding*. The lawyer must also remove himself from multiple representation at any time when an actual conflict of interest arises during a transaction.

2. **Seller and buyer:** Even though the interests of seller and buyer are directly adverse, dual representation at closing is permissible. The attorney must withdraw, however, if a dispute over closing procedures arises. *In re Lanza*, 322 A.2d 445 (N.J. 1974) (attorney violated ethics rules by not withdrawing from dual representation in a dispute when buyer gave seller postdated check for part of price and subsequently claimed foundation of house was not watertight).

3. **Payment of fees:** A lawyer may be paid *from a source other than the client* as long as the client is informed and consents, and as long as this does not impair the professional duty of the lawyer. Lenders typically require that the borrower pay the lender's attorneys' fees.

   a. **The attorney as adverse party:** The attorney must be careful to avoid putting himself in a position that may be adverse to the client and that would thereby violate the duty owed to the client.

      Example: Kirstin contracts to purchase property, which she plans to develop as a waterfront condominium development with 100 units. The project budget is $30 million, and units are expected to sell for twice their cost when the project is completed in two years. Kirstin engages Jenny to be her lawyer for the entire project. They agree to an hourly rate for Jenny at $250 per hour plus a bonus arrangement giving Jenny a free option to acquire up to three units at Kirstin's cost. During the construction phase of the project, Kirstin encounters a number of points of disagreement with her lender and with some of the construction subcontractors. Kirstin is contemplating an abandonment of the entire project; she might just take a write-off on it and get on with another venture. She needs legal advice and counsel from her lawyer, Jenny. The problem here is that Jenny stands to make a lot of money from the exercise of the unit purchase options if the deal is completed. This raises a direct *conflict of interest* with the advice she might give her client, Kirstin. At this point, Jenny should withdraw from representing Kirstin. When they entered into the fee arrangement, Jenny should have disclosed the possibility of such a conflict arising in the future as a result of the option.

B. **Duty to nonclients:** When an attorney expressly represents one party and another party to the transaction is unrepresented by counsel, two separate problems may arise.

   1. **Implied or informal representation:** Dual representation may result inadvertently when the unrepresented party believes the attorney is protecting his interests. This may result because the attorney misleads the party or fails to correct the party's misunderstanding. Implied representation, however, is difficult to establish. *Hacker v. Holland*, 570 N.E.2d 951 (Ind. Ct. App. 1991) (dual representation does not result merely from conduct of buyer's attorney in preparing closing documents and presiding over closing).

   2. **Duty not to further client's wrongful conduct:** Occasionally, an unrepresented party will have such a bad deal that it appears the executory contract is tainted either by unconscionability or by fraud. The attorney who assists the client in closing the transaction without warning the unrepresented party may be guilty of ethical misconduct. *Florida Bar v. Belleville*, 591 So. 2d 170 (Fla. 1991) (unrepresented elderly seller who traded apartment building and home for unsecured promissory note).

      Example: Bert contracts to sell property to Ernie. At closing, neither Bert nor Ernie has an attorney, but Heather represents the bank that is providing mortgage financing for Ernie. Heather explains the basic provisions of the loan documents. Ernie asks a few routine questions about the deed and the status of his title, which she answers. Ernie sees from the settlement statement that he is paying Heather a $300 attorneys' fee. After the closing, Bert and Ernie leave the building together, and Bert says, "Gee, Ernie, you sure had a very nice lawyer." Ernie responds, "Yes, I liked her, too; she made my loan documents easy to understand." Due to her conduct, Heather may have entered into an attorney-client relationship with Ernie or may owe him some other sort of duty. She should have explained that she represented only the bank. Ideally, Heather should make a disclosure of non-representation to Bert and Ernie in writing, and ask them to acknowledge the disclosure in writing, as well.

III. DOCTRINE OF MERGER

Promises, representations, and conditions from the ***executory contract*** are merged into the deed and other instruments signed at closing. "Merger" means they are extinguished and are no longer enforceable. The merger doctrine applies to both title covenants in the executory contract and covenants related to physical condition or quality. Along with caveat emptor, merger puts the entire risk of quality on the buyer after closing.

Example: Juan contracts to sell property to Rosita, promising to convey title by a special warranty deed. At closing, Juan signs and delivers a standard-form general warranty deed that he purchased at the local bookstore. Three months later, Rosita learns of a title defect created not by Juan, but by an earlier owner of the property. She sues Juan for damages, even though he would not be liable for the defect had he given only a special warranty deed. Juan claims he should be held only to his contract obligation, but he loses on the ***doctrine of merger***. Juan had an opportunity to prepare and review the deed prior to the completion of closing. A similar result should follow were the situation reversed: Juan contracts to deliver a general warranty deed, but Rosita accepts a special warranty deed.

A. **Exceptions to the doctrine of merger:** The three primary exceptions to the doctrine of merger relate to collateral matters, fraud, and mutual mistake.

　　1. **Collateral matters:** Modern courts often say merger is based on the parties' presumed intent. Thus, if there is sufficient evidence that the parties intended a particular undertaking to survive closing, merger does not apply. Typically, this exception applies only to nontitle matters, such as the need to repair part of the property. When merger does not apply, the matter is said to be collateral to the closing. Title matters, such as the quality of the estate conveyed or the type of deed used, will not survive closing and the operation of the doctrine of merger. The rationale is that title matters are not collateral and are more likely to have a third-party impact, and third parties need to have the ability to rely on the documents of record without having to reference prior contractual undertakings, which may not even be ascertainable.

　　　　Example: In a contract of sale, Juan warrants to the buyer, Rosita, that the swimming pool on the property is in good working order, having no leaks and a properly operating water filter system. The contract contains an express provision wherein both parties agree that the above contract term shall survive the closing of the contract and the exchange of the deed for the payment of the purchase price. At closing, Juan conveys the property to Rosita. Several days later, the pool is found to have a broken pump and filter system. Investigation indicates that the defect existed prior to closing. Rosita sues Juan. As to the defects with the pool, these are collateral to the conveyance of title and can survive the closing and the operation of the doctrine of merger, since the parties have expressed a clear intent as such.

2. **Fraud:** If a party has committed fraud in closing the transaction, he cannot use the doctrine of merger to relieve him of an earlier obligation.

3. **Mutual mistake:** If the parties operated under a mutual mistake as to the content of the closing documents, reformation is available despite the doctrine of merger. Unilateral mistake does not suffice. In the first example in this section, Juan may claim that both parties thought the document he presented was in fact the proper form for a special warranty deed. Note the difficulty of proof, especially because Rosita now has no incentive to say she was mistaken. See *Embassy Group, Inc. v Hatch*, 865 P.2d 1366 (Utah Ct. App. 1993) (seller failed to persuade court that parties made mutual mistake when buyer paid $40,000 for conveyance of land; seller asserted that the parties had two contracts, each calling for payment of $40,000; at closing, buyer paid $40,000 and seller delivered a deed conveying all the land; seller asserted the agreement was really for two payments of $40,000 each but failed to prove mutual mistake—that contracts contemplated two-step purchase, with total price of $80,000 due, thus merger prevented the post-closing claim for an additional $40,000).

IV. ESCROW

The term "escrow" has three popular meanings: a loan escrow, a closing escrow, and a contingency escrow.

A. **Loan escrow:** Lenders use the loan escrow to collect and hold money from the debtor for paying annual real property taxes, and fire and hazard insurance premiums. Loan escrows are widely used for residential loans and for many commercial loans as well. The debtor's monthly loan payment includes the pro rata escrow fee in addition to principal and interest. The lender has ***two primary goals***. First, it wants to ensure payment of these items because failure to pay jeopardizes its security. Second, most lenders earn a profit on escrows because they do not pay interest to the borrowers, even though they earn interest on the escrowed funds.

B. **Closing escrow:** This refers to a process for closing used in some states, such as California. Pursuant to an escrow agreement, the parties appoint an escrow agent, who handles the closing. The agent receives deeds and other instruments, collects funds, confirms that all steps necessary for the closing have occurred, records documents, and remits funds. Deeds and other instruments deposited in escrow are subject to the conditions specified in the escrow agreement. This is a proper method for making conditional deliveries.

Example: In *Miller v. Craig*, 558 P.2d 984 (Ariz. Ct. App. 1976), attorney Craig prepared a purchase and sale contract and also acted as an escrow agent for an escrow closing pursuant to the contract. In his capacity as escrow agent, he owed a duty to both parties to the purchase and sale contract. When he released a disputed $5,000 deposit amount to the buyer without consent from the seller, he violated his duty to seller. The court cited authority holding that the attorney has a duty to both parties when acting as an escrow agent in these circumstances.

C. **Contingency escrow:** A contingency escrow is used to resolve a problem that arises before or at closing. When the problem consists of an unperformed obligation of the seller, an escrow agent retains part of the purchase price pending the correction of the problem. The parties should enter into a written escrow agreement that addresses several important factors:

- Clearly identifies the problem to be corrected.

- Sets a cost or expenditure constraint (a dollar cap) on action that the party may have to take to correct or remedy the problem.

- Establishes a time period for completion of the corrective action.

- Sets a standard for evidence or proof of compliance (what the other side will accept as evidence of properly correcting the problem).

- Establishes a right of inspection, and a framework for objection to the offered evidence or proof.

- Sets out how, when, and to whom the money in escrow will be paid.

- Identifies the escrow agent for purposes of the agreement and sets out the agent's duties and obligations.

Example: Sean orders an inspection on a home he's buying from Marie. The inspection report discloses that the swimming pool has a broken water filter system. Estimated repair costs are between $1,000 and $1,500, and the work cannot be done before closing. The parties want to go ahead, but Sean insists on his contract right to have the system placed in good working order. They execute a contingency escrow agreement at closing, and $1,500 is retained from the price and paid into an escrow account. The seller is to correct the problem within 30 days, at her own expense, up to a cost of $1,500. Marie hires a pool company, which gives her two proposals: buy and install new filter equipment for $1,450 or repair the old filter for $400. The new system would have a five-year warranty, and the repair approach comes with a 45-day warranty. Marie elects the repair approach and pays the bill. Sean has the city water department conduct a water quality test the next day, and the water is declared to be of "acceptable quality." The escrow agreement, with the consent of both parties, pays $1,500 to seller. Two months later, the filter system fails. Sean learns Marie has taken the cheap approach and wants her to fix the problem properly. Marie successfully defends this claim. She did everything required under the contingency escrow, and it is obvious that she would be expected to pick the lowest-cost repair alternative to maximize the price she received. (Generally, the low-cost approach must still be considered reasonable.)

Quiz Yourself on
CLOSING THE CONTRACT

24. Mario is an attorney representing Donna, who has contracted to buy a home for $500,000. At the closing, a dispute arose concerning a home inspection report, which identified the home heating system as inoperable. Seller and Donna agreed to a contingency escrow, putting $3,000 into escrow for the repairs. Mario prepared the agreement and agreed to act as escrow agent. Within the time set to complete the work under the escrow agreement, nothing happened. Seller and Donna dispute the matter and argue about the right to the $3,000. Does Mario have any ethical problems? _____

25. Zeta signs a contract to purchase a home being sold by Lucy. Zeta has secured mortgage financing so that she can pay for the house. As they are signing documents at the closing on the contract and the mortgage financing, Zeta observes that her closing statement of costs indicates that she is being charged $650 for the attorney representing the bank. Can an attorney representing one party be paid by another party? _____

26. Hans contracts to sell 300 acres of forest land to Wu. In the contract, Hans represents that he is in sole possession of the property. Three months after closing, Wu engages a lumber company to inventory the tree types and lumber grades on the property. Wu gets a report that a squatter is on the land. Twelve years ago, the squatter built a small cabin and cleared an acre of land in the middle of the forest, where he has lived since. Independent of claims on the deed, Wu asserts that Hans is liable on his contract promise and thus must remove the squatter. Is Hans liable on the contract? _____

27. Big Development Company does residential housing projects. It contracts for the sale of homes and conveys them to buyers in fee simple absolute by special warranty deed. This is standard practice for developers of new housing in this region. Pauli contracts to buy one of Big's homes for $700,000, with the contract calling for Seller to convey title to Buyer by warranty deed at closing. Pauli believes that he will be getting a general warranty deed at closing. At closing Big delivers a special warranty deed granting a fee simple absolute estate interest and Pauli accepts it. Six months later a title defect is discovered. The defect is one that would have come within the scope of a general warranty deed but is not within the scope of a special warranty deed. Pauli asserts that he was honestly mistaken about his understanding of the type of warranty deed to be delivered at closing. Big says that it followed its normal practice and delivered what it promised. Can Pauli raise his claim, or is it too late because of the operation of the doctrine of merger? _____

28. Jim agrees to sell a house to Rita for $400,000 and Rita puts down a $10,000 deposit. Robin is employed as an escrow agent for the closing of the contract. In the course of the executory contract a dispute arises between Jim and Rita, and Rita asserts that she has an excuse because Jim has not met a condition precedent to her obligation to close. She puts her assertion in writing and sends it to Jim and Robin. A week later, after receiving no response from Jim, Robin releases the deposit to Rita and closes up his files. Three weeks later, Jim asks Robin to deliver the deposit to him. Robin informs Jim that the deposit has already been returned to Rita. Has Robin done anything wrong? _____

Answers

24. **Yes.** And his ethical problems started before the parties became active adversaries. When drafting the escrow agreement, he may have acted as attorney for both parties and failed to give full disclosure and obtain consents. Alternatively, if he continued to represent Donna only, Seller may have reasonably believed that Mario also represented him. Mario's agreeing to act as the escrow agent triggers further difficulty because an agent owes a duty to both parties. In addition, Mario has his own interest now, as escrow agent, which may further conflict with the interest of Donna. At present, Mario must withdraw from the conflict. This would be true even if he had previously made proper disclosure and obtained consents.

25. **Yes.** The lawyer owes a duty to the client, the bank in this case, but can be paid by a third party. The lawyer must make it clear that the third party understands that she is not the client, and there must be no conflict of interest. The lawyer needs to disclose the relationship and make sure that the third

party is informed and consents. It is important for the lawyer to understand that the third party may assume that there is an attorney-client relationship. The lawyer should take steps to avoid liability to the third-party nonclient.

26. **No.** The doctrine of merger puts an end to the cause of action on the contract. Wu is left with only those rights provided in the documents signed at closing.

27. **No.** Mistake is an exception to the operation of the doctrine of merger but it must be a mutual mistake as to the drafting of the documents. Here the asserted mistake does go to an understanding of the terms or form of the document of conveyance. The problem is that it is not a mutual mistake; it is a unilateral mistake made by Pauli. As such, any claim by Pauli has to be limited to the deed he accepted at closing. Both the general and special warranty deeds are forms of a warranty deed and each is fully capable of conveying a fee simple absolute estate. The difference is in warranty coverage and liability of the grantor.

28. **Yes.** As an escrow agent Robin owes a duty to both Jim and Rita. In carrying out this duty Robin is bound by the terms of the escrow agreement and by his fiduciary duties to each party. Robin should not release the deposit funds to either party without the consent of both parties. If the parties do not mutually agree to the release, Robin should place the money in court and have the parties determine the matter.

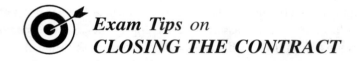

Exam Tips on
CLOSING THE CONTRACT

☞ **Avoid conflicts of interest and multiple representation:** In dealing with the ethical problems of multiple representation, one must be careful to identify the *relevant parties* at the outset. Be sure to distinguish between clients and nonclients. Then map out their potential *areas of conflict*. Don't forget that the lawyer may also have an adverse interest with the client under certain circumstances. Next, consider whether the attorney made *full disclosure* to each client, including information about the other party and about the potential risks stemming from multiple representation. Look for evidence that *all parties consented* to the multiple representation. In the absence of a writing (the best evidence of consent), seek consent in fact, but suggest that a writing is advisable. After this, see if there is a *change in circumstances*, which raises a conflict between the parties so that the attorney can no longer properly represent both clients.

☞ **Understand the doctrine of merger:** The doctrine of merger is the general rule that operates at closing, which you should apply first in your analysis. Once you properly address this issue, you should then proceed to discuss exceptions in an orderly manner. Be sure to cover all of the elements relevant to collateral matters. The fraud exception requires you to identify the elements of fraud from the facts. Finally, be careful with the mutual mistake exception. Remember it does not apply to all situations of mutual mistake. You must find a mutual mistake in drafting the documents for this to be applicable under the general rules.

☛ **Closing the transaction:** To handle a question focused on closing, it is useful to make a ***checklist*** of what each party agreed to do in the contract, checking off each item as it is satisfied or performed. You must spot any uncompleted elements of the bargain, as well as any under- or over-performance by either party. Remember that for any given party getting less than bargained for or giving more than agreed to can be a bad deal so over-performance is as important to spot as under-performance, depending upon which party you are asked to represent. In a similar vein, you must be sure that all of the elements of an effective conveyance are present.

☛ **Identify the proper type of escrow involved in a transaction:** Remember to check the fact pattern for facts that trigger the use of any of the three basic types of escrow. And consider what duties may be taken on, to which parties, in the event that there is an escrow situation. Also be sensitive to the possibility of using something like a contingency escrow to permit the parties to go forward with a closing, even if there are a couple of issues that need to be resolved.

Chapter 7

CONTRACT REMEDIES

ChapterScope

This chapter discusses the basic remedies available when dealing with the contract of purchase and sale.

- **Expectancy damages:** Expectancy damages are equal to the difference in the **contract price** and the **fair market value** of the property **at the time** of the breach.

- **Equitable remedies:** The **four main equitable remedies** are (1) reformation, (2) rescission, (3) specific performance, and (4) the vendor/vendee lien.

- **Liquidated damages:** *Liquidated damages* are agreed to by the parties at the time of contracting. They cannot operate as a penalty or a forfeiture.

- **Tort damages:** In an exceptional case, an injured party may recover **tort damages** as a result of a breach or default in the real estate transaction. This is unusual but significant because it permits punitive damages to be assessed and because it creates an opportunity to avoid the problem of lack of contract privity in certain situations.

- **Slander of title:** A landowner may bring a **slander of title action** if someone wrongfully clouds her title. This can happen if a document effecting title is wrongfully recorded against a property thereby "slandering" its good name.

- **Lis pendens:** A *lis pendens* allows a plaintiff to notify potential third parties that she claims an ownership interest in specific real property. It is a notice that is filed in the public records for real property, usually when a law suit is commenced in which the outcome of the case will have an impact on the title to the identified real estate.

I. DAMAGES AT LAW

The basic idea behind damages is *fungibility*. The injured party who receives money can enter the market to deal with another person. The buyer may purchase a substitute unit; the seller may resell to another buyer. Fungible property, such as oil or standard automobiles, lends itself to money damages because there is a ready market and price that can be reasonably well determined from that market. Unique property is by definition not readily fungible and easily substituted, so simply awarding money damages does not generally make an injured party whole.

A. Expectancy damages: Upon breach, either the buyer or the seller may recover expectancy damages. The object is to make the injured party whole by giving her the **benefit of her bargain**. The measure of expectancy damages is the difference between the contract price and the fair market value of the property at the time of breach. These contract damages are **not** supposed to be **punitive.**

    1. Resale by seller after buyer's breach: Under the traditional formula, the seller is not entitled to collect the difference between the contract price and the price obtained by the seller upon a resale. Resale price may be some evidence of value, but it will depend on a number of factors, including how quickly the property is resold after the breach. Damages are based on the contract price relative to the fair market value *at the time of the breach*, not on price or value at some later date. *Zareas v. Smith*, 404 A.2d 599 (N.H. 1979). Therefore, if the contract price is $100,000 with the fair market value at the time of the breach being $90,000, and seller is able to resell the property four months later at $80,000, the expectancy damages are $10,000 rather than $20,000.

B. Reliance damages: Reliance damages, or consequential or special damages, are awarded under general principles of contract law. They include *lost profits* and *out-of-pocket costs*, such as expenses incurred to fulfill contract promises relating to title searches and survey work. Generally, reliance and consequential damages are recoverable only if they are *foreseeable* to the breaching party.

C. Fair market value: The concept of fair market value, which is central to the formula for expectancy damages, can be divided into three components.

1. **Fair:** *Fairness* means we should use a reasonable market *comparison* for the type of property involved and an appropriate formula or set of variables for calculating the value of a loss. For example, is it fair to measure a loss by the reduction in the property's value or by the cost of correcting the problem so that the property complies with contract promises?

   Example: Peevyhouse contracts to let a coal company strip-mine its land. The contract obligates the company to reclaim the land by returning it to its natural state after completion of mining. The company breaches, and Peevyhouse sues for the cost of reclamation. Reclamation would cost between $25,000 and $29,000, but the loss in fair market value to the property, if not reclaimed, is only $300. The court allows Peevyhouse only the $300 loss in value because it views reclamation as a waste of resources. *Peevyhouse v. Garland Coal & Mining Co.*, 382 P.2d 109 (Okla. 1962).

2. **Market:** To determine fair market value, we must define the market that is *relevant* for the type of property involved in the parties' transaction. Geographic proximity is one issue. In addition, a unique property, such as a school or church, presents trouble in defining the market.

3. **Value:** There are three primary ways to determine value. Fairness requires that good reason be given for the selection of a specific method as the most appropriate method for assessing valuation in a given case.

   a. **Comparable sales:** Data is collected from sales of comparable properties in a defined market, with adjustments to take account of differences in the characteristics of the properties. Good comparables are easier to find in a strong real estate market, where there are a lot of sales and thus a lot more comparative information.

   b. **Replacement cost:** This method calculates the cost of rebuilding or replacing the property. Usually, an adjustment is made for depreciation of buildings and other improvements. This method is particularly useful when there are few or no good comparables for the property.

   c. **Income flow:** This method applies to properties that produce income or rents, such as shopping malls and apartment buildings. The net annual income is capitalized, meaning a calculation is made of the amount an investor would pay to acquire an asset that generates this amount of income, with the risk profile for a property of the type involved.

Example: Jax Inc. owns an office building, designed by the company founder decades ago and outfitted with special gold bathroom fixtures and a variety of other special details. The tax assessor, using the replacement method, values the building at $900,000 for purposes of property taxes. Jax challenges the tax assessment, presenting evidence that, based on the annual cash flow from leases, the property is worth only $600,000. This example shows how valuation is relevant to more issues than simply calculating damages in the event of breach.

4. **Time value of money:** Money has a value related to time, which must be accounted for when calculating the fair market value of property. Current payments and future payments are different. One must discount future payments to their present value.

Example: Gina, as buyer, breaches a contract to buy Sal's home for $200,000, payable in cash at closing. Sal finds information on several recent sales of similar homes, each for over $220,000, so Sal claims expectancy damages of $20,000. Gina responds that all of Sal's comparables are credit transactions where the seller took 10 to 15 percent of the purchase price at closing and financed the remaining amounts over 15 years. Gina shows that the present discounted value of the similar sales is around $190,000. Thus, Sal has not proven recoverable damages.

5. **Time of the breach:** It is often hard to measure damages at the time of the breach because comparable sales take place at different dates. Similarly, the resale price of a property may be the best evidence of its fair market value, but because it comes after the breach, it is less than perfect evidence of the value at the time of breach. This means one must make a strong case for the best way to infer value at the time of breach. The problem is more acute in a volatile market, where prices are either rising or falling rapidly.

D. **Lost profits:** To recover potential ***profits*** from a real estate venture, the plaintiff has the burden of proving that she would have earned profits and what the amount of those lost profits would be. Some courts do not permit a person who planned to start a new business or enterprise to recover lost profits due to the lack of a profit history. Other courts, however, allow recovery of lost profits for a new business, provided there is competent evidence of likely success. *Miami International Realty Co. v. Paynter*, 841 F.2d 348 (10th Cir. 1988) (malpractice recovery against attorney for lost profits for new time-share development).

II. EQUITABLE REMEDIES

Four major categories of equitable remedies of relevance to the real estate transaction are ***reformation***, which permits the parties to rewrite a contract or other document to reflect a different intent from that expressed in the contract language; ***rescission***, which allows the parties to put an end to their agreement; ***specific performance***, which forces the parties to complete the transaction; and the ***vendor/vendee lien***, which provides an enforcement mechanism with respect to credit in the transaction.

A. Reformation: Reformation is given when a party proves that the written contract or deed has an error or mistake and thus fails to reflect the actual intent of the parties. This must be a ***mutual mistake***, not a unilateral mistake or misunderstanding of one party.

Example: A contract for the sale of land provides for the seller to convey an easement over retained land to the buyer. The parties close their transaction and forget to include a grant of the easement in the deed. Merger does not apply, and the buyer is entitled to the equitable remedy of reformation. *Stack v. Commercial Towel & Uniform Services, Inc.*, 91 N.E.2d 790 (Ind. Ct. App. 1950).

B. Rescission: Rescission means one party has the right to terminate the contract, due to a material default, a material misrepresentation, or an unfulfilled condition by the other party. A buyer's mistaken belief about an element of the transaction is not grounds for rescission. *Geist v. Lehman*, 312 N.E.2d 42 (Ill. Ct. App. 1974) (denying rescission when buyer of home believed he would get a large yard based on appearance of landscaping, but actually got a much smaller yard under the deed of conveyance; contract did not guarantee quantity, and buyer alleged, but failed to prove, misrepresentation by seller or seller's broker).

C. Specific performance: This remedy forces a reluctant party to complete the transaction. The general rule is that both the buyer and the seller have the right to specific performance. For the buyer, the rationale is that every piece of land is ***unique***. For the seller, the rationale is ***mutuality of remedy***—if the buyer has the right to specific performance, so should the seller. An alternative explanation is that real property is often not liquid and a seller therefore often cannot be made whole with money damages at law, coupled with an ability to seek a resale. In order to obtain this remedy, the requesting party must be ready, willing, and able to perform all of her obligations under the agreement. Under a modern minority view, both buyer and seller must prove the circumstances that support specific performance, in particular the seller cannot simply assert mutuality of remedy as the basis for the remedy.

Example: The buyer under an executory contract does not have sufficient cash to close, and she attempts to raise financing by getting investors to participate in a joint venture. After the time for closing passes, the seller refuses to grant an extension, and the buyer sues for specific performance. The buyer is not entitled to relief unless she can establish she was ready, willing, and able to pay the price. To do this, she must prove that the prospective investors were firmly committed to the joint venture. *Steiner v. Brian Park Associates*, 582 A.2d 173 (Conn. 1990) (denying specific performance).

   1. Specific performance with abatement: Specific performance can also be granted with an abatement in the purchase price. If an abatement would substantially reduce the value of the transaction, a court may find that the matter is inappropriate for a remedy of specific performance.

D. Equitable liens

   1. Vendor's lien: The vendor's lien secures any amounts owed the seller or vendor, such as the purchase price or expectancy damages. Usually, this comes into play after closing, when the seller extends credit and fails to secure the remaining purchase price with a mortgage. The vendor may bring an action for judicial foreclosure, causing a sale of the property to satisfy the debt.

2. **Vendee's lien:** When the buyer or vendee obtains rescission, she may have the right to either the return of a down payment or the payment of reliance damages. By operation of law, she has a lien on the property to secure such debts, which she may foreclose.

   Example: A buyer agrees to purchase property, provided the seller obtains subdivision approval. The seller fails to get approval and refuses to refund the buyer's deposit. The buyer is entitled to a vendee's lien on the property, even though the contract does not expressly provide for this right. This allows the buyer to commence a foreclosure proceeding against the property to recover the deposit. *Mihranian v. Padula*, 342 A.2d 523 (N.J. App. Div. 1975).

III. LIQUIDATED DAMAGES

Liquidated damages are damages that the parties agree to and quantify in advance of any breach. They are, in other words, ***prearranged contract damages***.

A. **Actual damages not easy to ascertain:** A party is entitled to liquidated damages only if actual damages are difficult to predict ***at the time of contracting***. For real estate sales, due to difficulties in measuring fair market value and problems of liquidity, courts generally presume actual expectancy damages are not readily ascertainable.

B. **Reasonable amount:** Grossly excessive liquidated damages are considered to be a penalty and are not enforceable. For real estate sales, if the liquidated damages are 10 percent or less, it is very rare for courts to disallow them. *Pima Savings & Loan Association v. Rampello*, 812 P.2d 1115 (Ariz. Ct. App. 1991) (allowing liquidated damages equal to $290,000 on sale of 65 condominium units for $4.7 million; this is 6 percent).

   Example: Buyer in a luxury condominium building in New York City contracted to pay $32 million for two units. The contract called for a 25 percent down payment, which was not unusual for such high-end properties. Buyer then decided not to close on the contract and Seller kept the deposit. The trial court permitted Seller to keep up to 10 percent of the deposit as liquidated damages, and said that the remaining amount had to be evaluated in terms of a liquidated damages review as to reasonableness, foreseeability, and difficulty of determining actual damages at time of contract. On appeal, the court held that Seller could keep the full amount because all parties were experienced in business and because there was evidence of strong negotiation of contract terms (the contract price of $32 million reflected a drop in the original asking price by $7 million dollars). *Uzan v. 845 UN Limited Partnership*, 778 N.Y.S.2d 171 (App. Div. 2004).

IV. TORT REMEDIES

In tort, an injured party may recover damages for noneconomic losses and for punitive damages. Tort theories also dispense with the need to establish privity in order to get recovery under contract law.

A. **Negligence:** When a party's negligence causes harm to the other party and that harm is the foreseeable consequence of the negligent act, rather than sue on the contract the injured party may choose to recover on the basis of negligence.

B. Strict liability: Strict liability does not generally apply to real property sales. However, courts are likely to impose strict liability if they view real estate development as the manufacturing of a product. For this reason, in some states a builder selling a new home is strictly liable to buyers for material defects.

C. Emotional distress: When the seller is liable to the buyer, under either strict liability or negligence, in appropriate cases the buyer may also recover damages for emotional distress.

D. Punitive damages: An injured party may recover punitive damages when the breach is intentional or grossly negligent.

Example: Nancy contracts to pay RJ Homes $450,000 for a new home. RJ fails to do proper soil testing and does a poor job in configuring the water drainage system. After Nancy moves in, the floor shifts and cracks due to a defective foundation. Water seeps into cracks in the foundation and into spaces within the walls. The moisture leaves the home with a damp and musty smell. Nancy has tried to clear the smell from the home, but it only gets worse. Mildew gathers on the walls. RJ has made several attempts to fix the problem and has required Nancy to leave the premises for weeks at a time on three separate occasions. The problem has continued even after the repair attempts. In addition to having to leave the home, Nancy has been unable to entertain her friends and has had people tell her that her home "stinks." Nancy loses sleep, misses work, and becomes physically ill from stress. In addition to contract damages, Nancy may have the right to recover tort damages for emotional distress and for medical expenses, and perhaps punitive damages.

Example: In *Sexton v. St. Clair Federal Savings Bank*, 653 So. 2d 959 (Ala. 1995), the court addressed the grounds for holding a builder liable in tort to a home buyer. The facts involved a claim for mental anguish as a result of faulty and negligent construction of the home. The court found for the home buyer. In that case it was also suggested that a lender to the builder during construction might also find itself liable in tort to the home buyer in such a situation.

V. SLANDER OF TITLE AND LIS PENDENS

A. Slander of title: The tort action of slander of title protects the value of property when its character or reputation is maligned. Slander of title occurs when a person maliciously or intentionally files false claims against a property or clouds an owner's title by falsely asserting a conflicting ownership interest. See *Newmanik v. Realty Co. of America*, 1980 U.S. Dist. LEXIS 12959 (July 17, 1980).

B. Lis pendens: A lis pendens is a *notice* filed in the public records for real estate that states that litigation is currently pending, the outcome of which may affect the status of title to the property described in the notice. This procedural device is designed to give notice to any potential bona fide purchasers, thereby destroying their ability to take without knowledge of the pending dispute. A lis pendens puts a "cloud" on title, which may prevent the owner from dealing with the property until the matter is resolved. If a lis pendens is improperly filed, the owner may have the right to bring a slander of title action.

Example: Jane claims easement rights across a large tract of land owned by her neighbor Bruce. Bruce denies the claim and puts up a fence to keep Jane off the property. Jane claims that the previous owner of her lot and Bruce signed a document that created an easement benefiting her lot. Bruce denies this and says that, if there is such a document, it spoke in terms of a personal right or license in favor of the prior landowner and, as such, gave no right to Jane. Jane files suit against

Bruce and at the same time files a lis pendens in the real estate records. Bruce answers, denying her claim and counterclaiming for slander of title. If Jane wins, she will have an easement over Bruce's land, thus affecting his title. Thus, she has not committed slander of title. The lis pendens is a proper device for giving notice so that Bruce cannot sell his property to a later third party who would take free of the easement on the basis of being a bona fide purchaser. As long as Jane has a plausible claim, it does not matter if she actually wins or loses her litigation; the lis pendens would have been proper either way. See, e.g., *Palmer v. Zaklama*, 1 Cal. Rptr. 3d 116 (Cal. Ct. App., 5th Dist. 2003) (court upholds a claim for slander of title where party did not have a basis for filing a lis pendens, and the lis pendens held up a sale of the property for four years).

VI. OTHER REMEDIES

In addition to the general categories of remedies, other remedies may come into play. For instance, you may wish to prevent someone from taking action that may affect a property, and this might call for an ***injunction***. At other times, you may wish to have a dispute under a contract or other transactional document resolved by having the court declare a party's rights in a ***declaratory judgment***. If a party is wrongfully in possession of property, one might seek an ***ejectment*** action to have her removed from the property. Similarly one may seek remedies in ***tort law or criminal law*** if threats are made against a party, if violence breaks out, or if a law is broken (like trespass).

Quiz Yourself on CONTRACT REMEDIES

29. Donald contracts to sell a lakefront condominium to Nikki for $1.2 million. Nikki has made a deposit on the contract of $300,000. By the time set for closing, Nikki has seen a major drop in value of some of her investments and has had her net worth fall considerably. Nikki decides not to close on the contract. Donald resells the property eight weeks later for $1 million. Donald seeks to keep the deposit and collect $200,000 for loss of expectation damages on the resale contract price. Is Donald entitled to the deposit and the expectation damages? _____

30. In the above question, assume that Nikki breaches, prices are falling, and buyers are scarce due to a financial market collapse. Donald, instead of reselling, seeks an order of specific performance. Will he succeed? _____

31. In the above question, suppose that Nikki closes on the contract and moves into the property. After living in the home for about six months, Nikki notices a strong odor and develops breathing problems. Nikki runs up large medical bills trying to discover the cause of her breathing problems. She is ill and becomes emotionally distraught. It is soon discovered that the problem is being caused by mold in the walls of the home. The mold arose from water getting in between the walls of the master bathroom as a result of a negligent repair job done by Donald in trying to install some fancy new plumbing fixtures. Can she sue Donald to recover her costs and damages? _____

32. Assume that, in our above question, Nikki closes on the property and invites her cousin Vikki to live with her for a few months. Vikki gets really sick from the mold problem and sues Nikki. Knowing that the property is the only major asset that Nikki has, Vikki files a lis pendens against the property so that it will be available to satisfy any judgment that Vikki might get. Is the filing of the lis pendens proper? _____

33. JJ Construction contracts to build a shopping center for the B&B Investment Group at $20 million. The contract has a provision stating, "Time is of the essence and the completion date is August 1." B&B will invest a lot of money to promote a special grand opening day, and delay will be costly. The actual damages from a delay are impossible to determine in advance, so the parties agree that JJ will pay B&B $200,000 if the project is not done by August 1 and that JJ will pay an additional $30,000 per day thereafter for every additional day that the project is late in completion. JJ misses the August 1 date and finishes two weeks later. B&B demands the liquidated damages, which JJ refuses to pay. Should B&B be able to collect liquidated damages? _____

Answers

29. **Not necessarily.** Donald seeks expectancy damages. The measure is the difference between the contract price and the fair market value of the property at the time of the breach. The $200,000 difference between the contract price with Nikki and the resale price on the new contract might represent expectancy damages, but we must be careful. The resale price may or may not be a fair approximation of the value eight weeks earlier, at the time of the breach. Donald has to present evidence of stable prices during the time period. To do this, he likely needs additional evidence of sales of comparable homes in the relevant housing market. As to the deposit, Donald's ability to keep this may turn on the wording of the contract. Did the contract provide for the deposit to serve as liquidated damages or as a straight-up contract provision? Even if Donald had a contract right to the deposit, he probably would not get to keep the deposit plus get expectancy damages of $200,000.

30. **Yes.** Donald will argue entitlement to specific performance based on the traditional doctrine of mutuality of remedy. This approach, while followed by many courts, is slowly losing ground. Donald may have to show that his remedy at law (damages) is inadequate. If he has little hope for a prompt resale because the market has turned cold, he should be able to get specific performance.

31. **Maybe.** Perhaps Nikki can sue on the basis of some warranty of habitability or for failure to disclose a latent defect. The problem is that this is after closing and Nikki will have to find a way around the doctrine of merger. Would Donald's actions rise to the level of fraud? Is the condition of the bathroom plumbing a collateral matter, and does it survive closing if there is not express intent to this effect? Another approach might be to try an action in tort, which would allow a recovery of damages plus punitives, if appropriate.

32. **No.** The lis pendens is improper. Vikki's claim against Nikki is for an action in tort. Her claim is not one that goes to the status of title to the property, so it is not the proper basis for a lis pendens against the property. Nikki can respond with a counterclaim based on slander of title.

33. **B&B can probably collect the liquidated damages.** It is true that shopping centers make advance plans and spend a great deal to set up an opening day. There may also be costs and penalties payable by B&B to its lender for delays and to tenants in the shopping center, who expect a given opening day as part of their lease. These types of damages are often uncertain at the time of contracting because construction can take many months and the market at the time of completion may be hard to predict. B&B also cites evidence that August is a very important month for sales, as it is vital for

holding "back to school sales" and for positioning the shopping center with consumers who will shop during the biggest sales months of the year leading up to Christmas. The provision has a graduated scale for payments and may be considered reasonable. JJ will need to argue that it is a penalty and is unfair. JJ will also try to show that it bears no relationship to actual damages and that damages are not all that difficult or uncertain to determine.

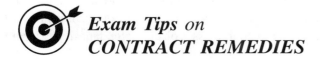

Exam Tips on CONTRACT REMEDIES

☞ **Expectation damages are calculated at the time of the breach:** In assessing expectation damages, be sure to consider facts at the time of the breach. Do not get confused by facts pointing to other times. This is the cause of common mistakes by many students. The relevant reference point is to compare the contract price to the fair market value *at the time* of the breach.

☞ **Define fair market value:** In addressing fair market value it is important to begin by defining the market. With reference to the defined market, address the fairness of the amount with reference to other properties and the three primary approaches to valuation (comparable sales, replacement cost, and income flow).

☞ **Equitable remedies are available:** Keep in mind that equitable remedies are only available when damages are inadequate. Equitable remedies are within the discretion of the court and can be denied if a party does not have "clean hands."

☞ **Know the types of equitable remedies:** Equitable remedies include reformation, rescission, specific performance, and equitable liens (vendor/vendee liens). Be sure to identify the remedy you seek in a given situation and explain the elements.

☞ **Specific performance:** In addressing specific performance, be sure to clarify the facts and your analysis with respect to the traditional and the modern approach. The traditional approach presumes that specific performance is available to both parties by invoking the doctrine of mutuality of remedy to benefit the seller. The modern approach requires both sides to demonstrate the need for specific performance without simply allowing a default to the doctrine of mutuality of remedy.

☞ **Avoid a penalty or forfeiture:** Watch for language in the contract that speaks in terms of penalty or forfeiture. These words, which often are used in contracts, may make a liquidated damages provision unenforceable. Also consider whether there is a ready market for the thing being sold. If so, liquidated damages are not appropriate because one can easily refer to the marketplace to determine the going price or value on any given date. In some contract settings, a formula for liquidated damages based on the duration of the breach is appropriate. For example, damages for delay in a construction project are more reasonable if structured on a daily basis rather than a flat amount ($20,000 per day for each day of delay, rather than $1 million owed at the moment of breach).

☛ **Consider privity and alternatives in the absence of privity:** When there are facts that focus on emotional distress as a result of a problem with the real estate or the transaction, consider the possibility of a tort remedy. Likewise, if there is a lack of privity on a contract claim, it may be possible to pursue a tort action for negligence and get around the contract privity issue. Remember that in contract law there is also the theory of third-party beneficiary to get around the privity constraint.

☛ **A lis pendens and a slander of title action are two other important legal devices:** A person entitled to a remedy can file a lis pendens in the public records for real estate at the time of starting a cause of action. In order to avoid a slander of title action, one must be careful to explain that the outcome of the matter in dispute will affect title to the property. In other words, there must be a connection to the status of title in order to properly file a lis pendens, and one cannot file a lis pendens just because certain property might be an available asset of the defendant in satisfying a claim.

☛ **Third-party issues:** Consider potential third-party remedies when there is a breach of the contract or a contract duty. Third-party "targets" for a potential recovery might include a title company, surveyor, lender, broker, or attorney. Evaluate potential claims under general rules of contract (for example, considering such issues as privity and third-party beneficiary theories) and tort law (considering such issues as a duty owed, foreseeability, breach of duty, and proximate cause). In other words, be certain to consider possible remedies against parties beyond the immediate ones to the contract itself.

CHAPTER 8

ALLOCATING TITLE RISK BY CONTRACT AND BY DEED

ChapterScope ━━

This chapter addresses how parties to a contract of sale handle title to the property. When real estate is sold, title risk is allocated and managed by the terms and conditions of the two prime documents, the contract of sale and the deed of conveyance. Under the contract of sale, the buyer has the right to marketable title. At closing, the contract provisions dealing with title are replaced by covenants of title set forth in the deed of conveyance. The doctrine of merger facilitates this replacement.

- ■ **Contract protection:** Under the real estate contract, buyer has the right to marketable title.

  - ■ **Record title:** Generally, marketable title means seller must have record title, established solely by reference to the public land records.

  - ■ **Encumbrances:** Encumbrances to title are very common. Most encumbrances impair title, making it unmarketable.

  - ■ **Zoning and land use regulations:** Generally, zoning and other public regulations are thought not to affect title.

- ■ **Deed protection:** Deeds have different allocations of title risk.

  - ■ **Quitclaim deed:** Buyer has all the risk of title defects, and seller has no risk.

  - ■ **Special warranty deed:** Buyer is protected from the risk of title defects created by seller.

  - ■ **General warranty deed:** Buyer has the greatest level of protection from risk, with seller generally liable under the standard types of title covenants.

I. TITLE UNDER THE REAL ESTATE CONTRACT

After a real estate contract is signed, the executory period begins and lasts until closing of the transaction. One of the primary reasons the real estate contract has an executory period is for the parties to handle title matters. The terms of the contract of sale that address title are of critical importance. In large part, these contract terms will determine the nature and scope of the title search and the allocation of risks with respect to title information that is discovered.

A. Implied term of marketable title: Most conditions in real estate contracts must be express. For example, the financing condition must be express in order for the buyer to terminate for the failure to obtain appropriate financing. Marketable title is an exception. It is both an implied condition and an implied promise. Buyer's obligation to close is conditioned on seller's title being marketable, and seller impliedly promises that his title will be marketable at closing.

1. **Definition:** Marketable title is best understood as title that is good in fact, subject to no encumbrances except those agreed to by the parties, and free from reasonable doubt.

    a. **Good in fact:** Title is good in fact when seller actually has the quality of title promised in the contract (fee simple absolute when this is the estate contracted for).

    b. **Subject to no encumbrances except those agreed to by the parties:** These are encumbrances permitted by the contract. Many contracts expressly provide that the buyer will take subject to certain enumerated encumbrances. By implication an agreement may also allow certain encumbrances. See the discussion of de minimis encumbrances and visible encumbrances in part I.C below.

       Example: Buyer deposited $50,000 to buy a 99-acre farm, and the title search revealed a "line-of-sight" easement granted by Seller six years earlier in connection with the sale of a neighboring parcel. The easement prohibited any building on the land under contract that was visible from the main residence on the neighbor's parcel. *Held*, the easement made title unmarketable, justifying rescission by Buyer, regardless of whether the land was still usable for residential purposes. *Haisfield v. Lape*, 570 S.E.2d 794 (Va. 2002).

    c. **Free from reasonable doubt:** There are no plausible claims of third parties concerning interests in the property. This means that buyer does not have to prove that a possible outstanding claim to the property is in fact valid in order to object that title is not marketable.

2. **Title-related matter:** A valid objection to title, of course, must identify a problem with respect to *seller's title* rather than some other property feature that may negatively affect its value. Buyers sometimes attempt to frame a problem as title-related when in fact it is not.

    Example: Jeff and Bessy contract to buy a house near a good elementary school, where they plan to send their two young sons. Just after signing, they learn that the school district is considering a new school assignment plan that may result in their children's assignment to a less attractive school. Their broker tells them that, until the school situation is resolved, all the homes in the neighborhood are no longer marketable. Can they back out of the contract on the basis that marketable title is impaired? No. The school uncertainty is not a title problem. The broker is using the word "marketable" in a different sense, referring to the practical question of how easy or hard it will be to sell the property.

3. **Timing:** Seller's title must be marketable at closing, not earlier. This is true not only for short-term sales contracts, but also for installment land contracts.

    a. **Buyer's title objections:** As a consequence, buyer cannot immediately terminate if he discovers a title defect. He must object and give seller a reasonable period of time to cure title. If the objection is made close to the time of closing, seller may have the right to an extension of the time for closing in order to cure title.

       Example: Logan contracts to buy Bobbi's house for $270,000. Logan searches the title and finds a lien filed by a contractor previously employed by Bobbi to work on the house. Logan promptly sends Bobbi a letter stating that he is terminating the contract because title is unmarketable and he wants all of his deposit back. Bobbi has a reasonable time to correct the problem, and Logan cannot object if Bobbi eliminates the encumbrance by the time of closing.

4. Buyer's knowledge: Generally, buyer's knowledge of a title defect at the time of entering into the contract will not preclude buyer from objecting to it.

B. Record title compared to marketable title: Generally, seller must have record title in order for title to be marketable.

    1. Problem of adverse possession: Sometimes, seller relies on adverse possession title as the basis for ownership of some or all of the property. When seller's adverse possession title is not confirmed by a court's judgment, seller lacks record title. When the contract is silent on the issue of whether record title is required, there is a split of authority.

        a. Record title is an implied requirement: Most courts hold a title must be demonstrated by the records to be marketable. Off-record claims, such as title by adverse possession, have an element of risk that buyer should not have to assume.

        b. Adverse possession with strong facts is sufficient: Other courts hold that adverse possession title is marketable when seller can demonstrate possession for a period of time appreciably in excess of the statutory period, with all elements of the adverse possession apparently satisfied. See *Conklin v. Davi*, 388 A.2d 598 (N.J. 1978), for the principle that when seller relies on title by adverse possession, it's a question of fact as to whether title is free from reasonable doubt and thus marketable.

C. Encumbrances: An encumbrance is a nonpossessory right or interest in the property held by a third party that reduces the property's market value, restricts its use, or imposes an obligation on the property owner. Encumbrances include easements, real covenants, equitable servitudes, marital property rights, mortgage liens, tax liens, and other liens and charges. Generally, marketable title means the property must be free of all encumbrances. Courts, however, have created exceptions to this rule. The following four types of encumbrances are often considered not to impair marketable title.

    1. De minimis encumbrances: Some courts hold a de minimis encumbrance does not impair marketable title. A de minimis encumbrance is one that does not have an appreciable effect on the value of the property or its use. Examples are real covenants and easements that are common to the neighborhood and do not interfere with present uses of the property. See *Caselli v. Messina*, 567 N.Y.S.2d 972 (App. Div. 1990), holding that title to a house is marketable despite restrictive covenants, when those covenants are not violated by the present structure or present use of property. Such covenants are consistent with the expectations of a reasonable buyer.

        a. Small lien: A lien would not be considered de minimis even if it secures a very small sum of money relative to the purchase price. Seller is expected to pay the debt to discharge the lien.

    2. Visible encumbrances: Some courts excuse visible encumbrances, such as overhead utility lines, on the theory that buyer saw them when he inspected the property and thus the parties implicitly agreed that they were permitted. When courts apply this rule for visible encumbrances, it is an exception to the principle that buyer's knowledge of title defects does not affect his right to insist on marketable title. The visible improvements imply that a third party has long-term property rights, and it is generally not reasonable to suppose the parties intended seller to bargain for a release of those rights.

3. **Superfluous encumbrances:** A superfluous "covenant" or "encumbrance" is written and recorded, but it does not impose any obligations on the landowner in addition to those otherwise required by law.

   Example: Sara contracts to buy Partyacre and finds a real covenant that provides the owner "shall not at any time cause, maintain, or permit a nuisance" on his lot. This covenant is superfluous and cannot form the basis for a title objection by Sara. It merely restates the tort of nuisance, with no extension or elaboration. The owner would owe precisely the same duty to his neighbors not to commit nuisances, even in the absence of the covenant.

4. **Obsolete encumbrances:** Covenants and other encumbrances in the chain of title are obsolete when it is clear they are no longer enforceable. Either they have an express time limit, such as 20 years, which has expired, or they are no longer enforceable for other legal reasons.

   Example: Title searches in older residential neighborhoods, if they go back far enough in time, often disclose old racial covenants that bar occupancy by members of racial or ethnic minorities. Such racial covenants are obsolete due to modern constitutional law and civil rights laws: for example, *Shelley v. Kraemer*, 334 U.S. 1 (1948); Fair Housing Act, 42 U.S.C. §§ 3601-3619.

D. **Encroachments:** Two types of encroachments may concern a buyer. Improvements on the land being purchased by buyer may encroach across a boundary line or across a setback line for yards. Alternatively, improvements on neighboring land may encroach on the land being purchased. Both types of problems are often said to render seller's title unmarketable.

   1. **Seller's improvements encroach:** In the first case, the owner may be forced to relocate the improvements or pay damages. In *Staley v. Stephens*, 404 N.E.2d 633 (Ind. Ct. App. 1980), the court found title to be unmarketable because a house slightly encroached on a sideyard setback line by either .1 or 1.6 feet, depending upon which restrictive covenant applied.

   2. **Seller's neighbor's improvements encroach:** In the second case, the owner may have lost title to the area covered by the encroachment either under the law of adverse possession or due to the application of principles of equity.

E. **Zoning and other public regulations:** Sometimes, after signing the real estate contract, the buyer discovers a problem related to zoning or other land use regulations that apply to the property. When this happens, a dispute may arise as to whether the seller's title is marketable.

   1. **Narrow view of title:** Some courts define title narrowly, looking only at fee simple interests and encumbrances like liens and private servitudes. This means zoning laws and other types of public regulations of use do not render title unmarketable, even if they are incompatible with buyer's intended use of the property. In *Voorheesville Rod & Gun Club v. E.W. Tompkins Co.*, 626 N.E.2d 917 (N.Y. 1993), the court held that the sale of part of the seller's land required subdivision approval by the local government, even though the buyer did not plan to add improvements to the land. The court, however, held that the seller's refusal to get subdivision approval did not make title unmarketable.

   2. **Broad view of title:** Other courts have used marketable title as a method to protect buyers whose expectations concerning property use and value are frustrated when zoning problems are encountered.

    a. Existing zoning violation: The broad view of marketable title is especially likely to apply when a zoning violation exists when the parties enter into the contract. The rationale is that buyer should not bear the risk of the government bringing a zoning enforcement action to seek an injunction or damages.

3. Non-title approaches: You should bear in mind that buyers who are disappointed by zoning or land use controls may assert claims other than lack of marketable title that sometimes have merit. In *Dover Pool & Racquet Club, Inc. v. Brooking*, 322 N.E.2d 168 (Mass. 1975), the buyer was entitled to rescission for mutual mistake of fact when it contracted to buy land for a tennis and swim club, but the government changed its zoning to require a special permit for such use.

F. Express contract provisions

1. Contract title: In many contracts, the parties replace the judicial definition of marketability with their own standard. For example, the parties may specify that only record title is acceptable, and they may agree to a list of encumbrances that are permitted and not objectionable to buyer.

2. Record title: Record title requires proof of the status of title, gathered solely from deeds and other instruments that are recorded in the public records. This means seller's title cannot depend on an unrecorded instrument or on title by adverse possession that is not yet litigated.

    a. Seller required to furnish abstract: Contracts sometimes provide that the seller shall provide the buyer with an abstract of title. Because abstracts are summaries of the public records, such a clause may be interpreted to require that the seller have record title. For example, in *Tri-State Hotel Company v. Sphinx Investment Co.*, 510 P.2d 1223 (Kan. 1973), the contract called for the seller to deliver abstracts of title that "shall disclose good and marketable title in fee simple." When the seller relied on title by adverse possession for a small part of the property under contract, the court found title unmarketable because the seller lacked record title to the adverse possession area.

3. Insurable title: Contracts often provide that buyer will obtain a title insurance policy. Depending on the language of the contract, the title insurance clause may replace the marketable title standard, with the issuance of an insurance commitment and policy replacing the marketable title standard. In effect, the insurance company rather than the court becomes the arbiter of marketability.

G. Buyer's remedies for title defects

1. English rule: Under the English rule, buyer generally cannot recover expectancy damages when seller breaches the promise of marketable title. Buyer is limited to restitution—the recovery of out-of-pocket costs, such as return of his deposit plus interest and expenses like the cost of title examination. The rationale is that titles are very difficult and many sellers are not fully aware of what problems may exist.

    a. Bad faith exception: The English rule has an exception when seller has acted in bad faith in connection with the title problem. The most common situation involving bad faith is the seller's failing to disclose a title defect known to the seller when the contract is signed. Then buyer is allowed expectancy damages.

2. American rule: Under the American rule, buyer can select among the full range of damage awards, including expectancy damages whenever the property value exceeds the contract price at the time of breach. The rationale is that the injury to buyer is the same, regardless of whether seller acted in good faith or bad faith. Moreover, it is hard to prove whether seller acted in good or bad faith and the American rule simplifies the law by making the inquiry unnecessary. See *Basilko v. Pargo Corporation*, 532 A.2d 1346 (D.C. Ct. App. 1987), holding that the purchaser at a foreclosure sale is entitled to expectancy damages when the sale was void because the borrower was not in default under the mortgage loan.

Example: When Seller signed the contract, he owned only an undivided half of the property, with his sister having the other half as Mama's other heir. Seller is unable to persuade Sis to agree to the contract, and Buyer sues for expectancy damages. Under the American rule, Buyer wins. Under the English rule, Buyer wins only if Seller acted in bad faith. If Buyer proves Seller knew he owned only half when he signed the contract, there's a good chance Buyer wins. However, even with this proof, bad faith is a question of fact. The fact finder might find good faith on the basis that Seller thought Sis would go along or that Seller was not aware that both heirs, as tenants in common, had to agree to a sale of the property.

II. FORMAL REQUIREMENTS FOR DEEDS

A. **Statute of frauds:** Oral transfers of title to land are prohibited by the statute of frauds, which requires a writing that:

- Identifies the parties.

- Identifies the land.

- Shows an intent to convey.

B. **Execution:** The deed must be signed by the grantor. Most deeds used in modern real estate practice are not signed by the grantee. Such a deed, signed only by the grantor, is called a ***deed poll***. An instrument of conveyance signed by both parties is known as a ***deed of indenture***. In some communities, attorneys tend to use deeds of indenture when the grantee undertakes affirmative obligations, such as assuming an existing indebtedness secured by a mortgage on the conveyed property or promising to abide by covenants set forth in the deed. See *Jeremiah 29:11, Inc. v. Seifert*, 161 P.3d 750 (Kan. 2007), in which a deed of indenture purported to restrict the land to residential use. Only the grantor signed the deed, even though the deed had a signature line for the grantee. The court held that a successor to the grantee was not subject to the restriction, reasoning that the deed did not impart constructive notice to the successor.

C. **Delivery:** The grantor must deliver the deed to the grantee. Usually it's a manual handing over of the instrument. In commercial transactions this is seldom a problem. A broader definition of delivery is any objective manifestation that the grantor intends the deed to be presently operative and to transfer ownership. In donative transfers, delivery is often a problem when a deed is used as a will substitute. Delivery may be called into question when the grantor never physically delivered the signed deed to the grantee, but the grantor gave the deed to a third person or stored it under circumstances indicating he may have intended it to be legally effective. See *Wiggill v. Cheney*, 597 P.2d 1351 (Utah 1979), finding there was no delivery when the grantor put a deed in her safety deposit box, instructing her co-depositor to give the deed to the grantee at the grantor's death.

D. Acceptance: The grantee must accept delivery of the deed. Acceptance is commonly presumed. With a deed poll, acceptance is the rationale for binding the nonsigning grantee to the terms of the deed.

E. Acknowledgment and recordation: In almost all states, a deed is effective upon delivery even if it is not acknowledged (usually by a notary public) or recorded. An unrecorded deed might not bind subsequent third parties, but it is operative as between grantor and grantee.

III. DEED CONSTRUCTIONAL RULES

Courts employ a number of rules of interpretation or construction to decide the meaning of language in deeds. Several of the most important tests are these:

A. Intent of the parties: The overall goal is to arrive at the parties' intent by looking at the whole deed.

B. Conflict between parts of deed: Occasionally, there will be a conflict or an apparent conflict between different parts of a deed, usually because of poor drafting. Courts may pick among several different rules to resolve such problems. The deed may be construed against the grantor on the ground that he is its author. Another rule accords priority to certain clauses: The ***granting clause*** and the ***habendum clause*** take precedence, and conflicting language found elsewhere is struck as repugnant to those clauses. Courts, however, have discretion over when to apply such rules, and they generally select rules that they believe effectuate the parties' probable intent. See *Barrier v. Randolph*, 133 S.E.2d 655 (N.C. 1963), where the court refused to apply the repugnancy doctrine even though the granting and habendum clauses had no exceptions. The middle part of the deed contained extensive conditions and restrictions agreed to by both parties.

C. Extrinsic evidence of the parties' real intent: To admit extrinsic evidence, the court must find ambiguity in the deed. The court cannot alter a deed that is plain on its face. The policy is to promote the reliability of the land records. Admitting extrinsic evidence impairs the paper records. This may disrupt reliance by bona fide purchasers (BFPs), defeating their expectations.

    1. Presumption against ambiguity: For this reason, courts sometimes strain to find a deed is not ambiguous. For example, in *Walters v. Tucker*, 281 S.W.2d 843 (Mo. 1955), the court found that a deed that conveyed the "west 50 feet" of a lot not to be ambiguous even though the line could be measured two different ways and there was conflicting evidence as to what the parties actually intended.

    2. Latent and patent ambiguity: Extrinsic evidence is admissible to resolve a latent ambiguity, but not a patent ambiguity.

D. Reformation: Where an unambiguous deed has an error or is wrong, an original party to the deed can bring an action for reformation, but this claim will not affect any BFP who is present (see Chapter 10 for a discussion of BFPs).

IV. DEFECTIVE DEEDS

A. Void deeds: A void deed has no legal effect at all. It is the same as if it was never made and did not exist.

1. **Forgery:** A forged deed is void and thus has no effect whatsoever. This means that a grantee or successor who relies on a forged deed has no right or title whatsoever: The original owner whose signature was forged still has title and the right to possession.

   a. **Grantee's damage action:** While the grantee claiming under a forged deed does not get title, he obviously has a cause of action for damages against the forger and may have an action against others who participated in the transaction. In *McDonald v. Plumb*, 90 Cal. Rptr. 822 (Ct. App. 1970), a notary public falsely acknowledged a forged signature by not requiring the personal appearance of the person who signed the deed. The court held the notary liable for damages to a subsequent purchaser.

2. **Lack of delivery:** A deed is not valid, even if signed by the proper person, until it is delivered. Thus, nondelivery if proven renders the deed void, just like a forged deed. This is fatal to the person claiming under the undelivered deed, even when that person is a BFP.

B. **Voidable deeds:** Some other types of defects are considered less serious—for example, when the grantee obtains the deed by duress or the grantor has an incapacity. Such defects make the deed only voidable, meaning the grantor has the right to rescind. The rescission right cannot be asserted against subsequent BFPs.

V. DEED COVENANTS OF TITLE

A. **Warranty deeds**

1. **General warranties:** General title warranties protect the grantee against any and all defects that may have arisen anytime during the entire chain of title up to the time of delivery.

2. **Special or limited warranties:** A special warranty deed or limited warranty deed protects the grantee only against defects arising while the grantor owned the property. Defects that arose prior to the grantor's acquisition of title are not covered by the warranties. Thus, the special or limited warranty deed reflects a sharing of title risk between grantor and grantee. In *Egli v. Troy*, 602 N.W.2d 329 (Iowa 1999), the court held that the grantor was not liable for the grantee's loss of title due to a neighbor's assertion of the doctrine of boundary by acquiescence if *all* of the acquiescence occurred prior to the grantor's acquisition of title.

B. **Quitclaim deeds:** A quitclaim deed has no covenants of title, so the grantee bears all risk associated with quality of title. If it turns out that the property is subject to liens, encumbrances, or other title defects, the grantor is not liable. A quitclaim deed, however, is completely effective to transfer to the grantee whatever title the grantor actually has.

C. **Types of covenants:** At common law, all title covenants in deeds must be express; none is implied. In many states today, use of a statutory form for a deed creates statutory implied title covenants.

1. **Present covenants:** Present title covenants do not run with the land. They are breached, if at all, at the time of delivery of the deed. This is when the statute of limitations begins to run.

   a. **Covenant of seisin:** The grantor promises he is seized of the estate the deed purports to convey. Today most courts view the covenant of seisin as a promise of good title to the estate. If the grantor is not in actual possession at the time of the conveyance, the immediate right to possession suffices.

b. **Right to convey:** The grantor promises that he has the legal right to convey the estate the deed purports to convey. This overlaps substantially with the covenant of seisin; the owner of an estate generally has an unqualified right of transfer.

c. **Covenant against encumbrances:** The grantor promises that there are no encumbrances on the land. If there are encumbrances that are not discharged at closing, the grantor should make sure that the deed has an express exception for the permitted encumbrances. It is sometimes difficult to determine the scope of the covenant against encumbrances. See *Magun v. Bombaci*, 492 A.2d 235 (Conn. Super. Ct. 1985), finding no encumbrance when part of a driveway and a sewer line that served a house on the lot conveyed to the grantee encroached on the neighbor's lot. The court noted that there is split of judicial authority on this issue.

2. **Future covenants:** These covenants run to subsequent grantees, provided they have not been breached at the time of the transfer of title to the subsequent grantee. A future covenant is breached by actual or constructive eviction of the grantee.

a. **Covenant of quiet enjoyment:** The grantor promises that the grantee may possess and quietly enjoy the land. The covenant of quiet enjoyment is breached if the grantee is actually or constructively evicted from all or part of the land by the grantor, by someone claiming under the grantor, or by someone with paramount title. An actual eviction occurs when the grantee is physically dispossessed from all or part of the premises. Events that infringe upon the grantee's possessory rights but are short of actual eviction are sometimes treated as *constructive eviction*, thereby affording the grantee a cause of action on the covenant of quiet enjoyment. Different standards may apply to determine whether a title-related problem rises to the level of a constructive eviction. Compare *Brown v. Lober*, 389 N.E.2d 1188 (Ill. 1979) (no constructive eviction when grantee cannot sell coal rights due to outstanding two-thirds interest in mineral rights) with *Booker T. Washington Construction & Design Co. v. Huntington Urban Renewal Authority*, 383 S.E.2d 41 (W. Va. 1989) (when grantor warrants a fee simple but has only a life estate and grantee has contracted to resell the property, constructive eviction occurs when grantee is sued for lack of marketable title).

b. **Covenant of warrant:** The grantor warrants the title to the grantee. Typically, the clause uses the terms *"warrant and forever defend"* the conveyed land. In most states, this covenant has the same scope as the covenant of quiet enjoyment; it is breached by an actual or constructive eviction of the grantee from all or part of the property. In many jurisdictions, there is a remedial distinction between the covenant of quiet enjoyment and the covenant of warranty. The latter covenant with its promise to defend obligates the grantor to pay the costs of defending title against third parties, including reasonable attorneys' fees.

c. **Covenant of further assurances:** The grantor promises to give whatever "further assurances" may be required in the future to vest the grantee with the title the deed purports to convey. If the deed is defective in some respect, this covenant obligates the grantor to execute a new, corrected deed. Often, this covenant also obligates the grantor to take reasonable measures to cure title by, for example, obtaining releases of interests held by third parties.

3. Remedies for breach of deed covenants

a. Damages: For the first five covenants listed above, the remedy for breach is damages. Most states limit the grantor's liability for damages to the purchase price received plus statutory interest from the date the price was paid. Some states are more generous to grantees, allowing damages in excess of purchase price under certain circumstances. See *Booker T. Washington Construction & Design Co. v. Huntington Urban Renewal Authority*, 383 S.E.2d 41 (W. Va. 1989), in which the court held the grantor liable for up to the value of the land at the time of conveyance, when the grantor donated the land to an urban renewal authority.

b. Specific relief: Only the covenant of further assurances provides specific relief. In appropriate cases if the grantor refuses to give further assurances, thus breaching the covenant, the remedy of specific performance is available as an alternative to damages. With this covenant, the grantor may be ordered to take steps to remove the defect or perfect the grantee's title.

VI. RELATIONSHIP BETWEEN TITLE UNDER CONTRACT AND DEED COVENANTS

Under the doctrine of merger, the title provisions of the executory contract are extinguished when the deed is delivered. The deed covenants take over at this point in time. In many transactions, there is a close match between the contract title provision and the scope of the deed covenants. However, they operate independently and sometimes diverge.

A. Quitclaim deed and marketable title: If a contract calls for the delivery of a quitclaim deed and is otherwise silent on the topic of title, the purchaser may raise a title objection prior to closing. Under the contract, the purchaser still has the implied right to marketable title up until closing.

Quiz Yourself on
ALLOCATING TITLE RISK BY CONTRACT AND BY DEED

34. Kali contracts to buy a house for $180,000 from Stump. The contract says nothing about title matters. The title search reveals a lien for an unpaid and past-due homeowners assessment in the amount of $200. Kali objects to the lien. Stump says the lien doesn't affect title, and anyway he has paid the assessment and can prove it. Kali continues to object. Who prevails? _____

35. Ariel and Troy enter into a contract for Ariel to buy Troy's house for $200,000, with the contract promising "good and perfect title in fee simple." Ariel orders a title search, which discloses a 10-foot-wide telephone easement that runs along the entire rear boundary line. Ariel objects to the easement, but Troy insists that the transaction go forward. Does Ariel have a valid title objection? _____

36. Tusk contracts to sell a ranch to Sanchez for $1.8 million, with the contract calling for delivery of a warranty deed at closing, which is to occur on October 2. The parties show up at closing, and Tusk produces and tenders a special warranty deed. Sanchez asks Tusk to show him written evidence that he has title to the ranch. Tusk refuses to do so, claiming he has fully discharged his title obligations by tendering the deed. Is Tusk right? _____

37. Same facts as prior question. Sanchez objects to the deed tendered by Tusk. He demands a general warranty deed. Does he have the right to a general warranty deed? _____

38. Same facts as the prior two questions. If you represented Sanchez in preparing the contract to buy Tusk's ranch, would you make any changes in drafting? _____

Answers

34. **Kali, probably.** Kali does have the right to marketable title. This is an implied term in every contract to purchase real property. The lien is an encumbrance. The dollar amount of the lien makes no difference. It is an encumbrance and impairs title whether it secures a huge or a tiny obligation. But whether Stump has paid the lien might matter. Until the homeowners association signs a release of lien, with the release recorded in the public records, Stump lacks marketable title *of record*. If the jurisdiction requires that marketable title be demonstrated by the records, Kali's objection is valid. Stump must cure the defect by obtaining and recording a release of lien. If, however, the jurisdiction allows proof of marketable title by other clear evidence (such as adverse possession by the seller), then proof by Stump that he fully paid the assessment is sufficient for him to comply with his contract obligations.

35. **Probably not.** The telephone line easement is clearly an encumbrance. While the parties are free to contract for something other than marketable title, their provision calling for "good and perfect title in fee simple" will very probably be interpreted as just restating the general implied standard of marketable title. This generally means that encumbrances are not permitted, even though Troy does have fee simple title to all of the real property. Thus, Ariel will argue that title is not perfect if it is blemished with an easement. Troy's response is that she has only the right to marketable title and this easement is common to the neighborhood, has no negative effect on property value, and does not interfere with use and enjoyment of the property. If the easement is visibly improved (e.g., there are poles and overhead wires), he will also say Ariel must have seen this when she looked at the property and she should have realized that they were located within an easement. Her response, even if there are visible wires, is that the contract doesn't expressly permit any easements, the court shouldn't read a title exception into the contract, and she may have thought the wires were located on the neighboring property, not on the land she was buying. This could go either way—courts split on the issue whether visible encumbrances impair marketable title.

36. **Yes.** Different parts of the country have different customs as to who usually arranges for a title search as between seller and buyer. Sanchez is out of luck on his last-minute demand to see proof of title unless the sale is in a community where the norm is for sellers to produce evidence of title *and* the court is willing to read this norm into the contract as an implied term.

37. **Probably not.** Generally, the seller drafts the warranty deed. Tusk will argue that it is up to him to decide which type of warranty deed to use. This argument may be persuasive—a special warranty deed is a warranty deed. However, Sanchez will point out that the contract provision cannot mean that the seller can put any words he wants into the deed, so long as it has the words "Warranty Deed" as

its caption. In order to avoid this dispute, the contract should specify whether the deed should be a general warranty deed or a special warranty deed.

38.   **Yes.** You should consider and draft provisions that (1) define the buyer's right to marketable title and (2) indicate who will arrange for a title search, when it will be completed and given to the buyer, and what process will be followed if the buyer decides to raise a title objection. As to the deed, you should specify what type of warranty deed and what title exceptions, if any, are permitted in the deed. You probably want to start from a strong position: "We want a general warranty deed, with all six of the standard covenants of title, and no exceptions except those expressly approved by the buyer after receiving the title report."

Exam Tips on
ALLOCATING TITLE RISK BY CONTRACT AND BY DEED

☛ **Marketable title:** Whenever you find an exam question with a title issue, you probably ought to discuss marketable title under the contract, even if you conclude there is another document (such as a deed or a title insurance policy) that is ultimately dispositive on the issue. Marketable title is a fundamental concept. In every contract, marketable title is an implied term. It's both an implied condition and an implied promise.

☛ **Express title provision:** If an exam question refers to a contract with an express clause dealing with title, it is essential that you study the clause carefully to determine which of the three types it is. Sometimes, a title clause is a hybrid—for example, it may provide both that the seller's title is of record *and* that it is insurable by a title insurance company. In addition, don't forget about the *implied* term of marketable title just because you have spotted an express title clause in the contract. While there is a good chance that the express clause has completely replaced the implied term, this is not necessarily true. Some courts are sufficiently fond of the general rules of marketable title that they will apply them, in addition to the express title terms of the contract, unless the parties have made it absolutely clear that they have displaced rather than supplemented the implied rules.

☛ **Defective deeds:** Certain defects, such as forgery or lack of delivery, are so severe that the deed has no legal effect—it's a void deed. Other defects are more minor—they make the deed voidable. This means the grantor may rescind the deed.

  ☞ **Defective vs. unrecorded deeds:** Don't confuse a defective deed with an unrecorded deed. Professors sometimes try to trick you with a question that implies that an unrecorded deed is ineffective or questionable. An unrecorded deed is perfectly valid to pass title from the grantor to the grantee. It's neither void nor voidable. A problem arises only if a third party is involved, who may qualify as a bona fide purchaser (BFP).

☛ **Deed covenants of title:** Be sure you know all six of the standard covenants:

☞ **Present covenants:** The three present covenants are the covenant of seisin, right to convey, and the covenant against encumbrances. They are breached, if at all, when the conveyance is made.

☞ **Future covenants:** The three future covenants are the covenant of quiet enjoyment, the covenant of warranty, and the covenant of further assurances. They run with the land, and are breached upon an eviction (actual or constructive) of the grantee.

If an essay question refers to a deed and the facts appear to point to some type of title problem, be prepared to list and discuss all six standard covenants of title (the three present covenants plus the three future covenants). Unless the facts clearly demonstrate that the deed is either a quitclaim deed or a warranty deed with less than the full set of six covenants, you should assume that all the covenants are present. If the deed language is set forth verbatim, then read it carefully to determine which covenants it contains.

☛ **Relationship between marketable title and deed covenants:** Be alert to the possibility that a good answer to the question will involve both marketable title under the contract and the analysis of covenants under the deed.

☞ **Merger:** When this happens, you should explain that marketable title governed the parties until delivery of the deed, at which point in time the deed covenants replaced the marketable title standard under the doctrine of merger.

CHAPTER 9

LAND DESCRIPTIONS

ChapterScope

This chapter examines written descriptions of land and the legal rules that address their sufficiency and interpretation. Land descriptions are pervasive in real estate documents. Every deed, contract of sale, and lease describes a certain parcel of real estate. This is also true of other instruments, such as restrictive covenants and grants of easements.

- **Land descriptions:** The three main types of land descriptions are:

  - Metes and bounds,

  - Government survey system, and

  - Subdivision plats.

- **Survey:** The "title survey" or "boundary survey" locates all the boundary lines of a tract on the ground.

- **Surveyor liability:** Surveyors, like other professionals, are liable to their clients for errors including negligent work. The trend is to permit a cause of action for third parties who rely on an erroneous survey to their detriment.

- **Statute of frauds requirement:** The statute of frauds requires a written description of the land for both contracts and deeds. Whenever possible, most modern courts strive to discern the parties' intent and uphold a land description even if it has flaws and is less than perfect.

I. TYPES OF DESCRIPTIONS

The goal of the land description is to describe one and only one parcel. In order to do this, the written description must provide a means of locating all the boundary lines of the parcel. There are three types of land descriptions that are in common use in real estate transactions.

A. Metes and bounds: This method describes every boundary line by length and direction. The description for each line, which may include references to monuments, is known as a *call*. In the United States, length or distance is usually given in feet. Straight lines are usually employed. Curved lines, such as along a road, are described by combinations of radius, arc, chord, and tangent. Irregular lines are not commonly used except when the boundary is a natural monument, such as a body of water (for example, "north along the western bank of Muddy Creek"). Direction, also called the *course*, is given in degrees east or west of north or south. There are 360 degrees in a circle.

Example: A simple metes and bounds description for a parcel of land having the shape of a trapezoid is set forth below. There's an error in one of the calls. Can you spot it?

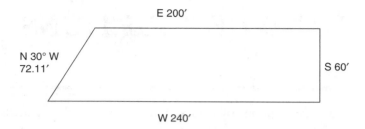

Surveys, like most other maps, are drawn with north at the top. The call for the western boundary of the parcel has the wrong direction. It must run northeast and should read ***N 30° E 70'***. A line running N 30° W from the bottom left-hand corner of the diagram must slant left. The calls, as shown on the diagram, result in a description that does not *close*. This means it does not form a closed geometric figure. Instead, it results in the following set of lines:

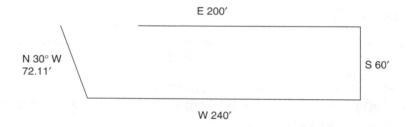

B. **Government survey system:** The federal government initiated this system in 1785. Among Thomas Jefferson's many talents was surveying. He adapted this system from earlier New England surveys for use for the public domain. The basic units are *sections* and *townships*, which are laid out using squares and rectangular grids. Each section has approximately 640 acres and is a square with sides of 1 mile each. Each township has 36 sections. The government survey system applies in most states except the original 13 colonies.

C. **Subdivision plats:** The plat or map shows a number of lots and is filed as part of the public land records. The local government, through its subdivision regulations, has standards for plats that the owner and her surveyor must follow. After the plat is recorded, parties then refer to the recorded plat in deeds, mortgages, and other instruments that create or transfer rights in the lots.

Example: A contract of sale describes the property to be conveyed as "Lot 7, Block 2 of Green Acres Estates, according to the plat recorded in Volume 189, Page 45, Plat Records, Malloy County, State of Chaos." At closing, the warranty deed will use this same description to convey the property to Buyer.

II. THE SURVEYOR

The purpose of the "title survey" or "boundary survey" is to locate all the boundary lines of a tract on the ground. The surveyor's work includes work on the ground and the study of documents. She makes field measurements and evaluates physical field evidence. She also reads instruments of record, including the chain of title for the tract and, to the extent they are available, she may study unrecorded documents, such as prior surveys on the same or neighboring properties.

A. Discretion: The professional surveyor exercises discretion. Often the surveyor must evaluate conflicting evidence and exercise judgment in deciding where a boundary line should be located.

B. Reasons for a survey: After signing a contract to purchase land, it is generally advisable that the buyer obtain a survey. The contract should expressly provide for a survey; for example, it may require that the seller obtain a survey and deliver it to the purchaser, or provide that the purchaser has the right to obtain a survey. The contract should indicate what will happen if the survey discloses a title problem or is otherwise not acceptable to the buyer.

1. **Existence of the property:** The survey confirms that the tract exists, that it has a certain quantity of acres or square feet, and that the legal description is sufficient.

2. **Relationship of the property to adjoining properties:** The survey may disclose whether the boundary lines of the surveyed tract are consistent with the descriptions of adjoining properties. If there are inconsistencies, there may be problems with overlaps or gores. An *overlap* means there is a strip or area that is within the descriptions of both adjoining properties. A *gore* means there is a small strip or area that separates or lies between the two properties that are thought to be adjoining.

3. **Relationship of occupied lines to record lines:** The surveyor should look at evidence of possession and occupation by the owner and her neighbors and compare the occupied lines to the deed record lines. Any mismatch should be shown on the survey.

4. **Location of physical improvements:** A complete survey should show the precise location of all buildings and other physical improvements on the tract. This is especially important for improvements that are located very near to the boundary lines, but a complete survey should also show the accurate location of all improvements on the tract.

5. **Unrecorded easements and other facts not of record:** The survey shows unrecorded physical features on the property that may be evidence of outstanding unrecorded property rights. Examples are utility lines, driveways, manhole covers, and drainage ditches.

C. Types of surveys

1. **Instructions:** A boundary survey is not a standardized product. Surveyors' codes and practices vary widely. For this reason, the client or attorney should specify the type of survey desired, the work the surveyor is expected to do, what the survey document should contain and disclose, and the nature of the surveyor's certificate.

2. **ALTA/ACSM standards:** These are uniform national standards for surveys that cover topics such as the location of buildings and other improvements, evidence of monuments, and discrepancies between record boundary lines and field measurements. The standards are promulgated as a joint project by the American Land Title Association (ALTA) and the American Congress on Surveying and Mapping (ACSM). The advantage of an ALTA/ACSM survey is that the owner or client has a standardized product, with clear expectations as to how the survey was prepared and its accuracy, which do not depend on state or local customs or practices. There are four types of ALTA/ACSM surveys:

   a. **Class A—urban surveys:** This is the most detailed and expensive to prepare. It is typically used for properties with high market values, whether developed or undeveloped.

   b. **Class B—suburban surveys:** This is used almost exclusively for single-family homes in residential subdivisions.

c. **Class C—rural surveys:** This is for farmland and other undeveloped land outside the suburban areas that may have a potential for future development.

d. **Class D—mountain and marshland surveys:** Normally used only for land in remote areas with difficult terrain with limited potential for development.

D. Surveyor liability

1. **Certificate:** The surveyor's certificate may promise that the survey has a particular degree of accuracy. Breach of an express representation or warranty may give rise to liability. See *Rozny v. Marnul*, 250 N.E.2d 656 (Ill. 1969), holding a surveyor liable for a defective survey when the certificate stated the "survey carries our absolute guarantee for accuracy."

2. **Negligence:** The surveyor is held to a standard of professional competence based on the norms and customs of the surveying profession. Failure to meet such standards is professional negligence.

    Example: A surveyor relies on field notes for land covered by a federal government survey. The surveyor finds monuments on the ground, which he rejects because they are inconsistent with the field notes. This is contrary to the legal rule, which provides that monuments on the ground prevail over calls in field notes. In *Hanneman v. Downer*, 871 P.2d 279 (Nev. 1994), the court found the surveyor committed negligence, relying on expert testimony of another surveyor.

3. **Persons who may recover**

    a. **Those in contract privity:** Under contract principles, the owner or lender who purchases a survey may recover for loss caused by the surveyor's breach of duty.

    b. **Third parties:** Most courts permit some class of third parties who reasonably and foreseeably rely on an erroneous survey to recover from the surveyor. Of these courts, some employ contract law (third-party beneficiary theory) and others use tort law.

       i. **Third-party beneficiary:** The person contracting with the surveyor may order the survey for the purpose of providing it to a third party, such as a prospective mortgagee or purchaser.

       ii. **Tort theories:** Third parties may recover based on tort theories, such as negligent misrepresentation. *Hanneman v. Downer*, 871 P.2d 279 (Nev. 1994), holding the surveyor has a duty to subsequent purchasers of the property. Purchasers who rely upon a survey to their detriment may recover for negligence.

4. **Statute of limitations:** A cause of action for breach of duty may be barred by the statute of limitations, whether the plaintiff is the client of the surveyor or a third party.

    a. **General statutes:** Depending upon the plaintiff's theory, the general statute of limitations for contract actions or the general statute of limitations for tort actions often will apply. Such statutes are often in the range of two to five years. In many states the statute will run from the time the surveyor did the work or made the error. In many areas of law, however, courts give plaintiffs the benefit of a ***discovery rule*** when the plaintiff does not discover the defect or error until much later. The discovery rule is sometimes applied to extend the statute of limitations for actions against surveyors. In *Hanneman v. Downer*, 871 P.2d 279 (Nev. 1994), an action was brought in 1984 against a surveyor, who negligently prepared a survey in 1965. Although a four-year statute applied, the action was timely because the subsequent purchaser did not discover the error until 1981.

    b. Specific surveyor statutes: A few states have specific statutes of limitations for surveyors, e.g., Tenn. Code Ann. § 28-3-114 (four years from date survey is completed in written form). Usually the legislative intent is to provide a bright-line rule that insulates surveyors from liability after a fixed period of time.

III. LEGAL ADEQUACY OF DESCRIPTION

    A. Descriptions in contract of sale: The major goal is to ascertain the parties' intent, yet the statute of frauds requires a written description of the land. There is tension between these two principles. Judicial approaches vary across a spectrum. The ends of the spectrum may be identified as:

    1. Formalism: The writing must completely describe the tract by permitting the location of all boundaries, with no ambiguity and no need to look to extrinsic evidence.

    Example: A contract of sale made by residents of the City of Lake, State of Anywhere, describes the property as 280 Lakeview Boulevard. No reference is made in the contract to the name of the city and state. Under formalism, this property description is not sufficient even though there is a street known as Lakeview Boulevard in Lake, Anywhere, and extrinsic evidence can prove that the seller owns a house at that address. See *O'Dell v. Pine Ridge Inv., L.L.C.*, 667 S.E.2d 912 (Ga. Ct. App. 2008), holding invalid a contract description of the land as "187.5 acres in Land Lot 170 Sumter County Georgia And containing 8,167,500 (187.5 acres) square feet of land, more or less." The land lot was much larger than 187.5 acres, and the contract provided no key for locating the property within the land lot. The court refused to allow parol evidence that the seller owned a particular 187.5-acre tract in that land lot or that the parties bargained with respect to the sale of a particular tract.

    2. Effectuating intent: Any written description suffices, with extrinsic evidence (written and oral) admissible to explain what the parties meant by their writing.

    Example: A written contract obligates Seller to sell property described as "the farm on Bayside Road." Under the approach of effectuating intent, this promise is enforceable, with extrinsic evidence proving both that Seller owns a farm on that road and the boundaries of that farm.

    3. Trend toward effectuating intent: The general trend in modern law is away from formalism and toward effectuating the parties' intent.

    Example: A contract provides for the sale of "40 acres of my property, including woods and pond on the northwest side of my property, further to be described in proper form." This is part of a 70-acre tract owned by the seller. The parties hire a surveyor, who creates a dividing line. The seller later refuses to go forward and close. The buyer is entitled to specific performance, even though the 40-acre portion could have been laid out many different ways. The court finds the contract description is sufficient to satisfy the statute of frauds. *Van Der Bent v. Gilling*, 143 N.Y.S. 1082 (App. Div. 1913), *aff'd*, 116 N.E. 1081 (1917).

    B. Descriptions in deeds and other recorded instruments: Courts have developed a number of rules to resolve apparent conflicts in deed language.

1. **Policy approach:** Courts tend to be stricter concerning the quality of the land descriptions in deeds and other recorded instruments than they are for land contracts. Deeds become part of the chain of title for the property, to be retrieved and evaluated for many decades. For this reason, successive owners come to rely on the descriptions in the chain of title, and they generally lack access to extrinsic evidence as to the original parties' actual intent.

    a. **Minimize use of extrinsic evidence:** For this reason, courts often craft rules that minimize or eliminate the use of extrinsic evidence.

       Example: In *Walters v. Tucker*, 281 S.W.2d 843 (Mo. 1955), a deed conveyed the "West 50 feet of Lot 13" in a subdivision. Thirty years later when successors owned both parts of Lot 13 a problem surfaced. Because the street fronting the lot was not perpendicular to the side lot lines, the 50 feet could be measured two ways—either perpendicular to the side lot line or as frontage along the street. The trial court found ambiguity in the deed as to how the parties intended the line to be measured, admitted extrinsic evidence, and ruled the parties intended 50 feet of street frontage. The supreme court reversed, holding the deed was not ambiguous and the line had to be measured perpendicular to the side line.

2. **Major rules of deed interpretation**

    a. **Prefer the grantee in cases of doubt or ambiguity:** The intent is to give the grantee the most land and the greatest estate possible. This is based on the common practice that the grantor drafts the deed and thus, if the deed has a problem, the grantor caused it.

    b. **Interpret deed so that it conveys some land:** If a deed, read literally, conveys no land at all, the court will strain to interpret it so that it conveys something. The fact that the grantor signed and delivered the deed and that the grantee accepted it shows they were intending to accomplish something, not engaging in a nullity.

       Example: This is illustrated by *Hoban v. Cable*, 60 N.W. 466 (Mich. 1894), which shows how a simple change of direction can make a description very different from what the parties intended. One call for a lot said "south 62 degrees 15 minutes west 158.96 feet to Market street" when it should have said "south 62 degrees 15 minutes *east* 158.96 feet to Market street." The description thus did not *close*: It did not describe a polygon (the last line didn't end up at the beginning point for the first line). The court nevertheless upheld the deed, focusing on the requirement that the line must go to Market street, an artificial monument.

    c. **Deeds may expressly incorporate other writings in order to show what land is granted:** The deed may refer to a prior deed in the chain of title, to a survey, or to another instrument. This incorporation by reference is valid. If the deed both contains a land description and incorporates another description by reference, in the event of a conflict usually the express description prevails over the incorporated description. When using incorporation by reference, there is no legal requirement that the referenced writing be recorded. However, if you are drafting a document that is to be recorded, such as a deed, you should refer only to recorded instruments. Otherwise, there is the risk that at some point in the future, a title problem will arise if the referenced instrument cannot be found or conclusively identified.

    d. **Specific language controls over general language:** If there is an apparent conflict between general language and specific language, the two are usually reconciled by giving effect to the specific language. This means the specific term is deemed to be an exception to the general term. This is likely to comport with the parties' intent.

Example: A deed conveys Blackacre along with "all appurtenances thereto," but also has a separate clause that excepts ownership in fee of a billboard located on Blackacre. The grantee may argue she owns all appurtenances and the billboard is an appurtenance. However, under this rule of interpretation, the billboard clause is the more specific term and it prevails. The grantee thus owns all appurtenances except the billboard. In drafting, to prevent the need to resort to this rule, the grantor should have modified the general term to convey "all appurtenances thereto except the billboard referred to below."

e. **Natural monuments control over artificial monuments:** Natural monuments are things like rivers, trees, and rocks. Artificial monuments are man-made objects like roads and fences; they also include monuments placed for surveying purposes like iron pins and wooden stakes. Natural monuments are often more permanent than artificial ones. The rule is also likely to effectuate intent; in cases of conflict, the parties more likely focused on the natural monuments when planning their transaction.

f. **Monuments control over calls (distances and courses):** This means that if there is a conflict between a monument and a call, the monument prevails. In *McGhee v. Young*, 606 So. 2d 1215 (Fla. Dist. Ct. App. 1992), the original surveyor set concrete monuments, which conflicted with metes and bounds descriptions set forth in deeds and in the subdivision plat. The court held that the monuments controlled, observing that it did not matter whether the original surveyor made a mistake in where he placed the monuments.

Example: One line of a metes and bounds description from a survey made 20 years ago says, "80 feet north 30 degrees west to an iron pin set in concrete." This week a new survey is made of the property, and the surveyor finds the iron pin and the proper starting point for this call. However, the line's correct call based on the pin location is "82.35 feet north 30 degrees 08 minutes west to an iron pin set in concrete." Under the rule that monuments control over calls, the new surveyor should use his new measurements and not relocate the iron pin.

Quiz Yourself on *LAND DESCRIPTIONS*

39. Fran is buying a ranch that is supposed to have 300 acres. She has a friend who is a broker who said she must make sure the contract describes the ranch using the government survey system in terms of sections, half-sections, quarter-sections, and so on. If she does this, her friend says she will not need to get a boundary survey. Is this advice sound? _____

40. Eduardo contracts to buy an industrial property for $1.5 million. In advance of closing, he hires Bonita, a licensed surveyor, to survey the property. Bonita's survey fails to refer to an unused public alley, which runs along the entire rear boundary line. Eduardo does not know about the alley, and he completes the purchase. The property is worth $50,000 less due to the presence of the alley. Is Eduardo entitled to recover damages from Bonita? _____

41. Casper contracts to buy a house from Suzanne. The contract describes the property as "155 Pitts Place, more particularly described in Exhibit A attached thereto." Suzanne lives at a house at this address in Littleton, Anystate. Suzanne listed this house for sale with a broker, who showed the house to Casper. The broker prepared the contract. He had a copy of the survey Suzanne got six years ago when she bought the house—he planned to attach this as Exhibit A, but he forgot. When Casper signed the contract, it had no Exhibit A attached. Casper refused to close the purchase, and Suzanne sued for specific performance. What defenses, if any, are likely to be raised by Casper? _____

Answers

39. **No.** The government survey system has the advantage of standardized units of quantity, and the monuments that mark section corners are generally quite reliable. It is not necessarily true, however, that a particular description within the government survey system is better than a particular metes and bounds description. Fran plans to buy 300 acres, which is less than a section of land (640 acres). Assuming the ranch is located in a government survey, a good legal description will refer to the section or sections in which the ranch is located. Depending on the ranch's location and configuration, a proper description may consist solely of government survey subsections, or it may also use metes and bounds to describe one or more boundary lines.

Fran should almost certainly add a survey contingency to the contract and get a survey from a reputable surveyor. Even if the land is properly described solely by reference to the government survey system, there are still a number of risks that a survey will eliminate or reduce—it will confirm the quantity, show the relationship of the ranch to neighboring properties, show the placement of fences and other improvements relative to the record boundaries, and disclose encroachments and possible title problems like adverse possession and prescriptive easements.

40. **No.** It's not clear whether omission of the alley on the survey represents an error. Eduardo's argument is that easements, roads, and alleys are generally shown on surveys, and that under local practice a survey is deficient if it fails to note an alley. But even if he is right, he's not entitled to recover damages. Eduardo has the burden of proving that Bonita's work was negligent. The facts do not point to negligence—there's no evidence that Bonita knew about the alley, or that it was visible on the ground, or that the scope of her work included a search of public records to uncover easements, alleys, or rights-of-way.

41. **Statute of frauds.** Casper will claim the statute of frauds bars enforcement because the contract lacks an adequate description of the property. A court that takes the formalities of the statute seriously may agree with Casper for two reasons: (1) The address does not indicate the city or state. Conceivably, there are other properties elsewhere in the world with the same address. (2) An address by itself does not indicate how much land at that address is to be conveyed. In other words, although it indicates some street frontage at a given address, it does not describe boundary lines for the side yards and backyard.

A court that is concerned about ascertaining the parties' actual intent, and cares less about formalities, will probably enforce the contract. It will admit extrinsic evidence to show Suzanne owns a house at this address in Littleton, Anystate; that she listed it for sale with a broker; and that Casper viewed this house. With respect to boundaries and quantity, it will presume that the contract covers all the land that Suzanne owns at this address up to the neighbors' boundary lines. Under this approach, there will be a serious problem only if Suzanne weakens her case by claiming she intended to sell less than all of her land to Casper.

The lack of Exhibit A is not likely to help either party much. Casper may claim the contract can't be enforced because the exhibit was never attached. But there is no express condition to this effect, and a court is likely to say that under the statute of frauds the issue is still whether *what is there*—the address—is sufficient. Suzanne may tender as evidence her survey as the parties' intended Exhibit A. However, since Casper never signed the survey nor the contract with a survey attached, the court should exclude this evidence. (Remember from Chapter 5 that multiple writings may satisfy the statute of frauds, but each writing must be signed by the party to be charged.)

Exam Tips on LAND DESCRIPTIONS

Most teachers do not test land descriptions in much detail. How much you ought to know, of course, depends upon the emphasis given to the topic during the course.

☛ **Types of land descriptions:** Remember, a parcel of land can be described by

☞ Metes and bounds,

☞ Use of the government survey system, or

☞ Reference to a lot shown on a subdivision plat.

They are alike in that each, when properly used, describes one and only one parcel of land.

☛ **Buyer should obtain survey:** If a question calls for you to advise a potential purchaser of land or critique a proposed contract from the buyer's point of view, don't forget about the value of getting a survey, coupled with drafting a good survey clause for the contract. This protects the client's expectations with respect to the quantity of the land and helps to safeguard against a variety of title defects and related problems.

☛ **Surveyor's liability:** A question dealing with a surveyor's potential liability for defective work is likely to raise an issue of standing to sue. Under the traditional view of privity of contract, only a client who hires a surveyor can sue for a negligent survey. The trend is to allow injured third parties, who detrimentally rely on an erroneous survey, to sue in contract (third-party beneficiary) or tort (negligent misrepresentation).

☛ **Statute of frauds:** Whenever a question refers to a contract of sale or a deed, there may be issues concerning the statute of frauds. It is easy to overlook the land description part of the statute of frauds. If, for example, the writing refers to property by street address, there is a good chance you will get credit for discussing whether the street address is legally sufficient.

CHAPTER 10

THE PUBLIC LAND RECORDS

ChapterScope ━━

This chapter examines the system for creating and maintaining public land records. Each state provides for the recordation of deeds and other instruments that affect title to land. Each state has its own recording statute, which establishes the system for that state.

- **Common law priorities:** The basic rule is "first in time, first in right."

- **Recording system:** The recording system provides methods for determining who owns a parcel of land and for ranking the priority of various interests.

- **Title search:** To search title, a person constructs a chain of title and then checks for adverse transfers.

- **Types of recording statutes:** The main types of recording acts are:

  - *Race statute:* The first to record wins.

  - *Notice statute:* The last bona fide purchaser (BFP) wins.

  - *Race-notice statute:* The first BFP to record wins.

- **Unrecorded valid interests:** Purchasers are subject to two main types of unrecorded interests:

  - Those interests that a good inspection of the land will reveal.

  - Those interests that are not recordable under the state recording statute.

- **Search problems:** Some interests, even though recorded, are hard or impossible to find.

━━━

I. COMMON LAW PRIORITY RULES

The basic common law rule for priorities is "first in time, first in right."

A. **Delivery:** The deed that is delivered first is "first in time." The date of signing by the grantor does not determine priority.

B. **Exception for prior equitable interest:** At common law, there is one circumstance where a subsequent interest takes priority over an earlier interest. An equitable claim is cut off by a subsequent purchaser who acquires legal title without notice of the prior equity.

C. **Significance of common law rules:** All states have recording acts that modify the common law priority rules, but the recording acts only partially displace the common law rules. Any subsequent purchaser who is not entitled to statutory protection is subject to the common law priority system.

II. FUNCTIONS OF RECORDING SYSTEM

A. Title assurance: The recording system provides a method for determining who owns any tract of land. Recorded instruments are public records that anyone is entitled to search and read.

B. Priority ranking: The recording system establishes relative priorities among successive transfers that do not directly conflict.

Example: A landowner leases her tract of land to a tenant for a term of 10 years, grants a right-of-way easement to a neighbor, and mortgages the land to secure a bank loan. These transfers are compatible—there is nothing wrong, dishonest, or unusual about a tract of land that is leased, mortgaged, and subject to an easement. It may be necessary, however, to determine priorities among the tenant, the easement holder, and the mortgagee. Does the easement owner have the right to use the right of way if the tenant objects? If the mortgagee forecloses, will the purchaser at the foreclosure take free and clear of the lease and the easement? We answer these questions by determining priority. If the easement is prior to the lease, the tenant cannot stop the easement owner from using the right of way. If the mortgage is prior to the easement and the lease, the foreclosure purchaser takes free of those interests.

III. TITLE SEARCH PROCESS

A. Construct chain of title: The searcher's first step is to construct the record chain of title, going back to a sovereign or a number of years (e.g., 40 or 50 years), consistent with local title practices.

B. Check for adverse recorded transfers: The searcher's second step is to check the records for adverse transfers by the present owner and by all previous owners in the chain of title.

C. Study recorded instruments: The searcher's third step is to read carefully all instruments found in steps 1 and 2.

D. Check other records: The searcher's last step is to check other records that may reflect adverse transfers, such as judgment liens, tax liens, and bankruptcy filings. See *O'Mara v. Town of Wappinger*, 879 N.E.2d 148 (N.Y. 2007), in which a subdivision plat approved in 1962 designated two lots to remain undeveloped as open space. A subsequent buyer of the lots was bound by the restriction, even though he did not know of the restriction and the plat was not recorded in the chain of title or referenced in the chain of title.

IV. TYPES OF RECORDING ACTS

All states have recording acts. They are alike in that subsequent takers sometimes beat prior valid interests. The distinctions among types of recording acts address when this happens.

A. Race statute: A subsequent purchaser who records first wins. Only three states have a race or "pure race" statute as their basic recording act.

Example: A jurisdiction's act provides: "No conveyance of land shall be valid to pass any property interest as against purchasers for a valuable consideration, but from the time of recordation."

B. Notice statute: A subsequent purchaser who takes without notice wins.

Example: A jurisdiction's act provides: "No conveyance or mortgage of real property shall be good against subsequent purchasers for value and without notice unless the same be recorded according to law."

C. Race-notice statute: A subsequent purchaser who takes without notice and who records first wins. This type of statute (compared to race and notice statutes) makes it the most difficult for BFPs to prevail.

Example: A jurisdiction's act provides: "No unrecorded conveyance or mortgage of real property shall be good against subsequent purchasers for value without notice, who shall first record."

D. Jurisdictions: Roughly half the states have notice statutes and the other half race-notice statutes. Only three states have a pure race statute as their general recording act: Delaware, Louisiana, and North Carolina.

V. BONA FIDE PURCHASER STATUS

A subsequent grantee or taker of an interest prevails against a prior-in-time interest if he is a bona fide purchaser (BFP). In notice and race-notice states, there are two requirements or prongs that a BFP must meet.

A. "Purchaser": The taker must pay value for the interest. More than nominal value is required.

1. **Mortgagee as purchaser:** When a mortgagee makes a loan, the money it lends generally counts as value under the recording acts.

   a. **Antecedent debt:** Taking a mortgage to secure a preexisting debt is not paying value. This creditor is a BFP for recording act purposes only if the creditor gives new consideration to the landowner in exchange for the mortgage (e.g., extension of due date, forbearance from collection efforts).

   Example: A landowner owes a creditor $50,000. This debt is unsecured. The creditor asks the landowner for security. The landowner grants the creditor a mortgage on her parcel to secure the debt. The antecedent debt is not "value" for purposes of making the mortgagee a BFP. The mortgagee takes subject to any prior unrecorded interests.

B. "Without notice"

1. **Actual notice:** The purchaser who has actual knowledge of a prior interest is disqualified. This is a state of mind test.

2. **Constructive notice:** The purchaser is charged with notice of all recorded interests. This is everything that a proper search of the public records should reveal.

   a. **Quitclaim deed:** Some older cases indicate that the presence of a quitclaim deed in the chain of title bars the taker from BFP status. Supposedly, it shows that in the past someone had doubts as to the quality of the title. Presently, this view is largely discredited.

3. **Inquiry notice:** When the purchaser has knowledge of facts that suggest that someone may have an unrecorded interest, he has the duty to inquire into the situation. This inquiry notice is less than actual notice that an unrecorded interest exists. The point is that inquiry may lead to actual notice of an interest.

   a. **Parties in possession:** The most important aspect of inquiry notice relates to inspecting the land. The purchaser has a duty to inspect the property and is charged with notice of the rights of parties in possession and other unrecorded interests that are visible from inspection.

      i. **Exception when record title and possession are consistent:** When a person's possession is consistent with the state of record title, usually there is no duty for the buyer to ask the possessor about the nature and extent of his claim. The buyer may assume that the possessor's claim matches the possessor's interest of record.

      Example: When property is owned by cotenants, whose estate is of record, a buyer does not have to inquire as to the rights of each cotenant. There is no duty to inquire, even if only one cotenant is in possession, because it is permissible and not unusual for cotenants to agree that all will not occupy. A different rule may apply, however, when the cotenants are former spouses. See *In re Weisman*, 5 F.3d 417 (9th Cir. 1993), finding a duty of inquiry when each former spouse still held an undivided one-half record interest to their former marital home, but the present possessors were the ex-husband and his new wife. The ex-wife had filed for bankruptcy, and the duty to inquire protected the ex-husband's interest under an unrecorded quitclaim deed to him from his ex-wife, executed as part of their property settlement.

   b. **Recorded instruments that point to other interests:** A purchaser may have a duty to go beyond the express terms of a recorded instrument to spot possible claims against the property. See *Pelfresne v. Village of Williams Bay*, 917 F.2d 1017 (7th Cir. 1990), in which the issue was whether a buyer of property took subject to a judgment ordering the razing of houses on the property. A judgment lien for $629, but not the judgment, was recorded. The court held that the buyer may have had the duty to look up the underlying judgment.

VI. OFF-RECORD RISKS

A. **Inquiry notice:** The doctrine of inquiry notice means the purchaser takes the risk of all unrecorded interests that he should have discovered.

B. **Unrecordable interests:** Recording acts protect BFPs only against an off-the-record interest that is capable of being recorded. Under every recording act, there are some interests in land that are not capable of being recorded. The scope of recording acts varies from state to state. The consequence of having nonrecordable rights in land is that a purchaser is bound by them, even though their existence is not ascertainable by a search of the records. There are two types of nonrecordable interests.

   1. **Interests that cannot be created by instrument:** Examples are claims of adverse possession, prescriptive easements, and marital property rights.

   2. **Instruments that are not eligible for recording:** The prime example is a statutory exception, which many states have, for short-term leases (e.g., one year or less).

Example: On July 5, Suzie agrees to rent her house to Travis for $500 per month for a one-year term to begin on August 1. On July 15, she sells the house to Pancho, who pays fair market value and takes and records a warranty deed. Suzie fails to tell Pancho about the lease. Pancho does not find out about the lease until August 1, when Travis shows up at the house and asks to take possession pursuant to his lease agreement. Travis's lease is an unrecordable interest. Thus, Pancho is not a BFP. Travis has the right to possession.

VII. BFP SHELTER RULE

Once a BFP cuts off a prior unrecorded interest, the BFP can transfer good title to any grantee. That grantee does not have to qualify as a BFP; he has "shelter" from the grantor BFP. It does not matter whether the grantee has notice of the prior interest. The old interest remains terminated.

A. Rationale: The reason the grantee who has notice of the old interest is sheltered is to protect the BFP. Without the BFP shelter rule, once the old interest becomes notorious or is recorded, the BFP's title would no longer be alienable. It would not be marketable because any successor would take subject to the old interest.

B. Exception for reacquisition by creator of prior interest: The BFP shelter rule does not apply when the BFP transfers title to the person who earlier created the prior unrecorded interest. The old interest is valid as against its creator. Otherwise, a person could rid herself of an obligation by "running title through" a BFP, i.e., arranging for a transfer and reacquisition for the purpose of cleansing title.

Example: Owner entered into a contract for deed (installment land contract), which was not recorded. Buyer under the contract for deed did not take possession of the property. Owner then borrowed $120,000, granting Lender a mortgage on the property to secure that loan. Owner then sold an undivided 70 percent interest in the property to X, who had actual notice of the unrecorded contract for deed. X later bought the mortgage from Lender, and claimed priority over Buyer. *Held*, even though Lender was a BFP whose mortgage was prior to Buyer's interest, X is not protected by the BFP shelter rule because he bought an ownership interest in the property with knowledge of the contract for deed. *Chergosky v. Crosstown Bell, Inc.*, 463 N.W.2d 522 (Minn. 1990). The court treated X the same as Owner for the purpose of not allowing an unfair "cleansing of title."

VIII. RECORDED INTERESTS THAT ARE DIFFICULT OR IMPOSSIBLE TO FIND

A. Name indexes: In most states, the public records are accessed through name indexes, sometimes also called *grantor-grantee indexes*. The searcher uses the name indexes to reconstruct the chain of title, then checks all record owners for the period of search for adverse conveyances. Some recorded documents are difficult or impossible to find this way.

1. Wild deed: A wild deed is both recorded and properly indexed in the name indexes, but cannot be found because the deed into the grantor is a missing link that was never recorded. This unrecorded deed into the grantor of the wild deed is an adverse conveyance vis-à-vis the chain of title being searched. Because the wild deed is completely impossible to find, courts treat it as unrecorded, even though it is actually recorded.

2. **Late-recorded deed:** A deed or other instrument is late recorded if there is a substantial gap in time between delivery and recordation and in the meantime the record owner has transferred ownership to someone else. The search difficulty is that the searcher will stop looking in the grantor indexes for adverse transfers after the time the record owner transferred to someone else.

3. **Early-recorded deed:** With an early-recorded deed, a person transfers an interest in land he does not own and subsequently acquires an estate in that land. If the grantor eventually gets title, the doctrine of *estoppel by deed* operates to transfer that title to the prior grantee.

4. **Effect of late-recorded and early-recorded deeds:** Courts split on whether late- and early-recorded deeds impart constructive notice. The policy choice is either (i) to reduce the time and costs of title searches by cutting off interests that are actually of record or (ii) to protect those who rely on early- and late-recorded instruments by expanding the scope of title searches.

B. **Tract indexes:** Tract indexes do not raise the search problems involving wild deeds and early- and late-recorded deeds because they reference all documents by legal description rather than name. Only a few states have official tract indexes. Title insurance companies and abstract companies, however, often produce and maintain their own tract indexes as part of the *title plant* they use in their business.

C. **Defective recorded instruments**

1. **Nondelivered deed:** This deed is void. See Chapter 8, part IV.A.2.

2. **Forged deed:** This deed is void. See Chapter 8, part IV.A.1.

3. **Improper acknowledgment:** All states limit recordation to documents that are properly acknowledged. Sometimes an unacknowledged or improperly acknowledged deed is nevertheless recorded. Most courts rule that a defectively acknowledged deed that is recorded does not impart constructive notice.

   a. **Latent versus patent defect:** Although many courts hold that all improperly acknowledged deeds fail to impart constructive notice, some courts distinguish between latent and patent defects. A deed with a latent defect imparts constructive notice, while a deed with a patent defect does not. The reason is that the title searcher cannot detect latent defects, but should spot patent defects.

   Example: Weaver signs a deed of trust to his property to secure a $400,000 loan. The deed of trust names a trustee, who holds title on behalf of the lender, as beneficiary. The trustee also acts as notary to acknowledge Weaver's signature on the deed of trust. This acknowledgment is improper—the trustee must act impartially, and state law does not allow the trustee to undertake another role in the transaction. This is a patent defect because by reading the deed of trust one can see that the trustee's name and the notary's name are identical. Subsequently, the federal government files a federal tax lien against Weaver. The federal tax lien is prior to the deed of trust because the latter instrument fails to impart constructive notice. *Metropolitan Nat'l Bank v. United States*, 901 F.2d 1297 (5th Cir. 1990).

4. **Misindexed deed:** Sometimes the recording office indexes a deed improperly, such as misspelling the grantor's last name, or even fails to make any entry for an instrument into the index. States split over whether a misindexed deed or an unindexed deed gives constructive notice.

   a. **Risk on searcher:** In most states, delivery for recording gives constructive notice even if not indexed or indexed incorrectly. Courts have interpreted the language of their recording statutes to hold that indexing is not required for recordation, despite the fact that the deed may be impossible for a title searcher to find. This is the same as the Uniform Commercial Code rule for indexing mistakes in financing statements, filed to perfect Article 9 security interests. UCC § 9-517.

   Example: Trustee held record title to a parcel of land, with the recorded deed to the trustee naming not only the trustee, but also the trust beneficiary. The trustee mortgaged the property. The recorder's office properly recorded the mortgage, but it wrongly indexed the mortgage by entering the beneficiary's name as mortgagor, rather than the trustee's name. The trustee subsequently sold the property to a buyer, whose title search failed to reveal the mortgage. *Held*, the buyer takes subject to the mortgage because under the recording statute, constructive notice to subsequent purchasers is based on recording the mortgage, not on its indexing. *First Citizens National Bank v. Sherwood*, 879 A.2d 178 (Pa. 2005).

   b. **Risk on recording party:** A growing number of states now interpret their recording acts to mandate proper indexing in order for a deed or other instrument to be legally recorded.

Quiz Yourself on
THE PUBLIC LAND RECORDS

42. On June 1, Aloysius, the owner of Blackacre, delivers to Barnacle a deed that purports to convey a present fee simple estate in Blackacre. On July 1, Aloysius leases Blackacre to Euripides for a five-year term. On August 1, Barnacle records his deed. On September 1, Euripides records his lease. None of the parties is in possession of any part of Blackacre during the time period these transactions took place. Does Euripides have a valid lease under:

    (a) a race statute? _____

    (b) a notice statute? _____

    (c) a race-notice statute? _____

43. Moe deeds Stoogeacre, a vacant five-acre tract of land, to Curly on April 1. On April 3, Curly is evicted from his apartment. He immediately drives to Stoogeacre and pitches a tent, where he begins to live. On April 5, Moe deeds Stoogeacre to Larry, who pays value in exchange for the conveyance. Larry has no knowledge of Moe's deed to Curly. On April 7, Larry records his deed. On April 9, Moe records his deed. Who owns Stoogeacre under:

    (a) a race statute? _____

    (b) a notice statute? _____

    (c) a race-notice statute? _____

44. Alice sells Greenacre to Brian, who pays a price equivalent to the property's fair market value. Alice delivers a deed to Brian, who does not record. Alice then borrows $20,000 from Carol, granting her a mortgage to secure the loan. Brian records. Carol records. Carol then sells her mortgage loan to David. He takes possession of the promissory note signed by Alice and records an assignment of mortgage signed by Carol. Alice defaults in paying the mortgage to David, who seeks to foreclose on Greenacre.

 (a) Is the mortgage valid under a race statute? _____

 (b) Is the mortgage valid under a race-notice statute? _____

 (c) Is the mortgage valid under a notice statute? _____

45. Same facts as prior question, except instead of selling Greenacre to Brian, Alice made a gift to him of Greenacre.

 (a) Is the mortgage valid under a race statute? _____

 (b) Is the mortgage valid under a race-notice statute? _____

 (c) Is the mortgage valid under a notice statute? _____

46. A deed contains a notarization that states that the instrument was signed in Georgia, but the grantor actually signed the instrument in the presence of the notary while in the State of Alabama. Is this a latent defect or a patent defect? _____

47. Monica deeds land to Bruno Hoopmaker. Hoopmaker takes the deed to the proper office for recording. The recording office uses name indexes, and the employee makes a mistake, indexing the deed under "Hopmaker, Bruno." Monica subsequently totals her Jeep Wrangler after letting her car insurance lapse. She defaults on her car loan. The lender obtains a default judgment against Monica and a judgment lien against all of her real estate. Is Hoopmaker's property subject to the judgment lien? _____

Answers

42. (a) No. Barnacle is first in time, so he prevails unless Euripides qualifies as a BFP. Euripides cannot be a BFP under a race statute because he recorded his lease after Barnacle recorded his deed.

 (b) Yes, probably. To qualify as a BFP under a notice statute, Euripides must have paid value for the lease without having notice of the conveyance to Barnacle. The facts don't suggest that Euripides had notice. Euripides' payment of rent qualifies as value.

 (c) No. Barnacle prevails under a race-notice statute because he recorded before Euripides.

43. (a) Larry. Under a race statute, a purchaser who records first prevails. When Larry recorded, Moe's deed was not yet recorded.

 (b) Curly. Although Larry had no knowledge of Moe's deed to Curly, Curly was living on Stoogeacre on April 5, when Larry purchased. Larry had inquiry notice from Curly's possession.

 (c) Curly. Although Larry recorded before Curly, this is not enough under a race-notice statute. Larry has notice of Curly's claim due to Curly's possession, just as in Question 43(b).

44. **(a) No.** Brian is "first in time," so he is first in right as against David under common law logic. To uphold his mortgage, David must rely on the state recording act. David, however, has no plausible claim that he is a BFP—he is the last guy on the scene, and when he bought the mortgage from Carol, Brian's deed was of record. To win, David must rely on the BFP shelter rule by claiming that his predecessor, Carol, qualified as a BFP. Carol, as mortgagee, is a "purchaser" for recording act purposes and clearly has paid value. Carol, however, is not protected under a race statute. She recorded the mortgage after Brian recorded his deed and thus has lost the race.

    (b) No. Just as for the race statute, Carol cannot qualify as a BFP because she recorded the mortgage after Brian recorded his deed. A race-notice statute only protects a BFP who records before the holder of the prior interest records.

    (c) Yes. Carol is a BFP under a notice statute, provided she lacked notice of the Alice-to-Brian transaction when she paid value by advancing the $20,000. At that time, Carol did not have constructive notice because Brian had not recorded. The facts do not indicate anything that would have given Carol actual or inquiry notice. Further research into the facts may be necessary. Many law teachers want students to identify what additional facts need to be investigated and why they may be relevant. Thus, a brief discussion of facts bearing on actual or inquiry notice may strengthen your answer.

45. **(a) No.** It does not matter whether Brian, the holder of the earlier-in-time interest, paid value or took the property as a gift. Under the recording act, it is only the subsequent purchaser who claims to be a BFP who must pay value. Thus, the analysis is completely the same whether Brian is a purchaser or a donee.

    (a) No. See answer to 45(a).

    (b) Yes. See answer to 45(a).

46. **Latent defect.** A latent defect in an acknowledgment is one that cannot be detected by only studying the instrument. To uncover the defect, one needs to obtain information that is not displayed on the deed. Here the deed states the grantor signed the deed in Georgia, with no clue on the face of the deed that the grantor actually signed in Alabama.

47. **Probably.** Hoopmaker's property is subject to the judgment lien. Most states follow the traditional rule that puts the risk of misindexing on the searcher. The rationale is that the recording act describes what is necessary for a person to record a deed, and the statute just says to present the instrument to the office for filing along with payment of the proper fee. Hoopmaker thus wins, and there is no need to evaluate the seriousness of the spelling mistake.

    In some states, indexing is considered legally part of the recording process. Thus, a completely unindexed deed is treated as unrecorded despite the fact that it physically was reproduced and maintained in a book or volume as part of the title records. For deeds like Hoopmaker's, which are in the index, but with some error, the case turns on the materiality of the error. Hoopmaker wins if the court determines a reasonable prudent searcher should have seen the entry "Hopmaker, Bruno" in the index. If the searcher had seen the entry, he would then have looked at the column for the "Legal Description" and would have seen that it affected the land he was searching. Hoopmaker may win on this fact issue, but the outcome cannot be predicted with confidence. In a small county that has printed "hard copy" alphabetized indexes, the entry for Hopmaker and Hoopmaker may be very close together on the same page, so a searcher scanning the list should easily spot the problem. In a large county, a hard copy index may have many names between Hoopmaker and Hopmaker, making the mistake hard to find. In modern systems that use computerized index databases rather than hard copy, the issues are whether the search software is set up to retrieve alternate spellings, whether Hoopmaker and Hopmaker would be considered alternate spellings, and whether the searcher has a duty on his own to search for possible variations in spelling.

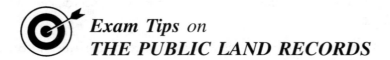

Exam Tips on
THE PUBLIC LAND RECORDS

☛ **Types of recording acts:** Be sure to know the three types of recording acts:

☞ **Race statute:** Under the race statute, the first to record wins.

☞ **Notice statute:** Under the notice statute, the subsequent purchaser who takes without notice wins.

☞ **Race-notice statute:** Under the race-notice statute, the subsequent purchaser who takes without notice and records first wins.

☛ **Consider each act:** Unless the exam question clearly tells you what type of recording act applies, give analysis for what happens under all three types.

☛ **Label the act:** If the facts give you the text of the jurisdiction's recording act, you of course are expected to categorize the act as one of the three basic types.

☛ **Evaluate BFP status:** When there are conflicting conveyances, be sure to discuss whether the *subsequent taker* meets the BFP requirements of (1) paying value and (2) taking without notice (in notice and race-notice jurisdictions). Remember that if a person takes by gift or by intestate succession (inheritance or a devise under a will), such a person can never qualify as a BFP.

☛ **Shelter rule:** Look out for the BFP shelter rule. Teachers like to slip this into the exam. The shelter rule protects any grantee who acquires title from a BFP, even if that grantee did not pay value or had notice of the prior unrecorded interest. The grantee is "sheltered" by the BFP.

☛ **Indexing problems:** Be prepared to distinguish a wild deed from a deed that is either late recorded or early recorded. The wild deed is completely unfindable in a name index system because there's a missing link. All courts treat wild deeds as unrecorded.

☞ **Late-recorded and early-recorded deed:** Conversely, the late-recorded deed and the early-recorded deed are recorded out of sequence, but they are nevertheless findable. The searcher just has to do more work by looking at more index books. There is a split of authority as to whether late-recorded and early-recorded instruments are considered to be recorded.

☛ **Constructive notice:** If the facts indicate a deed or other instrument is not acknowledged (not notarized), or there is something improper about the acknowledgment or notarization, you should discuss the possibility that the deed does not impart constructive notice. This means it is treated as if it were unrecorded.

CHAPTER 11

TITLE PRODUCTS

ChapterScope ─────────────────────────────────────

This chapter examines the three major types of title assurance, including abstracts, opinions, and insurance.

■ **Title abstract:** A title abstract is a summary report of all of the instruments of record for a particular tract of land. It purports to collect and report on all known and recorded information related to the title of a particular piece of property.

■ **Title opinion:** Title opinions are generally, but not always, issued by attorneys and are known as attorneys' title opinions and certificates. These reports are the opinion of the author, usually based on review of an abstract of title, and they inform the reader about the author's opinion as to the status of title to a property.

■ **Title insurance:** The two types of title insurance policies are the owner's policy and the lender's policy. The owner's policy insures the estate or interest of the title holder. The lender's policy insures the priority of a lender's lien and interest in the property.

───

I. TITLE ABSTRACTS

The abstract is a summary of all deeds and other instruments for a tract of land found by searching the public records. Other instruments might include, for example, leases, easements, mortgages, and liens.

A. **Types of abstracts:** There are several types of abstracts in use.

    1. **Complete abstract:** A complete abstract takes the chain of title back to the sovereign. This is sometimes referred to as an EPR (earliest public records) abstract.

    2. **Partial abstract:** Today, many searches go back only a customary period, such as 50 or 60 years (or in the case of many recently built subdivisions perhaps only 3-7 years). The time period may be based on a state statute or on local custom, or on insurance underwriting guidelines.

    3. **Updated abstract:** An abstract of title, once issued, is generally kept by the landowner who purchased it. The company issuing the update searches only the records from the date of the original abstract to the present; it does not check the records covered by the original abstract to make sure it is accurate. This is also sometimes referred to as a "continuation" abstract. An exception to this practice might arise when a property originally had a relatively low value at the time of a prior abstract and a planned change in use will make it significantly more valuable in the current economic context. For example, a title search might have been done 15 years earlier on a 100-acre farm valued at $300,000, and today a developer plans to acquire the property to build a $50 million golf course community. Such a change in use and escalation in value would likely prompt most title companies to go back behind the date of the last title abstract.

B. Standard for liability: An abstractor's liability for an erroneous title abstract generally is based on negligence. This is a professional malpractice standard that largely turns on community standards. *Bank of Cave City v. Abstract & Title Co.*, 828 S.W.2d 852 (Ark. Ct. App. 1992).

C. Who may rely on abstract

1. **Those in privity rule:** The traditional rule is that only the client who purchased the abstract may rely on it, based on privity of contract.

2. **Third-party beneficiaries:** Many courts expand liability to protect a third party when, at the time the abstract is ordered, it is clear the abstract will be given to a third party, like a buyer or mortgagee, who can be expected to rely on it. *First American Title Insurance Co. v. First Title Service Co.*, 457 So. 2d 467 (Fla. 1984).

3. **Subsequent buyers of land:** Under a tort theory of negligent misrepresentation, some courts extend liability to protect all subsequent buyers of the land who receive and rely on the title abstract to their detriment. *Williams v. Polgar*, 215 N.W.2d 149 (Mich. 1974).

   Example: A mortgage from Lady Godiva is recorded and indexed in the grantor index under "Gadiva, Lady." Suppose the state follows the view that the risk of misindexing is on the searcher. The abstractor does not find the mortgage, and this causes loss to a purchaser. The abstractor is liable only if negligent. Would a reasonable searcher checking for conveyances by Godiva have seen the entry under "Gadiva"? In an index with an appreciable number of entries under the letter "G," the answer is probably not. Abstractor wins.

II. ATTORNEYS' TITLE OPINIONS AND CERTIFICATES

The attorney's title opinion or title certificate, based on the evidence examined by the attorney, states a professional opinion as to the status and marketability of title to property. Normally, the attorney does not guarantee or warrant the title.

A. Standard for liability: When a title opinion is erroneous and the client suffers loss due to a title defect, the attorney's liability depends on proof of negligence. A professional liability standard applies, based on the norms established by and followed in the local community of real estate lawyers.

1. **Marketable title standard:** The attorney has a duty to disclose each item of record that is a *cloud* on title even if there is some basis for arguing that the possible adverse claim is not legitimate. *North Bay Council, Inc., Boy Scouts v. Bruckner*, 563 A.2d 428 (N.H. 1989). A cloud is a title matter that raises questions about the status of title to a property. It need not rise to the level of proving to be an actual defect, as long as it raises a question or a doubt about the quality of title. Title subject to a cloud does not meet the general marketability standard of title as implied in most contracts of purchase and sale (unless the contract provides otherwise).

2. **Attorney's representation of scope of work:** The opinion or certificate should clearly disclose the work the attorney had done in order to prepare the opinion. This provides appropriate information to the user as to information reviewed in forming the opinion, and it should be in writing to limit the potential liability of the attorney. For example, if the attorney only reviewed a partial title report, this should be expressly noted, and the opinion should be limited to items specifically in that title report.

B. **Who may rely on attorney's title opinion:** The principles here are much the same as for reliance on title abstracts.

1. **Those in privity:** Many courts limit recovery to the client to whom the title opinion is given. Some courts reject privity, imposing tort liability for negligent misrepresentation on the attorney on the theory that a third party has justifiably relied on the faulty title information.

2. **Third-party beneficiaries:** The attorney may know the client intends to give the opinion to a third party who will rely on it.

3. **Subsequent buyers of land:** Under the tort of negligent misrepresentation, an attorney may conceivably be liable to subsequent buyers who receive the title opinion and rely on it to their detriment.

III. TITLE INSURANCE: OWNERS' AND LENDERS' POLICIES

Title insurance is an alternative to an abstract of title or a lawyer's opinion. Gradually, title insurance has captured a greater and greater share of the market. A primary reason for this growth is the evolution of national markets for real estate finance since the 1960s.

A. **Primary functions:** Title insurance serves two primary functions.

1. **Search and disclosure:** The title insurer searches the records and discloses its findings to the insured by issuing a title commitment and later a title policy. In many ways, this is similar to the process of reviewing and preparing a title abstract. The difference is that this title report is related to the terms and conditions of the title insurance product and the regulations governing the title insurance industry.

2. **Risk spreading:** The title policy provides insurance for undisclosed risks. This is risk spreading among the pool of insured policyholders.

B. **Process of issuing title insurance policy:** The title insurance company takes several steps that lead up to the issuance of an owner's policy or a lender's policy.

1. **Title search:** First, the company either conducts or obtains a title search on the parcel.

2. **Title commitment:** Based on the title search, the company issues its written commitment. Based on the search results, the commitment often specifies curative action that must be taken before the company issues the policy. Curative action may require such things as getting a satisfaction of an outstanding lien or mortgage, or filing a corrective document to correct a typo in an earlier deed. A title commitment is generally issued prior to closing with the anticipation of a policy being issued after the closing.

3. **Title policy:** After closing on the transaction, the documents of title transfer are recorded, and a final policy of title insurance is issued. The policy shows the newly recorded documents and insures title in the new owner.

   Example: In the chain of title, the insurer finds that 10 years ago the land was deeded to "Jamie Smith" and six years ago "Jamie Smith Gonzalez" deeded the land to the next owner. The company should require curative action to establish that this is the same person so there is no break in the ***record chain of title***. Perhaps this name change is due to a change in marital status. The cure might consist of a notarized affidavit from this individual confirming the facts, or it might take the form of a correction deed from this individual.

    a. Specific exceptions: When the title search discloses outstanding interests in the property, they are listed on the commitment as specific exceptions to coverage. Easements, real covenants and servitudes, mortgages, and outstanding mineral rights are examples.

    b. Closing requirements: The commitment usually lists the documents needed at closing to establish the title the parties expect to be insured. These might include the need for a satisfaction of mortgage for an earlier mortgage, a deed from the grantor to the grantee, and a new mortgage for the buyer's lender.

C. Absolute liability: The insurer is absolutely liable to pay claims for insured defects covered by the policy. In contrast to abstracts of title and attorneys' opinions, the insured need not prove fault or negligence of the insurer in order to recover. Instead of proving fault, the insured must prove that the loss is covered by the terms of the insurance policy.

Example: A title company issued title insurance for a lender. After closing on the transaction and recording of the appropriate documents, a special taxing district levied a tax against the underlying property. The tax would have to be paid on sale of the property. When a sale was contemplated, the proposed buyer learned of the substantial tax payment and decided not to go ahead with the deal. The insured under the policy sought recovery for loss resulting from the imposition of the tax. The title company responded by denying coverage. The title company demonstrated that the policy effective date was the date of recording of the insured mortgages, and this was prior to the tax levy date. Under the title policy, an insured is only covered for items that predate the effective date of the policy. Consequently, the insured was not covered for this loss. *Vestin Mortgage, Inc. v. First American Title Insurance Co.*, 139 P.3d 1055 (Utah 2006).

D. Policy exclusions and general exceptions: All title insurance policies have preprinted exclusions and exceptions. Exclusions from coverage include such things as zoning and interests that arise after the effective date of the policy. Exceptions include such matters as outstanding real property taxes, matters that would be discovered by a survey, and the presence of adverse possessors. See *White v. Western Title Insurance Co.*, 710 P.2d 309 (Cal. 1985).

E. Off-record risks: A number of title risks that are not reflected by the public records are covered by title insurance policies. In *Kayfirst Corp. v. Washington Terminal Co.*, 813 F. Supp. 67 (D.D.C. 1993), title insurance covered a loss from a subsurface trespass.

    1. Survey exceptions: Policies generally have an exception for "matters which would be disclosed by an accurate survey." A good survey will disclose many types of off-record title risks if they are present. The company is willing to delete this exception if it receives a satisfactory new survey.

F. Who may rely on title insurance: Protection does not run to subsequent purchasers or grantees of the property. Each new owner must obtain a new policy. The policy contains a definition section that specifically describes the insured under the policy.

    1. Warrantor's coverage: When an insured owner conveys by warranty deed, the standard insurance policy protects the grantor if a title defect results in a claim against the grantor based on the deed covenants of title.

G. **Recovery on title insurance:** When a title risk is covered by a title insurance policy (not excluded or excepted), the title company is absolutely liable. Recovery is limited to an actual loss and to the stated amount of coverage provided in the policy.

H. **Tort liability:** Courts have split on the issue of whether a title insurer has an implied duty to conduct a reasonable search before issuing a policy. Generally, however, courts enforce the title commitment and policy as they are written, holding that the only basis for recovery is in contract.

1. **Significance of tort theory:** The action in tort allows for a higher recovery with no dollar limit. It also means that one is not limited by the contract exceptions and exclusions in the title insurance policy. Finally, it means that punitive damages are available.

I. **Ethical problems:** Ethical problems sometimes arise in connection with the issuance of title insurance.

1. **Conflicts of interest:** A conflict of interest may be present when an attorney or law firm serves as *agent* or as *examining counsel* for a title company and also represents another party to the real estate transaction, such as buyer or lender.

2. **Confidentiality:** A confidentiality problem may arise if the attorney learns of a title problem that is unknown to the title company.

3. **Good faith and fair dealing:** An insurance company owes its insured the duty of good faith and fair dealing.

Quiz Yourself on TITLE PRODUCTS

48. Jennifer purchased a waterfront property for $1 million. She purchased an abstract of title that was delivered just prior to closing on the property. The abstract did not identify any title problems or defects. After being on the property for about a month, she saw someone walking across her lot with a canoe to enter the water. Before the person, Frankie, got all the way to the water, Jennifer stopped him and asked him what he was doing trespassing on her property. Frankie seemed puzzled and said he was not trespassing but had been granted an easement of access by the prior owner, which he said had been duly recorded years ago. As it turned out, Frankie was telling the truth. The prior owner had granted an easement and it had been recorded. The problem was that the prior owner, Devon, inherited the property from his mother and prior to getting title of record had granted the easement to Frankie, who recorded. The abstract company failed to find the access easement granted by Devon to Frankie five years ago. The easement instrument is an early-recorded instrument because Devon granted it while his mother still owned the property (see Chapter 10). Four years ago, Devon's mother died, and Devon took title as her sole devisee and later sold the property to Jennifer. Can Jennifer recover from the abstract company? _____

49. Grace has lost title to the property she bought two years ago from Hank. A deed executed and recorded five years ago was forged, and the true owner, Karen, whose signature was forged, has repossessed the

property. In each situation below, please explain whether Grace has a right to recover damages for the loss of her property against the person who issued the title product. _____

(a) An abstract of title that she purchased that shows the chain of title for the past 50 years. The forged deed is abstracted, and the abstract says nothing about the deed being suspicious.

(b) An opinion letter from her attorney, in which she certifies "based upon my personal search of the public records, it is my opinion that you have marketable title. . . ."

(c) An owner's policy of title insurance issued to Hank two years ago. Does it matter whether Grace now has the original policy? Whether Hank formally assigned it to her?

(d) An owner's policy of title insurance that she purchased when she bought the property from Hank.

Answers

48. **Maybe.** First, we have to decide whether the easement is valid. In some states, an early-recorded instrument is outside of the chain of title and is cut off by a subsequent BFP who buys without notice of the interest. If this is the state's position, the easement is extinguished, and Jennifer has clear title and no loss, and thus cannot recover from the abstractor. If state law provides that early-recorded instruments are within the chain of title (i.e., they impart constructive notice), then the easement is valid, and Jennifer's title is encumbered by it. Now Jennifer can recover from the company. It had the duty to search for early-recorded instruments, and presumably, if it had done so in a nonnegligent fashion, it would have found and abstracted the easement

49. (a) **Grace has no privity problem because she purchased the abstract from the abstract company.** However, she must prove the abstract company committed negligence in failing to recognize the forgery. Grace loses unless there is something fishy concerning the appearance of the recorded forged deed. If, for example, the deed is not acknowledged at all and the abstract does not disclose this flaw, she has a good case.

(b) **Again Grace has no privity problem.** She can recover on the attorney's opinion only if she can prove negligence. The analysis here is precisely the same as for the abstract. Unless there is some defect on the face of the forged deed that should have prompted further inquiry, she loses.

(c) **Grace has no protection under Hank's policy of title insurance whether she has the original policy or a formal assignment.** She is not the "insured."

(d) **Grace may recover her loss under the owner's policy that she bought.** The policy provides absolute protection for covered risks. It does not matter whether the company was negligent in searching or in failing to uncover the forgery. This kind of a title problem is covered by the standard terms of an owner's policy. Since Grace has suffered a total loss of title, the face amount of the policy is the maximum amount she can recover. Her actual loss may be more than this amount but her maximum recovery on the policy is limited to the value stated in it. If she actually loses more than what can be recovered by the policy she may be able to go back against her grantor to recover under one of the standard deed warranties.

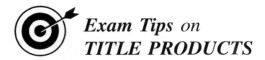

Exam Tips on TITLE PRODUCTS

☞ **Determine the form of title assurance (abstract, opinion, title insurance):** The first step in addressing title assurance is to determine which of the three types of products is being used: the abstract, title opinion, or title insurance. This should be compared to the contract to see if it is in compliance with the agreement between the parties.

☞ **Define the standard of liability:** Once you determine the type of title product being used, consider the standard of liability under each type and discuss the standard that applies to the given situation. The abstract and opinion are fault-based liability. Title insurance is strict liability for matters covered by the insurance.

☞ **Set the scope of liability:** In addition to discussing the standard of liability in each situation, one must be careful to address the scope of liability. In other words, once you know the standard you must identify the group of potential people capable of suing to recover on that standard. Think in terms of who has privity (a contract action), and also in terms of who is reasonably foreseeable in terms of reliance (a tort action).

☞ **Classify conflicting interest in terms of being on or off the public record:** Be sure to distinguish between on-record and off-record interests and to address the specific exception, exclusions, and limitations that may be contained in the facts or in the type of product used. Also consider the interplay of recording statutes, curative acts, and other title rules.

☞ **Consider the potential to raise the issue of attorney liability to a nonclient:** If it seems a third party has relied on an attorney's erroneous title opinion, study the facts carefully. As an example, an attorney for a lender may be explaining documents at closing to the borrower. There may be a claim of dual or multiple representation, which is an alternative theory for the disappointed owner who is harmed by the title defect. These are *alternative* theories of recovery. The owner pleads (1) based on the facts, "I reasonably expected that you were acting as my attorney in connection with the search, and (2) if you were not my attorney, you are liable to me under the principle of third-party beneficiary or negligent misrepresentation."

☞ **Consider alternative actions for recovery:** In addition to considering the ways to recover under a title insurance policy, abstract, or attorney opinion, always assess alternative paths to potential recovery for a loss. For example, losses due to a title defect may be covered by one of the traditional warranties in the deed of conveyance. Other defects that result in a loss may be exceptions to the doctrine of merger.

CHAPTER 12

IMPROVING THE EFFICIENCY OF THE TITLE SYSTEM

ChapterScope

This chapter considers the various measures used to improve the U.S. recording system. They include title standards, adverse possession, title curative statutes, marketable title acts, and Torrens legislation.

- ■ **Title standards:** Title standards reflect a bar-approved consensus on what title defects or flaws are bad enough to make title unmarketable.

- ■ **Adverse possession:** Adverse possession clears titles of old interests when the owner has been out of possession for a long time.

- ■ **Curative acts:** Title curative acts are state statutes that cure minor defects after a specified number of years.

- ■ **Marketable title acts:** A marketable title act extinguishes interests older than the root of title even if they are recorded.

- ■ **Torrens:** Under the Torrens system, used in a few states, the certificate of title issued by the government is conclusive on ownership.

I. TITLE STANDARDS

State bar organizations in about half of the states have adopted statewide standards for reviewing and approving titles. The standards reflect a bar-approved consensus of what defects or flaws are significant enough to impair marketable title.

A. Minor variations in names: Often, there are minor variations in names in recorded instruments. Standards address the significance of such variations, indicating that certain variations are very unlikely to present risk and should not be the basis of title objections.

    Example: A chain of title shows a deed conveying Whitewater to "William Clinton." Three years later "Wm. Clinton" deeded the same land to George Bush. Bar standards typically provide that customary abbreviations for names are permissible. Thus, Bush has marketable title.

B. Period of search: Bar standards often prescribe a recommended period of search. Georgia and Massachusetts, for example, recommend 50 years.

C. Legal effect: Bar title standards are not statutory and do not have the force of law. Courts often defer to them when deciding whether a particular problem is significant enough to impair marketable title, but the standards do not bind courts. In *Staley v. Stephens*, 404 N.E.2d 633 (Ind. Ct. App. 1980), a house built 10 years ago encroached on a setback line established by a restrictive covenant. The court ruled that title was unmarketable, rejecting a county bar standard that title was marketable if an encroachment was in place for at least two years.

D. Parties' incorporation of bar standards: Under a contract for the purchase of land, the buyer normally has the right to marketable title. See Chapter 8, part I.A. Under this implied rule, the courts may or may not defer to the bar title standards. Many standard-form contracts, however, explicitly define marketable title by reference to specified bar title standards. For example, a standard-form contract of sale used in Georgia provides: "Buyer shall have reasonable time within which to examine title and within which to furnish Seller with a written statement of objections affecting the marketability of said title, the validity of which shall be determined according to the title standards of the State Bar of Georgia." When the parties include such a clause, the title standards are normally dispositive of the buyer's right to make a title objection.

   1. Drafting consideration: If you review a contract that expressly incorporates state or local title standards, you should not accept this language unless you have read the standards and believe that you fully understand them. Bar standards are "one size fits all," and their allocation of risk between seller and buyer may not be best for your client. In particular, if you represent a buyer of valuable commercial property, your proper threshold of risk may be lower than that set by the bar standards.

II. ADVERSE POSSESSION

Adverse possession plays two principal roles that impact land titles. It is a two-edged sword with respect to the reliability of the paper records. One role improves record titles, and the second diminishes record titles.

A. Title-clearing function: Adverse possession strengthens titles to land by barring potential claims of persons who are not in possession of a parcel of land after a specified period of time has elapsed, provided that certain conditions are met. This defeats many old, stale interests of record.

   Example: Twenty-three years ago, Roscoe died intestate, survived by three daughters, Aviva, Brett, and Camilla. At the time of his death, Roscoe owned his house in fee simple, and Aviva and Brett lived with him. Camilla had moved to Australia long ago. Aviva and Brett took charge of Roscoe's estate, and six months after his death they sold the house to Sanchez. Camilla did not consent to or participate in the sale, and her sisters did not give her any of the sales proceeds. Sanchez recorded his deed, and he and his family took possession and have lived in the house ever since. If Sanchez has met the jurisdiction's requirements for adverse possession (which appears probable), Camilla's ownership interest as one of Roscoe's heirs is extinguished. This outcome makes Sanchez's record title secure; his deed, which purported to give him clear title to 100 percent of the property, now has that effect.

B. Modification of boundary lines: Adverse possession of a strip or area between neighboring landowners often changes the record boundary line, substituting a new boundary to conform to the line of actual possession. This undercuts the recording system by preferring the parties' actual possessions and expectations to the boundaries described in the records. A person conducting a title search will expect that the area and boundaries of the property will conform to the records, but the actual ownership will differ due to the impact of adverse possession.

III. TITLE CURATIVE ACTS

Many states have passed title curative acts to address the problems raised by defective instruments of record. These acts provide that instruments bearing certain defects are conclusively presumed valid after the passage of a specified number of years after recordation.

A. Types of defects: Problems commonly solved by curative acts include a missing or defective acknowledgment, the failure to pay the recording fee or a transfer tax, and lack of delivery. In *Bummer v. Collier,* 864 P.2d 453 (Wyo. 1993), the court held that Wyoming's curative act did not correct the failure of a lien instrument to provide a proper legal description of the property. After 10 years, the act cured defects and irregularities in the formalities of execution, recording, attestation, and acknowledgment of instruments. The land description was more than a formality because the cure of insufficient descriptions would make the records unreliable.

B. Period of time: The time that must pass for a defect to be cured is specified by the act and varies from state to state. Periods typically range from 3 to 21 years.

C. Legal effect: Unlike bar title standards, a title curative act is state legislation and binds the courts. There may of course be problems of statutory interpretation, but if the court decides the statute covers a particular defect, title is marketable—period, end of question.

Example: A curative act provides that after five years an instrument that is not acknowledged is valid as if it were duly acknowledged. Suppose your title search reveals an unacknowledged deed in the chain of title that has been on record for eight years. Title is plainly marketable because of the curative act. Without the act, the purchaser would have to make a judgment about whether to raise a title objection. If the purchaser objected, the seller might respond by trying to cure the problem, perhaps by getting a correction deed from the grantor. Alternatively, the seller might respond by claiming the objection was unreasonable, title was marketable despite the old unacknowledged deed, and thus seller had no duty to take curative action. Were litigation to result, in many states the outcome would be difficult to predict, given the typical broad, flexible definitions of marketable title (e.g., a title free from reasonable doubt).

IV. MARKETABLE TITLE ACTS

The basic concept is to extinguish interests that are older than *the root of title*. Sometimes the legislation is referred to as a *marketable record title act*. Twenty states presently have marketable title legislation: California, Connecticut, Florida, Illinois, Indiana, Iowa, Kansas, Michigan, Minnesota, Nebraska, North Carolina, North Dakota, Ohio, Oklahoma, Rhode Island, South Dakota, Utah, Vermont, Wisconsin, and Wyoming.

A. Goals: There are two primary goals of marketable title legislation:

1. Limited search: To limit the period of time covered by title searches to a set period, such as 30, 40, or 50 years. A searcher does not have to consult older indexes or read older documents.

2. Eliminate stale interests: To render more titles marketable by eliminating stale interests. A buyer cannot assert a valid title objection on the basis of an old interest extinguished by the legislation. See *H & F Land, Inc. v. Panama City-Bay County Airport and Industrial District,* 736 So. 2d 1167 (Fla. 1999), holding that Florida's act extinguishes a common law easement by necessity that is not asserted by its owner within the statutory period. But see *Blanton v. City of Pinellas Park*, 887 So. 2d 1224 (Fla. 2004), holding that Florida's act does not extinguish a statutory easement by necessity because entitlement to such an easement does not depend upon facts contained in the chain of title.

B. **Root of title:** The marketable title act operates to extinguish interests and defects that are older than the "root of title," which is the most recent deed or other instrument of title in the record chain of title that is more than 30 years old (or the statutory period).

C. **Function:** An interest created prior to the root of title no longer affects title unless it is referred to in the root or in a post-root instrument or reflected by possession after the root of title.

   1. **Preserving old interests:** The holder of an old interest can preserve that interest by rerecording the instrument or by filing a notice to continue that interest. A specific reference to the old interest in a post-root instrument also preserves the interest.

       Example: A 1925 subdivision plat, recorded in the public records, contains a setback restriction for the location of buildings on all lots. A 1951 deed is the root of title under the marketable title act. That deed and subsequent deeds refer to the subdivision plat to describe the land, and convey "subject to covenants and restrictions of record." This language preserves the restriction. The owner cannot construct a building in the setback area. *Sunshine Vista Homeowners Ass'n v. Caruana*, 623 So. 2d 490 (Fla. 1993).

D. **Exceptions:** All marketable title acts have express exceptions, which substantially undercut the fundamental goal. Many older interests are sheltered by exceptions, the most common ones being interests of the United States government, interests of state and local governments, utility and railroad easements, mineral rights, and visible easements.

V. TORRENS SYSTEM: TITLE REGISTRATION

The basic concept is that the government issues a certificate of title for each tract of land that is registered. This resembles a motor vehicle certificate of title. The Torrens certificate is intended to be conclusive as to ownership and the existence of all outstanding interests and encumbrances. It represents the government's affirmative statement as to ownership of the property. Interests other than fee ownership, such as mortgages and easements, are shown as **memorials.** Claims to the property not shown on the certificate are not supposed to exist.

A. **History:** The Torrens system dates from a system developed for Australia by Sir Robert Richard Torrens in the 1850s. He based his system on the system for the registration of ships.

B. **U.S. experience:** Nineteen states have adopted Torrens statutes, but in most of these states, their statutes have been repealed, or their systems have little or no current use. Substantial use today is in four states: Hawaii, Massachusetts, Minnesota, and Ohio.

C. **Weaknesses of Torrens in the United States:** Commentators have identified three principal weaknesses of the U.S. attempts to initiate Torrens systems, which have led to its very limited usage.

1. **Indemnity funds:** All Torrens systems have an indemnity fund to pay owners who lose interests due to mistakes in the process of registration and administration. In most states, the indemnity funds are inadequately capitalized and often it is difficult to collect on meritorious claims.

2. **Voluntary nature:** Unlike the British system for mandatory title registration, U.S. Torrens systems are voluntary. Owners usually decide that the cost of initial registration exceeds the benefits that may be realized in the short term. Initial registration requires a judicial proceeding, similar to a quiet title action. This costs at least several thousand dollars.

3. **Exceptions to conclusiveness of certificate:** All Torrens systems allow types of interests to be valid, even though they are not referenced on the certificate. This undercuts the value of the certificate.

   Example: A landowner uses a roadway on his neighbor's tract to haul timber and gravel for many years. The landowner's use is sufficient to give rise to a prescriptive easement. The neighbor registers his tract, obtaining a Torrens certificate, which does not refer to the easement. The neighbor sells his tract to a third party. That third party takes free of the easement only if he did not have actual knowledge of the easement at the time of his purchase. *Tetrault v. Bruscoe*, 497 N.E.2d 275 (Mass. 1986) (holding for purchaser due to lack of evidence of knowledge).

4. **Opposition of title professionals:** Title insurance companies and real estate title attorneys have tended to oppose Torrens systems, arguing that the present practices work reasonably well and the costs of a major reform like Torrens are not justifiable.

Quiz Yourself on
IMPROVING THE EFFICIENCY OF THE TITLE SYSTEM

50. Perry is a real estate attorney, and he does a title search for Yolanda, a client who buys a restaurant that is located on a big parcel of land with plenty of room for expansion. Perry searches back to a warranty deed that is a root of title that is 44 years old. He gives her an opinion letter stating that "based solely on my search of the public records I find title is marketable in [name of seller who has contracted to sell to Yolanda]." One year after closing her purchase, Yolanda wants to expand. Her lender orders a new title search, which takes title back to the sovereign. It reveals a pipeline easement, recorded 53 years ago, that traverses the middle of the portion earmarked for expansion. The easement is improved with a natural gas pipeline that is completely underground, with no evidence of its existence at the surface of the restaurant tract. This causes a big loss for Yolanda, and she sues Perry.

State bar standards prescribe a period of search of 40 years. What relevance, if any, does this fact have on Yolanda's claim and Perry's potential defenses? _____

51. Same facts as prior question. The period for gaining title by adverse possession is 21 years. What relevance, if any, does this fact have on Yolanda's claim and Perry's potential defenses? _____

52.   Same facts as prior question. A title curative act provides that after 10 years all defects related to acknowledgment, execution, and delivery are deemed to be cured. What relevance, if any, does this fact have on Yolanda's claim and Perry's potential defenses?   _____

53.   Same facts as prior question. The state has a marketable title act with a 30-year period. What relevance, if any, does this fact have on Yolanda's claim and Perry's potential defenses?   _____

54.   Same facts as prior question. The state has Torrens legislation. The restaurant tract has never been registered under the Torrens law, but it is eligible for registration. What relevance, if any, does this fact have on Yolanda's claim and Perry's potential defenses?   _____

Answers

50.   **This fact helps Perry.** Perry complied with the 40-year bar standard. This helps him establish that he conducted a reasonable title search, in accordance with the normal customs and procedures of local real estate attorneys. Due to the standard, it is less likely Perry will be found to have committed negligence. The standards are not dispositive, however. Yolanda has two arguments. First, it appears Perry did not tell Yolanda that he was searching back only 40 years and that her risk could be reduced by a longer, more expensive search. In essence, she claims it is malpractice for the lawyer not to disclose the bar standard to the client and lay out the choices. A second point is related. Perry knew Yolanda was buying a valuable commercial property that had room for expansion. While a 40-year search might generally be appropriate for residential properties and perhaps some completely developed commercial properties, for this property Perry should have known that an extended search was advisable and should have so told Yolanda.

51.   **This fact doesn't matter.** Adverse possession is not an issue here from any angle. It does not help Yolanda or Perry. The easement is by express grant, not prescription (akin to adverse possession). There is no claim that Yolanda's predecessor extinguished the easement through adverse possession by using the land surface. (Had the pipeline not been in place and had the restaurant owner interfered with its potential placement by maintaining surface improvements for more than 21 years, then there would be a plausible adverse possession argument.)

52.   **This fact doesn't matter.** This title curative act has nothing to do with the old pipeline easement. From what we know, the easement instrument was properly acknowledged, executed, and delivered. Even if we did an investigation and found something questionable with respect to the easement and one of these three acts, the title curative act would not help here. Title curative acts repair links in the chain of title; they do not cut off outstanding interests held by third parties.

53.   **This fact may help Perry.** The pipeline easement is older than the root of title, so it should be cut off by the 30-year marketable title act. However, marketable title acts have a list of statutory exceptions, and utility easements are a very common exception. Assuming the marketable title act has such an exception, the easement is valid, and Yolanda has suffered a loss. Perry will point to the marketable title act as evidence that his limited search was reasonable. The analysis and Yolanda's response are the same as discussed in Question 50 above for the 40-year bar standard. Perry, if competent, must know that the marketable title act has exceptions and that some purchasers, to reduce risk, should obtain searches beyond the period specified in the marketable title act.

54. **This fact probably doesn't matter.** The availability of Torrens should not matter. It is conceivable that, if Torrens is presently widely used in the city or community where the restaurant is located, Perry should have discussed with Yolanda the pros and cons of initiating a Torrens registration in connection with her purchase of her restaurant. However, this would not have solved the problem unless the Torrens registration was commenced prior to Yolanda's purchase and fortuitously the title search required for the Torrens registration happened to exceed 40 years. If the state now issues a Torrens certificate, it must list the easement as a valid interest.

Exam Tips *on* IMPROVING THE EFFICIENCY OF THE TITLE SYSTEM

☛ **Title standards:** Whenever a question concerns title searches or marketable title, you should consider the possibility that state or local title standards will affect the outcome.

☛ **Adverse possession:** Adverse possession is typically covered in detail in the first-year property course. For this reason, in this outline we have not covered the standard elements of adverse possession, such as open possession and continuous possession. Unless your real estate transactions professor has emphasized adverse possession, you should not expect to be heavily tested on it. Nevertheless, whenever there is a land title problem and someone has been in possession for many years (more than five), you should consider and discuss the possible impact of adverse possession law.

☛ **Title curative acts:** Be sure you understand how a title curative act differs from a title standard and from a marketable title act. A curative act resolves minor flaws in recorded documents, such as a missing or improper acknowledgment. A title standard is not legislation; it represents the consensus of the real estate bar as to how certain title problems should be treated. A marketable title act terminates old recorded interests by establishing a limited time for title searches. It does not matter whether the instruments that create the extinguished interests contain flaws.

☛ **Marketable title acts:** Expect to be tested on this if your state has a marketable title act, which your professor mentioned or your course materials discuss. Know the act's time period: how old a recorded interest must be for the act to extinguish it. You should also know the principal exceptions: those interests that are not extinguished, regardless of age. Even if your course has not concentrated on marketable title legislation, if a fact pattern on the exam includes a recorded interest that's more than 30 years old, mention the possibility that a marketable title act may apply.

☛ **Torrens system:** If you are in one of the four states that operates a Torrens system, you ought to know at least the basics. In addition, if you get a "thought question" asking you to evaluate the strengths and weaknesses of the recording system, you might do well by comparing the recording system and the Torrens system. Also, if your course has an international or comparative component, it's likely that you'll have the opportunity to say something about Torrens because most of the world has a recording system of that type.

CHAPTER 13

HOUSING MARKETS AND PRODUCTS

ChapterScope ━━

This chapter examines the primary types of housing products offered to buyers in the residential real estate market.

- ■ **A diverse market:** Housing markets in the United States are diverse and complex. There are many types of consumer needs and products to meet consumer demand.

- ■ **Single-family homes:** The single-family home occupies a central role in the American housing market, usually governed by *zoning* and *restrictive covenants*. While other housing products, such as condominiums, grow in appeal, the single-family home remains at the center of the "American dream."

- ■ **The planned unit development:** A planned unit development *(PUD)* generally imposes "life style" regulations on the entire development. These regulations are contained in the documents that organize the PUD. When people purchase a home in a PUD they also become members of a *homeowners association (HOA)*.

- ■ **The condominium:** The condominium form of ownership is based on statutory authority, not architectural appearance. Many condominium buildings look similar to apartment buildings, but it is important to know that a condominium is a form of ownership and not a building style. It offers the buyer an ownership interest in a specific housing unit together with an undivided interest in common elements.

- ■ **The cooperative:** In the cooperative form of ownership, the buyer acquires *stock* in a cooperative entity. The stock represents an ownership interest in a not-for-profit corporation; the basic asset of the corporation being the cooperative property. The stock gives the owner a right to a *proprietary lease* of space for a specific unit in the cooperative entity.

- ■ **The time-share:** Time-share products, usually employed for vacation properties, divide ownership of individual living units into *units of time as well as space*.

I. BASIC REAL ESTATE MARKET PROFILE

A. **Rate of home ownership:** The rate of home ownership in the United States has steadily increased over the years. In 1890, it was 47.8 percent, leveling off in the late 1990s at around 65 percent, and hitting approximately 70 percent by 2005. Changes in home financing practices and low interest rates (discussed in Chapter 15) have been a major reason for the rise in home ownership rates. Ownership rates dropped slightly after the mortgage market collapse of 2007-2009 as a result of mortgage defaults, foreclosures, and tighter credit markets.

B. **Median cost of housing:** In absolute and in constant dollar terms, the median cost of home ownership has risen dramatically in the United States. Based on the value of a 1990 dollar, the medium cost of a typical home has more than doubled since 1950. Housing prices rise and fall over time based on a variety of economic factors. In the early 2000s, prices were rising rapidly in high-demand communities, but prices rapidly deflated after the mortgage market collapse of 2007-2009.

C. **Product changes:** Part of the reason for rising housing costs relates to the changing nature of the housing product. The modern home is larger and has more amenities, including upgraded electrical and plumbing systems and energy-saving abilities.

D. **Variations in ownership rate:** Rates of home ownership vary based on race, gender, income, and education. Among all homeowners, Asians and Pacific Islanders tend to have the highest income and the highest levels of home value. Hispanics and African Americans have the lowest rates. Home ownership rates also correlate to income and education levels. Based on the 2000 census, home ownership rates by categories reported by the government included: 71 percent of whites; 47.2 percent of blacks; 46.3 percent of Hispanics; 56.2 percent of Native Americans; and 52.8 percent of Asians. Ownership rates dropped after the mortgage collapse of 2007-2009, with a disproportionate impact of this collapse falling on people who had newly entered the ranks of homeowners. This was particularly true of people who financed a home on a subprime mortgage (see Chapter 15). A disproportionate number of homeowners displaced by the mortgage market collapse and drop in housing values were minorities. Thus, some of the ownership gains recorded for minorities in the prior 5-10 years were wiped out by the mortgage and housing problems of 2007-2009.

E. **Access to housing:** The law prevents discrimination in housing. The Fair Housing Act, 42 U.S.C. § 3604, and other civil rights legislation make it illegal to refuse to sell to potential buyers based on race, gender, religion, and disability. See *Honorable v. Easy Life Real Estate System*, 100 F. Supp. 2d 885 (N.D. Ill. 2000). The prohibition includes activities that come under the terms "redlining" and "reverse redlining," as discussed in Chapter 15.

F. **Housing products:** Housing is a product that is typically sold in terms of the quality and amenities of the home, and in terms of a life style provided by a particular type of home or by its location. Particular housing products are directed at segmented elements of the market. This means that housing styles, sizes, and life style qualities can be targeted to different consumer preferences in the marketplace. Lawyers may help in the creation of products that are accessible to a diverse population, realizing that most home buyers enjoy a relatively privileged income.

II. THE SINGLE-FAMILY HOME

The single-family home on its own lot remains a mainstay in the home ownership market. It tends to be high priced relative to other types of ownership arrangements because of the high ratio of land to occupancy rate.

A. **Land use controls:** The two key types of regulations that affect most single-family homes are zoning and covenants. A special land use device known as the ***planned unit development or PUD*** governs many large housing developments.

1. **Zoning:** Zoning regulates land use by keeping conflicting uses apart from one another. Typical zoning also sets out requirements for minimum and maximum lot size and house size, and for location or position of the house on the lot.

2. **Covenants and restrictions:** Covenants and restrictions are private controls placed on the land by the owner or developer. Restrictions cover topics similar to zoning, but often go much further in an attempt to establish and ensure a particular "life style" within the community. These controls are part of the package being offered as a product; everyone who buys into the subdivision is on notice and is bound by the restrictions. Restrictions can limit the transferability of land as long as they do not place an unreasonable restraint on alienation. Valid restrictions may cover such things as house size and design, house colors, landscaping, and land use controls.

3. **Planned unit developments:** The planned unit development (PUD) is a special public control that allows a local government to approve a large development as an integrated and comprehensive land use. Sometimes, the device of ***mixed-use development*** is used if the project will integrate multifamily and commercial elements with single-family residences.

   Example: Carol buys a home in Sunset Gardens, a PUD with single-family detached homes, which has numerous recorded covenants and restrictions. They include the following: All homes must be one of three pre-approved styles consisting of between 2,500 and 3,000 square feet; exterior home colors are limited to white with black trim, blue with black trim, and yellow with black trim; all exteriors must be of high-grade cedar shake; all homes shall have an attached two-car garage; and no other structures may be placed on a lot. Three months after Carol and her two children move in, she does three things: paints the house exterior mint green with gold trim, installs a play yard with swings and a slide, and puts up a shed for storing the lawn mower and the yard tools. Carol is sued. Carol can be forced to change the color of her home back to an approved color, and she will have to remove the shed. Is the play yard a structure? Depending on how carefully the controls are drafted, this may be a debatable point. In subdivisions marketed to families with children, play yards may be allowed, but there may be specific requirements as to location, type, size, and quality.

B. **Owners associations:** In modern subdivisions, homeowners are generally made automatic members of a ***homeowners association (HOA)***. The association functions like a quasi-governmental body, enforcing land use controls within the subdivision and often enacting rules and regulations. Rules and regulations typically cover matters of conduct. Examples are pet restrictions, timing constraints for outside picnics or parties, time controls on lawn mowing, and limits on the volume of sound permitted from stereos, televisions, and musical instruments. These rules, which are not recorded, are often easier to amend than the recorded covenants and restrictions. A mere majority vote of the homeowners may suffice; sometimes the procedure requires a super majority vote. Usually one vote is allocated to each subdivision lot.

Example: Six months ago a PUD owners association, at an open meeting after giving notice to all owners, passed a rule preventing all owners from parking vehicles in driveways overnight; all vehicles must be garaged at night. Jerry and Inda, homeowners in the PUD, bring suit to enjoin enforcement of the new rule. The defendant owners association should prevail. This parking rule is reasonable because it promotes the aesthetics, safety, security, and convenience of all homeowners. *Holleman v. Mission Trace Homeowners Association*, 556 S.W.2d 632 (Tex. Civ. App. 1977).

III. CONDOMINIUM HOUSING

A condominium is a single unit in a multiunit project, together with an undivided interest in the *common elements* (the areas and facilities shared by all owners). The owner usually has fee ownership of the unit and an undivided percentage interest in the common elements. The condominium, as with other forms of property ownership, is determined by legal structure, not by architectural style. Condominiums can consist of apartment buildings, detached single-family homes, office or store space in a commercial building, boat slips at a marina, or parking spaces in a lot or garage.

A. **Creatures of statute:** All states have statutes governing the creation and operation of condominiums. The statutes are not uniform; they vary in terms and level of detail. The basic condominium documents are recorded in the local real estate records. The primary document is the *Declaration of Condominium*, which sets out the ownership interests, obligations, covenants, restrictions, provisions for governance, and all other matters required by statute. In addition to the Declaration, usually there are separate bylaws, rules and regulations, and documents establishing a not-for-profit *owners association*.

   Example: Sue is thinking about buying an apartment-style condominium unit in a high-rise building in a downtown urban area. She likes the unit and the building, and she sees that there is a parking garage adjoining the building. The sales representative tells her that every unit owner gets her own designated spot in the garage. He even shows her an unrecorded copy of the Declaration of Condominium with a map of the parking garage attached. Sue thinks the unit is a great deal, especially with the parking space included in the deal. When it comes time to close on the transaction, Sue learns that the parking space is not really part of the condominium she is buying. The developer decided to keep the garage as a separate piece of property and rents spaces on a first-come basis to anyone in the city. The developer had originally contemplated the inclusion of the garage in the condominium, as was indicated in the materials shown to Sue by the sales representative, but that set of documents was revised prior to final submission to and acceptance by the appropriate governing authority. The actual and effective Declaration of Condominium, filed in the public records, does not include the garage.

   Sue has no right to an ownership interest in a parking space. Everyone that seeks to buy, sell, lease, lend against, or otherwise deal with condominium property must be careful to review all of the statutes and all of the official documents, as recorded. In this case, Sue may have a cause of action for misrepresentation by the sales representative, but the right to bring such a suit is a poor substitute for getting proper information in the first instance.

B. **Ownership interests:** The three primary categories of ownership interests are the *unit*, the *common elements*, and the *limited common elements*. Each type must be properly defined in the Declaration of Condominium.

   1. **The unit:** Most frequently the condominium unit is held in fee simple, but other interests are encountered. In a housing project, the unit refers to the space occupied by the owner as living quarters—for an apartment-style building, the individual apartment. Generally, a buyer obtains fee ownership of the *interior space* of the unit and the *interior surfaces* of that space (walls, ceiling, and floor). The structure itself is not part of the fee estate.

   2. **Common elements:** Any property of the condominium project that is *not part of the unit* is common property. *Common elements*, which are shared by all owners, typically include

interior spaces beneath the surface of the units; exteriors of the structure; electrical, plumbing, heating, and cooling systems; hallways; stairways; lobby areas; elevators; parking; grass or open areas; and swimming pools or other amenities. Ownership of a unit entitles the owner to an undivided share or interest in the common property. Usually the percentage is proportional to the number of units in the project. Thus, if there are 10 units, each owner would get a 1/10 undivided interest in the common elements. In some instances, the share in the common elements reflects price differences of the units. Thus, assume we have a nine-unit building with eight units all priced the same, but the ninth unit is an extra-large penthouse apartment priced at twice the amount of the others. The first eight units may have a 1/10 interest in the common elements, with the penthouse unit coming with a 2/10 interest. ***The undivided interest in common elements cannot be partitioned***. Liability issues also generally follow with shared ownership; generally unit owners have joint and several liability for injury caused to a person in the common area as a result of improper care.

3. **Limited common elements:** Some common elements are designated for the ***exclusive use*** of a particular unit even though they are not included within the unit. Typical examples are patios, balconies, and designated parking spaces. These limited elements are owned in common and are the common responsibility of all unit owners in the same respect as other common elements. Only the use is limited.

Example: Anna went to visit her friend Bhaskar at the Mansfield Green Condominium. Bhaskar lived in unit 310 on the third floor of a five-story building. Anna decided not to take the elevator, but instead took the exposed stairway. The stairway consisted of steel steps connecting a series of walkways on each level of the building. Most people used the two elevators located at either end of the building rather than the stairway. On the walk up, a rusted-out step broke and gave way when Anna placed her foot on it. Anna fell and broke her leg and her hip. Anna wants to sue Bhaskar and anyone else that may be responsible.

Because the stairway is a common element, Anna is likely to have a claim against the condominium association that has managerial responsibility for the upkeep of the common property, acting on behalf of the unit owners. She should also be able to sue any or all of the unit owners, who are likely to be jointly and severally liable. To clarify actual liability, one has to look at the condominium statutes and at case law to see if joint and several liability has been modified. If the association has adequate insurance coverage on the common property, it may be possible to satisfy Anna's claims through the policy.

C. **Owners association:** Before the first unit is sold, an owners association is created to handle maintenance of the common property and to enforce the ***rules and regulations*** of the project. The association contracts for lawn care and engages people to check and repair plumbing, electrical, and other systems. Officers are elected by the unit owners, with each unit having either one vote per unit or a number of votes proportioned according to the percentage of ownership of the common property. Regular assessments, often payable monthly, are assessed to each owner to pay the association's expenses. In addition, the association has the power to levy special assessments to pay for atypical expenses. Assessments are levied in accordance with each unit owner's percentage of ownership of the common elements. In *Cedar Cove Efficiency Condominium Association v. Cedar Cove Properties*, 558 So. 2d 475 (Fla. Dist. Ct. App. 1980), the costs to repair balconies, which are limited common elements, were properly assessed to all unit owners even though some unit owners did not have balconies; the ***business judgment rule*** protected the Association with respect to its decision to assess all owners.

Example: Betty, a 67-year-old widow, lives in a large 500-unit condominium project that has a restriction limiting pets to fish and small caged birds. Betty has a cat, and the owners association notifies her that she must either remove the cat from the project or move out. Betty sues to prevent the association from enforcing the restriction, claiming that the rule is unreasonable and that her cat never leaves her unit, is quiet, and provides her with needed companionship in her old age. Betty will probably lose. In *Nahrstedt v. Lakeside Village Condominium Association*, 878 P.2d 1275 (Cal. 1994), the ban on cats was enforceable because owners bought with notice of restrictions in the Declaration of Condominium; restrictions are upheld if they are ***not arbitrary*** or in violation of public policy or fundamental constitutional right.

D. Right of first refusal: In many condominium projects, unit ownership is freely alienable, but in others, the association reserves a right of first refusal upon resale. The association can deny a sale to a person if it is willing to match the arms'-length contract price for the unit. The purpose is to allow the existing owners some control over who will enter the shared ownership community.

IV. COOPERATIVE HOUSING

A. Corporate form: Cooperative housing, another form of common ownership, depends on corporate law for its legal structure. A not-for-profit corporation takes title to the real estate project. Key corporate documents are the Articles of Incorporation and the Bylaws. As with a condominium, the cooperative form is a legal one rather than a recognizable architectural form.

B. Ownership interests: The ownership interests in a cooperative consist of the stock certificate and the lease.

1. Stock certificate: Each owner in the cooperative becomes a ***shareholder***. The corporation has stock certificates equal to the number of living units in the project. Thus, if there are 10 apartment-style units in the project, there will be 10 stock certificates. The stock is not a real property interest. It is personal property and is held and transferred in accordance with the law for stock transfers in such corporations.

2. Proprietary lease: Each shareholder has exclusive use of a specifically identified dwelling unit under a ***long-term lease*** from the corporation. The lease defines the extent of tenant rights in the property and delineates the interior spaces and facilities to which the leasehold interest extends. Anything outside the leased premises is common corporate property, owned in common by all shareholders.

3. Real or personal property: Some states treat the cooperative form of ownership as a mixed form of personal and real property. The stock ownership interest is personal property, and the lease is a real property interest such that the documentation has to properly reflect these different aspects of the transaction (the leasehold estate would be the collateral under a leasehold mortgage). Other states, such as New York, treat the entire interest in terms of personal property such that there would be no mortgage against the leasehold interest. In a state such as New York, one would expect to deal with a security agreement and not a real property mortgage.

Example: At closing, Antonia, the buyer of a unit in the Twin Parks Cooperative, is surprised when the seller refuses to give her a warranty deed. In this case, Antonia is confused. Rather than a deed, she should expect a transfer of a stock certificate and an assignment of the proprietary lease covering the unit to be occupied.

C. Corporate governance: The cooperative corporation has a board of directors and a mechanism for managing the property and enforcing the rules, regulations, and restrictions. Shareholders vote to elect board members, and they vote on policy matters, as described in the corporate documents. Common area expenses are financed by assessments against the unit owners in addition to or as part of the lease rents.

D. Right of approval: A cooperative reserves the right to approve all new owners. This right is more absolute than the right of first refusal sometimes used in condominiums. Because the cooperative form involves close living relationships *plus* shared financial commitments, the members have the discretion to exclude a potential buyer for any lawful reason, and they need not state any reason for denial. The only limit on this right of approval is that a stated reason cannot be one that violates the Constitution (it cannot be an unlawful reason for exclusion, for example, being based on one's race or religion).

Example: Peter is a successful New York criminal defense attorney with a lot of clients living in the very exclusive Uptown Cooperative. Peter decides that he would like to live in the cooperative, and when a unit goes up for sale, he puts in a contract offer at more than the asking price. The seller accepts the offer. Peter plans to buy the unit for cash, and he meets all of the income criteria of the cooperative review board. Peter is invited to interview with the board so that a better opinion can be formed concerning his acceptability. During the interview, one of the board members points out a previously overlooked matter concerning Peter's application. The board informs Peter that they do not accept criminal defense lawyers. This denial is proper. If the cooperative believes that criminal defense lawyers attract too much attention, are too likely to draw the wrong sort of discontented clients, and are likely to be too quick to litigate disputes within the cooperative, then the board can deny him approval. It is not unconstitutional to discriminate against attorneys.

E. Financing

1. **Cooperative mortgage:** With standard cooperative financing, the developer gets a loan secured by a *blanket mortgage* against the entire cooperative property. When shares are sold, the mortgage remains an obligation of the cooperative entity. Every shareholder is responsible for a pro rata share of the underlying mortgage expense.

2. **Individual unit mortgage:** In addition to the blanket mortgage, each owner can qualify for a home mortgage, secured by her stock and proprietary lease. This mortgage is the obligation of the individual only and is junior to the blanket mortgage unless the cooperative documents provide otherwise. A few states treat the stock and lease as personal property.

Example: Margaret plans to buy a cooperative unit by making a $50,000 down payment and borrowing $250,000 from Big Bank, to be secured by a home mortgage. There is already a blanket mortgage on the cooperative property, taken out by the developer when the project was built, with a present balance of $1 million. At closing, Big Bank gets a security interest under *Article 9* of the Uniform Commercial Code (UCC) in Margaret's stock in the cooperative corporation, and a real estate mortgage on her proprietary lease. At closing, Margaret also assumes liability for lease rents, which include a pro rata share of the blanket mortgage. Should Margaret become insolvent and default in paying rent to the cooperative and loan payments to Big Bank, there are two separate problems. As to the blanket mortgage, the unit owners have financial interdependence. The other owners must make up Margaret's shortfall, or the corporation will default on the blanket mortgage. Foreclosure on the project would wipe out each owner's rights, including termination of the leases, which are subsequent and junior to the mortgage. As to the home mortgage, Big Bank can foreclose on Margaret's stock and lease, but the other owners have no obligation or risk in this regard.

V. TIME-SHARE HOUSING

Time-share housing divides ownership into both space and time. A person buys an *interval of time* in a unit for one particular week each year (or for some other stated time period). Time sharing is often used in the vacation home market. With people coming and going, the project functions more like a hotel resort than a permanent residential neighborhood. There is a lot of overhead and management work in promoting and running a time-share project. This often shows up in high assessment fees and a markup of up to 30 to 40 percent in unit sales, costs that are unrelated to the physical value of the project.

A. Creatures of statute: Time-share projects are completely dependent on state statute. They do not exist at common law.

B. Ownership interests: An owners association is responsible for management and maintenance, taking on administrative requirements in the nature of a hotel or resort. The *three primary forms of structuring the time-share project* are a real property interest, a license, and a club membership.

   1. Real property interest: A time-share unit is sold as a fee interest that reoccurs periodically every year.

   2. License: The owner gets a license right to occupy a unit according to the terms specified in the license agreement.

   3. Club membership: With the most common type of club membership, the owner buys *club points*. If you acquire more points, you can, for example, get a bigger unit (two bedrooms rather than one), more time (two weeks rather than one), or a more expensive time of year (winter in Florida rather than summer).

C. Exchange features and swaps: Most time-share projects participate in exchange or swap programs. An owner can exchange her interest for one held in other time-share projects throughout the world. As a marketing tool, the exchange program is designed to overcome the buyer's fear of not wanting to vacation in the same spot every year. Issues of concern include the fees charged for the exchange service, how desirable your unit is in terms of the likelihood that someone else will want to exchange with you, and how long the exchange program will last after the developer sells all the time-share units.

D. Financing: A time-share owner can obtain a mortgage loan, but because of high overhead, loan-to-value ratios are usually lower than for single-family home mortgages, including condominium and cooperative financing. Also, many lenders refuse to make time-share loans due to their low value compared to other housing loans; in the alternative, they may charge higher fees for making the loan.

Quiz Yourself on
HOUSING MARKETS AND PRODUCTS

55. Josh contracts to purchase a cooperative housing unit from Celia for $900,000. He is not very familiar with the cooperative idea but has heard a few things about property from a friend who is a real estate sales person. Josh takes the contract to his lawyer and goes over the agreement. Josh says that his friend has told him that it is important to get a good deed from the seller when one buys a new home and asks the lawyer to explain which type of deed should be used in his transaction with Celia. Seeking to impress the attorney, Josh indicates that he knows that there are four types of deeds to choose from: general warranty deed, special warranty deed, quitclaim deed, and deed of trust or trust deed. Assume you are Josh's lawyer. Should you recommend the general warranty deed for this transaction because it has the broadest scope of protection for the buyer/grantee? _____

56. Tim and Patty bought a home in a new PUD made up of 100 single-family homes placed on quarter-acre lots. The PUD has various rules and regulations governing use of common areas as well as noise levels. When Tim and Patty moved in, it was a quiet and peaceful neighborhood composed of families with no children or very young children. Over the years, the families have stayed in place, and many of the children have become teenagers. Several families on the street with Tim and Patty have children who are budding rock stars. On most weekends, various rock bands are practicing in family garages for hours at a time. Tim and Patty no longer enjoy sitting out in their yard on the weekend; they cannot have guests over for a cookout because they cannot hear themselves think or talk, and the noise really upsets their pet bird. Tim and Patty have talked to the families involved, who say they do not understand the problem—the kids never start to practice before noon and always end by 7:00 P.M. Tim and Patty are fed up and they seek to put an end to all of this noise. They do a noise study and determine that the music exceeds the decibel restriction set out in the PUD Rules and Regulations. Can they stop the young rockers from playing? _____

57. Kara buys an expensive condominium that has detailed rules on the way the building must look from the street. After moving in, she changes all the curtain and window treatments from ivory white to light blue. The owners association tells Kara she must return to ivory white. Kara challenges this, arguing that she has the right to select her own curtain colors. Can Kara do this? _____

58. Claudia contracts to sell her cooperative housing unit to Ken. Ken will have to be approved by the board of the cooperative as part of the condition to closing the contract. Ken submits an application, submits an income statement, and does a phone interview. Having made it past these steps, he is invited to an in-person interview with the board. Ken goes to the interview and observes that all of the board members are white. He also discovered a week prior to the interview that all of the other 14 units in the cooperative are owned by white people. Ken is African American and would be the first person of that race to be a member of the cooperative, assuming the sale is approved and the contract closes. The interview covers a series of standard questions and lasts about 45 minutes. After Ken is excused from the meeting, the board deliberates for about 20 minutes and then issues a denial of the application without expressing any specific reason for the denial. This means that Claudia will need to find a new buyer and Ken will need to locate another home to purchase. Both Claudia and Ken would like to see this deal go through, so they jointly challenge the denial of Ken as a violation of the Fair Housing Act and an illegal act of racial discrimination. Are Ken and Claudia likely to win on their claim? _____

59. Liz owns a time-share unit in fee simple that entitles her to use unit 26 during the second week of May each year. This year Liz arrives for her annual weekly visit in the hopes of relaxing and enjoying a much-needed vacation. When she arrives, she finds that Kathleen is in the unit. Kathleen is the fee owner of the unit during the first week of May. Kathleen is still in the unit because she has been feeling ill and refuses to leave until she feels better able to travel. Can Liz have Kathleen removed?   _____

Answers

55. **No.** The direct answer is to point out to Josh that there is no deed involved in a cooperative purchase. Josh will get a stock certificate and this entitles him to a lease of his unit. The stock is a personal property matter while the lease is a real property matter. In states such as New York, the entire transaction is treated as a transfer of personal property. While types of deeds are not part of the answer to this question, they can be reviewed in Chapter 8. A deed of trust is actually a type of mortgage, discussed in Chapter 15.

56. **Yes.** They can enforce the noise controls in the PUD. They can bring an enforcement action to reduce the noise level to within the permitted range. If the noise level is within the permitted range, there would be nothing that they can do to stop it, other than suggesting a new noise control rule. They can try to get a group of like-minded neighbors together and use the machinery of the PUD government. At a homeowners association meeting, Tim and Patty can submit a proposal for a rule restricting the time, place, and hours of such music or limiting the decibel level. If the rule passes by the appropriate majority, it is enforceable on all owners in the PUD, as it would likely be considered reasonable. If they cannot get a rule passed, they should check to see if the public zoning code has any noise restrictions.

57. **No.** If the rules and regulations require ivory white, Kara is likely to lose any challenge. She has an obligation to read the rules before she moves in. Strict enforcement of a neat and uniform exterior appearance of the building will be perceived as reasonable.

58. **No.** Generally, the board determination will be upheld in these situations. The cooperative housing form is unique because all stockholders are jointly and severally liable for outstanding debts of the cooperative. There is a high degree of financial interdependence and for this reason the cooperative enjoys a right of approval. The board can deny approval for almost any reason, provided that the reason is not illegal. In general, a board is not even required to state a reason for denial. In this case no reason was given, so it will be difficult to prove that the denial was based on racial discrimination. Claudia and Ken are not likely to succeed. Remember that the right of approval is a stronger right than the right of first refusal that applies in many condominiums.

59. **Yes.** Liz should check both the statutes that provide for time-share developments and the time-share documents. The documents, if properly drafted, should address this issue. Liz has the rights of any fee property owner. She can seek eviction or ejectment, but this will have to be very quick if she hopes to enjoy any time in her unit.

Exam Tips *on*
HOUSING MARKETS AND PRODUCTS

☛ **Identify the source of regulation of single-family residential housing:** Pay close attention to the nature of any single-family residential property. Many homes located in older neighborhoods or in rural areas are not situated within subdivisions or PUDs. These homes, nonetheless, are likely to be governed by zoning or other public land use regulations. They also may be subject to restrictions in deeds and private covenants. Generally, such restrictions and covenants run with the land and bind future owners. Newer homes are more likely to be within a subdivision having covenants and restrictions. For questions regarding this type of ownership, you must carefully evaluate all references to zoning codes, covenants, restrictions, and rules and regulations. They are central in defining the rights of a homeowner.

☛ **Properly define the "unit" in a shared community housing project:** Focus on the shared nature of condominium ownership. Students sometimes forget the need to define an area in the project as a part of the unit, a common element, or a limited common element. Matters covered in the Declaration of Condominium are given more deference than matters provided for only in the rules and regulations.

☛ **Cooperatives need careful attention because of the mix of real property and non–real property elements:** For cooperatives, you must be sure to keep in mind the dual types of property involved in this form of ownership. The cooperative has a corporate structure. The buyer gets a stock certificate, not a deed of conveyance. There is also an important real property interest, the leasehold estate. In states that treat the cooperative form as a mixed transaction, one needs to consider all of the title, mortgage, and related issues discussed in earlier chapters of this book, as well as the steps related to the stock transfer as personal property.

☛ **Carefully consider the financial interdependence of the cooperative form:** Remember that the cooperative has a blanket mortgage against the full property. This makes the cooperative form of ownership financing very different from that of the condominium. Be sure to keep this in mind when answering questions about financing.

☛ **Classify time-share projects by type:** For time-share problems, first classify the type of time-share interest involved: fee ownership, license, or club membership. Then think clearly and carefully about the problems likely to be confronted with so many owners and the high rate of occupancy turnover.

☛ **Be prepared to contrast and compare:** When comparing different housing products be sure to keep in mind the difference in ownership interest, the difference in rules of transfer to a new buyer, and the difference in financing the purchase. Have in mind the different types of interests and documents related to each type of project.

CHAPTER 14

POSSESSION AND USE OF MORTGAGED PROPERTY

ChapterScope

This chapter considers the legal principles that govern possession and use of property while it is subject to a mortgage. The focus is on the relative rights and obligations of the borrower and lender. The main topics are the three mortgage theories, the doctrine of waste, the duties of the mortgagee in possession, assignments of rents, and receivership.

- **Nature of mortgage:** A mortgage transfers an interest in real property to secure the payment or performance of an obligation.

- **Mortgage theories:** The three mortgage theories are the *title theory*, the *lien theory*, and the *intermediate theory*.

- **Possession:** The right to possession generally is an incident of title, but under all three theories today, the mortgagor has the right to possession prior to default.

- **Waste:** The doctrine of waste safeguards the mortgagee who is out of possession against conduct by the mortgagor that reduces the value of the property.

- **Fiduciary duties:** The mortgagee in possession owes fiduciary duties to the borrower.

- **Assignment of rents:** Under an assignment of rents, the mortgagor assigns to the mortgagee the right to collect rents from tenants.

- **Receivership:** Upon a material default, the mortgagee may ask a court to appoint a receiver to take possession of the property.

I. NATURE AND PURPOSE OF MORTGAGE

A. **Mortgage defined:** A mortgage is a grant of an interest in real property to secure an obligation. Usually the obligation is a debt of the property owner, although a person may grant a mortgage on his land to secure an obligation owed by another person. Most often the debt arises from a loan transaction. A bank or other lender makes a loan and requests collateral; the property owner grants a mortgage to the lender to secure the repayment of the loan.

B. **Parties to the mortgage:** The real property owner who grants the mortgage is called the *mortgagor*. The holder of the obligation who has the benefit of the mortgage is called the *mortgagee*. The mortgage functions to make the property *collateral* to secure payment or performance of the obligation. This means that if there is a default in performance, the mortgagee has the right to resort to the collateral to satisfy all or part of the obligation.

C. **Written instrument:** A mortgage must comply with the *statute of frauds* because it is a conveyance of an interest in real property. Therefore, it must be in writing, must identify the parties, must contain a valid description of the real property (see Chapter 9), and must demonstrate an intent that the property secure an obligation. Most mortgage instruments have many additional clauses, and they are recorded in the public real property records, the same as warranty deeds and other instruments that bear on title to land.

D. Importance of possession and use in mortgage transactions: The essence of owning property is the right to possess and use that property. Possession and use rights are why property has economic value and is exchanged in markets. In order for a mortgage to have value, the mortgagee must have the ability to take control of possession and use rights. Thus, mortgage markets require legal rules that define possession and use rights as between mortgagor and mortgagee.

II. MORTGAGE THEORIES

The mortgage theories address whether the mortgagor or the mortgagee has title to the real property. The theories are the starting point for analyzing the competing possessory claims of mortgagor and mortgagee.

A. Title theory: Under the title theory, the signing of the mortgage transfers title to the real estate from the borrower to the lender, who retains title for the duration of the mortgage.

   1. English common law mortgage: The traditional English common law mortgage was a conveyance of title from the mortgagor to the mortgagee. The mortgagee had a freehold estate, typically in fee simple. The mortgagee's estate could be defeasible or indefeasible.

   a. Defeasible fee simple conveyance: At first the mortgagee normally took a defeasible fee simple, with the mortgagor retaining a future interest (either a possibility of reverter or a right of entry). The limitation or condition was that the mortgagor pay the debt by the specified due date, often called *law day*. The mortgagor who paid by law day then had the right to resume possession immediately. If not, then the mortgagee kept title to the land, with his estate becoming indefeasible, a fee simple absolute.

   b. Fee simple absolute with promise to reconvey: Later many English mortgagees bargained for fee simple absolute title, making a promise to reconvey to the mortgagor in the event he timely paid the debt. This gave the mortgagees more control over the termination of their rights in the land because the mortgagor's payment or tender of payment would not automatically strip the mortgagee of his right to possession. Instead, the lender had to affirmatively reconvey title back to the borrower.

   2. Title theory in the United States: The states originally adopted the English title theory of mortgages as part of their common law. A number of states, all of them in the eastern part of the United States, have retained the title theory.

   3. Effect on possession: The title theory implies that the mortgagee has the right to possession from the moment the mortgage is granted, based on the maxim that the right to possession follows the title.

   a. Express mortgage clause: Many mortgage instruments in title-theory states have an express clause that gives the mortgagor the right to possession up until the time of default.

   b. Implied term: In principle, in a title-theory state if the mortgage is silent on the issue of possession, the mortgagee should have the right to possession from the time the mortgage is granted. This outcome, however, would be so unusual that it would probably contravene the parties' expectations. Thus, a court would probably imply a mortgagor right to take and remain in possession, based on community practices.

    c. **Drafting consideration:** It is in the best interests of both lender and borrower to draft a mortgage that clearly defines the right to possession. Borrower of course wants the right to possession up until a default. Also, borrower would like to negotiate the right to remain in possession until lender notifies borrower of an event of default and a specified period of time thereafter, within which borrower has the right to cure the default. Lenders, however, often resist borrowers' requests for extensive notice requirements and generous cure provisions.

B. Lien theory: Most states follow the lien theory of mortgages, rejecting the title theory. Under the lien theory, the mortgagee prior to foreclosure has only a lien. The rationale is that the mortgagee does not need title to protect his interest in the property. The mortgagor keeps legal and equitable title to the estate after signing the mortgage, and the mortgagee's property rights are limited to the right to foreclose after default.

    1. Rationale: The rationale of the lien theory is that the mortgagee does not need title to protect his legitimate interests. The purpose of the mortgage is to secure payment of the debt, and a lien is sufficient to protect the lender's interest in security.

    2. Effect of mortgage language: Under the lien theory, the language used in the mortgage instrument is irrelevant. The lien theory rejects the parties' freedom to contract for the passage of title. The parties' title rights are defined by their status rather than by their agreement in fact.

    Example: Ida signs a mortgage that "conveys the fee simple in Restacre to Cain and his heirs" to secure her debt to him. In a lien-theory state, this granting clause is ignored. Cain has only a lien, just as if the mortgage had said Ida "grants a lien on Restacre to Cain and his heirs."

    3. Effect on possession: Under the lien theory, the mortgagor has the clear right to possess the property at all times prior to foreclosure.

C. Intermediate theory: A few states (e.g., Ohio, Pennsylvania) follow the intermediate theory or *hybrid theory* of mortgages. Under this view, the mortgagor retains title unless and until he defaults, and upon default, the mortgagee automatically gets title.

    1. Effect on possession: Under the intermediate theory, the mortgagor has the right to possession after signing the mortgage up until default. Retained possession by the mortgagor is the modern norm, and the intermediate theory, unlike the title theory, directly accomplishes this result.

    2. Creditor protection: Compared to the lien theory, the intermediate theory helps a mortgagee who seeks possession of the property after default, but prior to foreclosure. This may be significant because in many states foreclosure is not speedy.

III. EQUITY OF REDEMPTION

A. Hardship at law: The English common law mortgage sometimes imposed hardship on borrowers who failed to pay by law day. The mortgagee's title became absolute regardless of the reason for the borrower's failure to pay on time. At law, time always was of the essence.

B. Intervention of court of equity: Over time, the English Chancellor (the court of equity) intervened to protect borrowers who failed to pay their debts by law day. The court ruled that the debtor had the right to pay late, notwithstanding the terms of the mortgage deed. This right to pay late came to be recognized as the *equity of redemption*.

C. Anti-clogging rule: To protect the mortgagor's equity of redemption, the court of equity struck down mortgage clauses that waived the mortgagor's equity of redemption as contrary to public policy. Waivers and other terms or devices that would eliminate or restrict the borrower's equity of redemption are not enforceable. Such provisions are said to *"clog"* the equity of redemption and are invalid.

D. Late payment and foreclosure: The invention of the equity of redemption put a cloud on the mortgagee's title whenever the mortgagor failed to pay the debt by law day. Even if the mortgagee had possession, at some point in the future, the mortgagor might file a bill in equity asserting his equity of redemption.

    1. Strict foreclosure: During the seventeenth century, lenders became plaintiffs, filing bills alleging a mortgage default and asking for a decree ordering the borrower to pay by a fixed date or be forever barred from exercising the equity of redemption. The Chancellor responded favorably, setting a fixed date that he determined to be reasonable under the facts and circumstances. Such an action became known as *foreclosure*. It foreclosed, or barred, the mortgagor's redemption right.

        a. Retention of property by mortgagee: The procedure did not involve a sale of the land. If the mortgagor failed to redeem by the judicially set date, the mortgagee's title became absolute, at which point the mortgagee could elect to keep the land or sell it.

E. Relationship to mortgage theories: Although English courts developed the equity of redemption in the context of the title theory of mortgages, in the United States the principles and vocabulary of the equity of redemption also apply in lien-theory and intermediate-theory states. In a lien-theory state, while a mortgagee never gains title prior to foreclosure, the equity of redemption refers to the mortgagor's enduring right to obtain a release of lien at any time.

IV. DEED OF TRUST

In some states, such as California and Texas, the typical document used to secure a real estate loan is the deed of trust. The mortgage and the deed of trust are very similar, both serving the same purpose of granting the lender security in the real property.

A. Power of sale: The deed of trust adds a third party, the trustee, to the loan transaction. The trustee is given a power of sale, meaning that if the borrower defaults, the trustee is authorized to foreclose and conduct a private sale of the property.

B. Trustee's role: In principle, the trustee is to be a neutral person who will treat both the principal parties fairly and impartially. In reality, the lender selects the trustee and usually picks the lender's attorney or a title insurance company or some other entity with which the lender frequently conducts business.

V. POSSESSION BY MORTGAGOR

A. Doctrine of waste: Whenever the mortgagor is in possession of the mortgaged property, the doctrine of waste protects the mortgagee. The mortgagor owes the mortgagee the duty not to damage or destroy the property by way of voluntary or permissive waste.

    1. Balance: The modern law of waste seeks to achieve a balance between the rights of the possessor and the rights of the other owners. The basic goal is to preserve the economic value of the property for the nonpossessing owners. In the mortgage context, the goal is to preserve the economic value of the mortgagee's collateral, while allowing the mortgagor to use and enjoy the property.

    2. Voluntary waste: Voluntary waste is intentional conduct that substantially diminishes the value of the property. See *Bell v. First Columbus National Bank,* 493 So. 2d 964 (Miss. 1986), holding homeowners liable for waste when they removed and sold improvements and fixtures, including carpet, electrical fixtures, ceiling fans, closet doors, built-in appliances, and kitchen cabinets.

    3. Permissive waste: The mortgagor has affirmative duties that, if not performed, are permissive waste. Permissive waste means the owner's failure to act has diminished the property value.

        a. Duty to repair: The failure to make ordinary and necessary repairs to buildings and other structures is permissive waste.

        b. Duty to avoid legal risk: Certain neglect or omission by the mortgagor may threaten the lender with loss of title or other legal risk. Failure to pay real estate taxes on a timely basis, for instance, is permissive waste because it creates the risk of a tax sale.

        Example: Gustav bought a gas station from Sirhan, giving him a mortgage to secure part of the purchase price. After a year of pumping gas and fixing cars, Gustav gets tired of the gas station business. A recent environmental audit demonstrates that one of the station's underground storage tanks has developed a slow leak. Rather than repair the tank, Gustav plans to close the station, demolish the surface improvements, and turn the property into a surface parking lot. Gustav cannot legally do this without Sirhan's permission. Tearing down a valuable building is voluntary waste. Moreover, failing to get the tank fixed is permissive waste.

B. Relationship of waste to underlying debt: Mortgages often contain an express promise by the mortgagor not to commit waste. However, the law of waste is based on the tort principle that a person should not injure another person's property and thus is independent of contract. For this reason, a possessor of mortgaged property who is not personally liable on the mortgage debt or the mortgage covenants may be held liable for committing waste.

    1. Discharge in bankruptcy: A bankruptcy court may occasionally discharge the mortgagor from personal liability without causing the sale of the property or terminating the mortgage. The bankrupt mortgagor who remains in possession owes the mortgagee the duty not to commit waste. In *Bell v. First Columbus National Bank*, 493 So. 2d 964 (Miss. 1986), homeowners received a discharge in bankruptcy, but remained in possession of their home post-bankruptcy. The lender foreclosed and obtained a judgment for damages based on affirmative waste committed by the homeowners after the bankruptcy discharge.

2. **Nonrecourse loans:** Under a nonrecourse loan, the lender is limited to proceeding against the collateral if the mortgagor defaults. Loans may be nonrecourse for two reasons. The parties may expressly agree that the loan is nonrecourse; this is common for commercial loans. Second, in some states, certain residential loans are made nonrecourse by an anti-deficiency judgment statute. If foreclosure results in a deficiency, the mortgagor has no personal liability for the lender's loss. In many cases it will not be clear whether the mortgagor is personally liable for waste or whether the nonrecourse nature of the loan insulates the mortgagor from personal liability for waste.

   a. **Permissive waste:** Failure by a mortgagor to pay real estate taxes is permissive waste, but a nonrecourse provision in the loan documents may preclude the mortgagee from recovery. See *Chetek State Bank v. Barberg,* 489 N.W.2d 385 (Wis. Ct. App. 1992), holding the mortgagor partnership not personally liable for unpaid taxes under a nonrecourse loan. Although the mortgagor expressly promised to pay the taxes, the failure to pay was not "tortious waste" because it was not per se unreasonable and it did not result in physical damage to the property.

   b. **Bad faith waste:** Under California anti-deficiency judgment legislation applicable to purchase-money mortgages, the mortgagor is ordinarily not liable for damages for waste. Liability would conflict with the policy of protecting purchasers from a decline in property values. But there is personal liability if the mortgagor commits "bad faith" waste. See *Cornelison v. Kornbluth,* 542 P.2d 981 (Cal. 1975), where the lender alleged that the owner negligently failed to take care of the home. The court held the owner would be liable if he committed the waste in bad faith, defined as "reckless, intentional [or] malicious" and not the result of economic pressures.

   c. **Drafting consideration:** If you represent a lender who has agreed to make a nonrecourse mortgage loan, be sure to consider carefully what exceptions should be made to cover egregious cases of debtor misbehavior. Draft the loan documents accordingly. Obviously, the lender will want to make the borrower personally liable for at least some types of intentional misconduct, for example, fraud and affirmative waste such as removing and selling improvements and fixtures that are part of the mortgaged property.

VI. POSSESSION BY MORTGAGEE

A. **Mortgagee in possession:** A mortgagee who obtains possession of the property with the mortgagor's consent is known as a "mortgagee in possession."

B. **Fiduciary duties:** The mortgagee in possession owes fiduciary duties to the mortgagor. There are several components of fiduciary duties.

1. **Standard of care:** The mortgagee must manage the property in a reasonably prudent and careful manner. This includes making necessary repairs to the extent of income generated by the property.

2. **Duty to account:** The mortgagee has a duty to collect the rents and profits that accrue during his occupancy and apply them to the mortgage debt. The mortgagor is entitled to a periodic accounting for rents and profits.

3. **Third parties:** Ordinarily, the mortgagee's fiduciary duties run only to the mortgagor and are not enforceable by third parties who have dealt with the mortgagor. In *Myers-MaComber Engineers v. M.L.W. Construction Corp.*, 414 A.2d 357 (Pa. Super. Ct. 1979), the court did not allow a site contractor, who contracted with the mortgagor, to recover from the mortgagee in possession the balance due on its contract.

VII. ASSIGNMENT OF RENTS

Mortgages often contain a clause in which the mortgagor expressly assigns rents from the property to the mortgagee. This is especially likely for property that is leased to one or more tenants at the time the mortgage is given. For nonrental property, an assignment of rents clause (assuming it is drafted properly) will handle rents from any leases that the mortgagor may enter into in the future. The purpose of an assignment of rents is to allow the lender to collect rents directly from the tenant in the event the mortgagor defaults or some other event occurs that jeopardizes the lender's security.

A. **Express assignment of specific leases:** Sometimes, a lender requests a specific assignment of a particular named lease rather than relying only upon general language of the assignment of rents. In this event, the assignment is typically not put in the mortgage but a separate loan document is drafted, called an Assignment of Lease(s) or a Collateral Assignment of Lease(s).

B. **Types of assignments of rents:** Whether an assignment of rents is general or specific (naming a particular tenant and lease), the rights of the parties (debtor and lender) may turn on whether the assignment is classified as collateral or absolute.

   1. **Collateral assignment:** A collateral assignment creates a lien on or security interest in the rents, with the mortgagor still owning the rents and the right to collect them. Under a collateral assignment, the lender bargains for the right to collect rents if an event such as mortgagor default occurs. A collateral assignment is not presently operative when it is given. To invoke the assignment, the mortgagee must take some action, such as taking possession of the property or obtaining the appointment of a receiver.

   2. **Absolute assignment:** An absolute assignment passes title to the rents to the lender/assignee. It may be unconditional, with the lender collecting rents immediately, or it may be conditioned on a specified default or other event. In principle, an absolute assignment is inconsistent with the lien theory of mortgages, but many lien-theory states nevertheless allow the mortgagor to give an absolute assignment of rents.

   3. **Presumption of collateral assignment:** In states permitting both collateral and absolute assignments, in cases of ambiguity there is a presumption that the assignment is collateral. This presumption protects the borrower and, if the tenant has prepaid rents, may also protect the tenant from double liability.

      Example: The loan documents for the financing of an office building contain an assignment of rents, which they describe as "absolute." The documents, however, also give the borrower a license to collect rents, and they provide that the lender cannot collect rents unless it first terminates the borrower's license. The tenant wanted to terminate its lease early. It negotiated a "buy-out," pursuant to which it paid the borrower/landlord $1,050,000 to be released from its lease obligations. The borrower/landlord defaulted on its mortgage loan, and the lender brought an action to collect rents from the tenant, claiming it was not bound by the buy-out because the assignment was absolute. Because the assignment of rents was ambiguous, the lender was not entitled to summary judgment. *Oryx Energy Co. v. Union National Bank*, 895 S.W.2d 409 (Tex. Ct. App. 1995).

C. **Effect on leases of mortgagee taking possession:** Existing leases often heavily influence the value of real property. For this reason when the mortgagor/landlord defaults under the loan, the relative rights and duties between tenant and lender are very important. The starting point for analysis is to determine whether the lease or the mortgage is senior under recording act principles.

1. **Senior lease, junior mortgage:** When the lease is senior, the tenant's possession and other rights are not affected by the lender's action in taking possession, invoking an assignment of rents, or foreclosing. When a senior tenant receives proper notice that the lender has invoked a rent assignment, is entitled to collect the rents, or has foreclosed, the tenant generally is obligated to render future performance to the lender. Any prepayments of rent by the tenant and other lease modifications made before that time are binding on the lender.

2. **Junior lease, senior mortgage:** If the lease is junior to the mortgage, the parties' relative rights may turn at least in part on the mortgage theory followed by the state.

   a. **Title and intermediate theories:** Under both these theories, upon default by the mortgagor/landlord, the lender has the immediate right to possession of the property, which includes the leased premises. Thus, the lender can evict the junior tenant. Instead of exercising this right, the lender may insist that the tenant, if she wants to remain, pay rent under the existing lease or under such other terms as the lender may request. Any prepayments of rent by the tenant subject the tenant to risk because the lender may elect the remedy of eviction.

   b. **Lien theory:** Under the lien theory, the lender does not have the right to immediate possession, as against the borrower or a junior tenant, upon default by the borrower. The lender generally will have a valid lien on the rents, which it may act on after default and prior to foreclosure, or it may pursue other remedies, such as the judicial appointment of a receiver. The lender is bound by prepayments of rent and other lease modifications made by the tenant in good faith prior to the lender's exercise of remedy.

   Example: A shopping center landlord and tenant agreed that the tenant would perform work on the shopping center property in exchange for several years' worth of rental credits, to be applied to future rents due under the tenant's lease. The landlord defaulted on its mortgage loan, and a receiver took possession of the center. The receiver could neither evict the tenant nor demand rent for the period of time covered by the rental credits. *Kelley/Lehr & Associates, Inc. v. O'Brien*, 551 N.E.2d 419 (Ill. App. Ct. 1990).

D. **Drafting consideration:** When representing a mortgage lender, before drafting an assignment of rents it's important to research the relevant state law. Not all states permit an absolute assignment of rents, and the states that do may have different rules dealing with their creation and different characteristics. Moreover, the lender's counsel must consider whether the assignment will cover senior leases or only junior leases and must have an understanding of the lender's state-law rights respecting both types of tenants. In some situations, to protect the lender an assignment of rents alone isn't sufficient and the lender will need an express agreement with tenant(s). Depending upon its elements and form, such an agreement may be called an estoppel letter or certificate, a subordination agreement, or a Non-Disturbance, Attornment, and Subordination Agreement.

VIII. RECEIVERS

A receiver is a person who takes possession of mortgaged property at the instance of the lender. When this occurs, the property is said to be in *receivership*.

A. Judicial appointment: The mortgagee may ask a court to appoint a receiver to take possession of the mortgaged real estate. Receivership is available in all states as an incident to an action for foreclosure.

1. Procedure: Many states authorize the ex parte appointment of a receiver at any time after the mortgagor is served with a complaint in a foreclosure action.

B. Scope of receiver's powers: The court determines the scope of the receiver's powers. Often, the receiver is granted broad managerial discretion, including the right to enter into new leases and contracts. Sometimes, a receiver's role is more limited; for example, the receiver might only collect rents.

C. Advantages of receiver for lender: Receivership may protect the lender from the misbehavior of a mortgagor, who, if in possession, may fail to make repairs, may divert income from the property, or may otherwise "milk" the property.

1. Getting possession fast: In many states, getting possession through the foreclosure process can take a long time. Outside of foreclosure, a receiver can get speedy possession to protect the lender from borrower misbehavior.

2. Getting income from nonrental property: A receiver may generate income from property that is not presently rented.

3. Getting preforeclosure protection in lien-theory states: In some lien-theory states, a mortgagee lacks the right to take possession directly prior to foreclosure, even if the mortgage authorizes possession upon default. In these pro-mortgagor states, receivership is the mortgagee's only protection against waste and the only chance to get rents or income applied to the debt prior to foreclosure.

4. Avoiding fiduciary duties: A receiver spares the mortgagee from the obligations imposed on a mortgagee in possession, which are fiduciary in nature and often strict. When a court appoints a receiver, any liabilities arising out of the mismanagement by the receiver or other misconduct are the receiver's liabilities alone. Moreover, most lenders lack experience and expertise in managing real estate, which is a comparative advantage generally possessed by persons who are appointed as receivers.

D. Disadvantages of receiver for lender: There are several disadvantages, which the lender should consider before deciding to seek a receiver.

1. Paying receiver's fee: The receiver charges a fee, which is payable out of income and thus is not available to apply to the mortgage debt.

2. Going to court: Judicial action is necessary to appoint a receiver, which may be more costly than a lender's self-help alternatives.

3. Losing control: The lender loses control over the property while the receiver has possession. Because the receiver is not the mortgagee's agent, if the mortgagee is dissatisfied with the receiver's management of the property, the mortgagee's only recourse is to return to court.

E. Standards for appointment

1. **Proceeding in equity:** A petition for the appointment of a receiver is a proceeding in equity. Thus, the court has discretion to consider a number of factors.

2. **Default and other factors:** The lender must prove that the borrower has committed a material default. In addition, most courts require proof of additional facts that demonstrate the need for a receiver. Commonly used factors include the following: The value of the security is inadequate as compared to the debt; the doubtful financial standing of the borrower; fraudulent conduct of the borrower; imminent danger that property will be lost, concealed, or diminished in value; the probability that harm to plaintiff by denial of the appointment would be greater than the injury to the parties opposing appointment. In *Chase Manhattan Bank v. Turabo Shopping Center*, 683 F.2d 25 (1st Cir. 1982), the court upheld the trial court's appointment of a receiver when the value of the property was less than the debt. The borrower was lax in collecting rents from tenants who were the borrower's relatives, and the borrower diverted rents covered by an assignment of rents to hire attorneys to defend the lender's foreclosure action.

3. **Receivership clause:** Some mortgage documents have a receivership clause stating when a receiver is to be appointed. Usually, such a clause gives the mortgagee a right to have a receiver appointed, at the mortgagee's option, whenever there is a default. There are a variety of judicial approaches to such clauses.

   a. **Fully enforceable:** Some courts are deferential, enforcing such clauses as written, based on freedom of contract, regardless of whether the jurisdiction's normal criteria for appointing a receiver are satisfied.

   b. **One factor:** Other courts are less deferential, refusing to treat the clause as dispositive but treating it as one "plus factor" for the lender to be plugged into the jurisdiction's normal test for appointment of receivers. In *Barclays Bank v. Davidson Avenue Associates, Ltd.*, 644 A.2d 685 (N.J. Super. Ct. 1994), the court rejected the rationale of the trial judge, who appointed a rent receiver "based solely on the contractual agreement between the parties." The court nevertheless upheld the appointment, finding the borrower's failure to pay taxes and insurance premiums had exposed the lender to unreasonable risk.

4. **Unenforceable due to public policy:** Still other courts ignore receivership clauses completely. They view the jurisdiction's appointment standards as mandatory and perceive the clause as the lender's illegitimate attempt to dictate the rules of equity to the court. This is analogous to how courts often limit parties' attempts to alter the normal remedies for breach of contract for the sale of property; for example, liquidated damages clauses aren't enforceable when actual damages are easy to calculate.

5. **Relationship of appointment standard to receiver's functions:** In some states, a more lenient standard of proof for appointment applies if the receiver is to be assigned a limited role. The fewer management powers given to the receiver, the less the potential interference with the mortgagor's economic interest. It may be easier for the mortgagee to get a receiver appointed whose task is limited to collecting rents from one or more existing tenants.

Quiz Yourself on
POSSESSION AND USE OF MORTGAGED PROPERTY

60. Priscilla Pyromaniac grants a mortgage on her nonfireproof home to Lucky Lender. A fire destroys her home. After the fire department investigation, the prosecutor charges her with arson and obtains a conviction. What type of action, if any, may Lucky Lender bring against Pyromaniac? _____

61. When a deed of trust is signed, does the lender get title to the mortgaged real estate? _____

62. In the prior question, does it matter whether the state follows the title theory or the lien theory of mortgages? _____

63. Shopkeeper mortgages her shop to Great Bank to finance her purchase of new inventory. The loan requires monthly payments of principal and interest, due on the 10th of each month. One month, Shopkeeper defaults by failing to make any payment, and late on the night of the 18th, Great Bank responds by hiring a locksmith to change the locks on the shop. Is Shopkeeper surprised when she shows up to open her store the next morning! Great Bank refuses to give Shopkeeper the new keys unless she first pays the past-due amount plus the smith's costs, which she refuses to do. Shopkeeper promptly sues Great Bank for damages. Will Shopkeeper prevail in a lien-theory state? _____

64. Same facts as prior question, except the jurisdiction follows the title-theory of mortgages. Will Shopkeeper prevail? _____

65. A recorded mortgage provides as follows: "Borrower absolutely, unconditionally, and irrevocably assigns to Lender any and all rents and profits from the Mortgaged Property to secure the Indebtedness." After the mortgage is made, Borrower leases the property, which consists of a warehouse, to Tenant. The mortgage provides for monthly payments of $4,200, and the lease provides for net monthly rents of $5,000. Borrower defaults in paying the mortgage. Two weeks later, Lender notifies Tenant that all future rent payments should be made to Lender. Tenant does not respond. When next month's rent is due, Tenant's accounting department remits the sum to Borrower. Lender sues Tenant for this sum. Who should win? _____

66. Same facts as prior question, except Lender sues Borrower, asking the court to appoint a receiver to take possession and control of the property. Borrower resists the appointment. Who should win? _____

Answers

60. **Voluntary waste.** Pyromaniac's conviction demonstrates that she intentionally destroyed Lucky Lender's collateral. This affirmative, wrongful action constitutes the tort of voluntary waste.

61. **No.** The deed of trust does not convey title to the lender. The deed of trust purports to convey fee simple title from the borrower, as grantor, to the trustee, as grantee. The trustee is a third party who acts for the benefit of the lender.

62. **No.** The lender doesn't get legal title in any state. In a title-theory state, the conveyance is effective as written, and the trustee holds title. In a lien-theory state, the parties' intent is disregarded. This means that only a lien may be granted, so the trustee holds a lien for the lender's benefit.

63. **Yes.** Under the lien theory of mortgages, Great Bank's dispossession of Shopkeeper is wrongful. No matter how serious Shopkeeper's default is, Great Bank has only a lien up until foreclosure. A lien by definition is not a possessory interest. Great Bank has committed a trespass to real property and is liable for whatever damages Shopkeeper can prove.

64. **Probably not.** If the state follows the title theory or the intermediate theory of mortgages, Great Bank might have a good defense. Under property law, the general principle is that the right to possession follows title, and under both theories, after Shopkeeper's default Great Bank has fee simple title to the shop. This may be a winning argument for Great Bank, but its conduct was unusual and quite aggressive. Thus, even though Great Bank had title when it changed the locks, Shopkeeper might convince a court it acted wrongfully.

65. **Tenant, probably.** Lender should recover from Tenant if it had an absolute assignment of rents, but not if it held only a collateral assignment of rents. The phrase "absolutely, unconditionally" favors Lender, but is not dispositive. The phrase "to secure the Indebtedness" can be read to imply that Lender has a security interest, not present "title" to the rents. Also, the fact that before default Borrower collected rents from Tenant without protest by Lender supports the claim that this was really a collateral assignment of rents. Many states presume a collateral assignment in case of ambiguity or conflicting evidence. Tenant should win.

66. **Borrower.** Although Borrower has defaulted, there is no evidence of other facts that indicate Lender will suffer harm unless a receiver takes over. At the most, Lender might get a receiver appointed for the limited purpose of collecting the rent from Tenant and remitting it to Lender to apply to the outstanding loan balance.

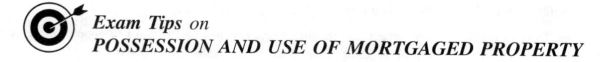

Exam Tips on
POSSESSION AND USE OF MORTGAGED PROPERTY

The three mortgage theories, the doctrine of waste, and the rules that protect the borrower's equity of redemption are basics, which all students should expect to have to know. What if anything you need to know about receivers and lenders' claims to rent prior to foreclosure depends upon the nature of your course. Courses that do not emphasize mortgage law (in particular, commercial mortgages) often do not include these two topics on the syllabus.

☛ **Mortgage theories:** Whenever you have a mortgage question, be sure to consider whether it could make a difference whether the jurisdiction follows the title theory, the lien theory, or the intermediate theory. If so, discuss all three.

☛ **Equity of redemption:** If the question describes a mortgage provision that makes it easier for a defaulting borrower to lose the property, be alert to the rule prohibiting clogging the equity of redemption. The borrower cannot waive her rights to the equity of redemption.

☛ **Possession disputes:** If there's a dispute over whether borrower or lender should have the right to possess and control the property prior to foreclosure, the first step is to read the mortgage to spot language that bears on the right to possession. Especially likely to be relevant is language that bears on the right to possession after default, and the remedies the mortgagee may exercise after default.

☛ **Waste:** Make sure that you can distinguish voluntary waste from permissive waste. Don't forget that the lender's ability to bring a tort action for waste can override nonrecourse mortgage provisions, which normally insulate the borrower from personal liability on the loan.

☛ **Leases:** The treatment of leases when the lender takes possession or forecloses is important. This is one of the most complicated topics in the course. If your teacher has made you responsible for this material, remember that:

    ☞ **Priority:** The first step is to determine whether the lease is senior to the mortgage or junior to the mortgage under recording act principles.

    ☞ **Assignment:** Next, you need to determine whether there is an assignment of rents or leases; and, if so, whether it's a collateral assignment or an absolute assignment.

    ☞ **Mortgage theory:** Finally, consider the possibility that the jurisdiction's mortgage theory (title, lien, or intermediate) will affect the outcome. This is especially likely if there is no assignment of rents.

☛ **Receivers:** If a receiver issue is on the exam, the area most likely to be tested is the standard for judicial appointment. Remember that most courts authorize a receiver only if, in addition to a material default by the borrower, there's at least one more risk factor, such as borrower insolvency or fraudulent conduct.

CHAPTER 15

RESIDENTIAL MORTGAGE MARKETS AND PRODUCTS

ChapterScope

This chapter examines the basic elements of the mortgage market and the types of mortgage products that are most frequently offered.

- ■ **Access to mortgage markets:** Access to mortgage markets varies according to race, education, income, and geographic location.

- ■ **Redlining and greenlining:** *Redlining* and *greenlining* affect access and are illegal.

- ■ **Secured credit:** *Secured credit* provides a lender with collateral and reduces the lender's risk. It is generally cheaper than unsecured credit to the borrower.

- ■ **Mortgage markets:** Capital for lending flows through *primary mortgage markets* and *secondary mortgage markets*.

- ■ **Home mortgage products:** There are a variety of home mortgage products. Home mortgage products vary in terms of interest rate, annual percentage rate (APR), points charged, loan expenses, insurance, and other factors.

I. ACCESS TO MORTGAGE MARKETS

Lending institutions control access to mortgage money. The lender views a potential mortgage loan as an *investment opportunity*. For each loan application, the lender assesses the applicant, the property that will be security, and the relevant market context of the transaction. Some mortgage terms are crucial to the lender's expectations as to profit and risk. They are unlikely to be changed, but other terms are more likely to be negotiable.

A. Security for the loan: Credit makes it easier for consumers to purchase things based on expected future income. It adds to the supply of money, and it supports industries and services that cater to the home ownership market. Credit may be secured or unsecured.

    1. Unsecured credit: With unsecured credit or general credit, the lender relies primarily on the promise of the borrower to repay the money. If the borrower defaults, the lender hopes to seize nonexempt assets of the borrower. To the extent it cannot find such assets, the debt will go unsatisfied. During the course of the loan, the lender must monitor the loan plus keep an eye on the borrower's other assets just in case it needs to take them to satisfy the debt.

    2. Secured credit: With secured credit, the borrower signs a promissory note and puts up specific collateral. For home mortgage lending, the lender takes a mortgage on the borrower's residence being purchased. If the borrower fails to pay, the lender has a direct claim against the property under the terms of the mortgage. Recording the mortgage establishes a priority for the lender, guaranteeing the availability of a specific asset. Due to this protection, the lender has lower monitoring costs and lower risk compared to an unsecured loan. This allows the lender to offer a cheaper interest rate, thus making borrowing for home ownership accessible to more potential consumers.

Example: Jena applies for a $100,000 loan to purchase a $150,000 home. She wants an unsecured loan, based on her general credit. She runs a small business and has savings in stocks and bank accounts. The bank agrees to the deal because Jena has been a good business customer for 10 years. Six months after the loan is made, Jena loses several major customer accounts when they shift their orders to a cheaper foreign producer. Unable to pay her debts, she sells her stocks and spends her savings, and then defaults on the home loan and on her credit arrangements with business suppliers. The bank and all 10 suppliers file claims in court. All of Jena's assets together are insufficient to pay even 50 percent of her total outstanding debts. Her home is in fact the only significant asset that she has at the time. In this setting, the bank must stand in line with all of the other creditors to see what amount of recovery, if any, it will get. In contrast, if the bank had taken a mortgage from Jena when it made the loan, it would have a claim to a specific asset, the home. Only if the home had a value that exceeded the bank's mortgage would anything be available for other creditors. Thus, secured credit makes it easier to keep track of the borrower's assets and reduces the risk of nonpayment and deficiency.

B. **Evaluating the loan applicant:** The two key factors for the lender's decision to extend credit are *ability* and *willingness* to pay the loan. Ability to pay involves an assessment of the *assets*, *income*, and *employment* situation and prospects of the borrower.

1. **Debt ratios:** Traditionally most lenders use two simple formulas. A borrower should not qualify for a loan requiring a mortgage payment in excess of 28 percent of gross monthly income. Second, a borrower should not have total debt payments (mortgage payments plus all other debts) exceeding 36 percent of gross income. Sometimes lenders vary these formulas, especially to accommodate high-cost regions of the country.

    Example: Zachary applies for a mortgage loan at Big Bank for which the monthly payment will be $1,800. How much annual income does Zachary need under the 28 percent and the 36 percent debt ratio tests? He needs a gross income of $77,143 in order to have a monthly income of $6,429, which is the amount that would make his $1,800 monthly mortgage payment qualify under the 28 percent rule. If Zachary has other debts, such as college loans and credit card expenses, he will need to show that his total monthly debt service will not exceed $2,314, which would be 36 percent of his $6,429 gross monthly income.

2. **Willingness to pay:** Willingness to pay is usually a more subjective determination than ability to pay. Credit and employment history must be evaluated, and any past credit problems or payment disputes with other parties must be cleared up to the lender's satisfaction.

3. **Race:** Various studies indicate that white loan applicants are substantially more likely to be approved for a mortgage loan than are black or Hispanic applicants. Much of the difference seems to relate to a greater willingness by loan officers to invest the time needed to solve problems for white applicants who have less than perfect credit histories. White and black applicants with ideal credit scores seem to do equally well in getting a loan approved.

C. **Market definition:** The lender's definition of its geographic market and its customer base impacts the evaluation of loan applications. This can raise serious issues of fairness and equality with respect to factors of race, gender, income, and education. Lenders tend to argue that they have a right to define the lending markets where they choose to operate. Housing advocates counter that lenders have an obligation to make loans available for all types of communities, not just those identified as most profitable.

1. **Redlining:** Redlining occurs when a lender refuses to make loans in a particular neighborhood because of its racial, social, or economic characteristics. Lenders defend nonracial redlining on the basis that loans in distressed areas (known for high levels of crime, unemployment, abandoned properties, and falling housing values) are poor investments. The problem is that such areas often correlate to lower income populations and therefore have a disproportionate impact on minority populations than on the white population. Loan denials ensure that these areas will continue to suffer from under capitalization.

2. **Fair Housing Act:** The Fair Housing Act (FHA) is interpreted to prohibit redlining that is based on the racial characteristics of the neighborhood where an applicant proposes to buy a home. In *Laufman v. Oakley Building & Loan Co.*, 408 F. Supp. 489 (S.D. Ohio 1976), redlining was found to violate the "otherwise make unavailable" language of FHA § 3604(a). In addition, advertising that conveys the implicit message that housing opportunities are not open to minorities violates the FHA. In *Housing Opportunities Made Equal v. Cincinnati Enquirer*, 731 F. Supp. 801 (S.D. Ohio 1990), no per se violation was found in ads that depict only white persons; the court found that plaintiff must introduce extrinsic evidence that bears on discriminatory intent, but the content of ads is reviewable.

3. **Greenlining:** Greenlining occurs when a lender identifies wealthy neighborhoods where it will pursue a customer base with financial products including mortgage loans. The lender might define its customer base in terms of income, education, car ownership, and other factors that have nothing to do with race, but that have a lot to do with expected profits. This concept, like redlining, excludes a disproportionate number of minorities from access to mortgage money and home ownership.

4. **Exploitation and predatory pricing:** Lenders must offer similar rates and opportunities to similarly situated borrowers without regard to race, gender, ethnicity, religion, geographic location, and other prohibited factors. In *Honorable v. Easy Life Real Estate System*, 100 F. Supp. 2d 885 (N.D. Ill. 2000), the court found that it was improper exploitation of consumers in a minority community to offer mortgage financing on less favorable terms than those offered to similarly situated white borrowers.

5. **Higher credit risk loans:** In the 2000s public policy favored increasing the rate of home ownership. This policy encouraged subprime lending and use of an "Alt-A" mortgage. Subprime lending involves making mortgage loans to borrowers who do not meet the traditional credit standards for a given mortgage. Because the borrowers have lower credit scores than prime borrowers, they are a higher risk for default and this makes these loans more expensive in terms of higher interest rates, points, or fees. The Alt-A mortgage was often a loan done with less documentation or given to a borrower that was not qualified for a prime rate, but not so risky as to be put in the subprime pool. If one were to simplify this and put it in terms of grading for a law school course, an "A" student qualifies for a prime loan, an "A–/B+" student might be an acceptable risk for an Alt-A loan, and a "B–"student might be eligible for a subprime mortgage. Many, but not all, of the loans that went into default during the mortgage market collapse of 2007-2009 were in the Alt-A and subprime categories.

6. **Market reform:** In response to the so-called mortgage market meltdown of 2007-2009, there have been a variety of short-term fixes and a lot of thinking about longer-term solutions to reducing risk in this market. Short-term measures have been directed at supporting weak lenders with cash infusions and regulatory protection. Likewise, various steps have been taken to protect borrowers from the full consequences of default, foreclosure, and bankruptcy as they lose their ability to pay for homes purchased during the housing bubble. Essentially, speculation fueled by rising housing values and lowered standards for Alt-A and subprime mortgages permitted too many people to purchase a home that they could not pay for once the bubble burst. After the crash, many home buyers were ***upside down***, meaning that they owed more on their mortgage than their home was worth. Other homeowners just could not make monthly payments on their mortgages once they had a rate adjustment on their loan. Many of these people went into their loans at low introductory rates subject to significant rate increases in years two or three of the mortgage. Many of these home buyers simply could not afford to make the increase in monthly payment brought on by the scheduled rate adjustments. A number of borrowers have benefited from programs to reduce their outstanding mortgage debt and reschedule payments, but many of the people receiving this benefit ultimately have defaulted again, even with a favorable adjustment. There are many regulatory proposals being discussed, with key issues being the need to assure better standards for extending credit to home buyers and for closer supervision of the loan origination process. There are also proposals to deal more specifically with the quality of information and complexity of products in the secondary mortgage market.

II. PRIMARY MORTGAGE MARKET

The primary mortgage market involves interplay between savers and borrowers, and the origination of home mortgage loans to home buyers.

A. **Savings:** Households and other investors save money, which becomes available as a source of funds for credit. Savers choose among a variety of investment opportunities, such as deposit accounts, certificates of deposit, money market funds, and commercial paper. These investments are generally short-term commitments, meaning that they can be withdrawn on relatively short notice.

B. **Intermediaries:** Financial institutions and other organizations that hold savings make mortgage loans. They serve as transactional facilitators in the overall economy. From the point of view of the intermediary, payments that must be made to attract investment from savers are a cost of raising capital or a cost of funds. They are the cost that must be paid in order to assemble the large sums of money needed to turn around and make loans available to borrowers.

C. **Borrowing:** Individuals and families borrow funds from the intermediaries to acquire or finance their homes. The intermediaries need to make enough money to cover their cost of funds and provide an adequate profit, called the ***return on investment***. There is an ***asymmetrical relationship*** between the short-term nature of savings and the long-term nature of mortgage lending. Dramatic instability in overall financial markets is felt more quickly on the ***cost-of-funds*** side of the equation. When inflation hits, for example, a lender is likely to experience rising costs and falling returns. This key risk affects intermediaries. To the extent we value the function of making money accessible for real estate activities, we may want to create mechanisms for protecting these intermediaries from undue exposure to such risk.

D. Alternative markets: Intermediaries have market choices and do not automatically channel money to the primary mortgage market. They consider *alternative capital markets* (e.g., the stock markets or mercantile exchanges), which represent alternative markets for investment activities. Intermediaries tend to specialize in particular types of financial markets. In the real estate transactions area we are most concerned with intermediaries that direct their attention to real estate markets, as opposed to alternative capital markets.

III. SECONDARY MORTGAGE MARKET

The federal government promoted the development of the secondary mortgage market to expand access to capital for residential loans. Since its start in the early 1980s, this market has grown to handle billions of dollars of transactions every year. Intermediaries in the secondary mortgage market think of mortgages as the right to streams of income represented by the obligation of the borrowers to make monthly mortgage payments. These streams can be organized and packaged to create investment opportunities capable of attracting resources and competing with investment opportunities in alternative capital markets. To gain economies of scale, an intermediary "packages or pools" similar mortgages together. A *mortgage pool* is created and treated as one large income stream. Securities and other investment devices can then be issued against the stream of cash flow and sold to investors. With a *pass-through security*, the monthly payment of principal and interest on each of the underlying mortgages merely passes from the party servicing the loans, less a fee for servicing, to the investor. Pass-through securities can also be issued as *partially or fully modified*. These involve protection for the amount of pass through available, even if actual payments drop as a result of loan defaults or loan prepayments. The two main objectives of these secondary mortgage market activities are to *diversify* lenders' investments and to *bring new money* into the real estate markets.

A. **Diversity of mortgage investments:** Local lenders generally make loans on properties within a given geographic area. These loans carry a substantial risk dependent on the swings in the fortunes of the local economy. To reduce risk, a local lender in Ohio may swap or sell its loans to a lender in Kansas, Florida, California, or Michigan. The secondary market also allows local lenders to diversify among regions of the country based on variations in savings rates and credit demands.

B. **New investment capital:** Many investors, such as insurance companies and pension funds, traditionally did not invest substantial amounts in residential real estate. Barriers included the peculiar nature of real estate, the variations in state mortgage laws, and the complexity of evaluating individual mortgage instruments. The secondary mortgage market has broken down such barriers by encouraging uniform mortgage documentation and by pooling individual mortgages and turning them into securities. This has attracted new investors from within and outside of the United States, increasing the money available for domestic mortgage lending.

C. **Intermediaries:** The secondary mortgage market intermediary facilitates the flow of resources among regions of the country and brings more investors into the market by bridging the gap between what local lenders originate and what market investors want to purchase. The intermediary connects the loan originators in the primary market to potential investors in the various capital markets. Securities issued by the intermediary, based on the cash flow of the underlying mortgage pool, are sold to investors, and the cash from purchase of the securities flows back to the intermediary, who in turn directs it to the primary market by way of buying additional mortgage pools. In some instances primary mortgage market pools will be delivered to the intermediary and returned to the primary lender as securities to be held in a more liquid form than the original collection of individual mortgages. For these services the intermediary is paid a fee, which is usually known in advance and factored into the loan closing costs paid by borrowers in the primary mortgage market. These can show up as *points* (see part IV.A.1 below) or other costs.

D. Direct sales to investors: In certain situations, a primary mortgage lender may be able to sell mortgage loans directly to investors in the secondary mortgage market. This usually involves larger commercial loans and takes the form of a direct sale of ownership or a sale of an interest in the loan by way of a loan participation.

E. Changing market dynamics: Prior to the development of the secondary mortgage market, lenders made loans and held them long-term as investments. Today, many originating lenders sell most of their residential home mortgages in the secondary market rather than holding them as individual long-term investments. This gives primary lenders access to a continuous flow of cash. They originate loans, sell them in the secondary market, and then use the cash generated from the sale to make additional loans in a repeating cycle. As a result, many lenders make much of their profit from charging loan origination fees and loan servicing fees rather than from holding loans as long-term investments. This drives primary lenders to be more focused on the needs and concerns of secondary market investors than on the individual needs of a particular home mortgage borrower. Another consequence of the changing market dynamic is that the access to a secondary market helps reduce the risk exposure inherent in the discrepancy between the long-term nature of mortgage loans and the short-term nature of the lender's cost of funds.

F. Secondary mortgage market financial products: Private and government-related entities are active in the secondary mortgage market. Based on the cash flow represented by the underlying mortgages in a mortgage pool, these entities issue securities that look like stocks and bonds. These mortgage-backed investments are sometimes generically referred to as collateralized mortgage obligations or mortgage-backed securities. They compete for investor attention along with other products in the financial markets. Sometimes a pool of mortgages will be used to support a securities offering and the pool will be organized in such a way as to create investment opportunities in different and smaller parts of the pool. By legally sorting out risks across the pool, for example, one might create different classes or grades of investments. This sorting out of a larger pool into smaller parts with different risk preferences is often referred to as creating different *tranches* for investment.

G. Derivatives and swaps: Derivatives are investments in the market that can include interest rate swaps. The interest rate swap is designed to reduce or eliminate the risk of swings in market rates of interest.

Example: Assume Robin borrows $2 million from Big Bank based on an adjustable-rate loan with a starting rate of 5 percent interest. Robin is planning his investment strategy on a fixed 5 percent cost of the loan. To achieve this result, Robin could do an interest rate swap with an investor like James Smith, wherein James agrees to pay Robin if rates go above 5 percent, and Robin agrees to pay James if and when rates drop below 5 percent. So if interest rates rise to 6 percent, James pays Robin 1 percent on the $2 million to cover the added cost on the adjustable-rate mortgage loan. On the other hand, if rates drop to 4 percent, Robin pays James 1 percent on the $2 million. The idea is that Robin wants to hedge against the risk of interest rate changes during the term of the loan and each party is betting on coming out ahead in terms of where rates actually go during the life of the loan. In this way Robin loses when rates go down but gains when rates go up. More important, Robin is able to turn his adjustable-rate loan into a fixed-rate loan that is easier to predict.

H. Secondary market provides funds for primary market: Seller and buyer contract for purchase and sale of a home, and buyer obtains mortgage financing from a lender. The lender sells that mortgage to a secondary market intermediary that puts the mortgage in a pool and issues a security based on the mortgages. These securities are then purchased by investors in the financial markets. Primary market lenders get funds from depositors and from sales of mortgages to the secondary market. These sources of funding enable them to continuously make new loans to new buyer/borrowers.

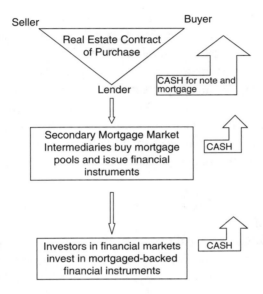

IV. MORTGAGE PRODUCTS

A. Preliminary matters: The concepts of points, annual percentage rate, and mortgage insurance apply to all mortgage loan products.

1. Points: Institutional lenders usually require that the borrower pay up-front fees called "points." Sometimes, points are called ***loan processing fees***, ***discount fees***, or ***origination fees***. One point is equal to 1 percent of the loan amount. One point also equals 100 ***basis points***. Points are used to cover processing costs for the loan, commissions for loan officers, and fees for transacting in the secondary mortgage market. The borrower often has the choice of paying additional points and reducing the stated interest rate on the loan.

2. Annual percentage rate: The annual percentage rate (APR) is a statement of the cost of a loan using a formula set forth in the *Real Estate Settlement Procedures Act (RESPA)*, 12 U.S.C. § 2601, and in furtherance of the *Truth in Lending Act*. To calculate the APR, lenders add to the stated interest rate a standard list of expenses and fees associated with the loan origination. The lender must disclose the APR to the prospective borrower, who then has a basis to do comparison shopping. Consumers should not be misled by quotes that might not reveal hidden expenses. The APR is for comparison and disclosure purposes; the actual interest rate on a promissory note for a loan will be the quoted mortgage rate and not the APR rate.

3. **Mortgage insurance:** Mortgage insurance protects the lender against risk of loss if a borrower defaults and the property is sold through foreclosure for a price less than the outstanding debt. Underwriting guidelines generally require insurance when the loan-to-value ratio exceeds 80 percent. The borrower pays for *private mortgage insurance (PMI)* by paying a monthly premium, along with principal and interest on the loan. *FHA insurance* and *VA guarantee programs* often require a full premium payment at the outset of the loan. PMI typically provides a 20 to 30 percent risk coverage; this means the insurer covers a 20 or 30 percent drop in property value, and the lender bears the remaining risk. FHA insurance, on the other hand, provides 100 percent coverage. Mortgage insurance makes it possible for people with only a small amount of savings or equity to get home mortgages.

Example: Gina goes to Big Bank for a mortgage to buy a new home. She needs to borrow $180,000 and will make a $12,000 down payment out of her own money. The bank offers Gina a 10 percent loan, with 2 points and an 11.5 percent APR, and says she will need PMI plus homeowners insurance and title insurance. To explain this to Gina, emphasize that each type of insurance is different. Homeowners insurance protects the property from such things as fire or other damage. Title insurance protects the lender from a loss in its mortgage priority or security as a result of a title defect. Mortgage insurance protects the lender from a drop in property value, which could cause a loss if Gina defaults and foreclosure ensues. It is required because Gina is paying less than 20 percent down on her house. She will pay a monthly PMI premium, added to her mortgage payments. As to the points, Gina must pay $3,600 at closing (2 percent of $180,000).

B. **Fixed-rate mortgages:** The fixed-rate mortgage has a set rate of interest, which applies throughout the life of the loan. Monthly mortgage payments never change. The loan is *self-amortizing*; with the very last payment, the loan is fully paid. During the early years, payments are allocated primarily toward interest. Most fixed-rate mortgages are for 15 or 30 years, but any *term* can be used. The fixed-rate mortgage puts on the lender the entire *risk of future increase* in market interest rates.

C. **Adjustable-rate mortgages:** The *adjustable-rate mortgage (ARM)* has an interest rate that changes periodically. Under a standard ARM, monthly payments are adjusted to reflect the interest rate change. The ARM puts on the borrower some or all of the *risk of future increase* in market interest rates. For this reason, lenders offer ARMs at significantly lower initial rates than comparable fixed-rate mortgages. Every ARM has three key features: the index, the adjustment period, and the cap. A fourth consideration for some ARMs is convertibility.

1. **Index:** The interest rate adjustment is based on an index described in the loan documents. An external index is outside the control of either party. Examples are Treasury bill rates, government or trade indexes of average mortgage costs for a region or the nation, and even international rates, such as the London Interbank Offer Rate (Libor). An internal index is subject to the lender's control; an example is a bank's prime rate. Such an index is more likely to present interpretational problems than an external index. See *Crowley v. Banking Center*, 1994 WL 685023 (Conn. Super. Ct. 1994), which involved the disputed interpretation of an index based on lender's "market rate" for adjustable-rate loans.

2. **Adjustment period:** The loan documents specify the timing and frequency of each interest rate adjustment. Common adjustment periods for ARMs are every six months, one year, or two years. This means that the index is checked during the agreed-to time frame and the interest rate is then adjusted up or down.

3. **Caps:** Many ARMs have *caps*, which limit the upward movement of interest changes. Caps protect borrowers from the uncertainty of an unlimited rise in their mortgage payments. As a matter of *symmetry*, caps usually work in both directions, also limiting downward adjustments. Caps may be in place for the life of the mortgage and for each adjustment period.

   Example: Giovanni goes to Big Bank and gets an ARM with an initial 7 percent interest rate, adjusted annually, with a 1 percent annual cap and a 4 percent lifetime cap. This means that Giovanni's interest rate cannot increase more than 1 percent in any given year. Therefore, the maximum rate in year two would be 8 percent, no matter what happens to the index. The highest rate that can ever apply is 11 percent, which cannot be reached, if at all, until year five of the mortgage. Similarly, if Giovanni's index drops by 3 percent in year two, his interest rate will decline only 1 percent for that time period.

4. **Convertibles:** A convertible loan permits the borrower to convert from an ARM to a fixed-rate mortgage at some predetermined time. A borrower might take an ARM during a time of high interest rates, expecting that rates will fall in three years when the economy adjusts to some new trend. In such a case, the borrower might bargain for a convertible mortgage, which allows her to exercise an option to convert to a fixed-rate mortgage on the third anniversary of the loan. The conversion would be at the then prevailing market rate of interest for fixed-rate mortgages, but the borrower would save on financing costs.

D. **Alternative mortgage instruments**

1. **Balloon mortgage:** The balloon mortgage provides for low periodic payments, with a much larger payment due when the term ends. For example, a balloon mortgage could provide for monthly payments based on a 30-year amortization schedule, but require the borrower to pay the loan balance in full three years after the date the loan is made. To avoid a default, the borrower must come up with cash or refinance at the end of three years. Balloon mortgages are often used for seller financing and in situations when the parties desire a *bridge loan*, with the expectation that in the short term the buyer will be able to get a better deal from another source of financing.

2. **Level payment adjustable-rate mortgage:** The level payment ARM provides a borrower with a stable and predictable monthly payment over the term of the mortgage, while giving the lender the benefit of interest rate adjustments. When the *effective interest rate* changes, the monthly payment remains the same, unlike the standard ARM, which modifies the amount of payment. Instead, the term of the level payment ARM adjusts, becoming shorter or longer, or a final balloon payment is required. If the level payments are not enough to cover the interest that accrues, *negative amortization* results, meaning the dollar amount of debt increases.

   Example: Dan gets a level payment ARM with a stated interest rate of 10 percent, requiring him to pay $500 per month on his 30-year mortgage. His effective interest rate is linked to a specific index, and an adjustment is made every six months. At the first adjustment, interest rates have risen, and his rate goes to 11 percent. Dan continues to pay only $500 per month, resulting in reduced amortization of principal. Conversely, if at the next adjustment Dan's rate has dropped to 9 percent, he still pays $500. During this time, he is making overpayments, which reduce the principal more quickly.

3. **Shared appreciation mortgage:** With the shared appreciation mortgage (SAM), the lender receives in addition to interest on the loan a percentage of the appreciation in value of the property over a specified time period. The borrower trades some of her *equity appreciation* in her property for a lower interest rate. For example, one might get a desired interest rate in

exchange for giving the lender a 30 percent interest in any equity appreciation that occurs within 10 years. If the home is sold earlier, the parties settle up based on the value at the time of sale.

4. **Reverse annuity mortgage:** The reverse annuity mortgage (RAM) is designed for senior citizens who have home equity and desire extra income. The homeowner receives a monthly annuity, secured by a mortgage on the equity value. Each month the amount of debt rises. The total annuity debt is capped, and the homeowner should ensure that if she outlives her expected time in the home, she will not be forced to leave.

E. **Purchase-money mortgage:** The purchase-money mortgage (PMM) is any type of mortgage provided by the seller of the property to the buyer. The seller therefore acts as the lender in the transaction and should take normal precautions, including getting a credit check and obtaining and recording standard loan documents. In some contexts, people refer to a PMM as any mortgage given to secure debt incurred to buy property. Under this definition, money from a third party is a PMM. In some states, a PMM has special status or priority, particularly when several mortgages are given simultaneously against a property.

F. **Deed of trust:** A deed of trust is a mortgage that includes a third-party trustee. The third-party trustee is named in the mortgage as an independent party to conduct a nonjudicial foreclosure sale after a default. Only certain states permit a nonjudicial foreclosure and thus it is only in such states that the use of a deed of trust will be given its intended effect. If such a form is used in a state that does not permit it by statute, it will generally be treated as a mortgage and will be subject to the rules in that state, including those that require a judicial foreclosure.

Quiz Yourself on
RESIDENTIAL MORTGAGE MARKETS AND PRODUCTS

67. Carrie invests in the secondary mortgage market. She recently purchased a major multi-million dollar investment in adjustable-rate mortgages. Carrie believes it is a good investment. The starting rate on the mortgages included in the adjustable rate pool is 5 percent. Carrie matches her investment against her liabilities and she wants to make sure that she gets 5 percent on this mortgage pool investment. Carrie has invested in an adjustable rate pool; this means the actual return over time could go up or down. Carrie does not want the down side risk. Can she reduce this risk? _____

68. Juanita makes $85,000 per year. She wants to buy a home and has saved $20,000 for a down payment. She has two questions. First, what is the maximum price she can pay for the home if she does not want to pay for private mortgage insurance? Second, what is the maximum mortgage payment for which she will likely qualify? _____

69. How has the secondary mortgage market changed the function of many primary mortgage market lenders and their relationship to their borrower clients? _____

70. Brian works for the U.S. Postal Service as a letter carrier. He receives a generous salary, but pay increases usually are budgeted at a steady rate of increase of 1 to 3 percent each year. Brian seeks to buy a new home. When he goes to apply for mortgage financing, he is confronted with a number of choices. He is offered an adjustable-rate mortgage, a level payment adjustable-rate mortgage, and

a fixed-rate mortgage. The fixed-rate mortgages will cost 1 point more than either of the other loans. Brian likes the idea of the level payment adjustable-rate mortgage. Is this the best choice for him? _____

71. Gary buys a new home for $200,000 and gets a SAM. It is at a fixed interest rate of 8 percent and gives the lender a 33 percent interest in any equity appreciation. Five years later Gary sells the home for $230,000. The lender claims a 33 percent interest in the $30,000 equity appreciation in the home. Gary argues that the lender is entitled to nothing because he spent $35,000 during that time repainting the house inside and out, repairing the plumbing and electrical systems, and putting on a new roof. What is the result? _____

Answers

67. **Yes.** Carrie can reduce the risk of an adjustable-rate investment by doing an interest rate swap in the derivatives markets. Carrie would look for and enter an agreement with someone willing to take a risk on interest rate swings. In the swap agreement, the swap investor would agree to cover Carrie in the event that interest rates went against her 5 percent return, and Carrie would cover the swap investor when returns were better than 5 percent. Thus, if Carrie wants to get a steady 5 percent return, she could do a swap agreement wherein she pays the swap investor any amounts that come in above 5 percent when the rate goes up, and likewise the swap investor would make up the difference and pay Carrie if the returns dropped below 5 percent as a result of an interest rate drop.

68. **First, Juanita can buy a $100,000 home and borrow $80,000 without having to pay for private mortgage insurance.** PMI is required if the **loan-to-value ratio** exceeds 80 percent. Second, Juanita makes $85,000 per year, which is $7,083 per month. Using the 28 percent rule, her maximum monthly payment cannot exceed $1,983. Her payment will naturally be determined by the type of mortgage she selects and its interest rate. Using the 36 percent test, Juanita must show that her total monthly debts, including the mortgage, are no more that $2,550.

69. **Before the secondary mortgage market developed, lenders raised money locally and made loans locally.** They held mortgages long term as investments and looked to the cash flow from the mortgages as their investment return. Now many lenders function primarily as loan originators, who make loans, package or pool them, and sell them to secondary market investors or intermediaries. Instead of holding mortgages as long-term investments, many primary lenders sell them quickly and make their money on the fees associated with the process of originating and servicing the loans. The secondary market allows local lenders to tap into regional, national, and international financial resources. The secondary mortgage market has fundamentally changed the lender and borrower relationship. Lenders must pay attention to the market demands of distant third-party investors. The types of loans they offer are now influenced by the secondary mortgage market as much as or more than by the needs of their local customers.

70. **Maybe.** Brian has a given income and an expectation that his future income is likely to be relatively stable, with perhaps annual adjustments that will cover the rise in the cost of living. People in this type of income situation are often served best by having a predictable and stable mortgage payment. The fixed-rate mortgage is the best way to assure a predictable payment as it will not change over the life of the loan. It is also self-amortizing so there is never a period of zero or negative amortization. The problem here is that it costs Brian one additional point to get this mortgage. This

is because the lender takes on all of the risk of potentially rising market rates of interest. On the other hand, Brian has a choice between two adjustable-rate mortgage plans. With the regular adjustable-rate mortgage, the mortgage interest rate and monthly payment adjusts with changes in the market. Brian is not sure he can handle such a risk. He is concerned that rates may go up quickly and he might not have enough income to cover a big jump in his mortgage payments. This risk can be reduced on the straight adjustable-rate mortgage by getting annual and lifetime caps on adjustments; the more limiting the adjustments and caps, however, the more this loan will cost. So by asking for these risk protections he will pay more and the difference in cost relative to the fixed-rate mortgage will be less. Also in the mix is the level payment adjustable-rate mortgage. This type of mortgage permits Brian to make the same payment every month without regard to the underlying interest rate changes. The problem here is that in months when the real interest rate is higher than the rate used to calculate his level monthly payment, the loan results in negative amortization (the debt builds up). Brian might end up owing more than he originally borrowed, based on what happens to the market rate of interest. Brian can ask for caps and limits on negative amortization, but this will reduce his risk while allocating more risk to the lender. The lender will charge more for limitations on this type of loan, so the cost differential with the fixed-rate mortgage will decrease. Brian may be best with the fixed rate or with an adjustable rate that limits the amount of risk exposure that he has from year to year. Limits on an adjustable-rate mortgage may cost something but it may still come in cheaper than the fixed-rate loan. The level payment adjustable-rate mortgage may be the worst option because of the potential to build negative amortization.

71. **This question points out a common problem with a SAM.** Gary claims that he has lost money on the sale because he has not recaptured all that he has invested. The lender replies that painting, doing repair work, and putting on a new roof are matters of upkeep and personal taste. They preserve rather than add to market value. The $30,000 rise in value for the property probably is due to general market trends, not Gary's expenditures. Gary has an uphill task; he must show that his work is properly classified as capital investment or capital repairs rather than ordinary maintenance. The documents must be carefully drafted and reviewed to see exactly how equity appreciation is to be calculated and what will be done in the event of a disagreement over that calculation. If they are unclear, they are likely to be interpreted against the lender, their drafter.

Exam Tips on
RESIDENTIAL MORTGAGE MARKETS AND PRODUCTS

☞ **Understand issues related to access to mortgage markets:** When considering access to mortgage markets, take a broad perspective. Consider the contract, property, and mortgage law involved. Think in terms of the market objectives, expectations, and dynamics that motivate lenders and borrowers in these market settings. Also, do not forget that people's constitutional rights are impacted by housing and mortgage markets. Thus, one should think of constitutional law implications as well as property law issues when looking at fact patterns related to access to mortgage financing.

☞ **Identify illegal exclusion efforts that deny access to mortgage markets:** Be sure to understand and explain the difference between redlining, greenlining, and exploitation theory. Many fact patterns will raise concerns that might be related to one or more of these illegal practices and one must be careful to distinguish them.

☞ **Know the relationship between primary and secondary mortgage markets:** Display your understanding of the dynamic relationships created by the primary and secondary mortgage markets. These networks facilitate the flow of capital among regions of the country and reduce local risk by facilitating diversification.

☞ **Secondary mortgage markets change the primary market relationship between borrower and lender:** Be able to explain how lending activities are transformed from long-term holding of local mortgages to origination, sale, and servicing of loans. Lenders must be concerned with the market objectives of distant and unknown third-party investors seeking to purchase mortgage-related securities. This is a change in focus from earlier days when the emphasis was almost exclusively on the needs of borrowers.

☞ **Be able to explain integrated financial markets:** You need to be able to explain that local real estate markets are susceptible to trends and changes in national and international financial markets. For example, the Japanese and European financial markets impact on the cost and availability of home mortgage loans in Mississippi and New Hampshire via integrated financial markets and the secondary mortgage market.

☞ **Understand and be able to explain the way in which different mortgage instruments meet different financial needs:** An exam is likely to test your understanding of what type of mortgage product is best for a given person under certain circumstances. This means you have to think carefully about the purpose of each type of loan. For example, a fixed-rate loan might be good for a risk-averse person, for a person on a fixed income, or for a person in a job with low annual pay increases. A fixed-rate mortgage might also be best when market interest rates are low and a person expects that they can only go higher. And a SAM may be attractive to a lender in a market with strong housing sales and a bright future, but may make little sense if the market is weak and housing values are steady or falling. Thus, you are taken back to the points raised in Chapter 1—you must understand the market context of your transaction.

☞ **You need to be able to distinguish a PMM from a PMSI:** Be careful and do not assume that a PMM (purchase-money mortgage) on real estate is treated the same as a *purchase-money security interest (PMSI)* under Article 9 of the Uniform Commercial Code (UCC § 9-103). This is a mistake; the Article 9 PMSI has specific priority rights and other consequences that do not carry over to the PMM. In many states a PMM has only the priority of its recording order and date; in other states it carries a presumption of priority only as in relationship to another loan funded at virtually the same time, and then only if it came from the seller. So the PMM will vary from state to state and can operate in a way that differs from the PMSI of the UCC.

CHAPTER 16

MORTGAGE OBLIGATIONS

ChapterScope ━━━━━━━━━━━━━━━━━━━━━━━━━━━━━━━━━━

This chapter explores the types of obligations secured by mortgages. Usually, the obligation is a debt, evidenced by a promissory note, but other obligations can also be secured by a mortgage. The legal rules include limits on interest charged by the lender (usury laws), and charges associated with late payment and early payment of the mortgage debt.

- ■ **Promissory note:** Mortgage debt is usually evidenced by a ***promissory note***.

- ■ **Usury:** Usury laws limit the amount of interest a lender may charge a borrower.

- ■ **Late charges:** Late payment charges are often expressly provided for in promissory notes. Most types of late charges are upheld as proper ***liquidated damages***.

- ■ **Prepayment:** A borrower has the right of prepayment only if the promissory note so states under the rule of ***perfect tender in time***.

- ■ **Nondebt obligations:** Mortgages may secure obligations other than debts, provided the obligation is described in the mortgage and its monetary value is reasonably capable of measurement.

I. FORM OF OBLIGATION

Every mortgage secures the payment or performance of an obligation. Usually, the obligation is a debt of the mortgagor owed to the mortgagee. A writing that is separate from the mortgage instrument usually evidences the debt. Most commonly the writing is a ***promissory note***.

II. USURY

A usury law limits the amount of interest a lender may charge a borrower. Most usury laws are state laws, either constitutional or statutory, and their content varies widely from state to state.

A. Traditional fixed limit: Traditional usury laws are not sensitive to market changes in the interest rate. Rather, they set a fixed maximum interest rate, such as 10 percent or 12 percent per annum for certain categories of loans. The limit is supposed to be high enough so that, in principle, there is sufficient room under the limit for reasonable and normal market fluctuations in the cost of money to occur.

B. Compounding of interest: The term "compounding" refers to how often interest on the loan is calculated. Interest may be compounded daily, monthly, annually, or at the end of any other period agreed to by the parties. The frequency of compounding affects how much interest the borrower owes. Frequent compounding raises the effective interest rate.

1. **Simple interest:** The term "simple interest" means that interest on the loan is compounded annually. A usury law with a fixed annual maximum rate is usually calculated based on simple interest. A lender that charges the maximum rate *and* compounds more frequently violates the usury law.

2. **Market customs:** Simple interest was once a very common method of compounding decades ago when many mortgage loans were not amortized; i.e., the borrower was obligated to make only one payment, when the loan matured. With ***installment loans***, almost always interest is compounded at the end of the period when an installment is due.

   Example: In a state with a 12 percent usury limit, Heidi makes a $100,000 loan calling for 12 percent annual interest, with all principal and interest due in one year. With simple interest, at the end of the year the borrower pays $112,000 ($100,000 principal + $12,000 interest). But if interest is compounded monthly, the borrower will have to pay $112,682.47 at the end of the year ($100,000 principal + $12,682.47 interest). This approach violates the 12 percent usury limit.

C. **Spreading interest over the loan term:** With many mortgage loans, the borrower's interest payments are not distributed equally over the loan term.

   1. **Prepaid interest:** Normally, interest is paid after it accrues, in arrears, but sometimes the parties contract for the borrower to prepay interest. When a borrower pays ***points*** up front to get a mortgage loan (see Chapter 15), this is a form of prepaid interest. It may cause a usury violation. However, most courts allow the spreading of interest if there is room under the usury limit when the points are added to the base interest rate. For example, in *Fleet Finance, Inc., of Georgia v. Jones*, 430 S.E.2d 352 (Ga. 1993), the court applied the spreading principle so that Fleet, which charged 19 percent interest per annum plus 22 to 27 points up front, did not violate a usury statute limit of 5 percent per month (i.e., 60 percent per annum). Without spreading, a usury violation would have occurred for the first month of the loan term (a point equals 1 percent of the loan amount, so the interest attributed to the first month would exceed 22 percent).

   2. **Adjustable interest rate:** A loan that calls for an adjustable or variable interest rate is open to challenge if it is subject to a usury law with a fixed maximum rate. The problem is that an upward adjustment may exceed the usury maximum. When this happens, some courts allow the spreading of interest, but others do not.

      Example: A loan obligates Borrower to pay interest at the ***prime rate*** announced by Big Bank, adjusted every month according to that bank's current rate. Suppose the loan is subject to a fixed 10 percent annual usury rate. Prime is now 6.5 percent so everything is fine. If, however, prime rises over 10 percent, there is a problem. Without spreading, the loan violates the limit as soon as prime exceeds 10 percent. With spreading, an average rate for the term of the loan is computed. This means the lender can collect interest in excess of 10 percent to the extent it previously charged interest at 6.5 percent and other rates below 10 percent.

      a. **Usury savings clauses:** Any lender who makes an adjustable-rate loan that is subject to a fixed usury limit should include a usury savings clause in the promissory note. There are two varieties of clauses.

         i. **Generic clause:** One is generic, saying in essence that the parties do not intend to violate the usury laws and regardless of the stated interest rate the borrower will not pay and the lender will not collect more than any applicable maximum rate. In some states, a generic usury clause is not effective. See *Swindell v. Federal National Mortgage Ass'n*, 409 S.E.2d 892 (N.C. 1991), holding a usury savings clause is against public policy because it puts the burden of determining the maximum lawful rate on the borrower, not on the lender, who is in a better position to know the law.

> **ii. Interest rate cap:** The other type of savings clause is specific: The lender looks up the specific usury limit and adds a life-of-the-loan maximum interest rate equal to this number.

b. Drafting consideration: When representing lenders in real estate transactions, it's essential that you become familiar with your state's usury laws. A generic usury clause may or may not be adequate to protect your client, but under some circumstances it's preferable. One advantage to the generic clause, compared to an interest rate cap, is its flexibility. If the state amends its usury law to remove or increase the fixed maximum rate, the loan documents allow the lender to take advantage of that change. With an interest rate cap, the lender takes on the financial risk that market rates may in the future exceed the cap. The lender who foresees this risk may add ***call protection***; while this solution reduces the risk, it adds complexity to the transaction and may not be ideal.

D. Time-price rule: When a seller of real estate extends financing to the buyer, he usually takes back a promissory note secured by a ***purchase-money mortgage*** (see Chapter 15). In some states, this loan must comply with any applicable usury laws, just as if a third-party lender supplied the financing. Many states, however, immunize purchase-money loans made by sellers from their usury laws under a rule called the ***time-price*** or ***credit-sale*** rule. This means the seller can quote both a cash price and a higher credit price without the difference between the two prices being construed as interest for usury purposes.

Example: Corky advertises his lakefront vacation condominium for sale, asking $300,000 all cash or $340,000 with seller financing, where he is taking back a purchase-money mortgage at 10 percent per annum. Suppose a state usury law generally allows only 10 percent annual interest for a mortgage loan of this type. Without the time-price rule, Corky has very probably violated the usury law, charging hidden interest equal to the price difference of $40,000 (like points) plus 10 percent. However, Corky is fine if the state applies the time-price principle.

E. Remedies for usury violations: The borrower's remedies for usury violations vary according to the state. At a minimum, the lender forfeits the interest that exceeds the usury limit. Many states levy harsher penalties to discourage usury:

1. Statutory damages: Some states require the lender to pay the borrower damages that are double or triple the amount of excess interest.

2. No interest: Some states do not allow the lender to collect any interest at all on a usurious loan. The lender may collect only the loan principal.

3. No further payments: In a few states, once the borrower proves usury, she is relieved of all further payments, not only interest, but also outstanding principal. The mortgage securing payment is then cancelled. In *Seidel v. 18 East 17th Street Owners, Inc.*, 598 N.E.2d 7 (N.Y. 1992), a statute limited the interest rate to 16 percent per annum. An individual financed a cooperative developer's purchase of a loft building, advancing $150,000 in funds and receiving a $225,000 bond plus the right to buy one floor in the building at a below-market price. This violated the statute, rendering the lender unable to collect the remaining principal balance.

F. Lender defenses: When a borrower establishes that his loan is usurious, the lender may have an affirmative defense. However, courts are usually stingy with affirmative defenses because usury laws are designed to protect borrowers who transact with unequal bargaining power or are otherwise preyed upon. See *Seidel v. 18 East 17th Street Owners, Inc.*, 598 N.E.2d 7 (N.Y. 1992), rejecting the affirmative defenses of waiver and estoppel. In *Seidel*, the successor entity to the original borrower had standing to assert usury although an unrelated purchaser who takes subject to a usurious loan may waive the right to complain of usury. An attorney acted both as principal in borrower and as counselor for lender, but this did not estop borrower from claiming usury.

G. Federal preemption: The Depository Institutions Deregulation and Monetary Control Act: In 1980, Congress passed the Depository Institutions Deregulation and Monetary Control Act, 12 U.S.C. § 1735f-7, to preempt state usury laws on almost all loans secured by first liens on residential real property.

1. **Property covered:** The law covers all single-family homes, apartments, other multifamily housing, manufactured homes, and cooperative housing.

2. **Federally related mortgage loan:** Under the Act, state-law usury preemption applies to every federally related mortgage loan. Such loans are those made by traditional institutional lenders, manufactured home sellers who regularly finance their purchasers, creditors who make or invest in residential loans aggregating more than $1 million per year, and individuals who finance the sale of their principal residence. With this broad definition, very few first-lien residential loans do not enjoy federal preemption.

    a. **Borrowers:** The borrower's identity makes no difference under the Act for preemption purposes.

3. **Junior mortgage loans:** Note the Act preempts only *first-lien* mortgage loans. Thus, all junior mortgage loans, including purchase-money second mortgages and home-equity loans are subject to state regulation of interest rates.

4. **Limits on points:** The law preempts not only state interest rate limits, but also state laws that limit discount points, origination fees, and similar up-front charges.

5. **State overrides:** The law authorized states to override federal preemption by acting within a three-year window that ended in 1983. Most states did not override federal preemption. During the window period, 15 states and Puerto Rico chose to reinstate their own usury laws.

III. LATE PAYMENT

When a mortgage borrower pays late, the lender is entitled to monetary compensation. The lender may also be entitled to proceed to foreclose on the mortgaged property under the terms of the mortgage (this topic is covered in Chapters 18 and 19). Under the mortgage terms, the additional compensation due from the borrower is usually also secured by the mortgage until paid by the borrower. The amount of compensation that the borrower must pay is based on general principles of damages and the express terms of the debt (the promissory note).

A. Interest on unpaid sum: The primary contract remedy for any person's failure to pay money when due is interest for the period of tardiness. This is the lender's only remedy unless the promissory note provides for additional remedies. Most promissory notes specify a rate of interest using language that indicates what rate applies between maturity and actual payment. Sometimes, this is the same basic rate that has applied prior to default.

Example: A promissory note provides for monthly payments of principal and interest of $1,000 for 15 years at a fixed "interest rate of 8 percent per annum on all amounts of principal until paid." Another sentence in the note says, "Any interest hereunder if not paid when due shall be added to principal." If the maker of the note fails to pay on time, the holder's remedy is to charge additional interest on the unpaid installment at 8 percent until paid.

1. **Higher default interest rate specified:** Some promissory notes require that the maker pay a higher interest rate upon the event of default. The clause may impose the higher rate on the entire loan balance, or if the entire loan is not yet matured only on unpaid past-due installments. See *Westmark Commercial Mortgage Fund IV v. Teenform Associates, L.P.*, 827 A.2d 1154 (N.J. Super. Ct. App. Div. 2003), holding the lender was entitled to enforce a clause raising the rate from 8 percent to 10 percent per annum.

2. **No default interest rate specified:** When the promissory note does not specify the rate of interest that should apply to a late payment, the rate of interest should be the market rate at the time of default. This amount will make the lender whole and cause the borrower to pay the loss she has caused. The market rate may be higher than the parties' contract rate. Conceivably, it could be lower if market rates have fallen.

B. Late payment charge: Many mortgage loans expressly provide for a late charge if the borrower fails to pay an installment after a specified grace period. This is true for commercial and residential loans, but is especially common for residential loans. The late charge is not an interest rate, but a specified fixed amount. Usually, it is equal to a percentage (such as 5 percent) of the unpaid installment.

1. **State statutory limits:** To protect borrowers from lenders who might try to assess high charges, many states have statutes that regulate late charges for residential mortgages. E.g.:

   - Cal. Civ. Code § 2954.4: late payment charge limited to greater of $5 or 6 percent of late installment; 10-day grace period.

   - N.Y. Real Prop. Law § 254-b: charge limited to 2 percent of late installment; 15-day grace period.

   - Wis. Stat. § 138.052(6): charge limited to 5 percent of late installment; 15-day grace period.

2. **Federal regulations:** At the federal level, residential mortgage lenders are subject to various regulations concerning late charges.

   a. **Conventional loans:** The Federal National Mortgage Association (Fannie Mae or FNMA) requires for conventional loans a late charge after 15 days equal to 4 percent of the late installment or such lesser amount permitted by state law. The Federal Home Loan Mortgage Corporation (Freddie Mac or FHLMC) authorizes, but does not require, a 5 percent late charge after 15 days.

    b. FHA and VA mortgage loans: Federal Housing Administration (FHA) and Veterans Administration (VA) mortgage loans bear late charges of 4 percent of the unpaid installment after 15 days. 24 C.F.R. § 203.25; 38 C.F.R. § 36.4212(d).

    c. Office of Thrift Supervision rule: The Office of Thrift Supervision (OTS), which regulates all federally chartered thrift institutions, authorizes its institutions to impose late charges on residential borrowers. 12 C.F.R. § 560.33. Its regulations generally preempt inconsistent state laws. The OTS regulation does not set a maximum charge, but it resembles some state statutes in its combination of disclosure principles and other substantive rules.

3. Liquidated damages: A late payment charge agreed on by the parties is a type of liquidated damages clause. As such, it is subject to judicial supervision. It must be a reasonable amount, and actual damages must be difficult or impossible to compute. Under this standard, courts have upheld some clauses but have struck down others.

    a. Amount of charge: In *Garrett v. Coast & Southern Federal Savings & Loan Ass'n*, 511 P.2d 1197 (Cal. 1973), the late charge for an unpaid installment was equal to 2 percent per annum for the period of delinquency assessed against the ***entire unpaid principal balance of the loan obligation***. The court held that this was an unenforceable penalty. To be a reasonable estimate of lender's actual damages, the charge must be calculated based on the amount of the unpaid installment.

    b. Difficulty of measuring actual damages: In principle, actual damages based on an appropriate interest factor for late loan payments are easy to calculate, and, thus, late payment charges should be unlawful. Courts nevertheless strain to enforce late payment charges they consider to be reasonable in amount. They stress two points. Actual damages from late payment are said to be hard to measure because the lender incurs administrative expenses in connection with the default, such as sending default notices to the borrower. Second, courts believe lenders should be able to encourage prompt payment (i.e., discourage default) by making borrowers pay appreciably more than their normal interest rate.

    Example: A commercial mortgage loan for $3,145,000 called for monthly payments of $23,077. The promissory note gave the lender the option to impose a late charge of 6 percent of any overdue installments. The court upheld the late charges assessed by the lender based on a presumption "that liquidated damages clauses in a commercial context between sophisticated parties" are reasonable. *Westmark Commercial Mortgage Fund IV v. Teenform Associates, L.P.*, 827 A.2d 1154, 1156 (N.J. Super. Ct. App. Div. 2003).

4. State usury laws: In some states, a late payment charge is considered interest for purposes of usury laws. The borrower will have a usury defense if the amount of the late charge exceeds the maximum permitted interest for the type of loan in question. In *Swindell v. Federal National Mortgage Association*, 409 S.E.2d 892 (N.C. 1991), a residential loan violated the state usury statute when the lender charged a 5 percent late charge on unpaid installments, but the state late charge statute authorized only a 4 percent charge. For a remedy, the court barred the lender from collecting any late charge or charging interest on past-due installments.

5. Effect of statutes and regulations on common law liquidated damages rules and usury rules: When a mortgage loan is subject to a state statute that protects the borrower by limiting a late charge, it is highly unlikely a court will find that a late charge that complies with the law is unreasonably high. At the federal level, the OTS regulations generally preempt state laws, which should include liquidated damages and usury principles, as well as state late-charge statutes.

IV. PREPAYMENT

A borrower might pay a promissory note on time, late, or early. The prior section discusses late payment. This section discusses early payment. Early payment is prepayment, when the borrower pays part or all of the principal before the due date specified in the promissory note.

A. Total prepayment: When the borrower pays the entire remaining loan balance before its due date, this is a total prepayment. The borrower pays accrued interest to the date of prepayment. The promissory note, being totally satisfied, is cancelled. For this reason the lender is required to release the mortgage.

B. Partial prepayment: A partial prepayment occurs when the borrower pays some, but not all, of the principal before it matures. This commonly happens for installment notes, when the borrower elects to pay one or more installments before they are due.

C. Voluntary prepayment: Prepayment is voluntary when the borrower decides to make a payment before the time specified in the note.

D. Involuntary prepayment: In contrast, involuntary prepayment occurs when the lender compels prepayment due to the borrower's default or the occurrence of some other event specified in the promissory note or in the mortgage instrument.

Example: The promissory note and mortgage contain a "due-on-sale" clause that prohibits the borrower from selling or transferring the property without the lender's prior written consent. If the borrower violates the due-on-sale clause, the lender has the right to accelerate maturity of the debt and thus compel prepayment by the borrower.

E. Borrower's right to prepay: Many promissory notes contain an express clause dealing with prepayment, and the first step in any dispute is to check the note for such a clause. Without such a clause, there are two implied rules.

   1. Perfect tender in time: The traditional implied rule, still followed by most U.S. jurisdictions, is that the borrower has no right to prepay a loan in the absence of an express prepayment clause. This rule is sometimes described as the rule of perfect tender in time: The promissory note specifies a payment date or payment schedule, and both parties have the right to insist that the performance comply exactly with the stated time.

      a. Effect on mortgage: When the lender has the right to reject a borrower's tender of full prepayment, the lender also has the general right to insist that the mortgaged property remain as security for the debt. This may restrict the borrower's property rights because the borrower is unable to free the property of the mortgage without the lender's consent. This may be significant when the borrower wants to sell the property or wants to devote it to a use not permitted by the mortgage.

   2. Implied right to prepay: The trend is for states, sometimes by statute and occasionally by judicial decision, to reject the rule of perfect tender in time. They follow the rule that, when the note is silent on prepayment, the borrower has the right to prepay the debt in full at any time without penalty or premium and with no further interest accruing on the debt after the date of prepayment. E.g., Wis. Stat. §138.052(2) (borrower may prepay residential mortgage loan "at any time in whole or in part").

3. **Express prepayment provisions:** The parties to the loan have the right to specify the terms and conditions under which the borrower shall have the right to prepay the loan, and many promissory notes contain express prepayment provisions. Some clauses favor the borrower, freely permitting total and partial prepayments. Most residential loans presently made in the United States have such pro-borrower provisions. Many *subprime residential mortgage loans* made since 2000, however, have contained prepayment penalties.

   a. **Prepayment penalty:** Many loans, especially commercial loans, restrict prepayment by the borrower. Often, prepayment is permitted only if the borrower pays a penalty or a premium, which is designed to compensate the lender for the loss of its bargain and its task in having to reinvest the loan proceeds earlier than anticipated. Sometimes, prepayment is prohibited completely for the first years of the loan. Often, the prepayment penalty is graduated, reducing in amount according to how long the loan has remained outstanding.

   b. **Enforceability:** Express prepayment clauses reflect the parties' allocation of risk with respect to future changes in market rates of interest and with respect to the borrower's desire to free the property of the mortgage. Courts generally enforce prepayment clauses in accordance with their terms. For example, in *Carlyle Apartments Joint Venture v. AIG Life Insurance Co.*, 635 A.2d 366 (Md. 1994), the court enforced a clause calling for a prepayment fee equal to the difference in yield between the contract rate set forth in the promissory note and the market rate for U.S. Treasury Notes at the time of prepayment. The *Carlyle* court rejected the borrower's argument that the clause constituted a liquidated damages clause and should be subjected to the normal judicial limitations for liquidated damages.

   Example: Nadia borrows $2 million from Lester to finance a small office building. The loan bears interest at 9 percent per annum and is repayable in equal monthly installments of principal and interest over 18 years. The promissory note expressly prohibits prepayment completely for the first four years. The note states that after the fourth year, prepayment in full is permitted but only on 60 days prior notice from borrower to lender and with payment to the lender of a premium equal to 4 percent of the then outstanding principal balance. The note provides that the prepayment premium is reduced by .5 percent for each succeeding year after the fifth year, but it never is reduced below 1 percent of the principal balance. Such a provision is generally enforceable in accordance with its terms. It does not matter whether the jurisdiction applies the rule of perfect tender in time or implies a borrower right to prepay mortgage debt. If, for example, during the seventh year Nadia decides to prepay the loan at a time when the principal balance is $1,600,000, she will owe a prepayment premium of $48,000 ($1,600,000 × 3 percent).

      i. **Prepayment resulting from lender's decision to accelerate debt:** Courts have split over whether a lender may collect a prepayment premium upon an involuntary prepayment resulting from the lender's decision to accelerate maturity of the debt after default by the borrower. See *Westmark Commercial Mortgage Fund IV v. Teenform Associates, L.P.*, 827 A.2d 1154 (N.J. Super. Ct. App. Div. 2003), following the

Restatement (Third) of Property, Mortgages §6.2 to allow a lender to collect the premium provided for in a commercial mortgage loan transaction.

V. NONDEBT OBLIGATIONS

Most mortgages secure debts held by the mortgagee. But a mortgage can secure other legally enforceable obligations as well.

A. Definition of debt: A **debt** is an obligation to pay a fixed amount of money with or without interest.

    1. Collateral promises: In addition to promising to pay the debt, the mortgagor usually makes other promises. These promises typically are set forth in the mortgage. These obligations are not themselves debts; they are collateral to the debt held by the mortgagee. Their purpose is to preserve the value of the security until the debt is paid. Once the debt is paid, these nondebt obligations vanish.

    Example: Martha owes Lucky $500,000, the debt being due on December 1. In the mortgage, Martha covenants to insure the gasoline station located on the mortgaged property. The insurance policy expires on June 1, and Martha decides not to renew it because she plans to demolish the improvements to build a gymnastics center. The debt is prepayable without restriction or penalty, and on May 30, Martha mails payment in full to Lucky, which he receives on June 3. Lucky learned of Martha's decision not to renew the insurance policy because the company sent him a notice of nonrenewal. Once Lucky receives payment in full, he has no legal right to insist that Martha insure the property. Nor can he collect damages for the failure to insure the property between June 1 and June 3, as he has suffered no injury. It does not matter that Lucky has not yet released the mortgage, so that the mortgage instrument still appears to be valid according to the public records.

B. Primary obligation is not a debt: A property owner may grant a mortgage to secure an obligation that is not a debt. For the mortgage to be enforceable, courts commonly impose several requirements.

    1. Written description of obligation: The mortgage must expressly describe the obligation it secures. The obligation itself does not have to be set forth in a separate writing, but it may be. A dollar amount for the obligation need not be stated.

    2. Definitely ascertainable amount: Most courts require that the nondebt obligation be capable of reduction to a definitely ascertainable amount so as to render the mortgage valid. The concern is that, if the obligation cannot be valued monetarily, it will not be possible to handle foreclosure properly in the event the mortgage at issue or another lien on the property is foreclosed. Courts usually do not say whether the amount must be ascertainable at the outset when the mortgage is granted, or only later when there is a foreclosure. The concern identified above suggests that valuation at the time of foreclosure should suffice.

    Example: A contractor who owned land subject to a first mortgage entered into a contract of sale, pursuant to which the contractor promised to construct an apartment building on that land. The buyer paid the contractor $25,000 in advance, and the contractor granted a second mortgage to the buyer to secure the contractor's obligations. The contractor defaulted under the first mortgage and under the construction agreement. The first mortgagee foreclosed, with the sale generating a surplus of $10,000. The court awarded the buyer this amount, holding that the second mortgage was valid. The buyer's claim was definitely ascertainable because the contractor owed the buyer at least the amount of the advance ($25,000) for breaching the construction contract. *Pawtucket Institution for Savings v. Gagnon,* 475 A.2d 1028 (R.I. 1984).

   a. Supplier of materials and labor: A person who supplies materials or labor for improvements to land may secure the purchase price or wages by getting an express mortgage. See *W.L. Development Corp. v. Trifort Realty, Inc.,* 377 N.E.2d 969 (N.Y. 1978), holding that the state procedure for mechanics' and materialmen's liens does not preclude the parties from securing the obligation with a mortgage.

   Example: Tenant rents an apartment building from Landlord for a period of 10 years. Tenant owns other real property named Westplace, which is subject to an existing first mortgage. In lieu of giving Landlord a security deposit, Tenant grants Landlord a second mortgage on Westplace "for the express purpose of securing Tenant's obligations under that certain Lease dated July 1, 2012, between . . . including Tenant's payment of all rent thereunder." This mortgage is probably enforceable. It adequately describes the secured obligation. An argument could arise as to whether Tenant's obligations under the lease can be reasonably valued or reduced to monetary terms. If the Lease provides for fixed rents for its term of 10 years, clearly valuation is practical and relatively simple. The case is harder if the Lease provides for percentage rent or for periodic rent adjustments based upon market factors.

C. Support mortgage: A support mortgage is a type of ***purchase-money mortgage*** in which the purchaser/mortgagor promises to provide financial support for the mortgagee/seller for the remainder of his life. It is used occasionally between family members when an older person transfers title to a daughter, son, or younger relative in exchange for a support commitment. The support obligation is generally not quantified in terms of dollars, but is interpreted judicially as ***reasonable*** support. Although such an obligation obviously is not reasonably quantifiable, courts nevertheless have enforced support mortgages. Thus, the support mortgage is an exception to the rule requiring that a nondebt obligation be reasonably ascertainable in monetary amount.

   1. Life estate compared: The support mortgage resembles a family transaction in which a property owner grants title and retains a life estate. It is distinguishable in that the grantee/mortgagor obtains the entire fee estate presently. Moreover, with a life estate, the life tenant is entitled to possession and the entire economic value of the property for the remainder of her life. With a support mortgage, there is sometimes the understanding when the property constitutes the grantor/mortgagee's home that she will continue to live there. However, the grantee/mortgagor is entitled to the all present rents and profits subject only to the duty to support the mortgagee.

   2. Planning consideration: A support mortgage is seldom used or encountered in modern real estate transactions. Regardless of its validity, the parties can almost always better accomplish their purposes by using a different structure. For example, the lawyer (whether she represents the present owner, the grantee, or both parties) can recommend an inter vivos trust, an installment sale of the property with the balance due to be forgiven at the grantor's death, or reverse annuity mortgage on the property (see Chapter 15) to provide monthly payments to the grantor.

Quiz Yourself on
MORTGAGE OBLIGATIONS

72. For a mortgage loan, what document describes the borrower's obligation to pay the debt? _____

73. Julio sells his ranch to Kelley, who pays $200,000 cash and gives Julio a promissory note with the face amount of $800,000. The note is payable in eight annual installments of $100,000. Interest is specified at 10 percent per annum for the first four years and then increases to 14 percent per annum for the next four years. Assume that a state usury law limits interest to 12 percent per annum for loans of this type. Is there a usury violation? _____

74. Joe Consumer goes to a bank, where he gets a loan, secured by a first-lien mortgage on his downtown condominium. Presently Joe is living in another state, and he's renting the condominium to his sister Jane under an oral month-to-month tenancy. Is this loan subject to any applicable state usury law? _____

75. A $200,000 commercial loan for a small apartment building provides for monthly payments over 15 years with an interest rate of 10 percent. A default provision states that, if any monthly payment is more than 10 days late, Borrower must pay a late charge of $100 plus interest on the past-due installment at 12 percent until paid. Borrower defaults, Lender demands the late charge, and Borrower claims it is not legally due. Must Borrower pay the $100 late charge? _____

76. Josef buys Karin's mink farm, giving her a promissory note for $1.2 million secured by a purchase-money mortgage. The note is payable in a lump-sum single payment, due in three years, with interest to accrue at 14 percent per annum. Sixteen months after buying the farm, interest rates have fallen, Josef has found investors who will refinance the debt, and he wants to prepay Karin. The note and mortgage are both silent on prepayment. Josef tenders prepayment. Karin refuses to accept it. Josef offers her $5,000 if she will accept and release the mortgage lien. Karin refuses, countering that if he pays an extra $150,000, she will take his money. Josef sues for a declaratory judgment that he is entitled to prepay. Who will prevail? _____

77. Your client Julio owns Rolling Rock subdivision, which is platted for 80 lots. It presently has no streets or other subdivision improvements. Julio wants to convey eight lots to Bucky Builder in exchange for Bucky's promise to put in the streets, sidewalks, and utilities for the entire subdivision. Can Julio get Bucky's obligations secured by a mortgage on the eight lots to be conveyed? _____

Answers

72. **The promissory note.** The mortgage refers to the promissory note, and may state the original principal amount of the note. The mortgage itself does not describe the debt in detail.

73. **Probably not.** Federal preemption does not apply because this is not residential real property, even if Kelley lives on the ranch. This is business property.

During the last four years of the loan, interest at 14 percent does exceed the state maximum of 12 percent. Julio has two potential defenses. First, if the state applies the time-price or credit-sale doctrine, this loan probably is not subject to the usury limit. The thinking is that, although the parties specified a price of $1,000,000 and an excessive interest rate, they could have bargained for a higher purchase price (such as $1,100,000) and a lower interest rate, thereby letting Julio lawfully collect the same dollars. Julio's second defense is that the total interest should be spread evenly among all eight years of the loan term, so that in the aggregate he is not getting in excess of 12 percent per annum. Many states would permit spreading the interest in this fashion.

74. **No.** Any state usury law that might otherwise apply is preempted by federal legislation (the Depository Institutions Deregulation and Monetary Control Act of 1980) because the bank holds a mortgage that is a first lien. This assumes the property is not located in one of the jurisdictions that passed laws to override federal preemption between 1980 and 1983.

   Joe's lease to his sister isn't relevant. This is clearly residential real estate under the federal act, and it doesn't matter whether the property is Joe's principal residence or whether he's holding it as rental property.

75. **Probably not.** If a state usury law applies to this loan, this late charge possibly violates the law. Borrower would claim the entire charge is interest. Lender would claim part or all is payment of damages for Lender's administrative costs and is not interest. Moreover, to the extent the charge is interest, Lender will claim it should be spread over the life of the loan to avoid a usury violation. Under liquidated damages analysis, it does not matter whether the late charge is characterized as interest. The parties will dispute whether the charge is unreasonably high, with the outcome difficult to predict. Borrower will claim that it is too high because it is unusual to combine a fixed charge (here $100) with additional interest, although each element, used alone, is standard practice. Lender will emphasize that the sum of the two, as applied to this loan, is not unreasonably high; that Borrower voluntarily defaulted; and that this is a commercial loan entered into with a borrower who agreed to pay this sum upon default.

76. **Karin in most jurisdictions.** Karin wins if the state applies the traditional rule of perfect tender in time. She has the right to insist on payment at the end of the three-year term, with all the accrued interest for that period. Because she has the right to reject Josef's offer of a prepayment penalty, it is unlikely that the court will scrutinize the amount of her counteroffer of $150,000 to see how it compares to the economic cost or loss to her of accepting prepayment.

   Josef wins if the state rejects the rule of perfect tender in time, instead implying a right of prepayment in the absence of agreement to the contrary. Since Karin rejected his offer of an extra $5,000, he now has the right to prepay without any premium at all.

77. **Yes.** With proper planning and drafting, Julio can obtain an enforceable mortgage. The mortgage must adequately describe Bucky's construction obligations. The value of Bucky's work has to be reasonably ascertainable. To eliminate any risk that a court might find it hard to value Bucky's obligations, the contract should specify a dollar amount just as if Julio had agreed to hire Bucky as a contractor and pay him cash as the work progressed. The specified amount may be expressed as liquidated damages in the event Bucky defaults.

Exam Tips *on* MORTGAGE OBLIGATIONS

- ☛ **Differences between obligation and mortgage:** Know the different functions performed by the promissory note and the mortgage instrument.

  - ☞ **Promissory note:** The promissory note evidences the debt, and provides details about the borrower's obligation to make payments of principal and interest.

  - ☞ **Mortgage:** The mortgage secures the debt—it makes the real property serve as collateral in case the debtor does not pay the debt.

- ☛ **Usury laws:** Usury is less important for real estate finance than it once was, due to federal preemption of state limits (Depository Institutions Deregulation and Monetary Control Act of 1980) and state law reforms.

  - ☞ **Federal preemption:** If the topic of usury is tested, you certainly need to know the basics of federal preemption: Almost all first-lien mortgages on residential property (single-family and multifamily) are sheltered by federal preemption.

- ☛ **Late charges:** Late payment charges are usually considered to be the proper method of liquidating damages because the lender's calculation of actual damages is not practical.

- ☛ **Prepayment:** If you have a dispute about the borrower's right to prepay a mortgage loan, be sure to discuss the split of authority:

  - ☞ **Perfect tender in time:** Under the rule of perfect tender in time, there is no right to prepay.

  - ☞ **Right to prepay:** A growing number of states (but still a minority) reject perfect tender in time, giving the borrower an implied right to prepay.

- ☛ **Nondebt obligations:** A debt is an obligation to pay a fixed sum of money. Remember that a mortgage can secure an obligation that is not a debt. The obligation does not have to be a fixed sum at the outset of the transaction, provided the amount can be definitely ascertained when the time comes for enforcement.

CHAPTER 17

TRANSFERS BY BORROWERS AND LENDERS

ChapterScope ——————————————————————————————

The chapter considers transfers of the property by borrowers and transfers of the debt and mortgage by lenders. Markets only function when property owners have the right and ability to sell or transfer their ownership interests. Much real property is mortgaged, and in every such case there are two valuable property rights that may be the subject of sale or transfer—the real property owned by the mortgagor, and the debt owned by the lender that is secured by the property. A complex set of legal rules define the rights and obligations of real estate borrowers and lenders who transfer their ownership interests.

When a mortgage continues after the borrower conveys ownership to another person, the grantee usually assumes the mortgage loan or takes subject to that loan. A due-on-sale clause in the mortgage may restrict the borrower's right to convey ownership. Lenders often sell or assign their mortgage loans. Those transfers sometimes implicate the rules concerning negotiable paper.

- ■ **Assumption:** A mortgage loan assumption means the buyer becomes personally liable to pay the seller's existing loan.

- ■ **Taking subject to:** A buyer who takes subject to the seller's mortgage loan is not personally liable.

- ■ **Seller as surety:** The seller of mortgaged property remains personally liable for the debt as a surety.

- ■ **Due-on-sale:** Many mortgages contain a due-on-sale clause.

- ■ **Lender's transfer:** The lender can sell or assign mortgages.

- ■ **Negotiable instruments:** Many real estate loans include a negotiable instrument under the Uniform Commercial Code.

I. TRANSFERS OF MORTGAGED PROPERTY

When mortgaged property is sold or transferred, one of two things happens. Either the mortgage debt is paid in full, with the mortgage released so it no longer affects title, or the debt and mortgage remain in place. When the existing debt remains in place, the grantee/buyer may agree to become responsible for that debt in one of two ways. She may *assume* the mortgage debt, or she may *take title subject to* that debt.

A. **Assumption of mortgage obligation:** Assumption means the buyer promises the seller that the buyer will pay all of the debt in accordance with its terms. Usually an assumption agreement is contained in the deed that conveys title from seller to buyer. An assumption results in a set of rights and obligations involving three parties: the seller, the assuming buyer, and the mortgagee. The following triangle encapsulates the parties' positions.

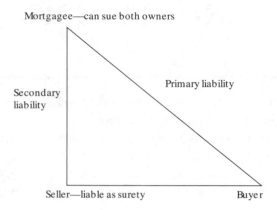

1. **Buyer's position:** Assuming mortgage debt means that the buyer is ***personally liable*** to pay the debt. The mortgagee may sue the buyer for failing to pay.

2. **Seller's position**

   a. **Primary liability of buyer:** The buyer is primarily liable to pay the debt. This is the intent of the assumption agreement between the seller and buyer.

   b. **Seller is surety:** The seller remains liable as the maker of the promissory note, but because the buyer is primarily liable, the seller's liability is secondary. The seller thus is a surety.

   c. **Surety's rights:** If the mortgagee sues the seller on the promissory note without foreclosing or threatening to do so, the seller usually has two choices:

      i. **Pay the debt:** In all states, the seller as surety may pay the debt to the mortgagee in accordance with its terms. Then through ***subrogation*** the seller obtains the mortgagee's rights to enforce the promissory note against the buyer and to foreclose on the real property.

      ii. **Sue the buyer on the assumption contract:** In most but not all states, the seller as surety has a second option. Instead of paying the debt, seller may sue buyer for breach of the promise to assume.

3. **Further transfer and assumption:** If the assuming buyer sells the property with her buyer assuming the existing debt, the original seller usually becomes a ***subsurety***. This means that as between the original seller and the first buyer, the first buyer is to bear the entire risk and cost of the second buyer's default. In *Swanson v. Krenik*, 868 P.2d 297 (Alaska 1994), after a sequence of two assumptions, the second buyer defaulted and the debt holder sued to foreclose, joining the original mortgagor and both buyers. The court rejected the first buyer's claim that she and the original mortgagor were cosureties with equal shared liability. Because the foreclosure sale resulted in a deficiency, the first buyer as primary surety was liable for the entire deficiency.

4. **Express release of liability:** When the seller is personally liable on the mortgage debt, the seller can avoid continuing liability as a surety only if the lender agrees. An express release of

liability accomplishes this objective. Courts will not find an implied release or waiver or estoppel just from the lender's knowledge of and consent to the transfer and assumption. In that situation, the lender is entitled to rely on the normal principle that the seller is becoming a surety. Both lender and seller are presumed to know this legal rule.

5. **Mortgagee's position:** The assuming buyer is personally liable to pay the debt to the mortgagee.

    a. **Direct contract between buyer and mortgagee:** In some cases of loan assumptions, an assumption agreement is entered into between the buyer and the mortgagee. Then the buyer's personal liability is a straightforward enforcement of this agreement. When the mortgagee has the right to approve or deny a requested assumption, the mortgagee sometimes insists upon the buyer's execution of such an assumption agreement.

    b. **No contract between buyer and mortgagee:** When there is no contract between the buyer and the mortgagee, two rationales are used to justify the mortgagee's right to enforce the buyer's assumption promise made to the seller.

        i. **Third-party beneficiary:** Some courts consider the mortgagee to be a third-party beneficiary of the assumption agreement between the seller and the buyer. This theory is well accepted, but it raises theoretical problems both under the creditor/donee beneficiary distinction of the Restatement of Contracts and the intended/incidental beneficiary distinction of the Restatement (Second) of Contracts.

        ii. **Derivative rights:** The second rationale is that the mortgagee has derivative rights against the assuming buyer: By *subrogation*, the mortgagee steps into the seller's shoes and enforces the buyer's promise to the seller to assume the debt.

B. **Taking subject to mortgage obligation:** Instead of assuming the debt, the buyer may take subject to the debt. This means that the buyer does not promise to pay the debt, but agrees that the mortgage is permitted as an exception to good title and that the seller is not responsible for paying the debt.

1. **Nonrecourse financing:** Taking property subject to existing debt means the buyer has no personal liability if he fails to pay the debt. This is a form of nonrecourse financing. The buyer who takes "subject to" usually pays the debt because, if he does not pay, he risks losing the property to the mortgagee, who may choose to foreclose.

2. **Relevance of amount of equity:** The higher the ratio of debt-to-value, the more important the distinction between assumption and taking subject to becomes. When the buyer pays a high percentage of the price in cash, the distinction is less important to both seller and buyer. The buyer who has a large amount of equity is less likely to default and walk away from the property. If a buyer with a lot of equity does default, there's a much better chance that the surety will not suffer a loss because the property value will be sufficient to pay the existing debt. Compare the sale of property for $300,000 with existing debt of (i) $290,000 or (ii) $180,000. In the former situation, it is more important to the seller to have the buyer assume the debt and, conversely, to the buyer to take subject to the debt.

C. **Modification and extension of mortgage debt:** Sometimes, the mortgagor conveys the property to a third person who assumes or takes subject to the debt, and subsequently the mortgagee and the buyer modify or extend the debt without including the mortgagor/seller in the agreement. The issue is whether the mortgagor is still personally liable on the debt, or whether the unconsented-to extension or modification has discharged the mortgagor's liability. In many states, the impact of an extension or modification may depend on whether the buyer assumed or took subject to the debt.

1. **Assumption: Discharge of surety:** Under suretyship principles, the general rule is that any *extension* of the maturity date for payment of the debt or modification discharges the surety unless the surety agrees to that extension. The rationale is that the extension adds to the surety's risk.

   a. **Other modifications:** The same discharge rule applies for modifications other than extensions that increase the surety's risk.

      Example: Diego, the original mortgagor, sells Draftacre to Emily, who assumes a fixed-rate mortgage loan providing for an interest rate of 8 percent per annum. Three months after the sale, Emily and the lender negotiate an increase in the rate to 9 percent. Up until the rate increase, Diego was a surety, with Emily primarily liable on the mortgage loan. The rate increase has the effect of totally discharging Diego from liability as a surety. The rate change increased the amount of debt and the probability that Emily would default, thus increasing the risk to Diego from his position as surety.

2. **Negotiable instruments and the UCC:** Some, but not all, mortgage obligations are evidenced by negotiable instruments. Article 3 of the Uniform Commercial Code governs negotiable instruments, including such instruments secured by a mortgage on real property.

   a. **Pre-1990 Article 3:** Prior to 1990, § 3-606 of the Uniform Commercial Code governed extensions and releases granted by the note holder, providing for a discharge when the holder "agrees to suspend the right to enforce" the instrument, and also providing for discharges under other circumstances. Most courts interpreted § 3-606 as codifying basic common law suretyship principles, including the rule that an extension made without the mortgagor's consent results in a total discharge, regardless of whether the mortgagor actually suffers loss. Some courts, however, interpreted § 3-606 to discharge the mortgagor only to the extent she proved that the extension or modification in fact caused actual harm or loss. The pre-1990 version of Article 3 is presently in effect only in New York.

   b. **Revised Article 3:** All states other than New York have adopted the 1990 revision to Article 3, with some also adopting the 2002 amendments to Article 3. Revised Article 3, as amended, extensively revised the discharge rules, but limited their scope to "accommodation parties" and "secondary obligors." A seller of property to an assuming party is neither an "accommodation party" nor a "secondary obligor." Thus, in states with Revised Article 3, resolution of the rights of makers of negotiable mortgage notes after a transfer of the mortgaged property turns on common law suretyship principles.

3. **Taking subject to debt:** States have adopted three different positions with regard to extensions and modifications when the buyer takes subject to mortgage debt (without assuming the debt).

   a. **Total discharge:** Some courts grant a total discharge, applying the same rule as they use for assumptions. The buyer's lack of personal liability is not a relevant factor. This also appears to be the rule for a negotiable instrument under revised UCC § 3-605(d), which deals with the discharge of secondary obligors by the lender's impairment of collateral. (But note that the seller is not a "secondary obligor" under Article 3, so this provision does not apply directly.)

b. No discharge: Other courts reach the opposite conclusion. An extension agreement with a nonassuming buyer does not discharge the mortgagor at all. Thus, she remains fully liable for the unpaid portion of the original debt.

c. Partial discharge: A number of states follow a middle ground, granting a partial discharge to the extent of the value of the real property at the time the mortgagee grants an extension to a nonassuming buyer. In *First Federal Savings and Loan Ass'n v. Arena*, 406 N.E.2d 1279 (Ind. Ct. App. 1980), the court applied this rule, with the result that the mortgagor was not liable when the mortgagee and buyer, who took subject to the debt, increased the interest rate.

4. **Reservation of rights clause:** Promissory notes and mortgages often have clauses stating that the mortgagee and a successor owner may extend or modify the debt without discharging the mortgagor from liability. These clauses are often enforceable, but they are strictly construed against the lender. See *First Federal Savings and Loan Ass'n v. Arena*, 406 N.E.2d 1279 (Ind. Ct. App. 1980), holding that the language of a reservation of rights clause authorized an extension of the debt, but not an increase in the interest rate.

D. Restrictions on transfer by mortgagor

1. **General rule of free alienability:** The general rule is that the mortgagor's interest in the property is freely alienable. This is true regardless of which mortgage law title theory the state follows. (For discussion of the title theory, lien theory, and intermediate theory, see Chapter 14.)

2. **Due-on-sale clause:** The parties by contract may restrict the mortgagor's right to alienate or transfer the mortgaged property. The most common type of restraint is the "due-on-sale" clause, which provides that, if the borrower sells the property without the lender's approval, the lender has the option to accelerate the loan (i.e., to declare that the entire principal balance of the loan is immediately due and payable).

3. **Federal rule on enforcement of due-on-sale clauses:** The Garn-St. Germain Depository Institutions Act, 12 U.S.C. § 1701j-3, enacted in 1982, preempts state laws that protected mortgagors from the lender's enforcement of due-on-sale clauses under certain circumstances. The Act makes the due-on-sale clause automatically enforceable. The Act is discussed in more detail below.

4. **Prior state law approaches:** Before the federal statute, state courts followed two radically different approaches to due-on-sale clauses.

a. Automatic enforceability: Most state courts followed the principle that due-on-sale clauses are automatically enforceable, which is now the federal national standard.

b. Impairment test: The state law trend was to reject the automatic enforcement theory of due-on-sale clauses, requiring that the lender act reasonably in the exercise of its rights. Under this minority rule, the lender had to observe standards of commercial reasonableness. Most courts said this meant that the lender could block a transfer only if the transfer would impair its security. The two most common reasons why the lender's security might be impaired were (1) the transferee was not creditworthy and thus was a greater risk to default than the present owner or (2) the transferee was more likely to commit waste, endanger the property, or change the use of the property in a manner likely to reduce its value. See *Wellenkamp v. Bank of America*, 582 P.2d 970 (Cal. 1978), holding that the due-on-sale clause is an unreasonable restraint on alienation "unless the lender can demonstrate that enforcement is reasonably necessary to protect against impairment to its security or the risk of default."

5. Garn-St. Germain Depository Institutions Act

a. **Automatic enforceability:** The Act adopts the automatic enforceability theory of due-on-sale clauses. The lender's reasons or motives for enforcement are not material. The lender generally has complete discretion to approve or disapprove a proposed transfer.

b. **Lender's conditions to transfers:** Because the lender can arbitrarily withhold consent, it also can impose any condition it wishes on a proposed transfer (i.e., bargain for a higher interest rate or additional collateral). For example, in *Destin State Bank v. Summerhouse of FWB, Inc.*, 579 So. 2d 232 (Fla. Dist. Ct. App. 1991), when the borrower requested approval of the sale of a restaurant, the lender demanded that the assuming purchaser put up additional collateral by granting a second mortgage on his home or pledging a $100,000 certificate of deposit. The court held that the lender's conduct was rightful under the federal Act. It did not matter whether the lender acted reasonably in making this demand.

c. **Express standard in due-on-sale clause:** Sometimes, borrowers bargain for an express standard that governs the standard to be used by the lender in deciding whether to grant or withhold consent to a transfer. Such clauses are enforceable.

   Example: A due-on-sale clause for a mortgage loan to a food store has the following proviso: "Borrower has the right to sell the property to any food-store company with total annual gross sales of not less than $30 million. Lender shall not withhold consent for any transfer to such company." The parties have contracted for an exception to the federal rule that due-on-sale clauses are automatically enforceable.

d. **Act's scope: "Real property loan":** The Act applies to every *real property loan* defined as "a loan, mortgage, advance, or credit sale secured by a lien on real property, the stock allocated to a dwelling unit in a cooperative housing corporation, or a residential manufactured home, whether real or personal property." The identity of the lender does not matter; the Act covers all such loans whether made by institutional lenders or others.

e. **Office of Thrift Supervision (OTS) regulation:** The OTS has authority to issue rules and regulations and publish interpretations of the Act. It takes a broad view of preemption. The statutory definition of real property loan may be read as not extending to clauses in leasehold mortgages or installment land contracts. The OTS regulation asserts that the Act applies to due-on-sale clauses in these two transactions.

f. **Act's definition of "due-on-sale" clause:** The Act defines *due-on-sale clause* as "a contract provision which authorizes a lender, at its option, to declare due and payable sums secured by the lender's security instrument if all or any part of the property, or an interest therein, securing the real property loan is sold or transferred without the lender's prior written consent." Most clauses used by lenders meet this definition.

i. Automatic clause: Note that the definition speaks in terms of the lender's *option* to declare the loan due and payable. Occasionally, due-on-sale clauses are worded so it appears that if the owner transfers without consent, the loan balance is *automatically* due and payable in full without any option or action by the lender. Such a variant of the due-on-sale clause is arguably not covered by the federal Act and is thus subject to whatever state law rule applies.

g. Act's exemption for nonsubstantive transfers: The Act protects residential borrowers by prohibiting a lender from using a due-on-sale clause for certain transfers. These transfers, sometimes called *nonsubstantive transfers*, consist of:

- A lien or encumbrance subordinate to the lender's mortgage that does not relate to a transfer of rights of occupancy in the property.

- A purchase-money security interest for household appliances.

- A transfer by devise, descent, or operation of law on the death of a joint tenant or tenant by the entirety.

- A leasehold interest of three years or less not containing an option to purchase.

- A transfer to a relative resulting from the death of a borrower.

- A transfer where the spouse or children of the borrower become an owner of the property.

- A transfer resulting from a decree of a dissolution of marriage, legal separation agreement, or from an incidental property settlement agreement, by which the spouse of the borrower becomes an owner of the property.

- A transfer into an inter vivos trust in which the borrower is and remains a beneficiary and that does not relate to a transfer of rights of occupancy in the property.

- Any other transfer or disposition described in regulations prescribed by the Federal Home Loan Bank Board (now the OTS).

h. Effect of exemptions on state law: Prior to the federal Act, in many states, the right of the lender to accelerate for transfers of the types federally exempted was unclear. In some of the states following the automatic enforcement theory for due-on-sale clauses, it seems that acceleration would be permitted. The Act preempts state law permitting such acceleration.

Example: Lacy moves to another city, renting his condominium to Tennille for one year. At Tennille's request, Lacy gives her a right of first refusal should he decide to sell the condominium while the lease is in effect. Lacy's mortgage loan has a standard broad due-on-sale clause. This lease is a transfer under the terms of the clause, but it is within the federal exemption. Tennille's leasehold is "three years or less" and while she has a right of first refusal, she doesn't have an option to purchase. The right of first refusal makes a sale less probable than would an option. Unlike an option, with the right of first refusal Tennille has no right to buy unless Lacy first decides to sell.

i. Representing the borrower: The federal exemptions for "nonsubstantive transfers" only apply to residential loans. In commercial loans, borrowers are often confronted with loan documents with very broad due-on-sale clauses. The borrower's attorney wants to restrict the scope of the due-on-sale clause to the greatest extent possible. At the minimum, the attorney should seek express exceptions similar to those listed in the federal Act. When the borrower is an entity rather than one or more natural persons, the borrower wants the right to transfer to an affiliated entity (such as a parent corporation or subsidiary).

6. **Seller–buyer avoidance of due-on-sale clauses:** Mortgagors and buyers sometimes try to avoid the consequences of a lender's due-on-sale clause. This is especially likely, both for residential and commercial transactions, when the existing loan has a low interest rate compared to the current market rates. When the parties are not able to arrange a transfer that is outside the scope of the due-on-sale clause, they may try to hide the transfer from the lender. Such a transfer is sometimes called a *silent sale*.

   a. **Risk to seller:** The seller has potential liability to the lender for breach of contract. With many due-on-sale clauses, there is no express promise by the mortgagor to notify the lender prior to making a transfer; the clause simply gives the lender an option to accelerate if a transfer is made. A court, however, might imply a duty on the mortgagor/seller's part to notify the lender of a transfer. If the seller is found to have breached a promise, she will be liable for expectancy damages. These damages could consist of the difference in yield or interest rates between the assumed loan and the market rate at the time of transfer.

   b. **Risk to buyer:** The buyer is not a party to any contract with the lender. Nevertheless, under some circumstances the buyer might be liable to the lender for interference with the lender's contract rights. See Restatement of Torts (Second) § 766 (1977) (liability for intentionally and improperly inducing a person not to perform a contract with a third person).

   c. **Risk to lawyer:** A lawyer who represents seller, buyer, or both in connection with a silent sale must observe ethical rules. It is generally said that a lawyer may assist a client in breaching a contract, provided that the breach does not also constitute a crime. The lawyer must also disclose to the client the risks associated with the breach.

      i. **Fraud:** Under some circumstances, efforts of seller or buyer to preserve secrecy may amount to fraud—either fraudulent misrepresentation or fraudulent concealment. The lawyer is ethically obligated not to assist her client in the commission of fraud.

      ii. **Confidentiality:** The client's plan to transfer the property in violation of a due-on-sale clause is confidential information, which the lawyer must not reveal to the lender without the client's consent.

II. TRANSFERS OF MORTGAGE DEBT

There are large markets for the sale or transfer of mortgage loans in both the residential and the commercial sectors. Individual loans are often transferred. Many loans, especially residential loans, are transferred as part of a pool or package of loans that are grouped together for marketing purposes. The bundling, marketing, and sale of mortgage loan pools or packages is known as *securitization*.

A. **How mortgage loans are assigned:** The transfer of an ownership interest in a mortgage loan is often called an *assignment*. When a lender sells its entire interest in a loan, the standard operating procedure is for the parties to take four steps.

1. **Assignment:** The lender executes and delivers a written Assignment of the Note and Mortgage. This could be one or two documents. The Assignment of Mortgage is in recordable form (notarized).

2. **Endorsement:** The lender endorses the original promissory note.

3. **Delivery:** The lender delivers the original promissory note and the original mortgage to the assignee.

4. **Recordation:** The assignee records the assignment of the mortgage in the real property records in the county where the land is situated.

B. **Mortgage Electronic Registration System (MERS):** In the 1990s, several large participants in the mortgage industry developed the Mortgage Electronic Registration System (MERS) to facilitate transfers of ownership interests in residential mortgage loans. MERS acts as a nominee for loans owned by its members. The mortgage names MERS as the mortgagee of record and as the beneficiary. When a member assigns a loan to another MERS member, MERS tracks the assignment within its system, but remains the mortgagee of record. Because residential loans are often sold multiple times, MERS saves its members the time and expense of recording assignments in the public records.

C. **Mortgage follows obligation:** The obligation is primary in importance, and the mortgage exists only for the purpose of securing payment of the promissory note.

1. **Transfer of mortgage only:** A mortgagee cannot transfer the mortgage without transferring the underlying obligation (the promissory note). An attempt to do so would not convey anything to an assignee.

2. **Transfer of promissory note only:** If the mortgagee assigns and delivers only the note, the assignee will automatically own the mortgage anyway. That assignee can require that the mortgagee make a formal mortgage assignment later.

D. **Failure to record assignment of mortgage:** If the original mortgage is recorded, it has priority from its date of recordation. A transferee of the debt and mortgage enjoys the same priority date. The transferee steps into the shoes of the transferor with regard to priority. Thus, for priority purposes it does not matter when or whether the assignee records the assignment of mortgage.

Example: Henderson buys real estate, granting a first mortgage to Lender One, who records its mortgage. Two years later, Lender One assigns its mortgage to Assignee One, who records the assignment. Fifteen years later, Henderson grants a mortgage to Lender Two. The next month, Assignee One assigns the first mortgage to Assignee Two, who fails to record this assignment. Three years later, Lender Two forecloses. Who has the prior mortgage lien, Assignee Two or Lender Two? Assignee Two prevails. When a first mortgage is validly recorded, it's not necessary to record an assignment to preserve the priority of that mortgage over subsequent claimants. When Lender Two bargained for its mortgage, and later when it foreclosed, it had constructive notice of the first mortgage. *Bank Western v. Henderson*, 874 P.2d 632 (Kan. 1994).

E. **Types of assignments of mortgage debts**

1. **Outright sale:** With an outright sale, the mortgagee transfers her whole interest in the promissory note and other instruments.

2. **Security interest:** The mortgagee can pledge the promissory note—that is, borrow money and grant to that lender a security interest in the note and mortgage.

    a. **Perfection under the Uniform Commercial Code:** The creation and perfection of a security interest in a promissory note secured by a mortgage are governed by UCC Article 9. Recording an assignment of mortgage in the real property records is not sufficient to perfect the security interest in the note. In *Rodney v. Arizona Bank*, 836 P.2d 434 (Ariz. Ct. App. 1992), the promissory note was held in escrow at the time of the assignment. The assignee notified the escrow holder of the assignee's security interest and did not record an assignment of the deed of trust in the real property records. The assignee's notice was sufficient to perfect under Article 9 by taking possession of the collateral. Thus, the assignee had priority over a subsequent claimant.

F. **Negotiable instruments:** Some mortgage debts are evidenced by a writing that qualifies as a negotiable instrument under Article 3 of the Uniform Commercial Code. The distinction between negotiable and nonnegotiable obligations matters when the obligation is assigned.

    1. **Assignee of nonnegotiable debt:** The assignee of nonnegotiable debt generally takes subject to any defense the mortgagor has against the mortgagee. The mortgagor may raise the defense against the assignee just as she could against the mortgagee.

    2. **Assignee of negotiable instrument:** Risk to the assignee is reduced when the assignee holds a negotiable instrument *and* the assignee is a holder in due course because the holder in due course takes free of *personal defenses*. Personal defenses include failure of consideration, payment to the mortgagor, and fraud in the inducement. The holder in due course, however, takes the note subject to *real defenses* asserted by the mortgagor. Real defenses include incapacity, which makes the obligation void; duress; and fraud in fact. UCC § 3-305(a). *Wilson v. Steele*, 259 Cal. Rptr. 851 (Cal. Ct. App. 1989), recognized another type of real defense. An unlicensed contractor assigned a contract to an assignee, who was a holder in due course. The *Wilson* court held that a contract made by an unlicensed contractor is void and illegal, which could be asserted as a real defense against the holder in due course.

    3. **Negotiation of mortgage:** When a negotiable instrument is assigned to a holder in due course, it is completely clear that if the holder sues to collect the instrument the mortgagor-payor cannot raise personal defenses. If instead the holder of the instrument seeks to foreclose the mortgage, the issue is whether the mortgage is also negotiable.

        a. **Majority view:** The mortgage follows the instrument. In almost all states if the instrument is negotiable, so is the mortgage. This means the mortgagor cannot assert personal defenses in a foreclosure action.

        b. **Minority view:** Mortgages aren't negotiable. A few states hold that a mortgage cannot be negotiable even though it secures a negotiable instrument. This means the mortgagor can assert personal defenses in a foreclosure action brought by the holder, but not in an action on the debt. Functionally, the holder has lost her security to the extent the mortgagor establishes a personal defense.

    4. **When is an instrument negotiable?** An instrument is negotiable when it meets the requirements of Article 3 of the UCC.

        a. **"Orders," "promises," and "notes":** Negotiable instruments include both "orders" and "promises" as defined in Article 3. An "order" is a "written instruction to pay money signed by the person giving the instruction," UCC § 3-103(a)(8); for example, a cashier's check or a personal check. A "promise" is a "written undertaking to pay money signed by the person undertaking to pay." UCC § 3-103(a)(12). Under Article 3, a promise is also called a "note." UCC § 3-104(e). In real estate transactions, we are principally concerned with Article 3 "notes" because they, rather than orders, are used for financing property.

b. Requirements for note to be negotiable: Not all writings called "notes" or "promissory notes" are negotiable under the standards of UCC Article 3. To qualify as a negotiable instrument the writing must first meet the definition of a "promise" set forth above and satisfy the following criteria:

   i. Payable to bearer or to order: The writing must be "payable to bearer or to order." UCC § 3-104(a)(1). If the note says it is "payable to bearer," this means the person who possesses the note is entitled to payment. If the note says it is payable "to the order of Joe," then Joe must indorse the note in order for another person to acquire the right to payment. Instruments payable to bearer may be secured by a mortgage, but this is rare. In mortgage transactions, almost all instruments expressly name a seller or a third party as the person to be paid, and thus they are not bearer paper but may qualify as "payable to order."

   ii. Unconditional obligation: The maker must have an unconditional obligation to pay a "fixed amount of money." UCC § 3-104(a). This requirement is usually the problem for mortgage notes that are not negotiable. Either the maker's duty to pay is subject to a condition, or the amount payable varies according to future events. The 1990 revision to Article 3 makes standard adjustable-rate notes negotiable. UCC § 3-112(b).

   iii. No additional obligations: The writing cannot contain additional undertakings of the maker besides the payment of money, with narrow exceptions. The writing, however, may state that the maker's obligation to pay is secured by a mortgage on real property or by other collateral. UCC § 3-104(a)(3).

5. Who is a holder in due course? To be a holder in due course, an assignee of a negotiable instrument must meet four requirements:

   a. Possession: The assignee must have possession of the instrument.

   b. Transfer by negotiation: The transfer must be by "negotiation." UCC § 3-201 (instrument payable to identified person is negotiated by transfer of possession plus indorsement; instrument payable to bearer is negotiated by transfer of possession alone).

   c. Value: The assignee must pay value for the instrument.

   d. Good faith: The holder must take the instrument in good faith, without notice of any defenses or claims or that the instrument is overdue or has been dishonored.

6. Statutory and regulatory restrictions on rights of holder in due course: State and federal laws sometimes protect the mortgagor from the normal consequences of assignments of negotiable instruments to holders in due course.

   a. State consumer legislation: Most states limit the holder-in-due-course doctrine in consumer mortgage loans. The statutes vary considerably. A uniform act, the Uniform Consumer Credit Code (the UCCC or U3C), applies in 12 states.

    i. Consumer credit sale: Under the UCCC, a ***consumer credit sale*** includes the sale of an interest in land when the price (adjusted for inflation) does not exceed $25,000 and the interest rate exceeds 12 percent. The Act prohibits creditors from taking negotiable instruments in consumer credit sales. If a creditor obtains a negotiable instrument in violation of the Act, an assignee of an instrument given in a consumer credit sale takes subject to all defenses of the consumer.

    ii. Consumer loan: Under the UCCC, a ***consumer loan*** includes a mortgage loan when the price (adjusted for inflation) does not exceed $25,000 and the interest rate exceeds 12 percent. A lender who makes a consumer loan to enable a consumer to buy property or services is ***sometimes*** subject to real defenses. The lender takes subject to those defenses if (1) the lender knows that the seller arranged for the extension of credit by the lender for a commission or fee, (2) the lender is a person related to the seller, (3) the seller guarantees the loan or otherwise assumes the risk of loss by the lender upon the loan, (4) the lender directly supplies the seller with the loan document used by the parties, (5) the loan is conditioned upon the consumer's purchase from a particular seller, or (6) the lender before making the consumer loan has notice of substantial complaints by other buyers of the seller's failure to perform his contracts and to remedy his defaults within a reasonable time after notice to him of the complaints.

b. Federal Trade Commission regulation: Regulations promulgated by the Federal Trade Commission in 1975 protect certain consumers. 16 C.F.R. §§ 433.1 to 433.3.

    i. Consumer purchases: A consumer is a "natural person who seeks or acquires goods or services for personal, family, or household use." This affects real estate finance because goods and services include purchasing fixtures and contracting for home repairs, improvements, and additions.

    ii. Mandatory notice: The FTC regulation requires that a creditor who sells such goods and services to a consumer must include in the contract the following notice:

> ANY HOLDER OF THIS CONSUMER CREDIT CONTRACT IS SUBJECT TO ALL CLAIMS AND DEFENSES WHICH THE DEBTOR COULD ASSERT AGAINST THE SELLER OF GOODS OR SERVICES OBTAINED PURSUANT HERETO OR WITH THE PROCEEDS HEREOF. RECOVERY HEREUNDER BY THE DEBTOR SHALL NOT EXCEED AMOUNTS PAID BY THE DEBTOR HEREUNDER.

Failure to include this notice is a deceptive or unfair trade practice.

Quiz Yourself on
TRANSFERS BY BORROWERS AND LENDERS

78. Cleveland is looking into buying a pawn shop. A broker tells him it can be had for a price of $80,000, consisting of $10,000 down plus taking over an existing mortgage loan of $70,000. With the broker's help, Cleveland turns in an offer with the price term being "$2,000 paid in escrow today, $8,000 more cash due at closing, and I agree to pay Seller's existing $70,000 mortgage." If this purchase closes, will Cleveland become personally liable on Seller's existing mortgage? _____

79. Abby buys a house from Grant, assuming a mortgage loan with a balance of $90,000. This is a balloon loan obtained by Grant two years ago. It is payable in monthly installments amortized over 20 years, but all principal and interest are due in three years. One year after buying, Abby renegotiates the loan with its holder, paying $2,000 in exchange for the holder waiving the balloon feature. Thus, monthly payments will continue for 17 more years until the monthly payments fully amortize the loan balance. What effect does this loan modification have on Grant's obligations? _____

80. Sancho, the owner of a successful bike shop for the past four years, has a mortgage for $180,000 with a standard due-on-sale clause that also says, "Lender agrees not to withhold consent unreasonably." Sancho wants to go to law school so he arranges to sell his bike shop to his cousin Ricardo. Ricardo is between jobs, having been laid off from his job as an aircraft mechanic. Although he's a mountain bike aficionado and has a good credit history, he's never owned or worked in a bike shop before. Sancho and Ricardo present the proposed sale and loan assumption to Lender, who withholds consent. The cousins sue Lender for injunctive relief and damages. Will they prevail? _____

81. Speedy Homelender makes home mortgage loans, both fixed-rate loans and those with adjustable rates (ARMs). Speedy then sells both types of loans to purchasers through the secondary mortgage market. Are those purchasers holders in due course of negotiable instruments, and why might it matter? _____

82. Fab Furnaces contracts to replace Veronica's heat pump, which just died at her house. Fab Furnaces offers financing, and Veronica agrees to pay $200 down and pay $2,800 spread over three years in monthly installments. May Fab Furnaces have Veronica sign a negotiable instrument to evidence the loan? _____

Answers

78. **Yes.** Cleveland will become personally liable if he "assumes" the loan or uses other words that have that effect; that is, "I agree to pay the loan in accordance with its terms." On the other hand, if at closing the documents indicate that Cleveland "takes subject to" the loan and mortgage, he will not become personally liable. Thus, care needs to be taken to have closing documents reflect the contract.

79. **Grant has a discharge.** Upon the sale and assumption, Grant became a surety. Elimination of the balloon feature is an extension of the maturity date. This increases Grant's risk as surety because it will be many more years before he knows whether Abby will pay off the loan or default. Because Grant did not agree to the extension, he is totally discharged from liability.

80. **Maybe the cousins will win.** The Garn-St. Germain Depository Institutions Act does not immunize Lender from liability. Due to the parties' contract, the clause isn't automatically enforceable under the federal law. Also, it doesn't matter whether the transaction is in a state that follows the view that due-on-sale clauses are automatically enforceable or the competing view that the lender must prove impairment of security in order to block a transfer. It is a question of fact as to whether Lender has behaved reasonably. Both parties will seek to introduce evidence bearing on commercial lending standards for borrowers who purchase businesses without having had prior experience in that particular business.

81. **Assuming Speedy uses standard-form promissory notes to document its loans, purchasers of the fixed-rate loans clearly qualify as holders in due course.** With respect to the ARMs, most courts prior to the 1990 revision to UCC Article 3 held that adjustable-rate instruments are not negotiable because they did not set forth an unconditional duty to pay a fixed sum. All states except New York have enacted the 1990 revision, and New York has amended its Article 3 to make ARMs negotiable.

The purchasers of Speedy's mortgage loans have reduced risk if they are holders in due course of negotiable instruments. They take free of any personal claims or defenses that the mortgagors may have against Speedy arising out of the mortgage transaction.

82. **No.** There may be state consumer legislation, such as the UCCC, that prohibits the use of a negotiable instrument in such a transaction. Regardless of state law, under the Federal Trade Commission regulation, Fab Furnaces must include a bold-type notice in the contract or instrument that makes the paper nonnegotiable.

Exam Tips *on*
TRANSFERS BY BORROWERS AND LENDERS

For almost all courses, the rules governing transfers by borrowers are basic material, which you are expected to know. Conversely, many courses do not cover transfers by lenders; or if they do, not much emphasis is placed on lender transfers. One reason is lender transfers are often covered in other parts of the curriculum, such as courses on commercial paper or payment systems.

☞ **Assumption vs. taking subject to a mortgage:** This is a key distinction. Whenever a fact pattern involves the sale or conveyance of mortgaged property, consider whether it matters if there is an assumption or a transfer subject to the mortgage.

　☞ **Personal liability:** A buyer who assumes a mortgage becomes personally liable, but a buyer who takes subject to the mortgage has no personal liability. The "taking subject to" buyer, however, is expected to pay the mortgage debt. If the buyer fails to do so, the buyer very probably will lose the property in foreclosure.

　☞ **Ambiguity:** Look to see if there's any ambiguity. If the language of the conveyance is ambiguous, the court will have to decide whether the buyer has assumed or taken subject to the debt.

☞ **Mortgagee can sue assuming buyer:** If a buyer who assumes a mortgage loan fails to pay, the mortgagee can bring an action for the debt against the buyer. This is true even if there is no contract between the mortgagee and the buyer.

☞ **Seller becomes a surety:** Instead of pursuing the buyer, the mortgagee has the right to collect from the seller, provided there is no release of liability. This is because the seller is a surety for the debt. If the mortgagee collects all or part of the debt from the seller, the seller can sue the buyer.

☞ **Due-on-sale clause:** If an exam question includes a due-on-sale clause, be sure to discuss the federal legislation (the Garn-St. Germain Act), which makes the clause automatically enforceable.

☞ **Particular language of clause:** A lender may limit its right to invoke a due-on-sale clause by specifying a standard for its use in the mortgage. Be sure to pay attention to the facts.

☛ **Lender's sale of mortgage loan:** When a lender sells a loan, the buyer customarily records an assignment of mortgage in the public records.

☞ **Priority:** Failure to record the assignment, however, has no effect on the priority status of the assigned mortgage. If the original lender/assignor recorded that mortgage, it keeps that priority date.

☛ **Holder in due course:** If there is a dispute between a mortgagor and an assignee of the mortgagee, be sure to consider whether the assignee might qualify as a holder in due course.

☞ **Negotiable instrument:** To be a holder in due course, the promissory note must meet the standards for a negotiable instrument.

☞ **Consumer transactions:** If the mortgagor is a consumer, the assignee might not be able to use the holder-in-due-course doctrine to cut off the consumer's personal defenses. State and federal laws often prohibit or restrict the use of negotiable instruments when consumers borrow money or buy property or services.

CHAPTER 18

DEFAULT AND ACCELERATION

ChapterScope ───────────────────────────

This chapter deals with issues surrounding default by the borrower and the lender's decision to accelerate the mortgage debt. Default includes not only failure to make loan payments on time, but other events defined in the loan documents. Related material is in Chapter 16, dealing with late payment charges, which may be imposed when the borrower defaults. Default and acceleration often lead to foreclosure, which is treated in Chapter 19.

- ■ **Default defined:** The promissory note, mortgage instrument, and other loan documents define *default*.

- ■ **Acceleration:** *Acceleration* means the entire principal balance of the loan is made immediately due and payable.

- ■ **Defenses to acceleration:** The most common defenses to acceleration are these:

  - ■ The lender has a history of *accepting late payments*.

  - ■ The default is technical and *not material*.

  - ■ The default has *not impaired the lender's security* for the debt.

- ■ **Equity:** General principles of *equity* protect the borrower from hardship, forfeiture, or a penalty.

- ■ **Prepayment penalty:** Generally, the lender cannot collect a prepayment penalty provided for in the loan documents when it accelerates maturity of the debt.

- ■ **Late charges:** A number of courts refuse to permit the lender to collect late charges for the time period after acceleration.

I. SETTING FOR DEFAULT

A. Market role: Mortgages perform the market function of reducing risk for creditors. Risk reduction only occurs when law provides a process for creditors to reach the mortgaged property if the debtor fails to perform her obligation to pay. Default and acceleration of the debt relate directly to the debt obligation (the promissory note), yet they are the first two major steps in the process that leads to creditors' obtaining value from the mortgaged property through foreclosure.

B. Importance for parties: When a mortgage loan default occurs, both lender and borrower often have hard decisions to make. Default threatens the lender's expectations that it has properly evaluated risk and that the loan would be profitable. In default scenarios, the borrower's point of view tends to be very different from the lender's. The borrower's expectations about the future also may not have been realized, whether she is a homeowner, investor, or entrepreneur. A bad economy, loss of a job, divorce, or high medical expenses may have led to a financial setback. The borrower may dispute the lender's contention that a default has occurred or that the default is material. The lender has discretion about how to proceed. Its decision is highly important because a decision to accelerate the loan and invoke loan remedies will very likely result in the borrower's loss of the property. If, however, the lender proceeds but can't prove it acted rightly, it has liability to the borrower. If the lender delays acting, however, its eventual losses may mount if the borrower is ***milking the property***, or the borrower has no realistic chance of recovery, or the property is declining in value. Decision making by both parties takes place in a highly charged atmosphere. Stress levels among the principals are often high. A lawyer who represents either party should assist her client in making a careful evaluation of the present situation and exploring the alternatives.

II. DEFAULT CLAUSES

A. **Purpose:** The purpose of the default clause is to allow the mortgagee to exercise one or more of the remedies provided for by the mortgage, including foreclosure. In a loan with standard documentation, default clauses are set forth in the promissory note and the mortgage instrument. In more complex loans other documents may also apply. The mortgage may refer to other documents, such as a collateral assignment of leases or a loan agreement, to specify events of default.

Example: Marcia owns a warehouse, which is divided into three spaces and rented to tenants. She has a mortgage loan with Money Haus, with one of the loan documents being a Collateral Assignment of Leases. Under the Collateral Assignment, she promises not to amend any of the warehouse leases without the express consent of Money Haus. Marcia and Tenant Tim's lease has two and one-half years remaining in the term. Without notice to or the consent of Money Haus, they renegotiate their lease, agreeing to a five-year extension at fixed rents equal to those presently paid by Tim. Marcia has defaulted under the Collateral Assignment. If Money Haus has properly drafted the mortgage instrument, there is a ***cross-default provision*** that allows Money Haus to accelerate the debt and pursue remedies under the mortgage.

B. **Lender's decision making:** For minor or technical defaults, lenders often have some patience and forbear resorting to remedies. For material or serious defaults, lenders usually try to evaluate the borrower's behavior in order to decide how to respond.

   1. **Foreclosure:** The lender will move to foreclose quickly or seek possession if it believes the borrower has intentionally defaulted, is threatening the value of the security, or has no realistic hope of being able to pay the loan installments in the near future.

   2. **Workout potential:** The lender will seek a workout with the borrower to get the loan back on track if it believes the borrower has suffered a hardship, he is willing to pay the debt, and there is a good prospect that he will be able to do so.

C. **Interpretation of default clauses:** The promissory note, mortgage, and other loan instruments almost always contain default clauses. They are interpreted in accordance with standard principles of contract law.

   1. **Place and manner of payment:** Under most promissory notes, payment is made upon actual receipt by the lender. The ***mailbox rule*** used in other legal contexts does not apply. *Moseley v. First Community Bank*, 649 So. 2d 1274 (Ala. 1994), rejected a borrower's attempt to use the mailbox rule. The court allowed the lender to foreclose when the borrower sent payment to the lender by certified mail on the due date, which the lender received four days later.

III. ACCELERATION

Acceleration means that the entire principal balance of the loan, together with all accrued interest, is made immediately due and payable. It applies to installment loans, which are payable in monthly installments or according to another schedule, and to loans with a single payment due at maturity.

Example: Hans borrows $100,000, promising to repay it in one year at an interest rate of 14 percent per annum. No payments are due until the expiration of the year. Hans secures the loan by granting a mortgage on his bakery. He promises to pay the real estate taxes on the bakery. He defaults on this promise five months into the loan term, and the lender accelerates maturity of the loan. Right now Hans owes the $100,000, together with interest calculated to the date of acceleration (not an entire year's worth of interest at 14 percent).

A. Types of acceleration clauses

1. **Automatic acceleration:** The clause provides that the entire debt shall be due and payable if a specified event happens, such as a certain type of default. The parties' language is such that acceleration happens automatically if the event occurs.

   Example: A due-on-sale clause provides: "If Borrower shall sell or transfer the Property or any interest therein without Lender's prior written consent, the entire principal balance hereunder together with all accrued interest shall become immediately due and payable." Under this language, an unconsented-to transfer automatically triggers acceleration. No act or choice by Lender is necessary. Acceleration will happen even though Lender, at the moment of the unconsented-to transfer, will probably not then know what Borrower has done.

2. **Optional acceleration:** Today, most acceleration clauses give the lender the option to accelerate maturity of the debt. The lender has the choice; it may declare an acceleration, insisting that the borrower pay the debt in full, or it may forbear.

   a. **Advantages:** Most lenders believe the optional acceleration clause is preferable to an automatic acceleration provision because it gives the lender more flexibility and control. This is true for two reasons. First, many defaults are not serious and can be promptly cured by the borrower, assuming she is willing to do so. If acceleration nevertheless occurs automatically but the parties want to continue their relationship, it will be necessary to unwind this act in order to reinstate the loan. Second, when the loan provides for a favorable interest rate, from the lender's point of view, the lender has an economic interest in *not* accelerating. Instead, if it is practical it wants to keep the loan outstanding and encourage or cause the borrower to cure defaults. Otherwise, if it accelerates and collects the full debt, it will lend this money out to another borrower at a lower, market interest rate.

B. Lack of acceleration clause

1. **No acceleration:** Almost all courts say that the maturity of future installments cannot be accelerated when the loan documents lack an express acceleration provision. The mortgagee must either attempt to collect the installments as they fall due or wait until final maturity of the debt.

2. **Anticipatory repudiation theory:** A few courts have accepted a lender's argument that failure to pay a series of installments amounts to anticipatory repudiation, justifying a lender's action for damages equal to the entire debt.

C. Procedure for acceleration

1. **Automatic acceleration clause:** With an automatic acceleration clause, the lender does not need to take any action to accelerate the loan. To insist on full payment, all the lender needs to do is to tell the borrower that acceleration has occurred.

2. **Optional acceleration clause:** With an optional acceleration clause, the lender must take some affirmative action that demonstrates its intent to accelerate. The requirements vary according to the language of the acceleration clause and state and federal law that applies.

    Example: Greypartners failed to renew the fire insurance policy on Greystone Apartments, and its lender sent Greypartners two notices demanding that it procure the policy and deliver to the lender proof of coverage and payment of the insurance premium immediately. Greypartners failed to cure the problem, and the lender's loan committee voted to accelerate the loan, with a secretary memorializing this decision in minutes for the committee meeting. The next day, before the lender gave Greypartners notice of this decision, Greypartners delivered to the lender by courier the new policy and evidence of payment. The loan is nevertheless validly accelerated, assuming that the loan documents have a standard optional acceleration clause with no borrower notice protections and that state law does not imply borrower notice protections, either by statute or by common law decision.

    a. **Notice to borrower:** The lender's notice to the borrower of intent to accelerate followed by an act evidencing acceleration is often required. In *Bodiford d/b/a Bodiford Investment Co. v. Parker*, 651 S.W.2d 338 (Tex. Ct. App. 1983), a promissory note provided that if the borrower defaulted, at the lender's option the entire debt would be immediately due and payable "without demand or notice of any character." The borrower defaulted, and 11 days later the lender sent a letter stating that the note was accelerated. The court held that acceleration was improper because the lender must give prior notice of intent to accelerate in order to provide the debtor an opportunity to cure her default prior to the harsh consequences of acceleration and foreclosure.

D. Defenses to acceleration

1. **History of late payments:** Waiver or estoppel may prevent acceleration when the lender in the past has accepted a number of late payments. In effect, the lender is ***estopped*** by its conduct to claim time is of the essence. See *Bodiford d/b/a Bodiford Investment Co. v. Parker*, 651 S.W.2d 338 (Tex. Ct. App. 1983), finding an implied waiver when the lender accepted the borrower's late payments a number of times in the past.

    a. **Anti-waiver clauses:** In an attempt to draft around this doctrine, many notes and mortgages have an ***anti-waiver clause***, which says that acceptance of one or more late payments will not waive or estop the lender from invoking remedies, including foreclosure for any future default in timely payment. Sometimes, courts give some effect to these anti-waiver clauses, either applying them as written or counting them as one factor to consider, along with the other circumstances, when deciding whether waiver or estoppel is appropriate. Some courts, however, say that a lender, by accepting late payments, waives the anti-waiver clause. This view just reads the clause out of the document.

    Example: Buyers purchased a house, giving Sellers a promissory note with a mortgage on the house. The note provided:

> If any monthly installment under this Note is not paid within fifteen (15) days of the due date, the entire principal amount outstanding and accrued interest and late charges thereon shall at once become due and payable without notice at the option of the Note holder. The Note holder may exercise this option to accelerate during any default by maker regardless of any prior forbearance. A late charge of five (5 percent) per cent of the overdue payment shall be due and payable with any delinquent payment.

For about a year, Buyers paid on time, but over the next 4 years, they made 27 late payments, including 5 after the 15-day grace period. Sellers did not exercise their option to accelerate the debt for any of these defaults, but when Buyers defaulted another time, Sellers notified Buyers that they were exercising their option to accelerate the debt. Four months later, Sellers filed a complaint for foreclosure. Buyers raised the affirmative defenses of waiver and estoppel, but lost on a motion for summary judgment. The court reasoned that Sellers "did nothing inconsistent or misleading with respect to their right to accelerate the mortgage debt. . . . The plain language of the note provides that the 'holder may exercise this option to accelerate during any default by maker regardless of any prior **forbearance**' (emphasis added). This language in the note effectively prevented the mere acceptance of late payments by the Kirkhams from operating as a waiver or giving rise to an estoppel in the event of subsequent defaults." *Kirkham v. Hansen,* 583 A.2d 1026 (Me. 1990).

b. **Lender's reinstatement of duty to make punctual payments:** To make timely payment of the essence again, the lender must notify the borrower that from now on payments must be made on time or else it will exercise its option to accelerate the loan.

2. **Materiality of default:** Most courts will safeguard borrowers from the harsh consequences of acceleration by evaluating how serious the default happens to be. When borrowers are protected from the hardship of acceleration, the common explanations are the default is technical, not material or substantial; or the event has not impaired the lender's security; or general principles of equity permit the court to intervene to protect the borrower from a penalty or a forfeiture.

Example: Borrower bought a house, promising in the mortgage to maintain insurance on the property and to deliver proof of insurance to Lender. Borrower failed to get insurance at the time of purchase, but obtained insurance two years later, which Borrower maintained for the next six years. The mortgage provided that if Borrower did not maintain insurance, Lender had the right to purchase insurance and add the premiums to the debt or demand reimbursement from Borrower. Pursuant to the provision, Lender obtained insurance for the first eight years of the loan term. During the eighth year of the loan term, Borrower sent a monthly payment late. Lender returned the payment, demanding an additional $2,000 as reimbursement for the insurance premiums. After Borrower failed to pay the $2,000, Lender accelerated the loan and brought a foreclosure action. The court did not allow acceleration or foreclosure because Lender never requested proof of insurance from Borrower prior to its demand for $2,000. *Mid-State Trust III v. Avriett,* 17 S.W.3d 500 (Ark. Ct. App. 2000).

3. **Borrowers' statutory rights to cure default:** Many states have statutes that protect defaulting mortgagors from acceleration. There are two types. One operates prior to acceleration: The lender must give the mortgagor notice prior to acceleration. The other type of statute operates after acceleration: The mortgagor is allowed to pay arrearages after

acceleration and thus reinstate the installment loan. Some statutes protect only residential mortgagors, but other statutes protect all mortgagors.

   a. Texas Property Code § 51.002(d): For debts secured by the debtor's residence, the mortgage servicer must send notice of default by certified mail, giving the debtor "at least 20 days to cure the default before notice of sale can be given."

   b. 735 Illinois Comp. Stat. 5/15-1602: After acceleration, the mortgagor may reinstate by curing all defaults and paying the lender's costs within 90 days after service of a judicial action to foreclose. The mortgagor may use this relief only once every five years.

   c. Pennsylvania Stat., title 41, § 404: After notice of foreclosure is given, the residential debtor may cure the default and avoid acceleration by paying the amount due, plus the lender's reasonable cost and late penalty, up to one hour prior to the judicial foreclosure sale. This right may not be exercised more than three times in any calendar year.

E. Amount payable upon acceleration: By definition, upon acceleration the entire principal balance of the loan, plus accrued interest, is due and payable. Often, the lender will also assert that additional amounts are due, such as prepayment premiums, late payment charges, attorneys' fees, and other lender costs.

   1. Prepayment premiums: Generally, the mortgagee cannot both accelerate and receive a prepayment penalty. This is because the mortgagee has decided to accelerate, and it is not the mortgagor's voluntary decision to end the loan transaction by prepaying the debt.

   a. Exception for intentional default: When the borrower's default is intentional, some courts permit the lender to collect a prepayment penalty, provided the prepayment clause is broadly worded so as to cover this situation. Courts split on this issue. See *Florida National Bank of Miami v. Bankatlantic*, 589 So. 2d 255 (Fla. 1991), allowing the lender to collect a prepayment charge, equal to 12 months interest on the amount of prepayment that exceeded 20 percent of the principal balance, when an apartment complex borrower intentionally defaulted in making installment payments. But see *Rodgers v. Rainier National Bank*, 757 P.2d 976 (Wash. 1988), rejecting a claim for a prepayment premium even though the borrower deliberately defaulted to avoid the prepayment premium.

   Example: Joanna's second mortgage prohibits prepayment absolutely for the entire eight-year term of the loan. Joanna wants to prepay, so she defaults in making monthly payments. Under an optional acceleration clause, her lender elects to accelerate and demands payment of the entire loan principal, accrued interest, plus damages stemming from the prepayment (loss from having to reinvest the principal at a lower yield plus income tax liability). Here, the lender has not bargained for a contractual prepayment penalty, and it will fail in its attempt to collect damages.

   2. Late payment charges: Under many promissory notes, a late charge is imposed if the borrower doesn't pay an installment on time or within a specified grace period after the due date. Upon acceleration, the borrower no longer has the obligation to make installment payments. Acceleration means that instead the entire debt is due. For this reason, courts have held that late charges cannot be imposed after a lender has accelerated payment of a note. In *Security Mutual Life Insurance Co. v. Contemporary Real Estate Associates*, 979 F.2d 329 (3d Cir. 1992), after the borrower's default, the lender accelerated the debt by filing an action to collect the debt. The trial court's judgment for the lender included late charges on unpaid monthly installments for the months preceding and following the filing of the complaint, up until the date of final judgment. The court of appeals reversed, holding no further late charges could be imposed after acceleration of the debt. It rejected the lender's argument that the borrower could have avoided the late charges by making monthly payments notwithstanding the acceleration of the note.

    a. Lender's drafting of documents: The cases denying lenders the right to assess late charges post-acceleration are based on the interpretation of specific late payment clauses. Through appropriate drafting, it's quite possible that the lender may succeed in imposing reasonable late charges after acceleration.

Quiz Yourself on
DEFAULT AND ACCELERATION

83. Borrower defaults in making the monthly payment for August, and the applicable five-day grace period expires. Three days later Borrower, having received no communication from Lender related to this default, shows up at Lender's office and tenders the past-due installment. Borrower is directed to Lender's assistant loan officer, who says, "Sorry, too late. We're not taking it. We've accelerated; the whole loan is due." Borrower disagrees, claiming (1) the loan is not validly accelerated and (2) Borrower should get credit for the August payment, without having to make a further payment, because Lender wrongfully refused the tender. What is the result? _____

84. Barney's 15-year loan to buy a resort condominium has a prepayment penalty equal to 6 percent of the principal being prepaid if prepayment occurs anytime during the first 10 years of the loan. After making punctual payments for two years, Barney incurs large debts for a new Mercedes-Benz and expensive South Seas vacations. Lacking sufficient income to pay all his debts, he keeps the Mercedes loan current because he values the wheels more than the condo. The holder of the mortgage on the condominium accelerates and demands payment of the prepayment penalty in addition to the principal balance and accrued interest. Assuming Barney finds a way to save the condo and pay off the debt, must he pay the prepayment premium? _____

85. Can a lender draft a late payment charge so that late charges are due for the period of time after acceleration of the loan balance until the loan is paid in full? _____

Answers

83. This monetary default is material. Unless state law provides borrower protection, either by judicial decision or by statute, Lender may accelerate without notice to Borrower. However, Lender needs to take some affirmative act prior to Borrower's tender of the past-due amount to evidence its exercise of the option. Lender needs a memorandum, note, or other tangible evidence that shows that, prior to the loan officer's discussion with Borrower, Lender had made the acceleration decision.

In many states, Borrower prevails because acceleration is not effective until Lender gives Borrower notice of default and intent to accelerate, notice of acceleration, or both. Also, for certain residential loans that are subject to federal regulation (e.g., made by federally chartered institutions or traded in the secondary mortgage market), default and acceleration notices are mandatory.

84. **Probably not.** The answer turns both on the precise language of the loan documents (the prepayment clause and the acceleration clause) and on the state's position on the relationship between acceleration and prepayment. In some states, Barney will win, and it will not matter what the loan documents say. The rationale is that prepayment penalties or premiums are due only if the borrower *voluntarily* prepays, and the lender cannot alter this precept by drafting. Other states focus on the risk of transactional misbehavior by debtors. In these states, there is an exception to the general rule that no prepayment premium may be collected upon acceleration when the debtor has intentionally defaulted.

85. **No.** Courts generally hold that late charges on unpaid loan installments no longer accrue after acceleration of maturity. Part of the rationale for a typical late charge that is a percentage of each unpaid installment is the lender's administrative expense in tracking each separate default and giving appropriate notices to the borrower. Once the loan is accelerated, the lender will no longer incur expenses in connection with the monthly tracking of the borrower's payments and nonpayments. Thus, a late charge that uses a different technique for the post-acceleration period—for example, a higher interest rate applied to the entire loan balance compared to the pre-default normal rate under the particular loan—is more likely to succeed.

Exam Tips on DEFAULT AND ACCELERATION

☞ **Analysis of the alleged default:** When answering an exam question involving default issues, pay very careful attention to the wording of the question. Sometimes, the existence of a material default is a "given." Based on the facts and what it is that you are being asked to do, you are to assume a default has occurred and go on to other issues immediately. Other times, the question will indicate that the lender *claimed* a default occurred or *notified the borrower* of a default. When this happens, the borrower might claim he has not defaulted, or at least has not materially defaulted. Then part of the analysis the professor wants to find may include argument, pro and con, on whether a default has in fact occurred.

☞ **Materiality of default:** Although it may be completely clear that a default has occurred, it is often hard to decide when it is material. There is no one standard definition of material, and courts often seem to make a "gut decision" on this issue. Some courts think of materiality in terms of impairment of security. This leads to "lender liability" decisions in which courts second-guess lender decisions that a default was sufficiently serious to justify acceleration and foreclosure.

☞ **Acceleration:** Acceleration means the entire principal balance of the loan is made immediately due and payable. There are two types of acceleration clauses contained in promissory notes:

   ☞ **The automatic acceleration clause:** This makes the debt payable automatically if a specified event happens.

☞ **The optional acceleration clause:** This gives the lender the option to accelerate maturity of the debt if a specified event happens. Most lenders use an optional acceleration clause. If an exam question doesn't indicate the type of clause contained in the loan documents, you should assume that it's an optional clause.

☛ **Lack of acceleration clause:** If the loan documents outlined in an exam question do not have an acceleration clause, remember that the lender may be unable to accelerate. Without an express clause, most courts don't permit the lender to accelerate maturity of the debt upon the borrower's default.

     ☞ **Anticipatory repudiation:** A few courts give relief to the lender through the doctrine of anticipatory repudiation.

☛ **How lender accelerates:** In a question involving a lender's attempt to collect a debt, whether or not it involves foreclosure, be sure to consider acceleration. The issue isn't always easy to spot. The facts may not use the words "accelerate" or "acceleration." With an optional acceleration clause, the lender must take some affirmative action that demonstrates its intent to accelerate. This must be accomplished *before* the borrower cures or tenders a cure of the default.

☛ **Defenses to acceleration:** Whenever acceleration is an issue on the exam, defenses are likely to be relevant. The most common borrower defenses to the lender's declaration of acceleration are:

     ☞ **Accepting late payments:** A history of the lender accepting late payments may result in waiver or estoppel so the lender can no longer accelerate for the most recent late payment.

     ☞ **Technical default:** The default is technical and not material.

     ☞ **Security not impaired:** The default has not impaired the lender's security for the debt.

     ☞ **Equity:** General principles of equity allow the court to protect the borrower from hardship, forfeiture, or a penalty.

☛ **Prepayment penalty:** Usually an exam tests the lender's ability to collect a prepayment penalty in a straightforward manner, but it can be hidden if there is an open-ended question asking you to list the lender's remedies available after the borrower's default. Generally, the lender cannot collect a prepayment penalty provided for in the loan documents when it accelerates maturity of the debt. Some courts have an exception for the borrower's intentional default.

☛ **Late payment charge:** Upon acceleration often the borrower doesn't pay the debt immediately, and months or years pass until payment is made or foreclosure is completed. A number of courts refuse to permit the lender to collect late charges for the time period after acceleration.

CHAPTER 19

FORECLOSURE

ChapterScope ───────────────────────────

This chapter examines the foreclosure of mortgages, focusing on judicial foreclosure and power of sale foreclosure. For judicial foreclosure, the key concepts are necessary parties and proper parties. For power of sale foreclosure, the key points involve compliance with statutory requirements for notice, advertising, and the conduct of the sale. For both types, the foreclosure may result in a deficiency or a surplus. For the foreclosure to be valid, a default by the borrower must precede the foreclosure. Thus, this chapter follows Chapter 18, dealing with default.

- **Foreclosure types:** The three main types of foreclosures are:

  - Judicial foreclosure,

  - Power of sale foreclosure, and

  - Strict foreclosure.

- **Deficiency or surplus:** A foreclosure sale yields a deficiency when the sales proceeds are less than the mortgage debt. When the proceeds exceed the debt, there is a surplus.

- **Necessary parties:** In judicial foreclosure, necessary parties are persons with junior interests.

- **Power of sale foreclosure:** To foreclose by power of sale, the mortgage must authorize this procedure, *and* the state must have a statute that regulates the procedure.

- **Equitable subrogation:** A lender who refinances a prior mortgage loan is entitled to equitable subrogation.

- **Statutory redemption:** Many states provide statutory redemption rights to protect the mortgagor and holders of junior interest. (Note that **equitable redemption** is discussed in Chapter 14.)

I. THE NATURE OF FORECLOSURE

A. **Purpose of foreclosure:** Foreclosure rules play a vital market role. They are a necessary condition for finance markets to operate on the basis of security. Having a mortgage to secure an obligation means there is property that the mortgagee has the right to obtain to satisfy the obligation in case the obligor cannot or does not perform. Foreclosure is simply the process by which the mortgagee gets the property and causes its value to be applied to the obligation.

B. **Types of foreclosure:** There are three primary types of foreclosures: strict foreclosure, judicial foreclosure, and power of sale (nonjudicial) foreclosure. With judicial and power of sale foreclosures, the mortgaged property is sold, with the sales proceeds applied to repay the debt. With strict foreclosure, the mortgagee keeps the property with no requirement of a sale.

II. STRICT FORECLOSURE

This is an action brought in equity by the mortgagee after default by the mortgagor. The purpose is to force payment of the debt or to cut off the mortgagor's *equity of redemption*. The court orders the mortgagor to pay the debt by a specified date. If the mortgagor fails to pay by that date, the mortgagor loses her equity of redemption, and the mortgagee's title becomes absolute.

A. Modern usage: Only two states, Connecticut and Vermont, still use strict foreclosure as the primary foreclosure method.

B. Specialized applications: In many states that use judicial foreclosure or power of sale foreclosure, strict foreclosure is available to handle specialized problems. For example, if a foreclosing mortgagee omits a necessary party, strict foreclosure may be available to cut off the necessary party's ownership interest. Similarly, with an installment land contract, if the purchaser defaults, the vendor may find it advantageous to clear title and end the relationship by bringing a strict foreclosure action against the purchaser.

Example: In a state that generally uses judicial foreclosure, Mainline Bank forecloses a mortgage on Jerry's Ranch. The foreclosure results in a sale of the ranch for $900,000 to Jolly Rancher. Prior to the time Mainline Bank commenced the foreclosure action, Jerry bought more cattle and granted a second mortgage on the ranch to Cattle Sellers to secure the unpaid part of the purchase price. In Mainline Bank's foreclosure action, Cattle Sellers is a necessary party, but Mainline's attorney failed to join Cattle Sellers as a party. As a consequence, Cattle Sellers still has a mortgage on the ranch, and this is a defect in Jolly Rancher's title. To solve the problem, Jolly Rancher may bring an action for strict foreclosure against Cattle Sellers. The court will set a deadline by which Cattle Sellers must "redeem" by paying Jolly Rancher the amount of Mainline Bank's debt. If Cattle Sellers does not make this payment on time, it loses its mortgage.

III. KEY CONCEPTS

A. Action on the debt: The mortgagee sues to get a judgment for damages where the damages are equal to the unpaid principal, interest, and other charges owed to the mortgagee.

B. Foreclosure action: The mortgagee seeks to change ownership of the property by erasing the mortgagor's equity of redemption. With judicial foreclosure, this is an action or bill in equity. With power of sale foreclosure, the process is extrajudicial.

C. Deficiency: If the value of the property is less than the debt, foreclosure will result in a deficiency. Often the mortgagee will seek a judgment equal to the shortfall, and this is called a deficiency judgment. The mortgagee must bring an action on the debt in order to get a deficiency judgment.

Example: Lassio owes Klaus $100,000, secured by a mortgage on his vacation home. Lassio defaults and Klaus forecloses, with the foreclosure sale resulting in net proceeds of $80,000. Klaus then brings an action on the debt against Lassio. He obtains a deficiency judgment for $20,000.

D. Surplus: If the value of the property is more than the debt, the mortgagor has equity. Foreclosure may result in a high bid that exceeds the debt plus the expenses of foreclosure. The difference is called surplus.

1. **Payment of surplus:** The surplus belongs to the mortgagor and is paid to the mortgagor if no other parties have a better claim to it. If there are other parties who own property rights that are terminated by the foreclosure, they are entitled to compensation before the mortgagor is paid. If there are multiple parties, their entitlements are ranked according to their priority under recording system principles.

   Example: Lenard loses his house through foreclosure. Three months before foreclosure, he had rented his house to Trudy under a written lease for one year. The foreclosure sale price is $100,000. The debt, together with accrued interest at the time of foreclosure, is $80,000. Foreclosure costs, including attorneys' fees, are $4,000. Trudy is promptly evicted by the foreclosure purchaser. There is a surplus of $16,000, which belongs to Lenard and the owners of junior interests that are terminated by the foreclosure. First, Trudy is compensated for whatever damages she has the right to claim against Lenard under the lease. The remainder of the $16,000 is paid to Lenard.

E. **Election of remedies:** Generally, the mortgagee may elect to bring an action on the debt or to foreclose. The remedies are not mutually exclusive.

   1. **Action on debt first:** The mortgagee may bring an action on the debt without trying to foreclose. In most states, this does not preclude a subsequent foreclosure action, provided that the judgment remains wholly or partially unsatisfied.

   2. **Foreclosure first:** The mortgagee may foreclose without seeking a judgment on the debt. If the foreclosure results in a deficiency, the mortgagee can sue the mortgagor for that amount.

   3. **Both remedies simultaneously:** With judicial foreclosure, the mortgagee may seek foreclosure and an action for a deficiency judgment simultaneously (see infra, one-action rule, part IX.A of this chapter).

IV. JUDICIAL FORECLOSURE

A. **Goal in terms of title:** The central goal of foreclosure is to give the purchaser the same title the mortgagor had at the moment the mortgage was granted.

B. **Necessary parties:** The persons who hold interests that are junior in priority to the mortgage being foreclosed are necessary parties. They are necessary in the sense that they have to be joined as defendants in order to accomplish the goal of transferring title to the buyer in the condition it was when the mortgage was granted.

   1. **Omitted necessary parties:** An omitted necessary party is an owner of a junior interest who is not joined as a defendant in the foreclosure action. The omitted necessary party is not bound by the foreclosure decree or the foreclosure sale. See *English v. Bankers Trust Co. of California, N.A.*, 895 So. 2d 1120 (Fla. Dist. Ct. App. 2005), holding void a foreclosure action brought against only the original mortgagor, after she had conveyed the property to a corporation.

      a. **Omitted party's rights:** The omitted party still has her property rights. If the omitted party is a junior lienor, she has the same two options that she had prior to the senior mortgagee's foreclosure:

    i. Foreclose the junior lien: The omitted party has the right to foreclose the junior lien. This revives the first mortgage, which is now held by the foreclosure purchaser.

    ii. Redeem the property: The omitted party may redeem the property by paying the foreclosure purchaser the amount of the first mortgage debt. This is a purchase transaction—the junior lienor has the right to buy the property. By redeeming, the junior gains fee title to the property in exchange for a price equal to the first debt.

    Example: Gustbank has a home equity mortgage on Hanna's home, securing a debt of $24,000. Gustbank's mortgage is a second lien. Hanna defaults on her first mortgage, and that lender forecloses, failing to join Gustbank as a necessary party. Gustbank's mortgage survives the foreclosure sale. Gustbank still has security and may choose to do nothing for the time being. For Gustbank to act, it will have to prove that Hanna has defaulted under her home equity loan. Even if Hanna has not committed a monetary default by failing to make payments to Gustbank, it is highly probable that the foreclosure sale of her house is a default. The loan documents must be read to be sure on this point. If Gustbank acts, it may either foreclose its home equity mortgage or redeem the property by paying the amount of the first mortgage debt to the foreclosure buyer.

  b. Foreclose purchaser's rights: The purchaser at foreclosure who finds there is an omitted junior interest has several options:

    i. Re-foreclose the senior mortgage: The purchaser may foreclose again, this time doing it properly by joining the omitted party. In *United States Department of Housing & Urban Development v. Union Mortgage Co.*, 661 A.2d 163 (Me. 1995), the court required this option. The purchaser wanted to limit an omitted junior mortgagee to the right to redeem the senior debt, but the court held that the omitted party could insist on a re-foreclosure of the senior mortgage.

    ii. Redeem the property: The purchaser may redeem by paying off the junior lien. This has priority over the junior lienor's redemption right described above, so if both parties say they want to redeem, it's the foreclosure purchaser who gets to buy out the junior lienor.

    iii. Use strict foreclosure: In some jurisdictions, the foreclosure purchaser may bring an action of strict foreclosure against the junior lienor. This forces the junior to use her redemption right by paying by the date set by the court or lose her interest.

  c. Intentionally omitted necessary party: Almost always a necessary party is omitted because the foreclosing lender or its agent made a mistake, either in searching title or for some other reason. If the foreclosing lender intentionally fails to join a necessary party, a court may refuse to grant relief. For example, in *Credithrift of America, Inc. v. Amsbaugh*, 773 P.2d 1287 (Okla. Ct. App. 1988), the court elevated a junior mortgagee who was intentionally not joined in a foreclosure proceeding to first lien status.

C. Proper parties: A proper party is a person who has rights or duties with respect to the property or the debt, but who is not a necessary party. A proper party can be joined as a defendant without her consent. Proper parties include holders of prior interests in the property and persons who are liable on the debt but who do not presently have an ownership interest in the mortgaged property.

D. Foreclosure of mortgages held by Mortgage Electronic Registration System (MERS): The collapse of housing markets beginning in 2007 led to a dramatic increase in the number of mortgage foreclosures brought against homeowners. Many recent mortgages have named the

Mortgage Electronic Registration System (MERS) as the mortgagee. MERS acts as a nominee of the originating lender, and when the mortgage is sold in the secondary market, MERS continues as the mortgagee of record. In many cases, homeowners have challenged foreclosures based on the involvement of MERS. They have generally failed, although in many states it appears that the foreclosure must be brought in the name of the real owner of the debt and cannot be brought by MERS as nominee. See *US Bank, N.A. v. Flynn*, 897 N.Y.S.2d 855 (Sup. Ct. Suffolk County 2010), in which the court allowed the foreclosure when MERS executed a written assignment of the note and mortgage to the beneficial owner two days before the filing of the foreclosure action. The court rejected the borrower's argument that the assignment was ineffective because MERS never had an ownership interest in the loan. The mortgage instrument conferred broad authority upon MERS to act with respect to the mortgage transaction.

V. POWER OF SALE FORECLOSURE

A. Goal in terms of title: The goal of power of sale foreclosure in terms of title is precisely the same as for judicial foreclosure—to give the purchaser exactly the same title the mortgagor had when the mortgage was granted.

B. Cheap and fast: Power of sale foreclosure is designed to be less costly and faster than judicial foreclosure. This is why roughly half the states have it. Both mortgagors and owners of junior interests generally have less protection, both procedural and substantive, in nonjudicial foreclosure.

   1. Notice to junior interests: In many, but not all, nonjudicial foreclosure states, junior interest owners are not entitled to notice of the foreclosure unless they have obtained such a right by contracting with the mortgagee.

C. Statutory procedures: State statutes govern nonjudicial foreclosure by specifying notice provisions, sales procedures, and other formalities the lender or its agent must observe.

   1. Strict compliance: The statutes are designed to protect mortgagors from the risks stemming from the fact that no disinterested third party such as a judge is supervising the foreclosure process. A deviation from statutory requirements generally means the foreclosure sale, even after completion, is subject to attack and invalidation.

   2. Harm presumed from statutory violation: Usually, any violation of the foreclosure statute is grounds for the court to set aside a nonjudicial sale. The borrower or other interested party does not have to prove injury in fact from the irregularity. *Henson v Fleet Mortgage Co.*, 892 S.W.2d 250 (Ark. 1995), set aside a sale when a substitution of trustee was recorded at the wrong office and the notice of foreclosure sale did not specify the courthouse at which the sale would occur.

D. Title risk

   1. Judicial foreclosure: When the foreclosure sale is confirmed by judicial decree, it becomes a final judgment once the time for motions and appeals is past. This means the foreclosure purchaser's title to the property is relatively safe.

   2. Nonjudicial foreclosure: Nonjudicial foreclosure results in titles that are weaker and shakier than judicial foreclosure titles. The foreclosure purchaser has greater title risk when there is no judicial determination that the sale was properly conducted. A disappointed mortgagor or third party may sue at any time after the sale, subject to any statute of limitations that may apply.

VI. PRIORITY OF MORTGAGE THAT REFINANCES PRIOR MORTGAGE

A. Equitable subrogation: Most states hold that a lender who pays the mortgage of another and takes a new mortgage as security is subrogated to the rights of the first mortgagee as against any intervening lienholder.

　　1. Notice of intervening interest: The doctrine of equitable subrogation protects a refinancing mortgagee who did not know of the junior claims at the time of the refinancing. Most courts refuse to protect a mortgagee who had actual knowledge of the intervening lien at the time of refinancing, but the Restatement allows subrogation even when there is actual knowledge. Restatement Third of Property, Mortgages § 7.6, comment e (1997).

　　2. Amount of debt: Equitable subrogation protects the refinancing mortgagee only to the extent of the senior mortgage that was repaid with the funds of the refinancing mortgagee. When the refinancing mortgagee makes a larger loan, the excess is not entitled to priority under the doctrine of equitable subrogation.

　　　　Example: Borrower granted a mortgage to secure a loan. Eight years later, Borrower refinanced the debt with a new $168,000 loan from New Lender, with $153,800 of the loan proceeds paid to retire the old loan. Several years earlier judgment creditors had filed judgment liens against Borrower. After Borrower defaulted, New Lender commenced foreclosure. Its title search had failed to disclose the liens; it thus had constructive, but not actual, notice of the intervening liens. The court applied equitable subrogation to give priority to New Lender over the judgment creditors, but only to the extent of $153,800. *Eastern Savings Bank v. Pappas*, 829 A.2d 953 (D.C. Ct. App. 2003).

　　3. Form of relief: When the court applies equitable subrogation, there are several different forms of relief that may be given to the refinancing mortgagee:

　　　　a. Re-foreclosure of senior mortgage: The refinancing mortgagee has the right to foreclose the senior mortgage.

　　　　b. Foreclosure of new mortgage given priority: When the refinancing mortgagee purports to foreclose its mortgage, not the senior mortgage, the court may give this mortgage priority. It is treated as if the mortgagee foreclosed the senior mortgage. *G.E. Capital Mortgage Services, Inc. v. Levenson*, 657 A.2d 1170 (Md. 1995), applied this rule to extinguish intervening judgment liens when the mortgagee foreclosed a mortgage that had refinanced a senior mortgage.

　　　　c. Revival of senior debt: When the refinancing mortgagee purports to foreclose its mortgage, not the senior mortgage, the court might revive the senior debt. (This was the position of the intermediate appellate court in *G.E. Capital Mortgage Services, Inc. v. Levenson*, 657 A.2d 1170 (Md. 1995), which the Maryland court of appeals rejected.)

B. Record priorities prevail: A few states reject equitable subrogation, ruling that the priority of a mortgage that refinances a prior debt is determined by normal recording act principles. Thus, the mortgage is junior to prior-in-time interests of which the mortgagee has notice (constructive, inquiry, or actual).

VII. DEED IN LIEU OF FORECLOSURE

After default, the borrower who is faced with foreclosure voluntarily conveys the property to the lender. The conveyance is accomplished by a deed in lieu of foreclosure. A standard warranty deed may be used, or the parties may draft an instrument that reflects the purpose of the transaction.

A. **Advantages for borrower:** In exchange for the transfer, the lender cancels part or all of the mortgage debt. The borrower is relieved of responsibility for the property and avoids being the target of foreclosure.

B. **Risks for borrower:** If the borrower has substantial equity in the property, this is lost by use of a deed in lieu of foreclosure. Thus, the biggest risk to the borrower is underpricing the property.

C. **Advantages for lender:** The lender gets title right away and avoids the time and expense of foreclosure proceedings. The lender may keep or sell the property however it wishes; for example, by listing it with a broker.

D. **Risks for lender**

    1. **Clogging equity of redemption:** The mortgagor may try to set aside the deed in lieu of foreclosure, claiming that the deed clogs her equity of redemption. Proper documentation of the reasons for the deed may protect the lender, but there's always the risk that the borrower may claim the transaction was intended not to terminate the loan relationship but to add to the lender's security as an attempt to avoid foreclosure.

    2. **Inadequate consideration or unconscionability:** The fairness of the exchange may be called into question due to extreme disparity of bargaining position. The risk is enhanced if the documents do not make it clear that the lender has released the borrower from personal liability on all or a substantial part of the debt.

    3. **Title risk:** The deed in lieu of foreclosure, unlike a properly conducted foreclosure, will not cut off junior interests that are subsequent to the mortgage.

    4. **Risk of mortgagor's bankruptcy or insolvency:** If the mortgagor files for bankruptcy or is pushed into bankruptcy within 90 days after the deed in lieu of foreclosure is given, the transfer may be set aside as a preference. Apart from bankruptcy, under the state law of fraudulent conveyances, there is the risk that other creditors of the mortgagor may attack the deed on the basis that it was given for less than market value.

VIII. ECONOMICS OF FORECLOSURE

A. **Problem of price adequacy:** Most foreclosure sales yield prices that are substantially less than the fair market value for ordinary arms'-length sales of comparable properties.

B. **Low price by itself does not invalidate sale:** The general rule is that a very low price by itself is not grounds for invalidating the foreclosure sale. This is true for judicial foreclosure, when the issue is whether the court should confirm the sale, and for nonjudicial foreclosure, when an action is brought to set aside the private sale. See *Greater Southwest Office Park, Ltd. v. Texas Commerce Bank National Association*, 786 S.W.2d 386 (Tex. Ct. App. 1990), holding that in the absence of an irregularity in the sale, the lender has no duty to bid a fair price.

C. **Grossly inadequate price coupled with mistake:** A court may refuse to confirm a foreclosure sale at a grossly inadequate price if the low price resulted from a good faith mistake made by the injured party in the foreclosure proceedings. In *RSR Investments, Inc. v. Barnett Bank*, 647 So. 2d 874 (Fla. Dist. Ct. App. 1994), the court overturned a foreclosure sale of property worth $107,000, sold for $5,000 when the lender's attorney made a clerical mistake on his calendar and failed to attend the sale.

D. **Inadequate price coupled with irregularity:** Whenever there is any irregularity, procedural or otherwise, in a foreclosure sale, there is the risk that the sale will be set aside. This is especially likely when the foreclosure price paid by the lender or a third party is very low. Courts strain to protect mortgagors and junior interest holders from the hardship of inadequate foreclosure prices.

IX. STATUTORY MORTGAGOR PROTECTIONS

A. **One-action rule:** Some states, including California, have a one-action rule. This limits the mortgagee to a single action that must include foreclosure and at the mortgagee's option may include a deficiency judgment. This prevents the borrower from having to defend multiple actions that arise from the same lending transaction.

B. **Statutory redemption:** Statutory redemption, permitted by 33 states, is the right to redeem the property after the foreclosure sale, whereas *equitable redemption* is a right to redeem before foreclosure, by paying the full, outstanding amount. Below are considerations for statutory redemption.

1. **Existence of right to redeem:** Some states allow redemption after both judicial and power of sale foreclosures. In others, statutory redemption is available only after one type of foreclosure and not the other. In almost all states, waiver of the right to redeem is invalid.

2. **Time period:** The time period varies from a few months to 18 months after the date of the foreclosure sale.

3. **Redemption price:** In almost all states, the price is the foreclosure sale price, plus interest and foreclosure costs. Usually, the interest rate is set by statute. In a few states, the redemptioner must pay the mortgage debt plus interest.

4. **Right to possession:** In most states, the mortgagor has the right to possession during the statutory period. In a few states, the mortgagor who remains in possession must post bond to protect against waste.

5. **Who can redeem?** In some states, only the mortgagor can redeem. In other states, junior lienors also have a statutory redemption right. Just like a mortgagor, a junior who redeems obtains title to the property.

6. **Competing redemptioners:** In states where junior lienors may redeem, two basic systems exist to handle competing redemptioners.

   a. **Priority approach:** The mortgagor has the first right to redeem within a set time period. If the mortgagor fails to redeem, each lienor has a short period (e.g., five days) to redeem in order of their priority.

   b. **Scramble approach:** Anyone can redeem at any time within the entire period. If the mortgagor ever redeems, this ends the process. Any junior may redeem, with the price to pay depending on the junior's rank and whether another junior has previously redeemed.

7. **Compliance with statutory requirements:** Substantial compliance with procedural requirements for redemption is generally sufficient. Minor flaws will not disqualify redeeming mortgagors and lienors. Redemption statutes are liberally construed to protect mortgagors and lienors. For example, in *Savoy v. Cascade County Sheriff's Department*, 887 P.2d 160 (Mont. 1994), a notice of redemption lacked a certified copy of the mortgage and an affidavit of the amount, which the statute required. Nonetheless, the notice contained sufficient information for exercising the lienor's right to redeem.

C. **Limits on deficiency judgments:** Many states have anti-deficiency judgment acts that bar lenders from obtaining deficiency judgments under certain circumstances. The statutes vary widely.

1. **Certain loans protected:** Some acts bar deficiency judgments only for purchase-money mortgages made by sellers. Others apply only to certain types of properties, such as owner-occupied residences and farms.

2. **Methods of foreclosure:** Some acts bar deficiency judgments only if the lender forecloses by power of sale, rather than by judicial action.

D. **Fair value rule:** Instead of banning deficiency judgments outright, fair value legislation permits a deficiency judgment, but only to the extent the debt exceeds the proven "fair value" of the property.

1. **Meaning of fair value:** Fair value is based on ordinary arms'-length sales. It ignores the fact that foreclosure sale prices are usually depressed. In *Gutherie v. Ford Equipment Leasing Co.*, 424 S.E.2d 889 (Ga. Ct. App. 1992), the court rejected the lender's claim that fair value of the property is the "quick sale" value obtained in the foreclosure context.

Quiz Yourself on *FORECLOSURE*

86. How likely is it that strict foreclosure will result in surplus proceeds being paid to the mortgagor? _____

87. Robert has a first mortgage on Blackacre, granted by the owner, Joe, and securing a $40,000 debt. After granting the mortgage, Joe had an auto accident and through his negligence injured Karen. Karen obtained a damage award that exceeded by $20,000 the amount of automobile liability insurance that Joe carried. Joe did not pay the excess, and Karen got a judgment lien on all of Joe's real property. Joe defaults on his mortgage, and Robert forecloses. Robert fails to join Karen as a party to the foreclosure action, and at the court-ordered sale, Starr buys the property for $35,000. What are the parties' rights and obligations? _____

88. If a lender has the choice of power of sale foreclosure, may it instead choose to pursue judicial foreclosure? Which option is the lender likely to pick? _____

89. Suzie has a mortgage loan, held by Big Bank, on her office building, which she took out five years ago in the original principal amount of $100,000. One year ago, she granted a second mortgage on the building to Federal Savings to finance restoration, getting a loan for $30,000. Interest rates have dropped, and Suzie refinances the Big Bank loan. The loan had a present balance of $80,000, and

Suzie prepaid it using proceeds from a new $90,000 mortgage loan from Small Bank. Suzie used the extra $10,000 as operating cash. Small Bank's title search failed to find the Federal Savings mortgage, which was validly of record. Suzie defaulted on the new Small Bank loan, and Small Bank seeks to foreclose. What priority will it have vis-à-vis Federal Savings? _____

90. A state law provides that the mortgagor has the right of statutory redemption for sixth months after the date the court confirms the foreclosure sale. A mortgagor loses her farm through foreclosure and tenders the notice of redemption along with the redemption price to the proper person. The mortgagor's tender is made shortly after the six-month period expires—three days late. She sues, seeking a declaration that her redemption right is enforceable because the minor delay has not prejudiced the purchaser. Should she prevail? _____

Answers

86. **It will not happen**, because under strict foreclosure there is no foreclosure sale, and thus there cannot be any surplus sales proceeds. Strict foreclosure means that, if the mortgagor does not pay the debt by the judicially set deadline, the mortgagee gets to keep the property. If the mortgagor has equity (the property is worth more than the debt), the mortgagee keeps this value—it is not considered "surplus" to be returned to the mortgagor.

87. **Karen is an *omitted necessary party*.** She still owns her judgment lien, and Starr owns fee simple title subject to that lien. Either Karen or Starr may take action to change the status quo. Karen has two rights or choices. (1) She may go to court and seek to foreclose her judgment lien. Starr will be a necessary party in Karen's foreclosure action. In that action, Starr, to protect her investment, will have the right to pay Karen the $20,000 plus costs and get the judgment lien cancelled. (2) Karen may seek to exercise her right as junior lienholder to redeem the property. To do this, she tenders $40,000, the amount of the first mortgage debt, to Starr. Starr gets this amount in exchange for title to the property. Karen now owns the property free and clear of all liens. Starr may have a cause of action for damages against Robert. It depends on the type of deed she received and the state's remedies for breach of deed warranties.

Starr has three rights or choices: (1) Starr may re-foreclose the senior mortgage that Robert had owned, securing the $40,000 debt. This time Starr will be sure to join Karen, who is a necessary party. (2) Starr may redeem the property by paying the $20,000 to Karen. This results in the release of the judgment lien. Starr's redemption right has priority over Karen's redemption right mentioned in (2) above because Starr owns the fee simple. Thus, if Karen tenders the $35,000 to Starr and Starr tenders the $20,000 to Karen, the second exchange is the one that occurs. Starr will keep title and pay the $20,000. (3) Starr in some states may bring an action of strict foreclosure against Karen. This would give Karen a court-set deadline by which to exercise her redemption right by paying Starr $35,000 in exchange for title. Otherwise, the court extinguishes Karen's judgment lien. Starr will use strict foreclosure only if she is willing to sell the property to Karen, unless she strongly believes that Karen will not be able to come up with $35,000 by the deadline.

88. **In all states that authorize power of sale foreclosure, judicial foreclosure is also available.** However, the lender is very likely to choose power of sale foreclosure because it is quicker and less expensive.

89. Small Bank has priority for most of its loan. The real property records, in order of recording, reveal that Federal Savings now has the first mortgage and Small Bank is second in position. However, Small Bank can prove that most of its loan was used to refinance the prior Big Bank loan. In most states, this entitles Small Bank to use the doctrine of equitable subrogation. To prevent hardship to Small Bank, Small is subrogated to the priority that Big Bank had. Subrogation applies only to the extent of the refinancing. Small Bank refinanced a debt that, at the time of refinancing, was amortized to $80,000. Thus, under subrogation, Small Bank has first priority to the extent of $80,000 (plus accrued interest on this amount). Then Federal Savings has second priority for all of its loan. Finally, Small Bank has third priority to the extent of $10,000, its remaining debt (plus accrued interest).

90. No. The court probably will hold for the purchaser and against the mortgagor, who is attempting to redeem late. While there are cases that protect mortgagors by holding that substantial compliance with the statutory requirements is sufficient, these cases involve mortgagors who gave notice and made some efforts to redeem before the period for statutory redemption expired. Here the mortgagor did nothing until three days after the period expired.

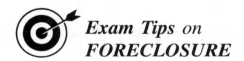 *Exam Tips on*
FORECLOSURE

☛ **Local law:** Foreclosure laws vary widely from state to state, and they can be quite technical. If your teacher has given you information on your state's foreclosure laws and practices, don't neglect to study it.

☛ **First, determine what type of foreclosure is taking place:** This dramatically influences the parties' rights. The three types of foreclosures are:

🖙 **Judicial foreclosure:** The mortgagee brings an action in court, serving the mortgagor/owner and the holders of junior interests as necessary parties. The court supervises the foreclosure proceedings. The debt is ascertained, and if the mortgagee proves it has the right to foreclose, the court arranges for the sale of the mortgaged property. The sale is a public auction. At the end of the process the court confirms the sale.

🖙 **Power of sale foreclosure (also called nonjudicial foreclosure):** Without going to court, the lender or a third party such as a trustee handles the foreclosure. Like a judicial foreclosure, the sale is advertised and held at a public auction.

🖙 **Strict foreclosure:** This was the original English foreclosure process. The mortgagee brings an action in court. The court sets a deadline by which the mortgagor must redeem the property by paying the debt in full. Otherwise, the mortgagor's equity of redemption is foreclosed. With strict foreclosure, the property is not sold. The mortgagee has no duty to account for any equity or surplus value in the property. Strict foreclosure is presently used in only two U.S. states as the primary method of foreclosure.

☞ Because strict foreclosure is uncommon, if the exam question does not indicate the type of foreclosure, you should assume it will cause a sale of the property through either judicial or power of sale foreclosure.

☛ **Action on the debt vs. foreclosure:** Pay attention to what remedy the lender is pursuing. The two main remedies the mortgagee may pursue against a defaulting mortgagor are an ***action on the debt*** (seeks judgment in court for the debt) or a ***foreclosure action*** (judicial or power of sale). It is important to be able to distinguish between the action on the debt and the foreclosure action. An exam question might not directly say whether the creditor has or has not brought an action on the debt. You nevertheless should be prepared to discuss the relevance of an action on the debt.

☛ **Deficiency:** With a foreclosure exam question, expect an issue concerning collection of a deficiency. If a foreclosure results in a sale for a price smaller than the debt, the mortgagee has a deficiency. The mortgagee may seek a ***deficiency judgment*** for the difference.

☛ **Surplus:** If a foreclosure results in a sale for a price greater than the debt, the surplus proceeds belong to the mortgagor. They are paid to the mortgagor or paid to owners of junior interests in the property.

☛ **Judicial foreclosure, necessary parties:** If there is a judicial foreclosure, check the facts to see if all necessary parties are in the litigation. Where there is a judicial foreclosure, necessary parties are persons who hold interests junior in priority to the mortgage being foreclosed.

☞ **Omitted necessary party:** A necessary party who isn't joined (made a defendant by proper service) is an omitted necessary party. The omitted necessary party retains her rights—she isn't bound by the foreclosure.

☛ **Power of sale foreclosure, statutory compliance:** If there's a power of sale foreclosure, statutory compliance is a likely issue. To foreclose by power of sale, the mortgage instrument must authorize this procedure ***and*** the state must have a statute that regulates the procedure. Statutory requirements for power of sale foreclosure are strictly construed. Thus, courts generally invalidate power of sale foreclosures whenever a procedural defect is proven. Generally, there is no need to prove that the defect affected the outcome; harm or the potential for harm to the mortgagor and other interested parties is presumed.

☛ **Equitable subrogation:** If the exam question facts mention a refinanced loan, you probably have to discuss equitable subrogation. A lender who refinances a prior mortgage loan is entitled to equitable subrogation. This means that if there is an intervening lien (between the refinanced mortgage and the new one), the new lender is entitled to the priority of the old refinanced mortgage.

☛ **Statutory redemption:** If your state has statutory redemption, it's more likely to come up on your exam. In many states, the mortgagor and owners of junior interests have the right, by statute, to redeem the property after the completion of a valid foreclosure sale. The statute specifies the period of time for redemption (such as six months or one year). The redemption price is the foreclosure sales price plus interest and foreclosure costs. Do not confuse the statutory right of redemption with the equitable right of redemption. The equitable right of redemption, discussed in Chapter 14, is available only before the final foreclosure, and requires payment in full of the debt.

CHAPTER 20

MORTGAGE SUBSTITUTES

ChapterScope ━━━━━━━━━━━━━━━━━━━━━━━━━━━━━━━━━━━━━━━

This chapter covers a number of financing arrangements that are alternatives to the standard promissory note secured by a mortgage or deed of trust. The main alternatives are the absolute deed intended as security, the negative pledge, and the installment land contract. They are called "mortgage substitutes" because they avoid use of the standard mortgage, but they perform a similar financing function.

- ■ **Mortgage substitutes:** Lenders sometimes prefer mortgage substitutes to get around mortgage laws that protect borrowers.

- ■ **Equitable mortgage:** An equitable mortgage or *disguised mortgage* is treated under mortgage law rather than under standard contract law.

- ■ **Absolute deed:** An absolute deed intended as security is recast as an equitable mortgage.

- ■ **Negative pledge:** With the negative pledge, the borrower promises the lender not to convey or encumber the property.

- ■ **Installment land contract:** With the installment land contract or contract for deed, the purchaser takes possession and pays the price over time.

I. THE USE OF MORTGAGE SUBSTITUTES

A. Market role: Mortgage substitutes are transactions that are like standard mortgages in that they perform a credit function. A person is extended credit in order to buy property or, with respect to property she already owns, to obtain loan funds for other purposes. Although mortgage substitutes are not traded in national markets like standard residential and commercial loans, they perform a valuable market role in expanding the amount of secured credit. The risk allocation between lender and borrower who use a mortgage substitute is often different than it would be had they used a standard mortgage loan. Many times the risk to the lender is higher than normal, either due to the amount of down payment or equity, the borrower's credit history or income, or the nature of the property. When this is the case, the mortgage substitute facilitates a credit transaction that may not have taken place absent the alternative vehicle.

B. Opting out of mortgage law: Parties sometimes use mortgage substitutes in credit transactions in which they could have selected a standard mortgage loan (a promissory note secured by a mortgage or mortgage variant, such as a deed of trust). To understand why parties make this choice, it is important to review several principles of mortgage law.

1. Mortgage as status: The parties to a mortgage are in a relationship where their status frequently determines their respective rights and duties. The law of mortgages limits their freedom of contract.

a. **Anti-clogging rule:** Express terms that restrict or clog the mortgagor's equity of redemption are void. This is often called the ***anti-clogging rule*** or the ***anti-clogging doctrine***. It doesn't matter whether the term that clogs the mortgagor's equity is set forth in the mortgage itself or only in a collateral document. It's invalid in either event.

Example: When the mortgage is signed, Mortgagor gives Mortgagee a deed conveying title to the mortgaged property, authorizing Mortgagee to record the deed upon any default. The deed is an invalid clog and has no effect on Mortgagor's equity of redemption. Assuming Mortgagor defaults and Mortgagee records the deed, Mortgagee still must foreclose in order to extinguish Mortgagor's equity of redemption.

b. **Foreclosure procedures:** The statutory procedures, including time period and notice provisions, cannot be waived because they are designed to protect mortgagors and third parties who have rights in the property.

Example: To secure a loan, Borrower signs a deed of trust that provides: Grantor hereby agrees that Trustee may sell the Property on any business day between the hours of 8:00 A.M. and 6:00 P.M. at any location in the county where the Property is located, provided the date and place of sale are disclosed in the notice referred to above. Grantor hereby waives and relinquishes the right to contest Trustee's selection of time and place of sale. The state foreclosure statute provides for foreclosure sales only on the first Tuesday of every month, to be held at the county courthouse. This deed of trust provision is unenforceable. The statute is designed to protect borrowers and third parties who have interests in the mortgaged property. When the community follows the statute, everyone knows when and where foreclosure sales are held. Holding a sale at a different time and place may result in confusion and reduce the likelihood that interested bidders will appear at the auction.

C. **Types of mortgage substitutes:** The most common types of mortgage substitutes are the absolute deed intended as security, the lease with option to purchase, the sale-leaseback, the negative pledge, and the installment land contract.

D. **Use of term "mortgage substitute":** The label "mortgage substitute" is neutral, and it does not tell you what law or principles a court will apply to the transaction. For some mortgage substitutes, courts will look to ***substance over form***, saying that the parties' labels are not determinative and mortgage law must apply. For other mortgage substitutes, courts will apply ***freedom of contract*** and defer to the parties' selection of form.

II. DISGUISED MORTGAGE

A disguised mortgage is any transaction that avoids the use of standard mortgage documents where the substance of the transaction is a debt secured by real property. The label "disguised mortgage" tells you that the court is applying mortgage law. It has seen through the disguise, perceiving the substance over the parties' form.

A. **Parties' motivations:** Usually, the lender is the party who desires to use a disguised mortgage device rather than standard documentation. The motive is risk reduction. The lender believes that mortgage law protects mortgagors too much. Sometimes, however, the borrower prefers the mortgage substitute. She wants to hide the fact that she needs money or is taking on debt.

B. Equitable mortgage: The term "equitable mortgage" is often used as a synonym for disguised mortgage. This reflects the history that a court of equity intervenes to declare that a transaction that appears not to be a mortgage really is one.

    1. Equitable mortgage to cure technical defects: The term "equitable mortgage" is also employed in one different context, when the parties intended a legal mortgage, but there was some defect either in the paperwork or in their implementation of the plan. Under this doctrine, courts have also enforced a borrower's express promise to grant a mortgage on specified property. In essence, this serves to make such a promise specifically enforceable.

    Example: Under the law of a particular state, a mortgage requires a witness to be valid. Mortgagor signs an unwitnessed mortgage to secure a loan. The instrument is defective, but if Mortgagee's rights are challenged either by Mortgagor or by a third party, courts usually protect Mortgagee. The explanation is that, while the mortgage is not legally valid, *in equity* Mortgagee merits protection; that is, the defective instrument is an enforceable *equitable mortgage*.

III. ABSOLUTE DEED INTENDED AS SECURITY

This is a common type of disguised mortgage where a party advances money to a landowner, taking a regular warranty deed to the property. If a dispute develops, the owner claims that the parties agreed that the owner could regain title by paying back the money plus an extra amount at a time in the future. The grantee under the deed often refutes this claim when there is no written evidence of the owner's right to regain title.

A. Written evidence of owner's right to regain title: If there is written evidence (e.g., the owner has a written option to repurchase at a specified price), the nature of the transaction will still be in dispute. The owner will argue it's a disguised mortgage, and the grantee will claim it's a bona fide sale coupled with a bona fide purchase option.

B. Parol evidence: Despite the statute of frauds, parol evidence is admissible to explain that an absolute deed was intended to secure a loan.

    Example: In *Smith v. Player*, 601 So. 2d 946 (Ala. 1992), a landowner defaulted on his mortgage loan after he lost his job. He asked an acquaintance for help in paying off the loan. The landowner conveyed the property to the acquaintance, using an absolute deed. The grantee paid off the debt. The grantor continued to live on the property after the conveyance. Later the grantor tried to repay the grantee, but the grantee refused to accept payment. The grantor brought suit, seeking to set aside the deed and reform it to a mortgage. The grantee introduced evidence that his attorney advised the parties that the transaction was a sale and not a mortgage. The court held for the grantor. The evidence as to the attorney's advice was not conclusive. Other evidence indicated that the parties actually intended the grantor to get his property back if he repaid the money advanced.

C. Factors: Factors that point toward a deed intended as security include:

    1. Prior loan transaction between the parties: Prior to delivery of the deed, the parties were borrower-lender. Courts sometimes use the phrase ***"once a mortgage, always a mortgage"*** when pointing to this fact.

Example: Two years ago, Freddie borrowed $60,000 from his cousin Moneybags to start a delicatessen business. The loan was unsecured, and at the end of each year Freddie was to repay $10,000 with interest until the loan was repaid. Freddie made the first year's payment plus interest in full. At the end of the second year, he paid only the interest plus $2,000 in principal and at the same time he gave Moneybags a warranty deed to his house. In litigation, Freddie claims he still owes $58,000 and his house is collateral. Moneybags claims she owns Freddie's house, there's no debt, and Freddie has no right to get title to the house back. The prior admitted borrower-lender relationship is a fact that counts in Freddie's favor.

2. **Unequal bargaining positions:** During negotiation of the transaction, the grantee may have had a much better bargaining position. This is especially likely if the grantor has great financial need. The grantor may have wanted a loan, and asked for a loan. The grantee, with a strong bargaining position, refused and insisted on a sale with an absolute deed, and the grantor acquiesced only to get the money.

Example: In the above example, Freddie is helped with evidence that he was in bad financial straits at the end of the second year when he signed and delivered the deed; that he didn't have the extra $8,000 so that he could make the entire principal payment; that he had no liquid investments that he could sell to raise this amount; that his credit rating was bad and he had no other opportunities to borrow $8,000. Moneybags of course is helped by contrary evidence—that Freddie had choices and the parties mutually decided to end the loan transaction and to enter into a sale.

3. **Price less than fair market value:** A low price compared to value suggests a debt rather than a true sale. However, the fact that the grantee makes a profitable resale years later does not necessarily indicate a loan. In *Duvall v. Laws, Swain & Murdoch, P.A.*, 797 S.W.2d 474 (Ark. Ct. App. 1990), a lawyer took a mineral deed from a client as payment for a legal fee. Five years later, the lawyer resold the property at large profit, and the court refused to find an equitable mortgage.

Example: In the above example, Freddie wants to prove his house was worth much more than $58,000 at the time of the alleged sale, and Moneybags wants to prove the opposite—that the parties' price was fair market value or within the range of plausible fair market value. In litigation, both sides are likely to hire real estate brokers as expert witnesses.

4. **Fiduciary relationship between the parties:** If the grantee/purchaser owes the grantor a fiduciary duty due to some special relationship, this may count in favor of the grantor who claims the transaction is a loan. The court may scrutinize the transaction more closely.

Example: In *Duvall v. Laws, Swain & Murdoch, P.A.*, 797 S.W.2d 474 (Ark. Ct. App. 1990), a lawyer's client was having trouble paying a legal fee. The lawyer took a mineral deed from the client as payment. Subsequently, the client claimed that the deed was intended as security. The court held for the lawyer because the transaction was bona fide. But the court scrutinized the transaction carefully due to the lawyer's fiduciary duties to his client. A dissenting judge argued that the attorney's ethical duties to the client mandated overturning the deed.

5. **Grantor retains possession:** With a true sale, the grantee takes possession at closing. Therefore, the grantor's retained possession suggests a mortgage loan.

Example: In the above example, if Freddie continued to live in his house after the alleged sale, this is some evidence of a mortgage loan. Moneybags will have to try to rebut this by saying

Freddie stayed with his permission and became his tenant. If there is neither a written lease nor a record of monthly rent payments, Moneybags' claim of a landlord-tenant relationship might not be believable. Conversely, if Freddie vacated possession shortly after the alleged sale and Moneybags moved in or held the house for rental, this would count strongly in her favor. In modern mortgage loan transactions, the owner/mortgagor virtually never relinquishes possession to the mortgagee in the absence of default.

6. **Existence of debt:** Courts often say that the existence of a debt owed by the grantor to the grantee is another important factor to consider. This is misleading because the existence or nonexistence of debt is a conclusion, not an underlying fact. If the fact finder can't identify a "debt," there can be no mortgage because there's nothing for it to secure. The debt need not be written. Oral loans are enforceable, and a debt may be inferred under proper circumstances.

IV. NEGATIVE PLEDGE

A. **Definition:** With the negative pledge, or ***negative covenant***, the borrower promises the lender not to convey or encumber specified property before the loan is repaid.

Example: Thomas, a homeowner, wants to borrow $40,000 to expand his retail book store. The lender agrees to make the loan if Thomas grants it a security interest in his equipment and inventory and signs a negative pledge agreement that covers his residence. In this agreement, he promises not to sell, convey, or encumber his residence until he repays the loan in full.

B. **Status as equitable mortgage:** Sometimes, the lender argues a negative pledge is an equitable mortgage. Other times, the borrower makes this argument in order to take advantage of a rule of mortgage law that favors mortgagors. Courts have split on the issue of whether the negative pledge is what it appears to be—a mere contract promise—or is in substance a mortgage.

C. **Factors:** Factors to consider in deciding whether a negative pledge creates an equitable mortgage include:

1. **Subjective intent:** If the parties believed the negative pledge in effect was a mortgage on the borrower's asset, the court may agree. This factor will seldom help much because the parties, if they're in litigation arguing opposite sides of the issue, will probably disagree on their subjective intent.

2. **Appropriateness of remedies:** If the buyer breaches her promise, the court may declare the transaction is an equitable mortgage if foreclosure against the property appears to be the most appropriate remedy.

Example: In *Coast Bank v. Minderhout*, 392 P.2d 265 (Cal. 1964), the borrower obtained a loan to improve his property and signed a negative covenant agreement. The borrower then conveyed the property in breach of this promise. In response, the lender used an acceleration clause and sought to foreclose. The borrower argued that foreclosure was not proper because the lender did not have a mortgage. The court held that the court allows foreclosure on the ground that the negative covenant amounted to an equitable mortgage. The court reasoned that alternative remedies were less desirable; an award of damages for breach of promise would entitle the lender to no more than it already possessed, the right to get a judgment for the full amount of the loan. Specific performance of the negative covenant might create an invalid restraint against alienation.

3. Construction against institutional lender: If an institutional lender selects a negative pledge form, ambiguity as to intent may be resolved against the lender.

Example: In *Tahoe Nat'l Bank v. Phillips*, 480 P.2d 320 (Cal. 1971), a borrower obtained a loan from a bank for capital needed for a real estate joint venture. The bank had the borrower sign an "Assignment of Rents and Agreement Not to Sell or Encumber Real Property," which covered her residence. Thereafter, the borrower filed for homestead protection on her residence and subsequently defaulted on the bank loan. The bank argued it had an equitable mortgage, which predated the homestead filing. The court held for the borrower. The court protected the borrower's homestead by construing the agreement against the bank, as a mere promise, which didn't amount to an equitable mortgage. The court distinguished *Coast Bank*, supra, on the basis that the *Coast Bank* loan was made to improve the property, had an acceleration clause, and involved a borrower's breach of the promise not to convey.

D. Parties' motivations: The lender hopes that, should the borrower default, the property will be available to pay the debt. The lender could proceed by suing on the debt, obtaining a judgment, and obtaining a judgment lien on the property. Ideally, the lender seeks a priority position. It hopes to be in the same position, with respect to proceeding against the property, as if it held a mortgage. However, legal questions surrounding the negative pledge may put the lender in a riskier position than if it had obtained a standard, enforceable mortgage. The upside for the lender may be the ability to avoid certain mortgage rules that protect the borrower by preserving the opportunity to argue that it has an unsecured loan if, based on future events, this position appears preferable.

1. Avoiding restrictions on borrower's mortgage of property: Sometimes lender and borrower agree to the negative pledge because the borrower cannot readily grant a mortgage on the property due to rights held by a third party or legal restrictions on transfer. The property may be subject to a due-on-sale clause that bars the owner from granting a second mortgage. The property may be marital property and not transferable without the consent of the borrower's spouse, or it may be homestead property and under state law not capable of being encumbered by any instrument that is not a purchase-money mortgage.

Example: Spenser owns an office building, subject to a 20-year mortgage loan. The mortgage has a due-on-sale clause that prohibits Spenser from selling, encumbering, or transferring any interest in the office building without the lender's prior written consent. It is clear this clause bars Spenser from granting a second mortgage on the building. Spenser wants to borrow $100,000 from Venture Bank to finance a new product line. Venture Bank wants collateral, and Spenser can prove he has $200,000 worth of equity in his office building (market value of $1 million, subject to existing debt of $800,000). Because Spenser and Venture Bank believe the first mortgagee will not consent to Spenser's grant of a second mortgage to Venture Bank, the bank makes a loan, with Spenser signing a negative covenant agreement.

V. INSTALLMENT LAND CONTRACT

A. Definition: An installment land contract, or ***contract for deed***, is an executory contract under which the purchaser pays the price in installments over a lengthy period of time.

1. Possession: The buyer goes into possession immediately, when the contract is signed.

2. Title retention and deed: While the contract is executory, the vendor or seller retains title. The vendor promises to deliver a deed to the purchaser when the last payment is made. Sometimes, instead the vendor signs the deed at the outset and it is held in escrow pending completion of the contract.

Example: Horace contracts to buy a small farm from Sinbad for $900,000, agreeing to pay $150,000 on October 1 for six consecutive years, with interest on the unpaid balance at 8 percent per annum. When Sinbad and Horace sign the installment land contract, Sinbad also signs a warranty deed that names Horace as grantee and gives the deed to Sinbad's attorney in escrow, with instructions to deliver it to Horace when he receives written evidence that Horace has paid the full contract price.

B. Market uses of installment land contract: Land contracts are used for seller financing in two primary market situations. Both involve consumer transactions, one consisting of nonmerchant sales and the other merchant sales: (1) when the purchaser buying from a nonmerchant individual does not qualify for standard institutional financing and (2) when the developer of a vacation or resort project is selling lots.

1. "Poor man's mortgage": One primary market role for the installment land contract is identified by the label "poor man's mortgage." The land contract often permits persons to buy property who do not qualify for standard institutional mortgage financing because they cannot make a substantial down payment or have a poor credit background. This benefits purchasers who otherwise would not be able to enter the market for buying real estate.

   a. Vendor's perspective: The vendor is willing to sell using an installment land contract because she expects that, if the purchaser defaults, terminating the contract and retaking possession will be cheap and easy.

2. Vacation and resort sales: A number of vacation and resort developments market their lots to purchasers through land contracts. This helps the developer to offer terms that include a very low down payment, with modest periodic payments. When the lot buyer is ready to build, the land contract is paid off as part of the buyer's financing for the house and related improvements. Occasionally, vacation and resort developers sell completed houses on land contracts, but this is much less common than for lot sales.

C. Vendor's remedies for purchaser's default

1. Forfeiture clause: Most installment land contracts expressly provide for forfeiture as a remedy for the purchaser's breach. This means that the purchaser's contract rights, as well as the purchaser's right to possession, are forfeited. The clause gives the vendor the option to declare forfeiture. Most courts apply contract analysis to evaluate forfeiture clauses.

   a. Traditional approach: Traditionally, forfeiture clauses are enforceable as written, absent contract defenses that apply to all contracts, such as fraud, duress, or undue influence.

   b. Modern trend: The trend is that forfeiture clauses are treated as a type of penalty, with courts refusing to enforce forfeiture if it would cause great hardship to the borrower (i.e., loss of substantial equity). Sometimes, this protection takes the form of a requirement that, in order to get forfeiture, the vendor must make ***restitution*** for the excess of payments received over damages. This is particularly true if the buyer has made substantial payments under the contract.

Example: Natasha contracts to buy Blueacre from Vinny for $100,000, to be paid in equal monthly installments of principal and interest over 10 years. In year four, when the principal balance on the contract is $80,000 and the fair market value of Blueacre is $120,000, Natasha defaults by missing three consecutive payments. Pursuant to the forfeiture clause in the contract, Vinny declares a forfeiture. Natasha, still in possession, refuses to leave, and Vinny sues for possession. Vinny prevails under the traditional contract approach. The trend today is for courts to protect Natasha. Restitution would mean Vinny must pay $40,000 to recover possession. Alternatively, Vinny may be required to proceed under the mortgage foreclosure rules discussed in Chapter 19.

2. **Expectancy damages:** Instead of declaring forfeiture, the vendor may have the remedy of terminating the contract and suing for expectancy damages. This gives the vendor the benefit of her bargain. The measure of damages is the difference between the contract price and the fair market value of the property at the time of breach.

3. **Restitution:** The vendor rescinds the contract and seeks to be put in his precontract economic position. This means he collects from the purchaser the value of possession from the date of the contract to the date of rescission, crediting the purchaser with the contract payments the purchaser had made.

4. **Purchaser's right of redemption:** In some states, the purchaser, after default, has the right to pay the vendor the unpaid contract balance and receive title. In *Petersen v. Hartell*, 707 P.2d 232 (Cal. 1985), the court ruled that a purchaser who has paid a substantial part of the price has the right to redemption, even when his default is willful.

5. **Foreclosure as a mortgage:** The vendor forecloses the contract as an equitable mortgage. This means the property is sold at an auction sale under standard judicial foreclosure procedures.

   a. **All contracts:** In a few states (e.g., Kentucky and Oklahoma), every installment land contract is an equitable mortgage. Then foreclosure is the only means by which the vendor can terminate the contract and regain the right to possession.

      i. **Practical effect:** In such a jurisdiction, it's foolish for a seller to ever use an installment land contract. A well-drafted promissory note and mortgage will better define the seller's rights and provide greater opportunity to protect the seller from risk related to purchaser default.

   b. **Substantial payment:** In some states, after the purchaser has made substantial payments, the forfeiture remedy is not available to the vendor, and the contract must be foreclosed as an equitable mortgage. In *Looney v. Farmers Home Administration*, 794 F.2d 310 (7th Cir. 1986), the court required foreclosure because $123,000 worth of payments on contract price of $250,000 was more than a minimal amount, even though virtually all those payments were interest, not principal.

D. **Transfers by purchaser**

1. **General rule:** As a general matter, the purchaser's rights under the installment land contract, including the right to possession, are freely alienable. This stems from both the property law policy that favors alienability and the modern contract notion that contract rights are assignable.

a. **Types of transfers:** The purchaser may engage in a range of transfers. She may assign her contract completely, retaining no rights; or she may make a limited transfer, such as a lease or a mortgage; or she may even enter into a subcontract (e.g., contracting to sell to another buyer).

2. **Express restrictions:** Installment land contracts sometimes expressly restrict transfers by the purchaser. Often the restriction is cast in the form of a "due-on-sale" clause, which is common for mortgage transactions.

3. **Relationship between vendor and purchaser's assignee:** The traditional position is that the vendor and the purchaser's assignee have no obligations to each other due to the *lack of privity*. This has led some courts to hold that the vendor has no duty to notify the assignee if the purchaser defaults and the vendor pursues a remedy such as forfeiture.

    a. **Trend to require notice:** When the vendor has notice that the purchaser has assigned some or all of his contract rights, the modern trend is to impose a duty on the vendor to notify the assignee prior to invoking a remedy for default. See *Yu v. Paperchase Partnership*, 845 P.2d 158 (N.M. 1992), holding that a vendor with actual knowledge that the vendee has assigned the contract to a subvendee must give the subvendee notice of a pending forfeiture.

    Example: Priscilla, the purchaser under an installment land contract for a mobile home site, rents her mobile home to Quigley, also giving Quigley an option to purchase the site and the home at the end of the one-year lease. Priscilla defaults in making the monthly contract payments, and the vendor declares forfeiture after notifying Priscilla of the default and giving her 10 days to cure the default. Quigley learns of Priscilla's wrong when he is served with an eviction notice from the sheriff. Quigley contacts the vendor, offering to cure Priscilla's default and to pay off the contract balance. The vendor refuses, which she has the right to do under traditional privity-based analysis. The trend is to protect a transferee such as Quigley, especially when the vendor had notice of the transferee when invoking the remedy.

Quiz Yourself on *MORTGAGE SUBSTITUTES*

91. Henrietta asks her rich cousin Louie for a loan for $50,000, offering to pay him $70,000 in one year when her ship comes in. Louie counters, "No. But deed me that nice mountain cabin you inherited from your father, and I'll give you $50,000 plus an option to repurchase it in one year for $70,000." They proceed on this basis, filling in the blanks for a warranty deed, which she signs and delivers. They document the option in a letter agreement. Henrietta misses the one-year deadline and tenders $70,000 plus statutory interest six months later. Louie refuses to take the money and deed back the property. What are the arguments for and against Louie having to accept late payment? _____

92. Ulrich signs a warranty deed conveying his farm to Carmine, who gives him a check for $200,000. Eight months later Ulrich sues Carmine, claiming the warranty deed really is a mortgage and he has the right to repay the $200,000 and keep the farm. Carmine claims that oral mortgages are invalid

under the statute of frauds and that, because the deed is recorded, the court should grant her motion for summary judgment. Should it? _____

93. Your client Julio has contracted to buy a 600-acre ranch from Frank. A title search reveals that three years ago Frank's grantor, Gretchen, signed a negative pledge agreement, promising not to sell, transfer, or encumber the ranch until she repaid a $100,000 loan. This agreement is recorded, and nothing else is of record bearing on this transaction. Is it safe for Julio to buy the ranch with title as it now stands? If not, what action should Julio take? _____

94. Two years ago, Edel used an installment contract to sell her resort condominium to Ferguson. He makes quarterly payments, all of which he has timely paid. But Edel just learned that he defaulted by failing to pay real estate taxes. The tax bill was still in Edel's name, as owner, and she forwarded it to him for payment five months ago. Last week, Edel paid the taxes, not wanting to be listed as a delinquent taxpayer. Edel comes to you for legal advice. The contract has a standard pro-vendor forfeiture clause. Edel wants her property back, plus damages. How should she proceed? _____

95. Bob is buying a mobile home under an installment land contract that runs for eight years. With substantial equity in the home, he wants to borrow money from his credit union, securing it by a second mortgage on his mobile home. The credit union generally makes second mortgage loans to its customers. Can this be done in Bob's case? _____

Answers

91. **Henrietta wants to argue the transaction is an equitable mortgage or disguised mortgage.** Louie wants the court to apply standard contract law so that the option expired, with no duty of the optionor to accept late payment. Facts that will bear on how the court decides include the parties' relative bargaining positions, including the extent to which Henrietta needed the money; the market value of the cabin at the time of the transaction in comparison to the $50,000 price and $70,000 option price; and which party used the cabin during the intervening year.

92. **No, not necessarily.** The statute of frauds does not bar Ulrich's action. While a mortgage, like other transfers of interests in real property, generally must be written, Ulrich is claiming that the written deed is really a mortgage. He is offering parol evidence to explain the writing, and this is considered acceptable under the statute of frauds. Nor does it matter that the deed is recorded. As between the parties, this is not relevant; Carmine is not a BFP under the recording act, and the deed being recorded does not increase her rights. For Carmine to get summary judgment, she must demonstrate that Ulrich does not have sufficient evidence, written or parol, that could justify a court in finding the parties agreed on a loan.

93. **No.** It is highly probable that the recorded negative pledge makes Julio's title unmarketable. Depending on the particulars of Gretchen's transaction, the negative pledge may be an equitable mortgage. This would mean that Julio as buyer would take the property subject to a lien for the balance of Gretchen's loan, assuming she has not paid it off.

Even if this negative pledge is not an equitable mortgage, that does not necessarily mean that title is marketable. The agreement still is of record, and Julio, as buyer, will have actual notice of it. The lender may argue that the negative pledge is a real covenant or equitable servitude, and thus binds Julio. This argument would probably fail in some states because it appears to be a covenant in gross (there is no land benefited by Gretchen's promise), but other states allow real covenants in gross. Based on the above, Julio should object to title and request that Frank get a written release of the negative pledge and record it.

94. **At the outset, you need to determine whether your state will treat this transaction as a contract or as an equitable mortgage.** If the latter, Edel can recover possession and clear up her title only by bringing a judicial foreclosure action against Ferguson. Edel is in a better position if contract law applies. She should be able to get the property back, plus damages. Your strategy should be to reduce the risk that the court will view Edel's use of the forfeiture clause as a penalty or an undue hardship on Ferguson.

95. **Yes.** The installment purchaser's rights are generally transferable, meaning they can be mortgaged to a lender as security for a loan. Strictly speaking, there is no first mortgage on the property, but functionally the credit union would be in a position like a second mortgagee; its rights would be subordinate to the seller's right to receive the remaining contract payments. It is important for Bob and the credit union to read the installment land contract to see if it restricts Bob from granting a mortgage or lien on his contract rights. If there is some type of restriction on purchaser transfers, then it will be necessary to decide whether the clause legally blocks this proposed mortgage.

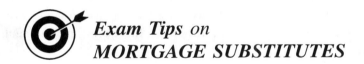

Exam Tips on MORTGAGE SUBSTITUTES

☞ **Mortgage substitutes:** If there's some type of mortgage substitute in the fact pattern, consider the parties' motivations. Lenders sometimes prefer mortgage substitutes to get around mortgage laws that protect borrowers like the doctrine against *clogging the equity of redemption* and foreclosure standards.

☞ **Equitable mortgage:** An equitable mortgage or *disguised mortgage* is a mortgage substitute that the court has decided should be treated under mortgage law rather than under standard contract law.

☞ **Absolute deed intended as security:** The owner gives a warranty deed to a person who advances money to the owner. This may be a sale of the property, but if the parties intend a loan with the deed as security, this is an equitable mortgage. Many factors bear on intent. Written evidence pointing to a loan or security isn't required. If the facts of an exam question clearly point to a sale, with no evidence that the parties considered a loan, then don't mention whether the deed might be intended as security. But if there are any facts pointing to a loan or a financing function, be sure to discuss this issue.

  ☞ **Primary factors:** Five factors are commonly used by courts: (1) prior loan between the parties, (2) unequal bargaining positions, (3) low price, (4) fiduciary relationship, and (5) the grantor's retained possession. If you spot an issue involving an absolute deed that might be a mortgage, be sure to discuss each one. This list however isn't exhaustive. In any particular transaction, other facts may have relevance. Thus, if you spot anything else in the question's facts that you think may have bearing, go ahead and mention it and explain why it may matter.

☞ **Negative pledge:** A negative pledge issue on an exam should not sneak up on you; the facts will raise it directly. With the negative pledge or negative covenant, the borrower promises the lender not to convey or encumber specified real property before the loan is repaid. Some courts treat the negative pledge as an equitable mortgage—the lender has a lien on the property and the right to foreclose. Other courts treat the negative pledge just as a contract, giving the lender no mortgage or lien.

    ☞ **Lack of authority:** In most states, there is no reported case law dealing with negative pledges or negative covenants. If you're asked a planning question, whether a lender should get a negative pledge in a particular transaction, you should highlight not only the risks identified above but also the likelihood that the transaction will take place in a state with no legal authorities whatsoever to guide the lawyer as planner and drafter.

☞ **Installment land contract:** Exam questions involving installment land contracts are quite popular because they prompt you to discuss both standard mortgage law principles and specialized rules for installment land contracts. With the installment land contract, also known as the contract for deed, the purchaser pays the price in installments over a lengthy period of time. The purchaser goes into possession at the outset, and receives title by deed only after paying the entire price.

    ☞ **Vendor's remedies:** When the purchaser defaults, a *forfeiture clause* permits the vendor to terminate the contract and retake possession.

    ☞ **Contract analysis:** Most courts analyze the vendor's remedies under contract law. Traditionally, forfeiture clauses were enforced as written, but the trend is to protect a purchaser who has substantial equity. Protection is sometimes achieved by invoking waiver or estoppel. More directly, some courts require that the vendor make *restitution* of the excess of payments received over the vendor's proven damages.

    ☞ **Equitable mortgage:** In any question involving breach by the purchaser and the vendor's remedies, don't assume that that court will follow the majority view and apply contract law (unless of course your teacher's question tells you to make that assumption). Be sure to indicate what happens if the court rules that the contract is an equitable mortgage. Some courts treat the installment land contract as an equitable mortgage, meaning the vendor must foreclose upon the purchaser's default. In some states, the contract is an equitable mortgage from the outset. In others, its status changes to equitable mortgage only after the purchaser has made substantial payments.

    ☞ **Transferable rights:** Both vendor and purchaser have transferable contract and property rights. Both can sell, transfer, or mortgage their respective interests in the property.

JUNIOR MORTGAGES

ChapterScope ─────────────────────────────────

This chapter examines the use of junior mortgages and secondary financing.

- ■ **The concept of leverage:** *Leverage* involves debt and equity financing that facilitates acquisition of property by permitting the buyer to put only a fraction of the price down in cash (out-of-pocket expenditure). Junior mortgages are frequently used for leverage because they permit a property owner to borrow against accumulated equity.

- ■ **Home equity loans:** Homeowners frequently obtain home equity loans, which are a type of junior mortgage. These loans are made against the collateral of the equity in the home.

- ■ **Marshalling of assets:** A court may order the equitable remedy of marshalling of assets to protect a junior lender from the foreclosure action of a senior lender. This constrains a senior lender that may have more than one property covered by the lien of its mortgage while a junior lender has a lien against only one of the same properties.

- ■ **Mortgage subordination:** The two main ways to accomplish subordination of an earlier mortgage to a later one are by express agreement, and by the order of recording (automatic subordination).

- ■ **The wrap-around mortgage:** A wrap-around mortgage is a junior mortgage in which the junior debt includes or "wraps" the senior debt.

───

I. LEVERAGING A DEAL

Leverage involves using debt or equity financing to increase investment potential beyond what it would be if the investment all had to be done for cash. This means that a property owner or developer is obtaining funds from lenders or investors to do a real estate project or to finance a completed project. When a property owner borrows against equity appreciation in a property, this also provides leverage and it is sometimes referred to as "mortgaging out" (borrowing money and getting cash by granting a mortgage against the equity).

A. Sources of leverage: Original mortgage financing helps people leverage a real estate transaction. This happens by, for example, permitting a borrower to own a property by only putting 20 percent down. The borrower leverages her investment by access to mortgage credit. This is leveraging your cash to acquire more than one might otherwise be able to afford. Junior mortgage loans are also a very common source of funds to increase leverage. With the junior mortgage, more debt is taken out behind a senior loan. It is also possible to refinance an existing first mortgage with a higher principal balance, taking advantage of equity in the property to increase the leverage. As an alternative to debt financing, equity financing is another alternative for leveraging ownership. It involves finding an investor willing to purchase an equity interest in the property or real estate project. An equity interest may be structured in different ways. The equity participant often becomes a partner, joint venturer, or shareholder; in all cases the equity investment can provide another source of leverage.

B. Leverage, risk, and return

1. **Rate of return:** The *rate of return* is the owner's annual profit or return on cash investment, expressed as a percentage. When a property is successful, higher leverage increases the rate of return to the developer or owner.

   Example: Carlos pays $500,000 cash for a restaurant that is subject to a long-term lease providing net annual rentals of $40,000. Carlos's rate of return is 8 percent ($40,000 divided by $500,000). Carlos can leverage his purchase by getting a purchase money mortgage from the seller. Suppose he obtains a $400,000 purchase money mortgage. Now his cash investment, which he pays at closing, is $100,000. Does this leverage increase Carlos's rate of return? It depends on the cost of borrowing the $400,000. If the interest rate on the loan is less than 8 percent, Carlos's rate of return rises; if it is more than 8 percent, his rate of return falls. Suppose his interest rate is 6 percent. Then the annual interest on the loan is $24,000 (assuming no amortization of the loan; if the loan amortizes, the analysis comes out the same, but is a bit more complicated). Carlos's return or profit, after paying the interest, is $16,000 per year ($40,000 rent less $24,000 interest). His return on investment is 16 percent ($16,000 divided by $100,000 cash investment), double the 8 percent return for an all-cash deal.

2. **Effect of leverage:** Higher leverage increases the risk for both lenders and owners. The risk to the lenders is greater because they have more capital at stake, and if the project is a failure, the property value may be less than the outstanding debts. Market evidence also indicates that one key correlation to mortgage default is the acquisition of junior debt by a borrower. Thus, leveraging requires caution.

II. THE MARKET FOR SECONDARY FINANCING

Junior mortgages, which are often second mortgages, are commonly made as purchase money mortgages (to enable a person to buy real estate). Junior mortgages that are not purchase money mortgages are also very common.

A. Rank of multiple mortgages: Junior mortgages are commonly *second mortgages*. This means there is a prior first mortgage in place. Some junior mortgages have lower priority; third and fourth mortgages are sometimes encountered. In general, mortgages are ranked in accordance with a first-in-time rule as modified by recording statutes.

B. Other junior finance devices: A mortgage is the most common method for a creditor to obtain a second priority position, but there are other devices available as well. Usually, the other devices present more risk for the lender than a standard second mortgage.

1. **Assignment of lease:** For rental property, a borrower/lessor may assign a lease to a lender. When there is a prior mortgage on the property, the mortgage is prior to the lease, so functionally the lease assignee is in a second priority position compared to the mortgagee.

2. **Pledge of ownership interest:** For property owned by an entity, a borrower may pledge ownership interests in the entity to secure a new loan.

3. **Negative pledge agreement:** The borrower may sign a negative pledge agreement, which promises the new lender that the borrower will not convey the property or grant any further mortgages or liens while the new loan is outstanding.

C. **Home equity loans:** Home equity lending has grown tremendously since the mid-1980s. Some home equity loans finance home improvements or repairs. Many home equity loans are for debt consolidation purposes, with the owner paying off credit cards, car loans, and other forms of consumer debt. Often, this reduces the debtor's overall monthly payments and simplifies her borrowing situation. Monthly payments can be reduced by consolidating the debt and moving it from unsecured credit to credit secured by a mortgage on real property. This move reduces risk and can therefore be translated into reduced interest rate charges and lower monthly payments.

1. **Loan terms:** Many home equity loans, secured by second mortgages, are amortized over a fixed term such as 5 to 15 years. In other words, home equity loans are generally shorter in term than the first mortgages that home buyers obtain when purchasing a home.

2. **Home equity line of credit:** Since the 1980s, home equity lines of credit have become very popular. A borrower who is approved for a home equity line of credit has the choice of how much actually to borrow, up to the maximum, at any time while the relationship continues. This can be like a revolving line of credit often obtained by businesses and differs from a regular mortgage loan, which makes a specified amount of credit available at one time and in the full amount of the loan.

3. **Income tax incentive:** For federal income tax purposes, a borrower may deduct interest paid on a home equity loan of up to $100,000. This gives homeowners a tax incentive to get a home equity loan, compared to an unsecured loan or a loan secured by other assets, such as an automobile. On a regular home mortgage, the interest paid also gives the homeowner a tax benefit.

4. **Bankruptcy impact:** Homeowners who enter bankruptcy often seek a plan to modify their debts under Chapter 13 of the Bankruptcy Code. Chapter 13 allows the debtor to modify loan terms *except for* any loan "secured only by a security interest in real property that is the debtor's principal residence." Bankruptcy Code § 1322(b)(2).

D. **Commercial market for junior mortgages:** For purchases of commercial properties, seller financing is often cast in the form of junior mortgages. There may be a prior loan on the property or the buyer may be getting financing from a commercial lender that wants a first position. Thus, seller's additional financing is in the form of a junior purchase money mortgage.

E. **Relationship between markets for first and second mortgages:** Secondary financing is an alternative to refinancing under a new first mortgage. Instead of getting a junior mortgage, an owner might get a further advance under a first mortgage, roll the first mortgage over into a new, larger first mortgage loan from the same lender, or simply pay off the first loan by borrowing from a new lender and taking on a larger debt.

III. PROTECTING THE JUNIOR MORTGAGE

A. **Contract terms and practices that reduce risk:** The junior mortgage holder takes risk into account in pricing the loan, charging higher interest or greater up-front fees due to the risk of default and foreclosure under the first mortgage. In addition, the junior mortgagee tries to reduce the risk of foreclosure under the senior loan by planning and monitoring.

1. **Planning:** The junior lender needs complete information about the first loan. It must also confirm the outstanding balance due on the first loan to ascertain the equity available to serve as security for the second loan.

    a. **Drafting junior loan documents:** The junior loan documents should contain borrower representations and warranties as to the outstanding loan amount, the completeness of the first loan documents given to the lender, and the fact that the loan is in full force and effect according to its terms (no current or outstanding defaults). The junior lender should seek an *estoppel letter* from the senior lender that confirms the borrower's representations and warranties as to the status of the senior loan. The junior loan documents should also contain promises as to the mortgagor's future behavior under the first mortgage. The junior documents should also have a *cross-default* provision; this makes it an event of default under the junior loan if the debtor fails to live up to all of her obligations under the earlier loan.

2. **Monitoring:** The junior lender should monitor the senior loan. It can do this by requiring the borrower to submit proof of payment for all installments due under the senior loan.

3. **State law protection of junior lienors:** The junior lienor is a necessary party to a judicial foreclosure. Generally, the foreclosing lender must make a search for junior lienors and join them in the judicial foreclosure proceeding.

B. **Marshalling of assets:** Sometimes, secured creditors, including mortgagees, have liens that attach to different properties and assets, but there is some overlap. A priority problem arises when the senior creditor seeks to foreclose and she has more assets as collateral than does the junior creditor. The junior lienor may be protected by the doctrine of marshalling of assets. This means that the court ranks or arranges the multiple properties and assets in order, requiring that the senior creditor first proceed against the asset that is not subject to a junior lien. The hope is that the senior creditor will be able to get satisfaction from the other properties, leaving some viable collateral for the junior creditor. This assumes that the senior creditor can be fully satisfied by proceeding against less than all of the assets covered by its lien.

IV. THE MORTGAGE SUBORDINATION

The *priority* of mortgages and other liens is generally determined by the principle of *first in time, first in right*, subject to modification by the state recording act in appropriate cases. Sometimes, a special rule grants priority to a particular type of lien, such as a mechanic's lien for work performed to improve real property or a purchase money security interest for a fixture under UCC Article 9. Owners of liens have contractual freedom to rearrange their priorities. Such a contractual arrangement is commonly called a *subordination agreement*. The primary purpose of this agreement is to alter the priority of the parties' liens from that provided by general principles of law.

A. **Methods of subordination:** In many states, the subordination can be accomplished simply by recording the two mortgages in the order of their intended priority. This process is sometimes called subordination by the act of recording. Subordination by the act of recording is occasionally called *automatic subordination*. Sometimes, a party executes a *subordination agreement* that expressly subordinates her mortgage to a superior mortgage described therein. The subordination agreement is recorded. This makes the dates of execution and sequence of recording of the two mortgages irrelevant for purposes of priority. Some states grant a ***special priority*** to a seller's purchase money mortgage as compared to other liens that attach simultaneously, including a third-party lender's purchase money mortgage. In these states, the seller's mortgage is prior in rank regardless of the order of recording. This means automatic subordination is not available, and the parties must use a written subordination agreement if they are to re-rank the priorities.

B. Other provisions besides priority rank: A subordination agreement may address a number of issues beyond priority. It might include requirements and conditions related to loan amount, term, interest rate, collateral, and future advances. When an agreement fails to cover a specific situation, a court is more likely to rule in favor of the subordinate or junior lienor.

C. Modification or extension of senior loan: When the senior lender and the borrower negotiate a loan modification or extension, the rights of junior lienors are often implicated. If the modification or extension is seen as prejudicing the junior's rights, the court is likely to rule that the modification or extension constitutes a ***novation***. This means that the new documents are sufficiently different from the earlier ones, and that the earlier ones are considered to be no longer in existence for purposes of priority. Thus, the junior lienor is now senior in rank.

Example: Giovanni has a senior mortgage loan with a balance of $300,000 payable in full in two years and a junior loan with a balance of $100,000. The fair market value of the property is $450,000. Giovanni and the senior lender renegotiate their loan: The lender advances Giovanni an additional $100,000, thus increasing the principal to $400,000 and extends the loan term from two to five years. The junior lender expected the property to be subject to only $300,000 in debt, which was to be paid in two years. To protect the junior's expectations, the court would probably rule that the modification, entered into without the junior's consent, constituted a novation. The result is that the junior loan is promoted to first priority. If, however, the senior loan documents as recorded provide express terms allowing modifications and future advances, the junior is likely to be held to notice of those terms and in such a case will remain junior in priority.

V. THE WRAP-AROUND MORTGAGE

A wrap-around mortgage is a special type of junior mortgage in which the junior debt includes or "wraps" the senior debt. Both of the debts are installment obligations. The borrower under the wrap-around mortgage pays the holder of the junior debt (the wrap-around loan), who in turn pays the holder of the senior debt (the wrapped loan). The wrap-around is an alternative to ordinary junior financing.

A. Purpose: The most common reason parties choose a wrap-around is to preserve the value of a below-market interest rate on the senior loan. Another time when the wrap-around is useful is when the senior loan cannot be prepaid, or cannot be prepaid without a substantial penalty.

B. Risk to wrap-around lender: Compared to other financings involving a standard junior mortgage, the wrap-around junior loan creates different risks. The wrap-around lender is generally in a safer position than a standard junior mortgagee because it makes payments on the first mortgage. The borrower pays the wrap lender an amount each month that covers the wrapped mortgage and the wrap. The wrap lender then forwards the wrapped lender its part of the payment.

Thus, the wrap lender has no problem of monitoring the borrower's payments on the first mortgage, as it would with a standard second mortgage.

C. **Risk to wrap-around borrower:** Compared to a borrower using a standard junior mortgage, the wrap-around borrower is at greater risk because she has appointed the wrap-around lender as agent or intermediary for making payments on the first mortgage. The borrower bears the risk that, even though she timely pays the wrap-around lender, that lender for some reason might fail to make installment payments on the first mortgage.

D. **Wrap-around note:** The wrap-around loan always involves an "overstated" promissory note because it includes the amount of the wrapped debt, as well as the amount of the new loan.

Example: Margaret has a first mortgage lien against her property for $100,000. Now she wants to borrow another $20,000 to be secured by the same property. Robin offers to do the loan as a wrap-around mortgage, with the deal structured as a $120,000 wrap mortgage and note. This means that there will be $20,000 of new debt wrapped around the original $100,000 debt. Margaret will make payment to Robin on the full wrap, and Robin will pay the holder of the first mortgage for the amount it has coming. The total debt is $120,000, even though the face of the documents may make it look like there are both a $100,000 debt and a $120,000 debt.

Quiz Yourself on JUNIOR MORTGAGES

96. Sean is thinking about buying a rental property in Discount City. It is a small house in moderate condition and will generate $10,000 of rental income for the year, after all expenses and the payments due on an already existing first mortgage. The seller wants $100,000 cash and for Sean to assume and agree to pay the first mortgage. Sean thinks he might be interested in the deal if he can get 80 percent seller financing under a purchase money mortgage. Based on the use of an 80 percent second mortgage, Sean can expect to make $6,000 in rental income after paying the underlying first mortgage and the $4,000 annual cost of the second mortgage. In terms of the concept of leverage, is the use of the purchase money second mortgage a good option for Sean? _____

97. Tiffany is considering lending $200,000 to a corporation that owns real estate in Rochester, which operates as a warehouse facility. The real estate is subject to a first mortgage with a balance of $280,000. The property is valued at $650,000. In this case, Tiffany is considering either taking a second mortgage or just lending against a pledge of the shares of stock in the corporation. Can Tiffany get a security interest in the stock? _____

98. The documents for a junior mortgage lack a cross-default clause. Does this create a problem for the junior lender in the event of a default on the senior loan? _____

99. Seller sells two adjoining undeveloped lots to Purchaser for $80,000. Purchaser pays with $10,000 in cash, giving Seller a promissory note for $20,000, secured by a mortgage on the lots. Purchaser borrows the remaining $50,000 from Big Bank, signing a promissory note and giving Big Bank a mortgage on the lots. Documents are recorded in the following order: (1) warranty deed from Seller to Purchaser, (2) mortgage from Purchaser to Seller, (3) mortgage from Purchaser to Big Bank. None of the documents discusses the priority of the mortgages, and there is no evidence as to why the documents were recorded in the above order. Is the Big Bank mortgage prior to that of the Seller? _____

100. Aaron sells Lakeacre to Baker, who gives Aaron a $100,000 purchase money mortgage. Baker sells Lakeacre to Cepeda, who gives Baker a $200,000 purchase money mortgage that wraps Aaron's mortgage. Cepeda sells Lakeacre to Doby, who gives Cepeda a $300,000 purchase money mortgage that wraps Baker's mortgage. How much debt presently encumbers Lakeacre? _____

Answers

96. **Yes.** On the all-cash deal, Sean makes a return of 10 percent. He pays $100,000 and gets a return of $10,000 in annual rent. With the purchase money mortgage, he pays 20 percent ($20,000) and assumes the underlying mortgage. In return he gets $6,000 in rent rather than the $10,000 on the all-cash arrangement, but his rate of return is much higher. With the purchase money second mortgage, his rate of return is 30 percent, as he gets $6,000 by paying $20,000. The result is that Sean has less equity in the property, but all things considered he gets a much higher rate of return on the cash he has to put down to own and control the property. Leveraging works to his benefit.

97. **Yes.** Tiffany can do either one of these options. In this context, both choices are types of secondary financing, presenting the same risk that foreclosure under the first mortgage might destroy the value of Tiffany's collateral. The two options are not equal, however, and generally the use of a second mortgage will be a better choice for someone such as Tiffany. With the pledge of shares, if the corporation loses title to its only significant asset through foreclosure, the shares are worthless, and Tiffany is secured by the stock, not the property. A properly drafted second mortgage is better than the pledge because it locks in Tiffany's position as second in priority against the property. Thus, if there is a foreclosure or other loss, Tiffany has her lien rights against the property. If Tiffany gets only a pledge of stock and no further rights, there is the risk that, due to the corporation's actions, a third party might get a lien on the property that will be second in rank, superior to Tiffany's position as pledgee of the shares.

98. **Yes.** A cross-default provision makes it an event of default under the junior loan if the debtor fails to live up to all of her obligations under the first mortgage loan. It is possible for the borrower to default under the first loan, but still make payments and perform all of the obligations of the second loan. In this event, the first mortgagee may declare a default, accelerate maturity of the first loan, and commence foreclosure. Without a cross-default clause, the junior lender may be unable to take similar measures to protect itself.

99. **No.** If the court applies the principle of automatic subordination, Seller's mortgage is prior. The principle is that, as between two mortgages granted at the same time, their priority is determined by the order of recording. Not all states apply this principle, and when courts apply it, usually there is some testimony that the parties recorded in a particular sequence with the purpose of subordination in mind. Here there is no evidence of whether the recording order was inadvertent or intentional. If both mortgages were created simultaneously, many states give lien priority to a seller's purchase money mortgage over other liens. Under this rule, Seller prevails even if Big Bank's mortgage was placed on record just prior to that of the Seller.

100. **$300,000.** The total debt is $300,000 even though three mortgages are outstanding with face amounts that total $600,000. Cepeda's $300,000 includes and wraps the two prior mortgages. The original mortgage is for $100,000. Then there is a $200,000 wrap, which includes the earlier $100,000 so the total is $200,000, and not $300,000. Then there is a $300,000 wrap that includes the earlier $200,000 so the total is $300,000. The confusion can come if you add the $100,000 to the $200,000 and then the $300,000 to get a face value of $600,000. Remember that with a wrap the outstanding debt is not the same as the face amount of the loan.

◎ *Exam Tips on* JUNIOR MORTGAGES

☞ **Refinancing with a home equity loan:** If you are asked to evaluate the risks and benefits of a home equity loan, be sure to consider the possibility that as an alternative the homeowner might refinance her first mortgage loan, getting a new loan in a larger principal amount. If the homeowner selects a home equity loan, this will be a junior mortgage, and you must address the risks and concerns of a junior lender when answering the question.

☞ **Thinking about subordinations:** If you get a question about mortgage subordination be sure to look at the facts carefully. Determine if it is a subordination by order of recording, or by agreement. Look for facts that indicate an intent to subordinate, and be careful to consider the potential risk of a simultaneous recording of more than one mortgage where one is a purchase money mortgage from the seller. When a lender's agreement is needed to subordinate its mortgage, that lender is in an ideal position to negotiate for contract provisions that reduce the risk of holding a junior mortgage. For example, as a condition to subordination, the lender may insist on the right to receive notices of default under the first mortgage and the opportunity to cure any default by the borrower.

☞ **When a senior mortgage covers more than one property:** Watch for fact patterns where a senior lender has a mortgage that covers more than one property and a potential foreclosure will involve a junior lienor with a lien on some but not all of the same property. In this situation, you need to address the equitable remedy of marshalling of assets.

☞ **Mortgage modification:** If the borrower negotiates a change in mortgage terms with the senior lender, be sure to consider the potential for this to be classified as a novation, thereby causing the senior to lose its priority to the junior.

☞ **The wrap-around mortgage:** Be careful with the wrap-around mortgage. As explained in part V above, one must keep track of the new money being put into the deal and not get fooled by the face amount stated on the wrap-around promissory note. One should be able to explain how this works, when it might be selected for use by the parties, and how it can help reduce the risk to the junior lender.

☞ **Leverage:** Be prepared to think about the value of leveraging an investment. In a leveraged deal, the buyer puts less of her own money into the deal. The idea is to get control of a property (having a right to future equity appreciation) and to get a favorable rate of return on the amount of money invested. Instead of having to come up with all cash, the investor can control/own a property for a reasonable amount down and use her additional resources to invest in other desirable projects. Leverage permits one to acquire assets on credit (so the asset can be purchased in a quicker and easier way), and it permits one to control an asset and have rights to future equity appreciation with only a fraction of the price being paid down at the time of purchase.

CHAPTER 22

THE COMMERCIAL REAL ESTATE MARKET

ChapterScope

This chapter discusses the basic elements of the commercial real estate market.

- **Special lending arrangements:** The standard commercial real estate transaction involves several special lending arrangements, including *construction lending* and *permanent lending*.

- **The three-party agreement:** Coordination of the relationship between the real estate developer and the construction and permanent lenders is often facilitated by the three-party agreement.

- **Entity selection:** The developer usually does a project in a legal form other than as an individual with full personal liability. The developer selects a legal form or entity, such as a corporation or limited liability company (LLC), to protect assets and reduce exposure to liability.

- **Personal property:** A commercial real estate project involves a number of non–real property assets. Many of these other assets are personal property (goods and intangibles), and the commercial lender must use Article 9 of the Uniform Commercial Code (UCC) to secure these assets. This is in addition to the mortgage to secure the real property.

- **Role of the lawyer:** Lawyers play a central role in coordinating the work of experts, managing risk within a legal framework, drafting and implementing various agreements, and giving or reviewing opinion letters.

I. FINANCING ARRANGEMENTS BY AND BETWEEN LENDERS

Commercial real estate projects are diverse. A project may be a shopping mall, office tower, restaurant, subdivision, condominium, time share, apartment building, country club, art museum, school, parking garage, boat marina, airport, amusement park, factory, or just about anything you can imagine as a possible land use. Experts involved in a project may include real estate brokers, accountants, surveyors, title examiners, insurance carriers, engineers, architects, planners, environmental consultants, contractors, marketing firms, suppliers, and lawyers. Commercial lenders, particularly the construction lender and the permanent lender, play a central role in the development process.

A. Construction loans

1. **Risk and term:** The construction loan is used to finance the construction of a building or other improvements on land. It is generally a high-risk loan because the project may not be finished, or the quality of the project may turn out to be less than anticipated. The developer might misuse funds or go bankrupt. Substandard construction may impair the project value. Even if the project is finished *in accordance with the approved plans and specifications*, the market for this type of project may slump by the time of project completion. Due to these risks, the interest rate is usually high compared to loan rates for mortgages on completed projects.

Typically the construction loan is short term: 6, 12, 18, or 24 months, depending on the nature and scope of the undertaking. At the end of the loan it must be paid off. This means that there is a need to have substantial resources available at the end of the short-term time period of the construction mortgage. Importantly, one must keep in mind that little or no revenue or equity appreciation may occur during the construction process. Developers are not likely simply to have cash to pay off the construction loan when it becomes due. Thus, they must make arrangements to have a long-term lender step in to pay off the construction loans and refinance the debt for a longer period; this is the role of a permanent lender.

2. **Structure:** Due to their high risk, construction loans typically are ***recourse***. This means that the borrower is held personally liable for repayment of the loan. In addition to having recourse to the value of the property, a recourse loan holds the borrower liable for the full debt, even though the full debt may exceed the value of the property in a foreclosure sale. If the borrower is a corporation or another limited liability entity, the lender sometimes requires a ***personal guarantee*** from the individuals involved with the entity. To reduce risk, construction loans are not fully funded at the outset. The borrower receives periodic ***draws*** (advances of part of the loan) as the project is built. Each draw (draw down) is paid against an established schedule of stages in completion of the construction project. By the end of the draw down schedule the full amount of the construction loan will be paid out to the borrower.

3. **Supervision:** The construction lender must have expertise in the planning, marketing, and construction of the type of project being financed. The developer's track record and financial ability to stand up to unexpected expenses or market shifts are also important. Once the project begins, careful monitoring is essential. The lender should supervise the job site to ensure that materials are of the quality specified and that construction accounting procedures are proper and complete. Government permits and approvals should be checked. Although the lender has a duty to its shareholders and to the public to control the risk on its lending activities, it must also be concerned with not getting so entangled with the project development that it becomes liable to third parties as a codeveloper or as a person with ***proprietary or managerial control***.

Example: Peg is approved for a $100 million construction loan for an office building. At the closing of the loan, Peg does not get $100 million because the building does not yet exist. As she develops the project, she gets loan advances, called ***progress payments***, pursuant to a prearranged schedule of draw downs agreed to by the parties. This structure provides a way for the construction lender to monitor the project. Prior to making each draw down payment, the construction lender will inspect the project for proper completion of the particular stage of work. The structure of progress payments also means that in some crude respect the amount of money disbursed is related to the asset value in the ground, on the property.

B. Permanent loans

1. **Risk and term:** The permanent loan is a long-term mortgage loan that finances a project when construction is completed. It is used to pay off the construction loan. It is less risky than the construction loan because the lender can evaluate an existing (completed) structure in a given market context. For income-producing property, there will be leases or sales contract revenue in place, which the permanent lender can assess at the time it funds the loan. For these reasons, the loan risk is lower and the interest charged on a permanent loan is significantly less than that charged on a construction loan for the same property. In addition to being lower risk, the

permanent loan is for a much longer term than the construction loan. Terms of 10 to 20 years or even longer are typical. This lets the borrower repay the loan out of income produced by the economic activity on the property.

2. **Structure:** Many permanent loans are ***nonrecourse*** due to the reduced risk to the lender. This means the borrower has no personal liability for repayment in the event of default. Another feature of a permanent loan is that the lender may have an ***equity participation***, consisting of a percentage of the cash flow or net income generated by the property. Sometimes, the equity participation is cast in the form of a ***convertible mortgage***, which gives the lender an option, exercisable during a stated time period, to convert some of the outstanding credit given under the loan into a percentage position in the equity of the project. Thus, a lender might exercise an option by forgoing $5 million of a $50 million loan in exchange for a 10 percent equity position in the project. A lender will exercise the option if the project is profitable. (Note: The convertible mortgage in the commercial setting is different from that discussed in the residential transaction. See Chapter 15 to compare.)

3. **Supervision:** The permanent lender requires different areas of expertise from the construction lender. The permanent lender must fully understand the management and operation of the particular type of project, including marketing to customers. It must also understand the borrower's cash flow accounting system so it can monitor performance of the project, and, if it has taken an equity interest, it needs to make sure it receives its fair share (for example, it needs to be certain the borrower is not keeping two sets of books).

Example: Big Bank makes a nonrecourse 20-year permanent loan for the new Waterside Shopping Mall project. In addition to interest payable on the loan principal of $200 million, Big Bank bargains for an equity participation, defined as 5 percent of net profits from Mall operations, payable quarterly throughout the life of the loan. After the Mall has its grand opening, some practices emerge that disturb the Bank. The Mall passes a policy of closing the weeks of Christmas, Easter, and Passover. During other weeks, some stores keep different hours and days of operation for a variety of religious, cultural, and personal preferences. The Mall owner claims to be sensitive to cultural differences in the population. But these practices reduce the potential profits from the Mall and thus lower its collateral value.

Big Bank needs to understand the mall business to prevent this from happening. Big Bank must obtain, in its permanent loan agreements, a binding legal obligation to have the Mall operate on a specific calendar, with minimum set hours. Every store must be required to be open during all hours and to cooperate in all promotions and other undertakings of Mall management. The point is that Big Bank, as a permanent lender, needs a different type of expertise from a construction lender. Big Bank is not simply making a permanent loan secured by the Mall as a physical building. It is making a loan to a "going concern." Whereas the construction lender had to be primarily concerned with getting the building done properly, the permanent lender must be primarily concerned with the Mall as an economic enterprise in which the building is only one part of total asset value.

C. **Loan coordination:** The construction lender will generally require that a permanent lender be committed to pay off the construction loan prior to making its own commitment to provide funding. The permanent lender will require knowledge about the construction loan before it makes a commitment. In practice, this means that the developer must work with both lenders simultaneously.

1. **Promoting comparative advantage:** In coordinating loan transactions, lenders utilize their respective comparative advantages. Not only do construction lenders and permanent lenders have different expertise, but lenders also seek comparative advantage by focusing on types of projects and developer relationships. Some lenders specialize in projects such as medium-size shopping malls rather than time-share housing. Others choose to lend to a particular developer, no matter what the range of projects undertaken. Here, the lender makes use of enhanced knowledge of the internal operation, accounting, and personality of the developer. In each case, expertise lowers risk and reduces information costs, and this is what provides the comparative advantage.

2. **Three-party agreement or buy-sell agreement:** The developer, construction lender, and permanent lender sign a comprehensive agreement providing for the permanent loan to repay the construction loan. This solves *privity* problems that either lender may have with respect to the other lender and gives each a right of *specific performance* against the other. Often, the permanent loan retires the construction loan, with a full set of new loan documents, including a permanent mortgage, signed at the closing of the permanent loan. Sometimes, however, the permanent lender prefers to take an assignment of the construction mortgage and perhaps also the construction promissory note. Then, the three-party agreement takes the form of a *buy-sell agreement* in which the construction lender sells its loan to the permanent lender.

3. **The take-out:** The arrangement by which the permanent lender pays off the construction loan is called the *take-out*. Three alternatives are the lock-in take-out, the stand-by take-out, and the open-ended take-out.

   a. **Lock-in:** The permanent lender issues a loan commitment that obligates both lender and borrower. The lender must make the loan on the stated terms, and the borrower is obligated or "locked in" to accept the funds and close. The object is to prevent the other party from shopping for new opportunities should the market change over the course of construction.

      Example: The permanent lender who issues a lock-in take-out views the transaction as an investment that is expected to yield a predetermined amount of profit. Problems can arise when lending markets change during the course of the project. If market interest rates for permanent financing drop, the developer may have the incentive to claim that the permanent lender is in breach so that it can seek cheaper financing elsewhere. See *Teachers Insurance & Annuity Association v. Ormesa Geothermal*, 791 F. Supp. 401 (S.D.N.Y. 1991), in which the court ruled that the developer under a lock-in commitment has a duty to negotiate in good faith so that the permanent loan would close; liability was found for expectancy damages for failure to accept funds.

   b. **Stand-by:** The permanent lender issues a loan commitment that the borrower has the option to use and close. The parties generally expect that the developer will obtain different or more favorable permanent financing by the time of project completion. Thus, the lender stands ready to fund on the stated terms if need be, but also agrees to accommodate alternative arrangements in the event of a favorable market change. A fee will be paid even if the borrower does end up getting permanent financing from a different lender.

   c. **Open-ended:** The borrower and construction lender agree not to obtain a permanent loan commitment for the time being. They plan to arrange for permanent financing later, when the project nears completion. The open-ended take-out is the most risky. It is usually used when the developer is very cash rich, the project has major preconstruction sales or leases, or the parties for a combination of other reasons believe the project's market potential merits the risk of proceeding without currently arranging for permanent financing.

II. SELECTING A DEVELOPMENT ENTITY

Developers have choices to make when they decide how to structure a commercial real estate development. Few developers wish to proceed in an individual capacity because of the liability exposure. In an attempt to *limit liability*, a developer has two key concerns. First, she wants to limit personal liability. Second, she wants to protect as many business assets as possible. These considerations lead a developer to select some form of limited liability entity as the legal form for doing business. Such entities include the corporation, limited partnership, and limited liability company (LLC). Sometimes, multiple entities are employed for a project. A developer may set up a limited partnership where the general partner is a corporation, for example. In structuring a development entity, in addition to liability issues one must examine tax consequences and *asset capitalization* requirements.

Example: Ed, Sol, Elmer, and Don are developers. They set up two corporations for purposes of conducting their business. One corporation makes a large loan to the other corporation, which serves as the vehicle for project development. They also make a smaller capital contribution to the development entity. The project fails, and the development entity has unsecured debt owed to a third party. The four developers have effectively limited their liability. In *American Discount Corp. v. Saratoga West, Inc.*, 537 P.2d 1056 (Wash. Ct. App. 1975), the court ruled that beneficial owners can choose to make a secured loan to the development entity rather than make capital contributions; the secured loan has priority over unsecured obligations of the entity; but if the limited liability entity is significantly undercapitalized, there may be grounds for liability. In other words, as long as the developer sets up a development entity with sufficient (but perhaps minimal) capitalization, the principals can either add capital to the business or make loans to it. Adding capital is like making money available in an unsecured manner. The alternative could be to lend additional sums and secure repayment by a mortgage. If they lend additional money to the company and secure it with a properly recorded mortgage, they will be secured creditors with priority over later unsecured creditors. In an attempt to upset this priority at a later date, after a default, a general and unsecured creditor may challenge the secured position of the developer-related investors, as in the *American Discount* case. The creditor may argue that the secured loan should really be treated as a capital contribution to the forming of the company. If it should have been part of the capitalization of the firm, the use of a loan form is really a sham. In such a case, the mortgage might be set aside and the investors would lose priority to later general creditors. This argument did not work in *American Discount* because the court held that the initial capitalization was adequate and therefore the additional funding on a mortgage loan basis was legitimate.

III. COMMERCIAL LENDING AND ARTICLE 9 OF THE UCC

Commercial real estate finance involves issues that extend beyond the boundaries of real property law. Several topics addressed by the UCC are highly relevant. The sale of a housing unit, office building, or other structure may include appliances or equipment subject to Article 2 of the UCC. Certain methods of payment, including promissory notes and checks, are covered by Articles 3 and 4 of the UCC. Article 9 of the UCC plays a critical role in protecting the lender's security for the loan. Both developer and lender have an interest in careful planning and negotiation over the nature and scope of the mortgage and security documents. While the lender desires as much control over the borrower's assets as possible, the developer naturally wants to keep a degree of flexibility and control.

A. Nature of the Article 9 interest: Many commercial real estate projects have a number of components that are not classified as real property. Most lenders see these other component interests as central to the security for their loans. Most of these other interests must be secured under Article 9.

Example: Eric and Donna plan to purchase a small bar in the city. They seek a $400,000 mortgage loan to finance the purchase, which Community Bank agrees to provide. The Bank wants Eric and Donna to sign a real estate mortgage plus an Article 9 security agreement. The Bank explains that the mortgage covers only real property and those things that are properly identified as fixtures. The value of the bar, as an economic enterprise, extends beyond such property. The Bank cares about the inventory and equipment (food, alcohol, glasses, plates, silverware, cash register, menus, etc.) and the intangible property, such as the liquor license, occupancy permit, the name of the bar, service contracts, insurance contracts, and a variety of other interests. In the event that the Bank has to take over the bar, it wants all of these rights so that it can operate or sell the property as a going concern. All of these non-real-property categories of interest must be secured under Article 9.

B. Security and priority for three categories of property: A commercial real estate transaction usually involves three categories of property.

1. Real property: Real property is secured in accordance with state mortgage law. The borrower executes a mortgage on the described real property, which the lender perfects by recording in the public records. Recording the mortgage is not necessary to create the security interest. Recording gives notice and establishes a priority.

2. Personal property: This category includes all property that is not real property, except for fixtures, discussed below. Goods and intangibles are included here. To obtain a security interest in personal property, a lender must have a security agreement granting a security interest in the property under Article 9 of the UCC. The lender must also perfect this interest in accordance with the rules and requirements of Article 9.

3. Fixtures: A fixture is an item of personal property that becomes attached to and identifiable with a particular piece of real property. When, and if, something becomes a fixture is determined by reference to non-UCC state law and is sometimes uncertain. Items that may be fixtures include the doors and windows of a building, elevators, walk-in freezers, furnaces, air conditioning units, factory equipment, conveyor belts, and mobile or portable buildings or structures. The lender gets a security interest in fixtures through an Article 9 security agreement or under a real estate mortgage. For complete protection under Article 9, a local fixture filing is made. Article 9 contains rules for addressing a conflict of interest in property held as collateral under both a real estate mortgage and an Article 9 security agreement (see § 9-334).

Example: A contract for the sale of land included a mobile home and a concrete ready-mix batch plant. The transfer documents described the mobile home and the concrete ready-mix batch plant as "goods, chattels, and personal property." The seller took back a mortgage to secure part of the payment. After the buyer defaulted, the question arose as to whether the mobile home and batch plant were covered under the mortgage as fixtures. Although normally these items would be considered fixtures, the parties' intent controls, making them purely personal property. *Lundgren v. Mohagen*, 426 N.W.2d 563 (N.D. 1988).

C. Priority issues: The point of getting a security interest and perfecting it is to establish a priority right to the property as collateral. With respect to ***real property***, the priority of competing claims is resolved under real property law, including the rules governing recording statutes. As to ***personal property***, the priority rules are in UCC Article 9. As to ***fixtures***, the rules for disputes among Article 9 claimants and real property claimants are in Article 9 (see § 9-334).

IV. THE LAWYER'S ROLE IN COMMERCIAL TRANSACTIONS

The lawyer performs a number of functions in the commercial real estate transaction. She must coordinate all aspects of the transaction for the client and interact with all of the parties. She has to deal with multiple areas of law, since the typical commercial transaction involves a number of different law school subjects.

A. Opinion letters: In many commercial transactions, lawyers are expected to give opinion letters on aspects of the project, such as the status of title, zoning and environmental compliance, the enforceability of loan documents, the perfection of mortgages and security interests, and the proper formation and authorization of legal entities. The opinion letter is a formal legal document that expresses the lawyer's professionally informed opinion as to the legal status of specific elements of the transaction. The lawyer may be liable for malpractice if the opinion proves incorrect. A carefully drafted opinion letter has appropriate qualifications and makes specific reference to the materials on which the lawyer has based her opinion. The letter should be addressed to a specific party in an attempt to limit the scope of persons legally entitled to rely on it.

B. Conflicts: With so many parties involved in the commercial transaction, a lawyer may unintentionally walk into a conflict of interest unless close attention is paid to this matter. ***Dual and multiple representation*** requires proper disclosure and consent. Other areas of conflict emerge from the nature of the commercial real estate transaction. Sometimes, a developer is forming one or more legal entities and asks the lawyer to serve as an officer. At other times, a developer may offer her lawyer an interest in the project in exchange for reduced legal fees. Such situations present risk. The lawyer should not take a position that may compromise her independent professional judgment.

Example: Umberto is a lawyer for Celia, who is a major developer of shopping malls. For a new project, Celia has lined up two partners. Umberto represents Celia in all aspects of the project, and her two partners have their own legal counsel. A corporation is to be formed to protect the partners from unlimited liability. Celia asks Umberto to serve as president, at least until the project is completed. Umberto agrees. Each partner becomes an equal shareholder in the corporation. As the project goes forward, Celia and her partners suffer a falling out. Various disputes arise with respect to investment contributions to the capitalization of the corporation. In the midst of these disputes, Umberto is charged by Celia's two partners with having a conflict of interest. They argue that as the president of the corporation he owes a duty to all of the shareholders and cannot therefore represent all of them and Celia at the same time. They are right. Unfortunately for Umberto, his desire to accommodate his client has put him in a very bad ethical position.

Quiz Yourself on
THE COMMERCIAL REAL ESTATE MARKET

101. Do a construction lender and a permanent lender for an office building share the same focus on risk and transactional dynamics? _____

102. What are the primary legal functions of a three-party or buy-sell agreement? _____

103. What is the nature of the capitalization question involved in setting up a limited liability entity, such as a corporation? _____

104. Big Bank is providing construction financing for an office tower. Part of the financing is for the cost of special copper piping for the complex plumbing and fire prevention system to be installed in the building. One million dollars is budgeted for this part of the project. Big Bank says it has determined that under state law the pipe will be a fixture when installed. Thus, it will secure a mortgage interest in the pipe to cover it, once installed. Big Bank wonders, however, about the time period from manufacturing of the special piping to actual installation. Should it do anything to secure the pipe beyond recording the mortgage? _____

105. Viki is asked to give an opinion letter on title to a 200-acre tract of land being developed as a residential subdivision by Robert, her client. The lenders require this letter in addition to title insurance and a survey. Viki reads the title insurance commitment and submits an opinion stating: "Based on my own independent review of various title information in the above referenced transaction, I am of the opinion that the property is held in fee simple absolute by Robert subject only to those items specifically mentioned in that certain title insurance commitment/policy #776543 prepared by Safe Title Company for this transaction." It turns out that the property is subject to a major easement that cuts across the property, interfering with development plans and substantially lowering the value of the project. The title insurer accidentally left the easement off its commitment and policy even though the survey notes the easement. Big Bank says that it did not pay closer attention to the survey information because Viki had given her title opinion. Big Bank sues Viki for malpractice on the opinion letter. Should Viki be liable? _____

Answers

101. **No.** The construction lender focuses on the high-risk activity of bringing a planned building into reality in accordance with the approved plans and specifications. The permanent lender, on the other hand, focuses on the project operating as a viable economic enterprise over an extended period of time after its physical completion. As a consequence of these different positions, the construction lender and the permanent lender structure their respective roles with slightly different emphases.

102. **There are two primary functions.** The two primary functions are to put all of the parties (developer, construction lender, and permanent lender) into privity with each other and to give each a right of specific performance against the others.

103. **Proper capitalization supports limited liability.** One must be sure to comply with all legal formalities and to provide adequate asset capitalization. If the entity is undercapitalized, it may end up having its corporate veil pierced. This could result in unlimited liability for the individual principals. When principals use other entities that they control to make loans to the development corporation, it is possible that such loans will be set aside, with respect to other claimants, if the entity is not sufficiently capitalized.

104. **Yes.** The special piping will become important potential collateral before installation is complete at the job. What will Big Bank do if the developer defaults while the piping is sitting at the factory waiting to be shipped or if the pipe is stored at the work site, but not yet installed? Certainly, prior to installation, the pipe is not real property or a fixture. Big Bank must comply with Article 9 to take and perfect a security interest in advance of installation. This action should be coordinated with a properly prepared mortgage so that the pipe is secure once it becomes part of the property.

105. **Probably yes.** Viki is not an insurer of the project just because she gives a professional opinion, but she can be held liable if she has failed to use the appropriate professional standard of care. Viki should be liable because of the way she wrote her opinion letter. She apparently reviewed only the title commitment/policy, yet she did not say that was the exclusive basis of her opinion. She said she reviewed various pieces of title information and reached a specific conclusion. She also stated that she did an "independent review," and this is likely to require a review of the survey and of the information available in the public records. If she has not done a true independent review, she needs to be careful and restrict her opinion to the specific items actually reviewed.

Exam Tips on
THE COMMERCIAL REAL ESTATE MARKET

☞ **Identify the parties and know their function in the transaction:** When you see a commercial lending problem, be sure to identify clearly all of the parties. Keep in mind the nature of the role to be performed by each party. Without an appreciation for the different risks and objectives of the construction lender, the permanent lender, and other parties, you will miss subtle elements of an examination problem.

☞ **Identify Article 9 issues:** While the details of Article 9 are beyond the typical scope of a real estate transactions examination, it is easy to test for a basic understanding of the relationship between mortgage law and Article 9. Begin by thinking about how the various types of potential collateral might be categorized as real property, fixtures, or personal property. Once these are categorized, you can then deal with how the lender obtains and perfects a security interest in the particular collateral. The key to most real estate examination questions in this area is your ability to identify the items that can and cannot be covered by a real estate mortgage. As to Article 9 issues, you should generally recognize what types of issues are covered by Article 9, but one will not likely need to know specific code sections or details unless they have been covered as such in one's particular course.

☞ **Clarify the relationship between construction loans and permanent loans:** It is important to understand the relationship between the construction loan and the permanent loan, including the various types of take-out arrangements. Pay close attention to facts that set the conditions for a take-out and the coordination of terms between the construction and permanent lender.

☛ **Entity selection for the development vehicle:** It is important to consider facts related to the developer's selection and use of a development entity. Make sure that the entity is properly formed and capitalized or it may not be effective.

☛ **Identify underlying transactional issues:** Keep in mind that even though you may be looking at a commercial real estate problem many of the underlying issues and concerns are ones discussed in the residential transaction. Therefore, do not forget to think of issues related to the statute of frauds, recording statutes, mortgages, title, and other issues studied in the residential area and determine if any of these issues arise in your commercial setting.

CHAPTER 23

COMMERCIAL REAL ESTATE FINANCING

ChapterScope ━━━━━━━━━━━━━━━━━━━━━━━━━━━━━━━━━━━━━

This chapter builds on the information set out in Chapter 22. It provides more detail concerning the relationship between the construction lender and the permanent lender, and it discusses some of the major elements of the commercial financing arrangement.

- ■ **Five phases of project development:** A commercial real estate project goes through five major phases, which correspond to financing and capital needs. These include planning, acquisition, development, construction, and completion.

- ■ **Equity contribution:** The developer seeks investors to capitalize the ownership entity and to provide an equity contribution. The equity contribution is needed when 100 percent financing is not available.

- ■ **Sale and lease schedules:** The permanent lender establishes a schedule for sales and leases and guidelines for *price maintenance*.

- ■ **Retainage:** A construction lender takes retainage out of draw payments and requires the developer to meet *performance standards* for the project. A retainage is a *holdback* of a set percentage of a scheduled draw payment.

- ■ **Loan participations:** Lenders may seek investors to join in the financing of a large commercial transaction under a loan participation. These loan participations are secondary mortgage market activities as discussed in Chapter 15.

- ■ **Leasing:** Commercial real estate transactions offer a variety of options for leasing arrangements.

━━━

I. MARKET COORDINATION OF COMMERCIAL DEVELOPMENT

A. **Project phases:** A commercial project emerges in five major phases, which follow a time path and are interrelated. Most projects follow a process that includes planning, acquisition, development, construction, and completion. These phases represent a circular process in which one moves from planning to completion, and then moves on with the planning of the next project (starting the process all over again). Full-time developers are continuously looking for new projects and moving through these phases on each one.

1. **Planning:** In the planning phase, the developer finds a location for a particular project idea, such as a hotel or condominium, or finds a use for a previously identified piece of property. Market research and feasibility studies are done to determine the prospects for a successful project. Drawings and plans are prepared so the developer can interest prospective investors and lenders.

2. **Acquisition:** If the developer does not already own the land for the project, acquisition is negotiated. The contract of purchase is usually complex because the developer wants a substantial number of contract conditions, which coordinate the purchase with steps for project approval and financing.

3. **Development:** Development involves regulatory approvals (land use and environmental) and basic site improvements, such as clearing and grading, drainage, basic utility services, and roads. Development funding usually comes as a specifically identified part of the construction loan.

4. **Construction:** This phase consists of construction of buildings and related facilities, such as parking lots. Large expenditures are made, while the project produces no income.

5. **Completion:** At completion of construction, the project begins to produce income. Space is leased or units are sold. Permanent lending takes out the construction loan.

B. **Loan relationship:** The financial needs of the project vary with the different phases. The financing of the permanent loan is coordinated in advance by way of commitments and contracts with extensive conditions. This means that the permanent loan has to be in place before or at the same time as arrangements are made for a construction loan. Simply put, most developers do not want to get committed to a project without knowing that they have the end financing in place at the outset. They do not want to take on a project and a lot of liability unless they know that there will be a source for paying off, or refinancing, the construction loan. Thus, developers carefully coordinate their loans and link their obligations together using complex agreements.

1. **Investors:** During the planning stage, the developer looks for investors to capitalize the development entity. Usually, the developer needs investors to make an equity contribution because mortgage financing will provide less than 100 percent of the project costs. This involves the use of equity leverage and can be organized in several ways. Two common ways of doing this involve either selling stock in a corporate entity or limited partnership interests in a limited partnership entity. As the purchaser and owner of stock or a limited partnership interest, an investor contributes equity to the financing of the project and gets a return on that equity when the project becomes profitable. There may also be tax benefits from certain types of investments.

2. **Acquisition, development, and construction funding:** Sometimes, the seller provides financing for the land acquisition, secured by a ***purchase-money mortgage (PMM)*** (discussed in Chapter 15). For the project to go forward, the seller will generally have to agree to ***subordinate*** the PMM to the later construction financing (subordination is discussed in Chapter 21). This is because most major lenders on a project will want to have a first lien. Another common way to structure financing for these phases is to get an "acquisition, development, and construction loan" ***(ADC loan)***. For construction loan financing, a lender generally must label its loan as a "construction loan" and must clearly identify how much of the loan is allocated for the independent purposes of acquisition, development, and construction. This provides important information to other potential creditors. It is important, for instance, for potential creditors to know that a $100 million construction loan includes $20 million for acquisition; otherwise, it may appear that the full $100 million is available to provide funding for labor and materials at the project when in fact only $80 million of loan funds will be available for these purposes. This is needed to protect the lien of the loan against the possible claims of other creditors. For example, Article 9 of the Uniform Commercial Code grants priority to the lien

with respect to fixtures to the extent that the loan funds are incurred for the construction of improvements, provided certain conditions are met. UCC § 9-334(h).

3. **Permanent financing:** When construction of an income-producing project is complete, the permanent lender takes out the construction loan all at once and replaces it with a long-term mortgage (discussed in Chapter 22). Payments are then made on the long-term mortgage obligation. With a for-sale project, such as a residential subdivision or condominium where units are sold, the process usually involves a series of *mini take-outs*. As each unit is sold, the developer pays a portion of the construction loan, pursuant to a formula in a *release schedule* agreed to by the parties. The lender signs a *partial mortgage release* for each unit as its required release amount is paid. When the developer sells the last units, the project ends with the construction lender fully paid and the construction mortgage entirely released. In its place will be whatever financing an individual unit buyer may have secured to acquire her individual unit.

II. COMMON DEVICES FOR STRUCTURING LOANS

A. **Retainage and holdbacks:** Draw down payments under construction loans are usually subject to retainage, which is also called holdback. The amount, typically 10-15 percent of each draw payment, is an important point of negotiation between lender and developer. Holdbacks serve two objectives. First, they create an incentive for the developer to finish the project because he is paid the holdback balance at completion. Second, the lender may use holdbacks to satisfy any lien claims that arise during construction. Lenders attempt to monitor developers' timely payment of all suppliers, contractors, and workers, but sometimes problems arise, which holdbacks can help to resolve.

B. **Performance standards:** Both the construction lender and the permanent lender are likely to set performance standards, which are in addition to construction and completion goals. Performance standards require that the developer meet targets for leasing or selling units. For example, the standards may specify that an office building must be 10 percent leased at commencement of construction, 20 percent leased after the foundation and structural steel are in place, 30 percent leased after the structure is enclosed, and 80 percent leased at completion. Such standards force the developer to engage in active marketing, and they improve the lenders' security because leases and sales contracts become part of the collateral. The standards also provide continuous market feedback for the project. If the developer cannot meet the goals, the lenders may propose changes. For example, perhaps the rents are too high, and a design calling for luxury appointments throughout the building can be scaled back to offer simpler and less costly space.

C. **Price maintenance:** When lenders set performance standards, they must also establish criteria for leases and sales contracts. A developer who has only a percentage goal may offer sales contracts and leases at deep discounts in order to reach the goal. This behavior severely undercuts the value of the performance standards to the lender. Consequently, lenders set minimum rent and price standards and try to police compliance so as to prevent unauthorized discounts or side deals between a developer and tenants or buyers.

D. **Release schedules:** As the project moves toward completion, the developer turns over possession of units to users and buyers. To preserve the security for their loan, the lenders want to compel the developer generally to release units of lower value prior to releasing ones of high value. Therefore a schedule will be worked out and agreed to in advance of making the loan.

Example: RPM is developing a high-rise oceanfront condominium project with 60 units. Half are ocean-view units, and half overlook a garden and pool area. RPM's financing consists of an ADC loan and a commitment from another lender to provide home mortgages to unit buyers, which will function as a series of mini take-outs of the construction loan. The construction loan totals $27 million and is scheduled for disbursement in 10 draws based on construction progress, subject to a 10 percent holdback. Completion for take-out purposes is required to take place within 22 months of initial funding, and completion is defined as receiving the certificate of occupancy from the local government authority and a certification from the architect that all work is at least 96 percent complete with reference to the approved plans and specifications for the project. Performance standards require at least 65 percent of the units to be under contract by the date of completion. Minimum prices are $700,000 for ocean-view units and $500,000 for garden-view units, and all sales contracts must be on a form approved by the lender. When the project is complete, the closings with buyers must occur in a specific pattern: two-thirds of the completed sales must consist of garden-side units until all the garden-side units are sold.

Here we see all of the standard loan devices at work. The loan is structured to control the outflow of cash and to preserve a measure of safety in the 10 percent holdback. Completion is defined, and sales targets, as well as construction goals, are set. The minimum prices will maintain the value of the contracts obtained to meet the performance standards. Finally, the closing of unit contracts upon completion of construction is covered by a release schedule. This schedule for closing the sales contracts preserves the lender's lien on many ocean-side units until the end so that, if the developer defaults, the lender will foreclose on the most valuable assets of the project.

III. GAP FINANCING

For two reasons, a developer may face a gap in financing between the construction loan and the permanent loan. First, a cost overrun during construction may result in a debt on the construction loan that exceeds the dollar amount of the permanent lender's commitment. Unless the developer has cash to cover the difference, additional financing, called *gap financing*, is needed. Second, when the developer has a stand-by or open-ended take-out and has not yet found desirable permanent financing, he may need to bridge the gap in time while he continues to seek permanent financing. This second type of gap financing is also known as a *bridge loan*.

A. **Future advance:** Many commercial mortgages have a *future advance clause*, which allows for the extension of additional credit at a later date. The advance is secured by the same mortgage and has the same priority as the original loan. With a construction mortgage, this clause is useful as a way of dealing with cost overrun issues. Coordination with the permanent loan is important. The three-party agreement should specify how much, if any, additional debt under a future advance clause is acceptable as part of an expanded obligation to take out the construction loan.

IV. LOAN PARTICIPATIONS

A lender who finances a project may offer to sell interests in the loan to other investors. This is called a loan participation and is a counterpart to the developer getting investors for his project. The original lender, known as the *lead lender*, manages and administers the loan and earns extra fees for undertaking these duties.

A. Spreading risk: A loan participation reduces a lender's risk because it puts less of its money on the line with one developer and one particular project. By selling participations, the lender brings in other lenders to help with the financing and gains a more diversified loan portfolio. By structuring a participation, each participating lender has less at risk in the transaction than if they financed the entire project individually. This reduces the risk to the lender in the event of a developer having serious financial trouble, and in the event of the developer or project going under.

B. Lending requirements: Institutional lenders have *regulatory limits* on the amount of money they can lend to any one customer, and on the amount they can commit to any one project. These limits vary according to several factors, including the lender's total assets. For an expensive project, the regulations may compel the lead lender to sell loan participations, even though it might prefer to lend the full amount.

Example: *Penthouse International, Ltd. v. Dominion Federal Savings & Loan Association*, 855 F.2d 963 (2d Cir. 1988), illustrates the difficulties that may be encountered in coordinating financing arrangements. Penthouse set up a subsidiary to develop a hotel and casino. After beginning the land acquisition, Penthouse sought financing through a mortgage broker. It obtained a $97 million construction loan and a coordinated permanent loan take-out from Queen City Savings and Loan. Arranging a loan participation, Queen City provided $7 million in funding and sold $90 million to 11 other lenders. Dominion Federal Savings and Loan, the biggest participant at $35 million, insisted on being a co-lead lender with Queen City. Disputes arose between Penthouse and the lead lenders over conditions precedent to funding the loan. Queen City was willing to waive all of the conditions, but Dominion refused to go forward. Penthouse sued the other lenders for anticipatory repudiation, getting a trial court damage award of $128.7 million. Upon appeal, the circuit court reversed, finding no anticipatory repudiation because the conditions to funding were not met. The court also explained some of the legal duties of a lead lender. It explained that a lead lender such as Queen City generally has day-to-day management responsibility for a loan participation and cannot unilaterally waive conditions without consulting the other loan participants. Because Queen City was acting as an independent contractor in its role as a lead lender, it was not authorized to waive conditions to loan funding. A lead lender would need to be operating as the agent of the participating lenders in order to waive express loan requirements for the group. As an agent rather than an independent contractor, a lead lender may have an ability to waive conditions but must do so in a context of having a fiduciary duty to all of the loan participants. This probably means that the condition should not be material. In practice, it is best to make the loan participation agreement clear as to the duties of the lead lender and the types of actions that require a lead lender to first obtain the consent of the other loan participants. In the *Penthouse* case the participation agreement did not make the lead lender an agent for the other lenders; thus, there was no basis for Queen City to act on its own to waive express conditions to funding the loan. The case illustrates the need for careful drafting in preparing the loan participation agreement, and establishing the legal relationship between lead and participating lenders.

V. LEASING CONSIDERATIONS IN COMMERCIAL TRANSACTIONS

A. Space leasing: In a commercial project where units are not for sale, space is usually leased to tenants for uses such as office space or retail space (stores). Apartment buildings offer residential leases. A lease is less costly for the occupant than a fee interest in comparable space. The standard lease gives no equity to the tenant, leaving the developer as owner, who may benefit from appreciation over time. The lease must be carefully negotiated, and if it is for a reasonably long term, it will need to provide for rent adjustments. The owner will want adjustments to be able to raise rent as the cost of living rises over time.

B. Ground lease: A landowner, rather than selling property, sometimes conveys a long-term leasehold to a developer. The lease term extends for the expected useful life of the building or for a time sufficient for the developer to recoup its investment. Terms of 40 to 99 years are common. The owner, as landlord, receives rents, usually payable monthly, quarterly, or annually. The developer, as tenant, is given primary control over the property and builds the real estate project. Any leasing of space, such as stores in a mall, is structured as a sublease between the developer and the subtenant. The ground lease lowers the developer's cost of land acquisition because he pays rent over time rather than the full purchase price up front. The ground lease, due to its long-term nature, usually provides for future rent adjustments to reflect inflation and increasing land values. The ground lease must be drafted to permit construction lending and permanent lending so that the developer can finance the construction and operation of the project.

C. Sale-leaseback: One financing alternative to a standard mortgage is a sale and leaseback. The owner sells the property to an investor and simultaneously leases it back. The investor serves as landlord and collects rent. By avoiding a mortgage, the parties follow a different set of legal rules and accounting rules. The investor has fee ownership, which is very secure and compares favorably to the position of a lender who holds a mortgage lien. Finally, the parties may achieve a mutually advantageous exchange of tax benefits, with the investor being treated as the owner for tax purposes and taking depreciation deductions on the building. For a combination of these reasons, the seller may get access to needed credit through a sale-leaseback on economic terms that are more favorable than those available on a straight mortgage deal.

D. Leasehold mortgage: A lender can secure a mortgage against a leasehold estate. In the event of a foreclosure, the lender proceeds against the leasehold in the same way that it might proceed against a mortgaged fee simple in a standard mortgage transaction. Since the tenant's leasehold is the collateral, the lender must carefully review the lease and ascertain that it is current and in full force and effect. The lease should guarantee that the lender gets notice of any default by the tenant along with the opportunity to cure that default.

    1. Attornment and nondisturbance agreement: When a mortgage covers rental property, the lender must consider the relationship it will have with the tenants in the event of a default and foreclosure. If the mortgage has priority over the leases, foreclosure may terminate those leases. If the leases have priority over the mortgage, foreclosure may allow the tenants to vacate possession (the lender is not the person with whom the tenants established their leases). The attornment and nondisturbance agreement deals with these problems. The tenant agrees to ***attorn*** to or recognize the lender as the new landlord in the event the lender takes over this position. Thus, the tenant cannot use the occasion to escape from an undesirable lease or to renegotiate a more favorable rent. The ***nondisturbance agreement*** obligates the lender, upon taking over the property, to leave the tenant in peaceful possession in accordance with the original lease terms.

Quiz Yourself on
COMMERCIAL REAL ESTATE FINANCING

106. How is the role of a developer in seeking equity investors similar to the role of a lead lender in a loan participation? _____

107. Developer gets a $5 million draw down construction loan for a condominium project. Draws are set to be in 10 equal distributions with 10 percent retainage. Assuming that Developer meets all conditions precedent to each draw, how much money can he expect to get from each draw payment? _____

108. Developer in the above problem has a construction loan with performance standards that require a specific number of pre-completion purchase contracts for condominium units. Developer must obtain binding sales contracts with deposits as follows: 5 percent of units prior to funding, 10 percent by the second draw, 30 percent by the fifth draw, 40 percent by the eighth draw, and 50 percent by the last draw. Based on your knowledge of markets and risk, do you think that buyers who contract prior to the funding of the project will pay the same price as the buyers who contract 18 months later, after the project is successfully completed? _____

109. Developer in our above problems obtains a construction loan with a future advance clause that allows for an additional $1 million. Given that a lender is willing to provide extra money at a later date, why should the parties set it up as a future advance clause rather than just doing an additional loan as needed in the future? _____

110. Polar Ice Co. needs a quick cash infusion to keep the business growing. It produces bottled water at its water springs and bottling plant. It has a $1 million equity in its plant. It learns that Big Bank will make a mortgage loan no larger than $700,000 using the plant as collateral. Is there an alternative way for Polar to get the cash it needs? Might it get more than $700,000? _____

111. JCS, a real estate development company, is building a casino and has acquired a 99-year ground lease for the property. The ground lease names JCS as the tenant and RPM Inc. as the landlord. JCS will build a 10-story hotel and casino structure on the property. JCS is negotiating with Big Bank concerning an ADC loan and with Metro Bank for the permanent loan. Big Bank is concerned about the ground lease and asks if its loan will be protected in the event of a default on the ground lease. Does Big Bank need to be concerned about a default in the ground lease after it funds the loan? _____

112. In the casino project that JCS is undertaking in the above question, it intends to lease out space to a few restaurants, a jewelry store, and an art gallery; all to be on the main floor of the project. Assuming the ground lease and the ADC loan are in place at the time JCS signs leases with these other businesses that will operate in his building, should the tenants have any special concerns as to the ground lease and the ADC loan? _____

Answers

106. Both developer and lead lender need capital from investors to pursue what they expect to be a value-creating enterprise. The developer has to promote a project idea in the hopes of bringing in equity investors and then lenders. The lead lender in a loan participation needs to promote the project idea to other lenders as a viable investment for mortgage loan funding. The developer will undertake a leadership role in the day-to-day operation and running of the project, while his investors hope for a return on their investment. Likewise, a lead lender will take on the leadership and management role in the financing of the transaction, and the other lenders, as investors, will be in the background, looking for a profitable return.

107. $450,000. The 10 percent retainage or holdback is standard. Out of each draw of $500,000, the lender places $50,000 in a special account for holdbacks. Thus, Developer has access to $450,000 from each draw. Upon completion, he will receive the total of what remains in the $500,000 account after the lender deals with any unpaid claims.

108. No. They should not pay the same price, all other things remaining constant. Early buyers take risk attributable to the construction process. The project may never be completed, it may be completed to a lesser quality than was hoped for, or it may come on line during a down market. These risks mean that the price of the first units has to be lower than that expected for sales at completion. If the project is successful, the early buyers will have a very good return on their contract investment. Remember that, even as to preconstruction contract prices, the loan documents are likely to require a minimum floor price that must be maintained in meeting the performance standards.

109. Each alternative works, but there are two advantages to the future advance. First, other than drafting an additional promissory note and a few other items, a new set of loan documents is not needed. This saves time and money. Second, as a future advance, the money is entitled to the same priority as the original funding. This is key because priority issues are fundamental in disputes after a default.

110. Yes. A sale-leaseback transaction might be a good alternative. Polar would sell the plant to Big Bank or some other investor for an amount exceeding $700,000, and Polar would lease it back. The lease payments would be structured to provide the new owner with a return of the purchase price with interest. Polar could bargain for an option to buy back the property at the end of the lease. The arrangement allows for different accounting classifications and tax implications than the mortgage approach. These considerations may be valuable enough to the parties to make this a viable funding option. Note: Tax planning issues need to be accounted for in structuring a viable transaction.

111. Yes. Big Bank has a major concern with respect to the ground lease. Basically, the loan will be secured by JCS's interest in the ground lease; thus, if the lease goes into default and JCS can have its interest terminated, there will be no collateral for the loan. The ground lease is prior to the loan and if JCS violates a term of the lease and goes into default, the leasehold estate may terminate. Inasmuch as the leasehold estate may be terminated, the loan would then become unsecured with respect to the real property. Therefore, Big Bank will probably want to insist that the ground lease be subordinated to the loan. This will require the cooperation of RPM.

112. Yes. Each of the businesses will really be on a sublease and be subtenants to JCS, who is the tenant on the ground lease. Each will want to make sure that JCS has permission to sublease and to determine if there are any restrictions on the types of businesses or mix of businesses that can be in the building—the type and mix of businesses being a key element in the success of such projects. In addition, if either the ground lease or loan go into default, since both are prior in time to the subleases, their leases will be terminated. The businesses may wish to get the prior interests subordinated to their leases. Unlike the construction lender who will most likely get a subordination of the ground lease so that the project can go forward, these businesses are unlikely to have that much clout. They should probably be looking to negotiate a nondisturbance agreement that will let them stay in place if a party with priority takes over the project after a default. This may be a possibility for a business considered to be a major draw to the location. In most cases, however, the major players will not be very motivated to make such a deal with a typical subtenant. At the same time, the major players may seek an attornment agreement from the businesses (inserting such a provision into any lease to be used and approved for JCS to sublease to these parties). The attornment agreement will require the subtenants to stay with the project if JCS is removed from it; they will not be released unless the prior parties consent to it.

Exam Tips on
COMMERCIAL REAL ESTATE FINANCING

☛ **Identify the five phases of the project and the one(s) relevant to your problem:** To prepare a well-organized answer without missing any issues, you should identify the five phases of the project and position your facts and issues within one or more of these phases. Be sure to link the phases with the different types of financing arrangements suitable to each phase.

☛ **Understand the lease:** Begin a lease problem by focusing on the two immediate parties, landlord and tenant. Analyze the terms of the lease, and consider the purpose it serves in the transaction. Also pay attention to third-party interests. Some leases will be of interest to a lender, who may have a lot to say about the terms of a lease. Satisfying the lender may be central to the objectives of the two immediate parties because there may be no deal without the lender.

☛ **Use planning tools:** When presented with a "planning" type question, remember to think about tools that can be used to structure a transactional relationship. In addition to having a draw down loan, as discussed in Chapter 22, you should think about tools discussed in this chapter such as the ideas of retainage, performance standards, gap financing, bridge loans, future advance clauses, and the use of leases as substitutes for financing (as in the sale and leaseback).

☞ **Use the proper vocabulary:** Demonstrate that you know the vocabulary of commercial transactions and use the terms identified in this chapter and in earlier chapters as you construct your answers.

Exam Questions

QUESTION 1:   RPM owns a $2 million property. RPM is going to sell the property and decides to enter into an exclusive agency listing agreement with Easy Brokers. The agreement calls for a 6 percent commission and lasts for a six-month period. Easy does a little advertising of the property and shows it to several parties, but it is a slow market and no purchase contract emerges. About three months after listing with Easy, RPM meets Jim, a broker with Quick Flip Real Estate. Jim says that Quick Flip can move the property at the asking price for a simple 2 percent commission. RPM, always looking to save some money, signs an open listing agreement with Quick Flip. Two weeks later, Jim brings a potential buyer to see the property, and a contract of purchase and sale is signed. RPM agrees to sell the property to the buyer secured by Quick Flip Real Estate. At the closing, RPM pays Quick Flip the 2 percent commission, but Easy Brokers also demands that it be paid a 6 percent commission. Does RPM owe a commission to Easy Brokers?

QUESTION 2:   On November 20, Robin contracts to sell his home to Jim for $400,000. The contract is set to close on December 12. On December 5, while Robin is still in possession, the house is destroyed by fire through no fault of either party. Must Jim close on the contract or is he excused from performance because the subject matter of the contract has been destroyed by an act of nature?

QUESTION 3:   On October 10, Robin conveys a 30-foot wide easement to Gina for travel across his 20-acre property. The easement runs along the western lot line of the property for a distance of 400 yards. On December 8, Robin sells the property and conveys it to Jim for $600,000. Robin conveys the property in fee simple by special warranty deed. Jim does not know about the prior granted easement to Gina. Jim records his deed on December 9. Upon learning of the situation, Gina records her easement on December 23. It is now December 30. Jim sues Robin over this title issue. Robin responds by asserting that he might have some liability if he had conveyed by a general warranty deed, but as he conveyed by a special warranty deed, he has no liability for any loss that Jim might have as a result of Gina's easement right. What is the status of the title here, considering race, notice, and race-notice jurisdictions?

QUESTION 4:   Your client borrows money to finance the purchase of a residential home. The client agrees to an adjustable-rate mortgage and note with a starting interest rate of 10 percent. The rate will be adjusted annually according to a Treasury bills index, which will provide the "market rate" to be applied to each annual adjustment. In pertinent part, the note provides as follows:

CHANGE IN INTEREST RATE

The yearly changes: By signing below, I agree that you can change the interest rate for the note each year. Here is how you will do that: Each year on the first day of the calendar month just before the anniversary date of the note, you will look to see what your market rate for adjustable-rate mortgage loans is. If your market rate is different from my existing rate for the note, you will increase or decrease the interest rate for the note to your market rate.

Changes in the interest rate on the note shall take effect on the first day of the month following an anniversary date.

During the life of the loan, you will make no single annual increase or decrease that is greater than 1 percentage point, regardless of what your market rate is. But this shall be true only so long as the existing rate for the note is the same or more than the original rate for the note.

If the existing rate is less than the original rate, then you will increase the interest rate for the note as follows: If the difference between the existing rate and the original rate is more than 1 percentage point, you will increase the interest rate for the note to the original rate or your market rate, whichever results in the smallest increase.

At the end of year one of the loan, the market rate has gone up 2 percent. At the end of year two, the market rate drops 4 percent from the previous year's market rate. At the end of year three, the market rate drops 1 percent from the previous year's market rate. At the end of year four, the market rate drops another 1 percent. At the end of year five, the market rate is up 5 percent from the previous year's market rate. What is the interest rate that should be applied to the client's note for the next year?

QUESTION 5: Robin is thinking about investing in some real estate. His investment will be $355,000. The project he is investing in is a small office building. The return on his money that he anticipates is 12 percent. An alternative investment option for his money involves stocks that have an expected return of 15 percent. The rate of return on similar office building projects is 8 percent, and the rate of return on similar stock investments is 17 percent. Explain the potential value of these investments to Robin in terms of a comparison between accounting and economic profits.

QUESTION 6: Paige telephoned you this morning to enlist your aid in connection with a proposed purchase of a restaurant known as Burrito Brothers. Paige informed you that she signed a contract for the purchase of the restaurant 15 days ago. Since signing the contract, Paige has inspected the restaurant more thoroughly, with the help of a friend who is an engineer. The inspection revealed the roof is in bad shape and will require substantial repair in the near future. Also, Paige noticed that the restaurant does not have a fire sprinkler system, and she expressed concern about potential liability to injured persons in the event of fire. Despite the condition of the roof and lack of sprinklers, Paige is still very interested in the property because of its excellent potential for appreciation. In not too many years, she plans either to construct a much larger restaurant on the property or to pursue other development alternatives for the property. The contract signed by the owners and Paige is set forth below.

REAL ESTATE PURCHASE CONTRACT

1. The undersigned Buyer agrees to buy and the undersigned Seller agrees to sell, upon the terms hereinafter set forth, the real estate known as 1400 Main Street, located in Pine City, State of Confusion.

2. The purchase price shall be $1,000,000. Buyer has deposited with Broker the sum of $20,000, which deposit shall be applied to the purchase price at the closing.

3. Seller shall furnish and pay for an owner's title insurance commitment and policy in the amount of the purchase price. The title policy shall insure in Buyer good and indefeasible title in fee simple free and clear of all liens and encumbrances except (a) those created by or assumed by Buyer; (b) those specifically set forth in this contract; (c) zoning ordinances; (d) rights of tenants, if any; and (e) covenants, restrictions, conditions, and easements of record that do not render title unmarketable. If Buyer desires a survey, Buyer shall pay the cost thereof.

4. Seller shall convey to Buyer marketable title in fee simple by transferable and recordable general warranty deed, free and clear of all liens and encumbrances not excepted by this contract.

5. Adjustments shall be made through date of closing for (a) taxes and assessments; (b) rentals; (c) interest on any mortgage assumed by Buyer; and (d) transferable insurance policies, if Buyer so elects.

6. Risk of loss to the real estate and appurtenances shall be borne by Seller until closing.

7. This contract shall be performed and this transaction closed within 30 days after acceptance hereof.

8. Seller shall pay a brokerage fee of 5 percent of the purchase price in connection with this transaction to Brenda Baker.

9. This contract constitutes the entire agreement, and there are no representations, oral or written, that have not been incorporated herein. Time is of the essence of all provisions of this contract.

You will meet with Paige this afternoon. She wants to know if she can require the sellers to repair the roof and install a sprinkler system or, in the alternative, to reduce the purchase price by the estimated cost of such repair and installation. Prepare a memorandum setting forth your advice (and the reasons for your advice).

QUESTION 7: Gary is a doctor, and he is performing surgery on Brad. Gary gets into a major conversation with an assisting doctor during the surgery and messes up the operation because he was not paying attention. Brad suffers permanent scarring from the procedure due to the negligence of Gary. Brad hires you to sue Gary for malpractice. You discover that Gary has some major real estate interests and figure that, since Gary is self-insured, you will probably be looking at the real estate as the major asset available to satisfy a judgment. You consider filing a lis pendens against the property. In this way, you will put people on notice while establishing the priority of your claim against the real estate. Is this a good strategy in this situation?

QUESTION 8: Mary has retained you to defend her in an action to quiet title to 77 Sunset Road, Pine City, Bliss. The plaintiff in the action is Zittman Corporation. The other defendants are Lucy and Price. Mary had never heard of the other litigants until she was served with the complaint.

Mary purchased 77 Sunset Road in 2003 for $60,000 from Drake. At that time, the property was unimproved. In 2005, Mary, with the help of friends, built a small log cabin on the property. She was not represented by counsel when she bought the property. Accordingly, no title examination was made at the time, and she has no title insurance policy. You ordered a title report for the property from Pine City Title Company, and it disclosed the following documents of record purporting to affect the property:

1. Patent from State of Bliss to Andrew, dated November 5, 1920, and recorded on December 2, 1920, in Volume 11, Page 7 of the Deed Records of Green County, Bliss.

2. Warranty Deed from Boyd to Zittman Corporation, dated December 27, 1940, and recorded on December 31, 1940, in Volume 39, Page 1, of the Deed Records of Green County, Bliss.

3. Warranty Deed from Andrew to Boyd, dated June 8, 1945, and recorded on July 2, 1945, in Volume 44, Page 82, of the Deed Records of Green County, Bliss.

4. Quitclaim Deed from Boyd to Camilla, dated May 21, 1950, and recorded on May 29, 1950, in Volume 49, Page 26, of the Deed Records of Green County, Bliss.

5. Warranty Deed from Camilla to Lucy, dated September 1, 1970, and recorded on September 3, 1978, in Volume 72, Page 55, of the Deed Records of Green County, Bliss.

6. Warranty Deed from Camilla to Drake, dated April 7, 1971, and recorded on April 8, 1971, in Volume 61, Page 7, of the Deed Records of Green County, Bliss.

7. Warranty Deed from Norton to Otto, dated April 20, 1971, and recorded on May 1, 1971, in Volume 61, Page 72, of the Deed Records of Green County, Bliss.

8. Unobstructed utility easement ten feet (10') wide along rear boundary of lot, granted to Capital City Power Company, by instrument dated July 1, 1975, and recorded on July 10, 1975, in Volume 68, Page 20, of the Deed Records of Green County, Bliss.

9. Warranty Deed from Otto to Price, dated August 17, 1990, and recorded on August 20, 1990, in Volume 91, Page 82, of the Deed Records of Green County, Bliss.

10. Warranty Deed from Drake to Mary, dated October 10, 2003, and recorded on November 17, 2003, in Volume 128, Page 58, of the Deed Records of Green County, Bliss.

Each of these deeds purports to convey a fee simple title, is in proper form for recording, and recites receipt of a valuable consideration. You have not yet conducted any pretrial discovery, so you do not know whether Price can produce an unrecorded deed purporting to convey title to Norton.

All the defendants have filed counterclaims to quiet title in themselves. What arguments can your client and each of the other parties make to support their respective claims of ownership? In your opinion, who has the better chance of prevailing and why?

Note: The official real estate records in Green County, Bliss, are indexed only by the names of the grantors and grantees. The Bliss recording statute reads: "Section 425. No instrument affecting real estate is of any validity against subsequent purchasers for a valuable consideration, without notice, unless filed in the office of the county recorder."

QUESTION 9:   You are a lawyer for Big Bank. You represent the Bank at all of its loan closings. In 95 percent of the cases, the borrower comes to closing without a lawyer. In one typical situation, the borrower, Karen, asks you a lot of questions about what the various mortgage documents say and mean. You give her general guidance. She also asks about the purchase price and the quality of the home and her title. She is buying a home in a new planned subdivision. She seems nervous and asks, "The Bank really checked the place out, didn't they? This place is going to be perfect for me and my family. After all, they wouldn't be giving me $225,000 if this wasn't a good deal, right?" In order to move things along and to seem pleasant, you smile back at Karen and say, "Yes, sure, the Bank always checks these things out before they make a loan." In such a setting, might you owe a professional duty to Karen, and if so, what are the implications?

QUESTION 10:   Moesha comes to you and asks you to represent her in the purchase of a unit in the Brandypath Cooperative. Moesha says that she has read that there are different types of deeds that have different types of warranty protection. She asks you which type of deed she will get at the closing. Tell Moesha what she can expect.

QUESTION 11:   You represent Mary, who is bargaining to obtain a permanent loan commitment from Bank to build a medical office building on a hospital campus. Mary plans to form a new corporation, to be named "Mary 2012 Inc.," which will be developer and borrower for this project. Mary 2012 Inc. will be wholly owned by an existing closely held corporation, of which Mary is the majority shareholder. Bank has sent you a proposed Loan Commitment Letter, with the following provision:

> 7. *Transfer of Property.* Borrower shall not sell or transfer title to the Property in any manner whatsoever, either directly or indirectly, without prior written consent of Bank. This prohibition

shall apply to any sale or transfer of stock or partnership interest of the Borrower, if Borrower is a corporation or partnership. Any such transfer shall be deemed an event of default and shall render the full balance of the Loan due and payable.

1. Analyze this provision and explain how it allocates risk between the parties. Include an explanation of the rights your client would have in the absence of a provision dealing with this subject.
2. What changes, if any, do you propose for Mary's benefit? Please be explicit, and if you recommend retaining the provision with modifications, rewrite the clause in your answer.
3. Suppose instead that you were representing Bank. Would you recommend any changes for Bank's benefit? Again, explicitly describe any suggested changes.

QUESTION 12: MVP, Inc., is doing a shopping mall development project. In arranging the financing for the project, MVP lines up a construction lender and a permanent lender with a lock-in take-out agreement. As one of the closing documents on the loans, the construction lender, the permanent lender, and MVP all sign a three-party agreement. Explain the nature of the three-party agreement, and identify its two primary legal functions.

QUESTION 13: Your client is New Bank, and it is expanding its operations in a new part of the country. It is targeting Beltway City as a high-income urban area with a strong growth potential. New Bank seeks your advice on what types of strategies might or might not get it in trouble. The Bank's main concern is that it make as much profit as it can with the least amount of cost. The Bank hires you because it is a conservative bank and does not want to violate the law or get bad press from trying to test the limits of permitted behavior. New Bank is considering several strategies and asks your advice about each. Consider the three strategies below and briefly comment on each.

1. New Bank wants to open branches in several of the densely populated suburban areas where many highly paid college graduates live and a branch in a very "upscale" section of Beltway City. Even though the population in each of these areas is 90 percent white, New Bank considers only the income and service potential of its customer base with respect to economic demographics for each area without regard for the racial makeup.
2. New Bank wants to advertise in several small-circulation newspapers that serve the individual suburban markets and in a local gourmet cooking magazine read by a high percentage of people living in the upscale neighborhood of Beltway City. It does not want to advertise in a newspaper of general circulation even though that would be cheaper because it would not be as effective at reaching the target group.
3. New Bank was founded three years ago by a group of Asian American investors. It wants to target funds for Asian Americans in the Beltway City area. Because Asian Americans have had difficulty getting credit in the past, it will place 90 percent of its loans with Asian Americans living in the target areas. Its advertising will use only Asian American models in an effort to entice this underserved market segment to come to its branches rather than going to competitors.

QUESTION 14: Can a lawyer ethically represent both the vendor and the purchaser in connection with the preparation of an installment land contract? Why or why not?

QUESTION 15: You represent Judy, who is buying a brand-new custom-built house from Frank for $450,000. Closing is scheduled for tomorrow, which is the last day Judy can close without losing a favorable interest rate on her mortgage loan commitment. At the "walk-through" of the house this morning,

Judy found everything to be fine, except that three major kitchen appliances (oven/range, refrigerator, and dishwasher) are not installed. These are top-of-the-line, commercial-grade appliances, which Frank ordered from an out-of-state supplier. At the walk-through, Frank told Judy that the supplier was late in shipping, the appliances should arrive in five to seven days, and then he'll put them in. Judy asks what she should do with respect to the closing in light of the missing appliances. Explain any risks that you foresee, and give Judy your recommendation.

QUESTION 16:   Gina agrees to buy a home from Giovanni for $250,000. During the executory contract period, the economy goes into a slump, and local housing prices are falling rapidly. On the date set for closing, Gina never shows up. Giovanni declares Gina to be in default, and he wants to sue her for either specific performance or damages. He has no prospects lined up for a resale to a new buyer, although he has been told by his broker that he might be able to get a new purchase contract on the deal if he is willing to drop the asking price to $210,000. He also has expenses of $400 for a survey and $700 for title information generated as part of his performance under the contract with Gina. His broker is also asking for payment of a $17,000 commission on the grounds that the fee was earned when the contract was signed between Gina and Giovanni. Assess the likely remedies that Giovanni has available to him.

QUESTION 17:   Sheila, the record owner of Blackacre in fee simple, signed a broker's contract with Julio in May. Blackacre is a vacation home in the mountains. The contract listed Blackacre for sale for $110,000, with a commission payable at the rate of 5 percent of the sale price. Julio found a prospective buyer named Ben, and negotiations resulted in the execution of a contract of sale between Sheila and Ben. In the contract, signed May 24, they agreed Ben would pay Sheila $20,000 down and would pay the remaining $80,000 in one year. At closing on June 21, Sheila delivered a warranty deed with all six covenants to Ben. The warranty deed is a standard form except that the consideration clause provides: "This deed is given for and in consideration of the sum of $100,000, part of which Grantee has on this day paid to Grantor, the remainder of which is due in one year and shall be secured by a mortgage to be given by Grantee on the property herein conveyed." Ben promptly recorded the deed. Ben never signed a mortgage instrument.

Although Ben paid Sheila the $20,000 down payment, at closing she refused to pay any of the $5,000 broker's commission to Julio, claiming the broker's contract requires that he find a buyer who would pay the listed price of $110,000 and that, in any event, the commission is not payable until the buyer pays the full purchase price. In July, Julio, who still had not been paid any part of his commission, signed and had notarized a document called "Affidavit of Lien." In this document, Julio claimed a lien on Blackacre (with a proper land description) to secure payment of his $5,000 commission. The Affidavit has a copy of the broker's contract attached as an exhibit. Julio promptly recorded the Affidavit of Lien.

For some time, one of Ben's creditors, Aggressive Loan Co., had been hounding him on outstanding personal loans totaling $15,000. To get Aggressive off his back, on September 1 Ben granted Aggressive a mortgage on Blackacre. Ben did not tell Aggressive about the unpaid amount due to Sheila. On September 18, Aggressive recorded its mortgage. The clerk at the recording office properly recorded this instrument, but made a mistake in the name indexes by entering the name as *Aggression* Loan Co.

Sheila vacated possession of Blackacre in June, just after the transfer to Ben. Blackacre was vacant for several months, and on September 7, Ben took possession and has remained in possession continuously thereafter.

In October, Ben decided he wanted to improve Blackacre by adding a swimming pool. To finance this improvement, he borrowed $30,000 from Money Inc., secured by a mortgage, which was immediately recorded. Ben did not tell Money Inc. about the unpaid amount due to Sheila or the mortgage to Aggressive.

In December, Aggressive Loan Co. filed a complaint against Ben to foreclose its mortgage on Blackacre. Sheila, Julio, and Money Inc. are also parties to the foreclosure action. Each of these parties alleges that it has a lien on Blackacre that is entitled to first priority.

1. At this point in time, which of the above parties have valid liens on Blackacre and why?
2. Of the parties that have liens, what arguments can each party make to support the claim of first priority?
3. Resolve the conflicting claims of priority, and indicate the order in which the liens should be ranked.
4. Which of the above parties are necessary parties, and which are proper parties in Aggressive's foreclosure action?

Note: The recording statute in the state provides: "Every conveyance of real property which shall not be recorded as provided by law shall be void as against any subsequent purchaser in good faith and for a valuable consideration whose conveyance shall be first duly recorded."

Sample Answers to Exam Questions

SAMPLE ANSWER TO QUESTION 1

RPM is the owner of the property and engages Easy Brokers to list the property. They enter into an exclusive agency agreement. Such an agreement obligates RPM to pay the 6 percent commission to Easy Broker in all cases other than where RPM sells the property on its own. The listing is for six months. RPM later, but within the six-month period, engages Quick Flip and agrees to a 2 percent commission on an open listing. The open listing provides for paying a commission to a given broker if that broker is the procuring cause of the sale. The facts indicate that Quick Flip identified the buyer and brought the parties to contract and closing with RPM. Quick Flip has earned a commission as the procuring broker for the sale. RPM owes 2 percent to Quick Flip and pays this amount at the closing. Easy Broker did not procure the buyer but wants a 6 percent commission on the sale. It is important to note that the later agreement with Quick Flip for an open listing does not modify or amend the earlier agreement with Easy Brokers. Consequently, RPM owes Easy Brokers a 6 percent commission on the transaction, because it had agreed to pay such a commission if the property was sold by anyone other than RPM. Thus, RPM is obligated to pay Easy Brokers 6 percent and Quick Flip 2 percent.

SAMPLE ANSWER TO QUESTION 2

The traditional default rule assigns the risk of loss to the buyer from the moment of signing the contract, provided that the contract is specifically enforceable. This is a consequence of the doctrine of equitable conversion, which treats the buyer as the holder of equitable title. In the absence of a contract term to the contrary, the general rule is still that risk is on the buyer under the contract. It is of course a simple matter to add the words, "risk of loss is on the seller until closing," and this would keep the risk on the legal title holder. Assuming that there was no express term in the contract, Jim has the risk during the executory contract. Because Jim has the risk, he could have obtained insurance to cover this risk. The risk of a house burning is foreseeable, and under the traditional rule Jim will suffer the loss. He will need to pay the full contract price.

There are some variations to consider on the traditional risk of loss rule. In a jurisdiction with the Uniform Vendor and Purchaser Risk Act, the risk would be on Robin because Robin is in possession of the property at the time of the fire and he has not yet conveyed title to Jim. In addition, some states might modify the traditional rule by requiring Jim to close on the contract but making Robin turn over any insurance proceeds collected through his owner's insurance. This can be done by arguing that the funds are held in a constructive trust for the benefit of a buyer in such a circumstance. Strictly speaking, however, this is a fiction because insurance is a personal contract for the benefit of the person who acquires it. In those states willing to use the fiction, if Robin forces Jim to close, Jim must pay the contract price and Robin must turn over the insurance proceeds as a "substitute" for the improvement that used to be on the property. Another approach to this problem is to assert a mutual mistake on the grounds that both parties contracted with the contemplation of the home existing on the property. This, of course, is just a way to say that the risk of loss is on the seller because mutual mistake would let buyer off the hook, and seller will be stuck with the property with no home on it as a result of the fire. Some states will turn to mutual mistake if the facts seem to merit it for purposes of fairness. Unless one knows the specific law in a given jurisdiction, it is probably best to base the answer on the traditional rule. If one knows that the Uniform Act is in place, one should go with the Act. Likewise, pay attention to any contract terms, because an express allocation of risk in the contract should generally control. Mutual mistake is a "hard sell" unless you know that it's common in a given jurisdiction or you have approached the issue this way in your own specific course.

SAMPLE ANSWER TO QUESTION 3

Robin grants the easement to Gina prior to conveying the property to Jim. Robin grants the easement to Gina on October 10. On December 8, Robin strikes a deal with Jim and conveys the property to Jim in fee simple using a special warranty deed. At the time of the conveyance, Jim pays value and has no notice or knowledge of Gina's interest. Jim records the next day, on December 9. Later Gina learns about the sale to Jim and records her grant of an easement on December 23. Now it is December 30, and Jim asserts that Robin is liable to him for any loss from this dispute over title.

Under the traditional default rule, one might argue that "first in time is first in right." Technically, once Robin conveys the easement to Gina (prior to the conveyance to Jim), Robin no longer has that interest available to transfer to Jim. Basically, Gina is first in time and therefore first in right, as opposed to Jim. This old rule has been modified by the various recording statutes adopted by the different states. Thus, one needs to apply the recording statutes to the facts to see if they might result in a different outcome. In general, the recording statutes condition a first in time, first in right rule to the terms of the rule. Recording acts explain how to apply a priority rule to these disputes. Looking at the chain of events, Jim wins against any adverse claim by Gina under all three types of recording acts. Under a pure race statute, Jim is the first to record. A race statute does not require one to be a BFP. Under a pure notice recording act, Jim is the last BFP so he wins. Under a race-notice statute, Jim wins because he is the first BFP to record. Thus, in a title dispute between Jim and Gina, Jim should win. Jim should not have a loss.

Robin's response that there is no liability because of the use of a special warranty deed rather than a general warranty deed must also be addressed. Robin is incorrect. A special warranty deed has the same warranties as a general warranty deed, only the scope of coverage under the warranties is narrower. Under a general warranty deed, the warranties go to the successful claims of any person whomsoever. In the special warranty deed, the coverage extends only to those successful claimants claiming by, through, or under the grantor. In this case, Robin is the grantor on both the easement to Gina and the conveyance to Jim. Thus, the claim from Gina is covered by the warranties in the special warranty deed used by Robin to convey to Jim. In this case, the type of deed makes no difference because both types would cover this situation if there were to be an actual loss. In the end, Jim wins under the recording acts. Gina loses, and the law is not generally sympathetic to her because she "slept on her rights." She could have avoided this by recording right away and putting the world, and in particular Jim, on notice of her rights in the property.

SAMPLE ANSWER TO QUESTION 4

The answer is 10 percent. This is an adjustable-rate mortgage (ARM), with annual adjustments tied to a Treasury bills index identified as the "market rate." The rate is based on the rate on the first day of the month before the anniversary date of the mortgage, and that rate is effective on the first day of the month following the anniversary of the loan. This ARM also has an annual interest rate adjustment cap, but no lifetime cap. The annual cap is set at 1 percent, but this is qualified such that an annual increase might be more than 1 percent if the existing rate, at the time of the adjustment, is below the original or starting rate of interest.

Applying the language of the note to the added facts on market activity in the years after the loan, we can determine the rate of interest for the mortgage. At the end of year one, the market interest rate has gone up 2 percent to 12 percent, but we have a 1 percent cap, so the mortgage rate would rise only 1 percent to 11 percent. At the end of year two, the market rate drops 4 percent from the prior year market rate, and this would equal 8 percent, but the adjustment is limited to a 1 percent drop back to 10 percent from the prior 11 percent. In year three, the market rate drops 1 percent from the prior year, and this makes the market rate 7 percent, so borrower benefits by a 1 percent drop and the mortgage rate falls to 9 percent. At the end of year four, the market rate drops another 1 percent to 6 percent, and the mortgage rate falls 1 percent to 8 percent. In year five, the market rate is up 5 percent from the prior year rate of 6 percent to a new market rate of 11 percent. This results in a mortgage rate increase of 2 percent to the original 10 percent rate. This is because the 8 percent rate is below the original rate, so the lender is not within the 1 percent cap. Here, according to the language in the note, the lender can raise the rate to the original rate (10 percent) or the market rate (11 percent), whichever results in the smallest increase. Thus, the rate rises to the original rate of 10 percent.

SAMPLE ANSWER TO QUESTION 5

Remember that accounting and economic profits are different. Accounting profits measure positive cash flow, whereas economic profits compare the expected rate of return against other similar market opportunities. Economic profits, in other words, take into account opportunity costs. In terms of accounting profits, both of the options indicate a positive return. The stock investment returns 15 percent and the office building 12 percent. In terms of economic profits, we conclude that the building makes a 4 percent economic profit, while the stock generates a 2 percent loss. Compared to similar investment opportunities, Robin gets a 12 percent rather than an 8 percent return on the building (this is the 4 percent profit), but he gets only 15 percent on the stock, when other similar stocks return 17 percent (this is the 2 percent economic loss). When considering the dynamics of a transaction or the regulation of an activity, we must be careful to consider economic profits and losses, as well as accounting ones, so as to properly understand the economic motivations for the deal.

SAMPLE ANSWER TO QUESTION 6

The traditional rule of caveat emptor means that there are no implied warranties under a contract of sale as to the physical quality of improvements to real estate. This means that a purchaser such as Paige should inspect before contracting or add express provisions to the contract that address physical condition. The contract could provide for inspections of the improvements, including the roof. The contract also could have warranties of quality—for example, that the roof does not leak. The contract signed by Paige has no such provisions. It has no explicit "As Is" clause, but a court is still likely to apply caveat emptor. This is especially true because this is a commercial sale. Courts are more prone to avoid the application of caveat emptor for residential purchasers.

There are various doctrines Paige may try to use to get around caveat emptor. Tort law principles of intentional or negligent misrepresentation or fraudulent concealment sometimes succeed. Further investigation of the facts might support such a claim. In some states, sellers of real estate have a duty to disclose material latent defects to purchasers. This is less likely for commercial sales, and the integration clause in paragraph 9 of the contract may serve to negate such a duty. If, however, the sellers have such a duty, then the issue is whether the roof condition is a latent or patent defect. How noticeable was the poor condition of the roof? Was deterioration visible from outside the restaurant? Were stains from leaks evident from the inside?

The lack of sprinklers is not likely to be considered a building defect even if the sellers have a duty to disclose material defects. Moreover, the absence of sprinklers is likely to be considered patent, not latent. Paige's best chance here is to find a violation of a state or local law. If the lack of sprinklers violates a zoning or building code, the sellers may have a duty to install them. The violation may be said to impair marketable title. Notice that the parties' contract, in paragraph 3, excepts zoning laws, not violations thereof, from the sellers' title duties.

SAMPLE ANSWER TO QUESTION 7

No, this is not a good strategy; in fact, it may lead to liability in an action for slander of title. Here the legal action is one in tort for malpractice. This is not a suit about the status of the real estate. A lis pendens can be properly filed when the status of the title to the property may be affected by the outcome of the pending litigation. This does not mean that the plaintiff needs to actually win. The plaintiff needs to have a meritorious or colorable claim. Since the lawsuit itself has nothing to do with the status of the real estate, the filing of a lis pendens against the property is improper. Such an improper filing may also form the basis for a slander of title action against Brad because it will place a cloud on the title to the property.

SAMPLE ANSWER TO QUESTION 8

This is a complex title question with a number of facets. Good organization is essential. An organized answer could proceed party by party or chronologically, deed #1 through deed #10.

Zittman recorded its deed in 1940, five years before its grantor, Boyd, acquired title. This raises the doctrine of estoppel by deed, also called the doctrine of after-acquired title. Under this doctrine, when Boyd took title in 1945, title passed to Zittman. Most courts say that title automatically passes to a grantee like Zittman who has a warranty deed. This prevents a breach of Boyd's covenants of title. Zittman's theory is that he is "first in time, first in right" compared to the other claimants. Zittman's deed is early recorded. Because Bliss uses name indexes, a searcher might not find this deed if she looks for adverse conveyances from Boyd only for the years 1945 to 1950, his period of record ownership. There is a split of case authority here. Some states treat early-recorded deeds as validly recorded. Others treat them as unrecorded because of the added burden it would place on searchers to find such instruments. Under the former rule, Zittman wins the case—Zittman still has good title. Under the latter rule, Zittman wins only if none of the subsequent grantees qualifies as a bona fide purchaser. The language of the Bliss recording act shows it is a notice act. Camilla or Drake may have been a BFP—paying value and taking without actual or inquiry notice of Zittman's claim. Then Mary could prevail under the BFP shelter rule. But it seems Mary does not need to prove this. She is a BFP—she paid value, and the facts say she had never heard of Zittman prior to litigation.

In a few states, Camilla, because she takes by quitclaim deed, is disqualified from asserting BFP status. Camilla's successors, Drake and Mary, each got a warranty deed. Camilla's quitclaim deed should not affect Drake's or Mary's status as a potential BFP.

Lucy has an unlikely path to success. She recorded in 1978, eight years after taking a deed from Camilla. If Zittman's early-recorded deed is deemed unrecorded, Lucy has a better claim than Zittman, provided that Camilla or Lucy was a BFP (paid value without notice of Zittman). However, Drake took a deed and recorded it in 1971 before Lucy recorded. If Drake is a BFP, this cuts off Lucy's title. If Drake is not a BFP, then Mary may be a BFP as against Lucy. There is a split of authority on whether late-recorded deeds are validly recorded, just as there is for early-recorded deeds. If Lucy's deed is deemed unrecorded, Mary apparently is a BFP. For Lucy to prevail, (1) Drake must not be a BFP, (2) the state must treat Zittman's early-recorded deed as unrecorded, and (3) the state must treat Lucy's late-recorded deed as validly recorded. The combination of (2) and (3) is possible, though unlikely, because the policy concerns related to the expanded search burdens appear to be the same in both cases.

Price definitely should not prevail, whether or not he paid value for the property in the belief his grantor, Otto, had good title. The prior link in his chain of title, the Norton-Otto deed, is a wild deed. Because Bliss uses name indexes, it would be impossible for a person searching title to the property, using the name "Drake" and working back (or using the state and working forward) to find either the Otto deed or the Price deed. Thus, both deeds are wild deeds and are deemed unrecorded. Mary is a BFP—she paid value, she had no actual notice of Price's claim, and no facts point to inquiry notice. Thus, Mary prevails as against Price. It does not matter whether Price can produce a deed from Drake or someone else to Norton. While such a deed could link Price to the chain of title, it is too late. The issue is whether Mary could have found Price's interest by searching the records when she bought in 2003.

The utility easement is not relevant to the question asked. The easement is apparently valid, and none of the parties is contesting the easement (the company is not a party to the quiet title litigation).

SAMPLE ANSWER TO QUESTION 9

Karen is not your client. You do not have privity with her, and your client is the Bank. At the same time, you may owe a duty to Karen in such a situation where you know that she is not represented by an attorney and you have reason to know that she may be relying on you for legal advice. In such a case, you may have a legal duty to explain the transactions more fully to Karen, and this would include informing her that the Bank's interest is not the same as hers. The Bank has a different interest in the loan documents, such as wanting a prepayment penalty or the like. Karen might be better served by a mortgage without such a penalty or with different terms. Furthermore, the Bank is interested in the value of the property, but she may be interested in uses or restrictions affecting the home. These may be contained in other documents and may be of little interest to the Bank. An example might be a restriction on owning pets or on parking a vehicle on the street overnight. In order to reduce this risk, one should give a full notice and disclaimer to Karen, making sure that she understands that you represent the Bank, that her interests may not be the same as the Bank's, and that she should seek independent counsel. If you are deemed to owe her a duty, you are also in the bind of dual representation because you then owe duties to parties that have conflicting interests in the transaction.

SAMPLE ANSWER TO QUESTION 10

You should tell Moesha that she will not be getting a deed in her transaction. A cooperative unit involves a special kind of ownership. The entire project is held by a not-for-profit corporation, and the individual residents buy stock in the cooperative entity. The stock that will be assigned to her at closing will give her a right to a lease of the designated unit that she has contracted to buy. She will assume responsibility for her percentage share of any blanket mortgage on the entire property plus any mortgage that she takes out and secures by her stock and leasehold rights to the unit she is buying. Thus, she will get a stock interest and a leasehold interest, not a deed.

SAMPLE ANSWER TO QUESTION 11

1. The "Transfer of Property" provision is a type of "due-on-sale" clause, which serves to protect the Bank from risks associated with a transfer of ownership of the mortgaged property to another person. The Bank has dealt with Mary in connection with its assessment of the medical office building project. Its willingness to make the loan is based in part on an expectation that after project completion Mary will manage the property competently and responsibly, thereby generating funds to be used to repay the permanent mortgage loan. This provision is intended to give the Bank the right to approve or disapprove any transfer that it believes might result in less competent

management. From Mary's perspective, this provision increases risk for her because it makes her asset much less liquid. In the absence of an express restriction, a mortgagor has the right to sell the mortgaged property, at any time to any person, without the need to obtain the mortgagee's consent. Mary could sell the office building, with her buyer agreeing to assume the Bank's mortgage or to take title subject to that mortgage.

2. Mary's preference would be deletion of the provision in its entirety. As indicated above, the default rule as to a borrower's right to transfer the collateral is one of free alienability: She could sell the building at any time, without having to obtain the Bank's consent or prepay the mortgage. It is unlikely that the Bank will agree to wholesale deletion. Instead, as Mary's attorney, our strategy should be to propose revisions that specify the conditions under which she will be entitled to sell or transfer all or part of her ownership interest. For example, language could be added specifying that the Bank will not unreasonably withhold its consent to a proposed transfer. In addition, the anti-transfer language of the provision is broad enough that it might be triggered by Mary's entering into leases of space in the building, junior mortgages, or even the grant of an easement across the property. As Mary's attorney, we may propose language that specifies our client's rights to engage in such transactions.

3. The Bank has several possible concerns. First, it's not clear whether the provision applies to involuntary transfers (such as a transfer pursuant to a judgment lien or incident to the borrower's bankruptcy) as well as transfers voluntarily made by the borrower. Second, the anti-transfer language might not be interpreted to extend to space leases and to junior mortgages. If the Bank in fact wants the right to approve leasing and junior financing, the language needs to be strengthened. Third, there is a loophole with respect to the sentence dealing with stock, which reads, "This prohibition shall apply to any sale or transfer of stock or partnership interest of the Borrower, if Borrower is a corporation or partnership." The facts state that Mary 2012 Inc. will be wholly owned by an existing closely held corporation, of which Mary is the majority shareholder. Although Mary will violate the prohibition if she causes her closely held corporation to sell shares of Mary 2012 Inc., nothing prohibits her from selling her shares in the existing closely held corporation.

SAMPLE ANSWER TO QUESTION 12

The three-party agreement is used to link all three of the parties together in recognition of the cooperative relationship that exists among them in completing the proposed project. The first of the two primary legal functions of the agreement is to put all of the parties in privity with each other. This gives each a direct contract action against any of the other parties if they do not live up to the transaction. The second legal function is to give each a right of specific performance against the other parties. The developer needs both loans to do the deal and avoid losing its equity. The construction lender wants to be sure it has the developer bound to the terms of its loan, and it also needs to know that the permanent lender is bound to do the take-out. If the permanent lender fails to do the take-out, the construction lender will not be paid off when expected. The permanent lender needs to know that the developer and the construction lender will not shop around for better (cheaper) long-term financing in the event of market changes during construction. The three-party agreement links all of the parties and their underlying undertakings.

SAMPLE ANSWER TO QUESTION 13

Each strategy poses a problem. A lender has an obligation, by regulation, to serve the community. At issue is the description or nature of that community and the service to be provided. Both redlining and greenlining are illegal. Redlining involves the identification of areas within the community in which the bank will not make loans. This is particularly problematic when the areas have a high correlation to race.

Greenlining is a more recent problem and raises questions about the ability of a business to define its own market. Illegal greenlining activities involve defining a market in such a way as to not serve given areas of a community that one should be serving. In other words, the government's definition of the community may be different from that of the Bank. If the pursuit of certain greenlined areas results in underservice to areas that have a high correlation to race, the Bank may be held to be committing racial discrimination in its lending practices. Strategy 1 is similar to a practice that was used by some banks in the Washington, D.C., area, and they got in trouble for not serving the community in which they operated. In other words, *community* is defined as a broad geographic space rather than a segmented market based on customer profiles. Strategy 2 has the same problems as strategy 1. The way the market is defined and the way the advertising takes place foster a result that ends up excluding people with identifiable racial characteristics. Strategy 3 seems to present an understandable attempt to remedy a past wrong. On the other hand, the Bank proposes taking actions based on race and will end up discriminating against a number of potential customers within the community. Note that the focus on lending to Asians would also work to exclude African Americans, Hispanics, and Native Americans, as well as whites. The Bank should be advised against each of the above strategies as presented.

SAMPLE ANSWER TO QUESTION 14

Dual representation is sometimes permissible in real estate transactions, subject to certain conditions. There are three prongs to the ethics rules that apply in this situation:

1. The lawyer must believe that dual representation will not have an adverse effect on either client, the vendor, or the purchaser.
2. The lawyer must disclose the fact of dual representation to both parties and apprise them of the risks entailed by dual representation.
3. Both parties must give their informed consent to the dual representation.

Provided the lawyer does these three things, she may represent both vendor and purchaser in drafting the installment land contract. She should not participate in the negotiation of contract terms. This is a high-risk endeavor, and many real estate attorneys would refuse to represent both parties in connection with an installment land contract. It will be hard to draw a line between drafting and negotiation. Moreover, the installment land contract raises special concerns for dual representation that are not present in the typical executory contract of sale. The long-term nature of the parties' relationship, remedies issues relating to forfeiture and redemption, and an imbalance of bargaining positions, which is often present between the parties (the land contract is called a "poor man's mortgage"), make dual representation problematic.

SAMPLE ANSWER TO QUESTION 15

This is a type of problem that's extremely common with respect to the sale of single-family homes, both used homes as well as new ones. Closing is just about to take place, and at the last minute a problem arises with respect to the condition of the property or the performance of some other obligation of the seller. Judy has the legal right to delay closing, telling Frank she will not close until he installs all three major kitchen appliances. This option, however, is not attractive because she will lose her favorable mortgage interest rate.

Judy might simply close her purchase tomorrow, trusting that Frank will keep his word and install all three major kitchen appliances within the next week or two. The risk is that once Frank has the entire price, he may lack the incentive to perform. He may delay, may do less than perfect installation work, or may even attempt to install a substitute appliance that isn't the same quality that Judy expects. If Judy doesn't get anything in writing with respect to Frank's post-closing obligation, it's even possible that Frank will argue that the parties agreed he did not have to supply the appliances, or that there was no deadline by which he had to make the installation. It's even possible that Frank will bring up the doctrine of merger, asserting that any obligation he had to install the appliances ended at closing (although a court would likely conclude that merger would not apply here, stating that a promise to install appliances is a "collateral promise" unrelated to title to the property).

Judy's best choice is to close tomorrow, with part of the purchase price put in escrow until Frank has properly installed the correct appliances. A title company or other independent professional should hold the escrowed funds pursuant to a written agreement among the three parties (Judy, Frank, escrow holder) that explains the terms of the escrow and what must take place before Frank receives the escrowed money. As to dollar amount, from Judy's point of view the escrowed funds should exceed the retail cost of the appliances and the installation cost that a third-party installer would charge, in the event Frank defaults. The escrow agent owes a duty to both parties and should only release the funds when all parties agree.

SAMPLE ANSWER TO QUESTION 16

First, we will consider the potential action for specific performance. This is an equitable remedy and is therefore entirely within the discretion of the court. Giovanni will have to show that he stands ready, willing, and able to deliver the property on the stated contract terms. This should be easy, since the down market has made a favorable resale unlikely. Giovanni will also have to show that he has completed the conditions required of him under the contract. It seems that he has in obtaining the survey and title information. Under the traditional rule, a buyer can get specific performance because each property is considered unique and not fungible. Under the doctrine of mutuality of remedy, this means that Giovanni could get specific performance because Gina would be able to get it if the tables were turned. Under the emerging modern rule, however, Giovanni would have to show that he has an independent basis for specific performance. This may have some chance if the market is so bad that a court can be persuaded to think of a contract buyer as an almost unique situation under the given circumstances. It may at least give the court reason to stick with the traditional rule or to focus on other elements in permitting Giovanni to get specific performance.

The remedy at law is for damages. Contract damages are to be compensatory and not punitive. They cover loss of bargain or lost expectation damages plus out-of-pocket costs. Damages are based on the difference between the contract price and the fair market value at the time of the breach. Here we have no firm evidence of the fair market value at the time of the breach. We do have the statement of the broker that might indicate something about the value of comparable sales at the time of the breach, but this is not by itself enough to show fair market value at the time of the breach. Thus, more evidence is needed here, but if we work with the broker price estimate, we will see a loss of $40,000 on the contract.

Giovanni should also get the cost of the survey and the title information. Because a seller has a duty to mitigate, Giovanni should try to resell the home and use the survey and title information for the new sale. This way, he can save some or all of the expense, offsetting the damages he can collect from Gina. Note that the longer the time period is between the breach and getting a new contract, the less informative the new contract price will be with reference to the fair market value of the property at the time of the breach.

As to the broker commission, the traditional rule holds that the broker earns a commission upon finding a ready, willing, and able buyer. The custom of paying the fee at the closing is merely a convenience to the customer, and closing is not a condition to earning the fee. Some courts now imply a successful closing as a condition, but in the absence of an express contract term, this remains a problem. The seller is fully responsible for the broker fee, but this cost may be a cost of the transaction that can be recovered as damages. Furthermore, some courts hold a buyer directly liable for the fee when the buyer wrongfully breaches based on third-party beneficiary theory. That is, the buyer knows that the broker will earn a fee as a result of the transaction, and when the buyer wrongfully breaches, she knows that the broker will have an economic injury. The broker is a third-party beneficiary under the contract between buyer and seller, so buyer should pay when, but for buyer's breach, the commission would have been earned.

SAMPLE ANSWER TO QUESTION 17

1. Ben owes Sheila $80,000, the unpaid purchase price. Sheila is an unsecured creditor unless she has a vendor's lien or an equitable mortgage. The issue is how to interpret the unusual language in the warranty deed. Did the parties intend Sheila would have no lien unless and until Ben signed a mortgage, or does Sheila presently have a lien? She has two theories: a vendor's lien and an equitable mortgage. First, whenever a person sells real property on credit, a vendor's lien is implied by operation of law to secure the unpaid price. Thus, Sheila has a vendor's lien unless the language of the deed is construed to waive it. Second, one type of equitable mortgage is a bargained-for promise to give a mortgage. In equity, the promise is enforceable. Sheila should be able to enforce the language in the deed, which seems to reflect a promise that Ben would give a mortgage. The doctrine of merger does not get Ben off the hook because the promise is set forth in the deed.

    Julio is a creditor because he is entitled to a $5,000 commission. Although the property did not sell for the listing price, Sheila accepted Ben's offer of $100,000. Since Julio found Ben, it does not matter whether the listing contract was an exclusive listing, an exclusive agency, or open listing. It also does not matter which rule the state follows on when a broker earns a commission (the traditional rule that the commission is earned upon finding a ready, willing, and able buyer or the rule that the sale must close before the commission is earned) because Sheila closed the sale. The financing extended to Ben does not affect Julio's commission; Julio can collect the entire commission now—he does not have to wait one year. Again, it does not matter which rule the state follows on when the broker earns the commission. Although Julio is a creditor, he has no lien, and he cannot get one by unilaterally filing an Affidavit of Lien. The timing of the filing of the Affidavit is not material; had Julio filed the Affidavit before the deed from Sheila to Ben, he still would not have a valid lien.

    Aggressive and Money both clearly have valid mortgages. The fact that Aggressive's mortgage secures antecedent debt does not invalidate the lien. It only impacts priority under certain circumstances.

2. Sheila argues that she is "first in time, first in right" and that the deed language suffices to record her vendor's lien or equitable mortgage.

    Aggressive, who is second in time, argues (a) Sheila has no lien or (b) the deed language is too ambiguous to impart constructive or inquiry notice of her lien to subsequent purchasers.

    Money has no plausible claim to first priority. At best, it is junior to Aggressive. The fact that Aggressive's mortgage secures antecedent debt does not give Money priority over Aggressive (the only function of antecedent debt is to disqualify Aggressive from being a BFP; this is not the issue here). The name misspelling is not material because it is in the *grantee's* name. A searcher looking for adverse conveyances from Ben will use the grantor's indexes. Aggressive is properly recorded even if the state follows the rule that accurate indexing is necessary for an item to be recorded.

3. The answer to part 2 demonstrates two plausible rankings of priority. The first is (1) Sheila, (2) Aggressive, (3) Money. The second priority scheme results if Sheila has a lien, but the deed language is not sufficient to give record notice of that lien: (1) Sheila is prior to Aggressive (it is

not a BFP because it took the mortgage to secure antecedent debt and did not extend new value), (2) Aggressive is prior to Money, (3) Money is prior to Sheila because Money qualifies as a BFP. This means we have circular priorities, a mess a court would have to sort out.

The statute is probably a race-notice act ("good faith" implies lack of notice), but might be interpreted as a race act. This choice does not affect the priorities; none of the lien claimants was in possession so as to give inquiry notice to successors. Nor is it relevant that Ben took possession on September 7. The deed covenants do not matter either.

4. A necessary party is a person who must be joined as a defendant in judicial foreclosure to give the purchaser at the foreclosure sale title in the shape it was in when the foreclosing mortgagee acquired its lien. Under the first alternative in part 3, Ben and Money are necessary parties. Both have interests that should be extinguished by the foreclosure. Sheila is a proper party. This allows a court to make certain her claim to a prior lien on the property. Under the second alternative (circular priorities), Ben, Sheila, and Money should all be considered necessary parties.

Glossary

Abstract of title.   A written distillation of information from the public records pertaining to the title of a particular piece of property.

Accounting profit.   The excess financial returns of a particular activity relative to the costs of that activity.

Adjustable-rate mortgage (ARM).   A mortgage loan in which the interest rate changes during the term of the loan.

Adverse possession.   The act of wrongly possessing land owned by another so as to begin the running of the statute of limitations against the true owner, provided that certain conditions are met.

Alt-A mortgage.   A loan made on slightly different terms than a standard prime mortgage loan. Generally, it is slightly more risky because it does not involve a full document package to support the loan, or because the borrower is a slightly greater credit risk than those in the pool for prime loans. An Alt-A mortgage is of lower quality than a standard prime rate mortgage loan but of higher quality than a subprime loan.

American Land Title Association (ALTA).   A trade organization that issues the vast majority of standardized title insurance policy forms.

Annual percentage rate (APR).   A calculation of the cost of a loan using a federal formula set forth in the Real Estate Settlement Procedures Act.

Anti-deficiency legislation.   A statute that transfers the risk of market declines in real estate values from borrowers to lenders by prohibiting a deficiency judgment upon foreclosure.

Appraisal.   A measurement of the fair market value for any particular type or parcel of property.

"As Is" term.   A real estate disclaimer clause utilized in real property sales, indicating that the property will be sold in its then existing physical condition.

Bona fide purchaser (BFP).   A good faith buyer who pays value without notice of any defects in the seller's title or competing claims.

Broker.   A properly licensed information specialist who facilitates real estate transactions.

Buyer's broker.   A broker who represents the buyer of property rather than the seller.

Buy-sell agreement.   See "three-party agreement."

Caveat emptor.   The common law rule of "buyer beware," where, in the absence of express agreement or misrepresentation, the purchaser of real property is expected to make his own examination and conclusions as to the condition of the land.

Chain of title.   The history of ownership of a parcel of land from its first link, usually the sovereign, to its last link, the present owner.

Closing.   The completion of a contract for the sale of land by the seller conveying the property and the purchaser paying the price.

Collateralized mortgage obligation.   A special type of mortgage-backed security issued against the income stream of a pool of mortgages.

Commitment.   A promise to fulfill the requirements and expectations of an agreement, as in a loan commitment where the lender agrees to make funds available on agreed terms and conditions.

Comprehensive Environmental Response, Compensation, and Liability Act (CERCLA).   A federal "Superfund" statute under which owners and operators of properties containing hazardous waste have statutory liability for the cost of cleanup.

Condemnation.   The governmental taking of private property for a public use, requiring just compensation payment.

Condominium.   A form of ownership where each owner acquires a single dwelling unit in a multiunit project, together with an undivided interest in the common areas and facilities.

Construction loan.   A short-term, high-risk loan funded against the expectation of success for a project that is to be built.

Contract for deed.   See "installment land contract."

Convertible mortgage.   In the residential context, an adjustable-rate mortgage that can be converted to a fixed-rate mortgage; in the commercial context, a lien position that can be converted, in full or part, to an equity position in the property.

Convey.   To transfer or pass an interest in real property from a grantor to a grantee.

Cooperative.   A form of joint ownership where title to all of the real estate is held by a corporation, with each shareholder having the right to a dwelling unit pursuant to a long-term lease from the corporation.

Cramdown.   Under the Bankruptcy Code, a Chapter 11 reorganization method affecting the undersecured creditor, whose debt is split into two parts: a secured portion equal to the fair market value of the collateral and an unsecured portion equal to the remaining debt.

Curative act.   A statutory provision under which instruments bearing certain defects are conclusively presumed valid after the passage of a specified number of years after recordation.

Deed.   An instrument that conveys an interest in real estate, effecting and documenting the transfer of title from the grantor to the grantee.

Deed in lieu of foreclosure.   When a borrower is upside down or under water, she may be willing to make a deal with a willing lender to simply deed the title to the property to the lender in return for a release from the mortgage obligation.

Deed of trust.   An instrument used to secure a loan by granting an interest in the real property to a trustee, who is authorized to foreclose for the lender's benefit.

Deficiency judgment.   The monetary claim a mortgagee has against a mortgagor when a foreclosure sale fails to satisfy the secured obligation.

Depreciation.   The decrease in value of land improvements, such as buildings, through physically wearing out or becoming obsolete.

Derivatives.   Financial investments related to secondary mortgage market activity. An interest rate swap is an example.

Draw down loan.   A loan in which the full loan amount is not released to the borrower at the time of closing, but is instead dispersed by scheduled amounts correlated with the value of improvements added to a property.

Due-on-sale clause.   A mortgage provision requiring the full payment of the outstanding loan amount if a borrower transfers the property covered by the mortgage.

Economic profit.   The excess financial returns available from a given market transaction relative to the returns available from other similar market choices.

Eminent domain.   The government power to take private property for public use through condemnation or expropriation.

Encumbrance.   A nonpossessory right or interest in the property held by a third person that reduces the property's market value, restricts its use, or imposes an obligation on the property owner.

Environmental audit.   An inspection of property for environmental purposes.

Equitable conversion.   The splitting of real property title upon the signing of a binding contract, where the seller retains legal title and the buyer acquires equitable title.

Equitable mortgage.   A lien on real property that a court of equity will recognize and enforce in accordance with the clearly ascertained intent of the parties.

Equitable subrogation.   A doctrine allowing a lender who refinances a senior mortgage loan to take over the senior's priority when foreclosing.

Equity of redemption.   The process by which a borrower redeems property after default by making full payment of the mortgage debt before foreclosure.

Equity participation.   A lender's right to share in the equity value of a property.

Escrow.   To hold money or documents for a stated purpose and under certain conditions.

Estoppel by deed.   A doctrine that provides that any title subsequently acquired by a grantor who has already warranted the title to the grantee passes directly to the grantee by virtue of the warranty.

Fair Housing Act (FHA).   A federal statute that prevents discrimination in the sale, rental, and financing of housing.

Fair value statute.   A statute that protects borrowers by permitting a deficiency judgment only to the extent the debt exceeds the proven fair value of the foreclosed property.

Fannie Mae (Federal National Mortgage Association).   A federally chartered corporation, owned by private shareholders, that facilitates the secondary mortgage market for residential loans.

Federal Housing Administration (FHA).   A federal agency created in 1934 to provide for the development of mortgage insurance programs; offers a variety of mortgage forms.

Federal Trade Commission (FTC).   A federal agency responsible for the protection of consumers who purchase goods and services for personal or household use.

Fixed-rate mortgage.   A mortgage loan in which the interest rate specified when the loan is made remains the same throughout the term of loan.

Fixture.   A chattel that becomes so related to particular real estate by virtue of affixation to the land that an interest in it arises under real estate law.

Foreclosure.   The process, after default, by which the lender gets value from the collateral to repay part or all of the debt.

Fraudulent conveyance.   A conveyance or transfer of property that has the purpose or effect of defrauding or hindering a creditor.

Freddie Mac (Federal Home Loan Mortgage Corporation).   A federally authorized corporation created to increase the marketability of all mortgages through development of uniform standards to facilitate the purchase and sale of mortgages in the secondary mortgage market.

Garn-St. Germain Depository Institutions Act.   A 1982 congressional act that preempts state laws that protected mortgagors from lender enforcement of due-on-sale clauses and that covers a variety of market reforms.

Ginnie Mae (Government National Mortgage Association).   A corporation established within the Department of Housing and Urban Development that concentrates on the secondary mortgage market to increase liquidity and investment opportunities among originators.

Greenlining.   An illegal discriminatory practice where lenders identify wealthy neighborhoods where they will pursue a customer base and, in the process, exclude a disproportionate number of racial minorities.

Ground lease.   An alternative financing arrangement where improvements are built on a long-term lease of the land or "ground" rather than on a fee simple estate.

Holder in due course.   A person who takes by negotiation a negotiable instrument, having possession of the instrument, taken in good faith, without notice of any defenses or claims or that the instrument is overdue or has been dishonored, through a negotiated transfer for which value is paid.

Home equity loan.   A loan secured by a second or junior mortgage upon the existence of adequate property value and sufficient borrower creditworthiness.

Home Mortgage Disclosure Act.   A 1975 federal statute requiring lending institutions to keep records and report on lending activities based on a number of factors, including the race of the loan applicant.

Homeowners association.   An organization that enforces recorded covenants and servitudes and often manages common areas and facilities and enacts rules and regulations.

Home Ownership and Equity Protection Act (HOEPA).   A federal statute that regulates certain high-cost residential mortgage loans.

Illinois land trust.   A legal form for holding property where the trustee is deemed to hold both the legal and the equitable title to the property, while the beneficiaries of the trust are considered to have only a personal property interest.

Implied warranty.   A warranty that arises from the situation or context in which a transaction takes place based on reasonable or fair expectations, given the nature of the exchange.

Installment land contract.   An executory contract under which the buyer takes possession at the contract signing and pays the purchase price in installments, with the seller being obligated to transfer title by deed when final payment is made.

Insurable title.   A title of sufficient quality that it is insurable by a reputable title insurance company.

Interim loan.   A short-term loan usually obtained to pay for construction costs or to bridge a gap between present and future loan commitments.

Interstate Land Sales Full Disclosure Act.   A 1968 federal disclosure statute applied to the sale of unimproved lots in subdivisions with 25 or more lots, requiring a developer to file a registration before offering any lots for sale and to provide each prospective purchaser a detailed property report.

Land description.   A description of land that must be contained in both real estate contracts and deeds, and that must be in written form to comply with the statute of frauds; generally described in terms of (1) metes and bounds, (2) a government survey, or (3) a subdivision plat.

Land trust.   A legal form for holding joint ownership of property, authorized by state common law or state statute, that places legal title in the name of a trustee.

Lease.   An agreement that gives rise to the relationship of landlord and tenant or lessor and lessee of real estate; an estate for a specific term.

Letter of intent.   A preliminary writing that seeks to map out the basis for a contractual undertaking; often it is unclear whether the parties intend to be legally bound prior to the subsequent execution of a formal contract.

Lien.   A right or claim against some interest in property to secure an obligation, created by an agreement or by operation of law.

Like-kind exchange.   A nontaxable event for income tax purposes that involves a person's exchange of real property for property that qualifies as like kind.

Lis pendens.   A method of asserting, on the public record, a potential claim or conflicting interest against title to real estate when litigation is filed and pending.

Loan participation.   The method of lender risk spreading where two or more lenders join in a loan, with each providing a portion of the amount to the borrower.

Market risk.   The risk associated with general market forces, such as temporal and transactional risk, that can affect the profitability of any given transaction.

Marketable record title act.   Legislation that limits the period of time covered by title searches and renders more titles marketable by eliminating stale interests.

Marketable title.   A title that enables the holder not only to hold the land, but also to hold it in peace, and if there is a wish to sell, to be reasonably sure that no flaw or doubt will come up to disturb its marketable value.

Marshalling of assets.   A rule of equity that protects a junior creditor when a senior creditor has access to multiple funds or multiple items of collateral; the assets are ranked in order, requiring that the senior creditor first proceed against the assets that are not available to the junior creditor.

Merchantable title.   See "marketable title."

Merger doctrine.   A doctrine that provides that everything that came before closing is merged into the documents exchanged at closing.

Mortgage.   An instrument used to secure a loan by granting the lender a security interest in the real property.

Mortgage-backed security.   The general term for a variety of secondary mortgage market securities issued against the value, based on the income flow, represented by a pool of real estate mortgages.

Mortgage broker.   An intermediary that connects prospective borrowers with lenders.

Mortgage Electronic Registration System (MERS).   A system that facilitates sales of residential mortgage loans by having MERS act as the mortgagee of record and as nominee for purchasers of loans.

Mortgage insurance.   The insurance generally required for any residential loan that exceeds 80 percent of the appraised value of the property; protects the lender against risk of loss in the event a borrower defaults and the property is sold through foreclosure for a price less than the outstanding debt.

Mortgagee.   One who takes or receives a mortgage—the lender.

Mortgagor.   One who grants a mortgage on his property—the borrower.

Mutuality of remedy.   A traditional rule positing that, for every type of remedy for breach or default under a real estate contract available to one party, a mutual remedy should be available to the other party.

Negative pledge.   A method of creating an unsecured loan where the lender identifies a particular asset owned by the borrower and the borrower promises not to convey or encumber that asset until the loan is repaid.

Note. See "promissory note."

One-action rule. A rule utilized by a handful of states that limits the mortgagee to a single action that must include foreclosure and may include, if appropriate, a deficiency judgment; the action proceeds against the promissory note and mortgage instrument together.

Parol evidence rule. A rule prohibiting the admission of prior written or prior contemporaneous oral evidence that adds to or that is inconsistent with the final written agreement between the parties.

Performance zoning. A regulation prescribing the use to which real estate within designated districts may be put, based on attaining particular performance outcomes with respect to the use.

Permanent loan. A commercial real estate loan with a term generally between 10 and 30 years, with the borrower making installment payments out of income revenue from the property.

Planned unit development (P.U.D.). A zoning technique where a developer organizes density and use allocations of property by establishing blanket restrictions affecting an entire community.

Points. Up-front fees for home mortgage loans charged in addition to the interest on the loan; one point is equal to 1 percent of the loan amount.

Predatory lending. Lending that exploits lower-income borrowers and generally treats one identifiable group of borrowers differently than similarly situated borrowers of another race or group.

Prepayment penalty. A monetary penalty for paying off a loan early; more common in commercial loans because many state statutes prohibit or limit residential loan prepayment penalties.

Promissory note. An instrument, separate and apart from a mortgage, evidencing the debtor's promise to pay the loan.

Purchase money mortgage (PMM). Any mortgage in which credit is extended to enable the debtor to buy or acquire the property on which the mortgage is placed; in common usage, generally denotes seller financing.

Quitclaim deed. A deed that has no covenants of title; the grantor makes no representations or warranties concerning the state of title, and the grantee bears all risk associated with the quality of title.

Real estate investment trust (REIT). A vehicle for real estate investing created by Congress; functions like a public real estate company, selling investment opportunities to the public and using the money to invest in the ownership, development, and management of commercial properties.

Real Estate Settlement Procedures Act (RESPA). A federal statute that regulates residential closings; under RESPA, prior to closing the lender must disclose to the borrower the annual percentage rate (APR) in addition to the quoted rate of interest that will appear in the promissory note.

Realtor. A broker who is a member of the National Association of Realtors, a trade association.

Reciprocal negative easement.   An implied servitude created when a subdivider begins selling lots, expressly imposing most lots with the same restrictive covenant pursuant to a common plan for the neighborhood; the subdivider's retained lots become similarly restricted by implication.

Record title.   A contract title requiring proof of the status of title, gathered solely from deeds and other instruments that are recorded in the public records for recording interests in real property.

Recording act.   A state statute modifying the common law "first in time, first in right" rule by setting up a recording system that provides for the recording of instruments that affect title to land; the three basic types of recording acts are the race, notice, and race-notice statutes.

Redlining.   An illegal discriminatory practice where lenders refuse to make mortgage loans on properties in specified neighborhoods with large minority populations because of alleged deteriorating conditions.

Rent seeking.   The manipulation of legal opportunities in the pursuit of economic gain where a person is willing to spend almost as much money on changing an unfavorable legal rule as he estimates that a favorable rule will add to the value of the property.

Retainage.   The process where a lender holds back some portion of loan disbursements due to the borrower, pending completion of a project in accordance with the plans and specifications and to the satisfaction of the lender.

Reverse annuity mortgage (RAM).   A mortgage marketed to senior citizens who own their homes as a major source of wealth subject to little or no mortgage debt; the homeowner is paid the value of the home over time as a way to provide supplemental retirement income.

Sale in gross.   A sale by tract without regard to quantity; lump-sum pricing or the presence of the words "more or less" evidences such sales.

Sale-leaseback.   An alternative form of financing where the owner of property sells the property for cash and leases it back under a long-term lease.

Second mortgage.   A mortgage of property secured by existing equity and ranking in priority below a first mortgage.

Secondary mortgage market.   The wide range of mortgage loan activities consisting of the packaging, pooling, buying, selling, and reselling of whole loans, loan participations, or bonds or securities backed by mortgages.

Secured transaction.   A method of collateralizing the obligation of the debtor by the creation of a security interest that is governed by Article 9 of the UCC.

Shared appreciation mortgage (SAM).   A mortgage in which a lender gives a borrower a favorable interest rate on a loan in exchange for a percentage interest in the equity appreciation of the property.

Short sale.   When a borrower is upside down or under water, she may try to sell her home for less than the mortgage amount, assuming that the lender will agree to a price. Lender may agree because a reasonably good payment on a short sale may be quicker and easier than the expected payout on a foreclosure.

Statute of frauds.   A statute that prohibits the enforcement of oral agreements unless there is a writing signed by the party to be charged; the writing must generally set out essential terms, such as the identification of the property to be exchanged, the price, and the names of the parties.

Statute of limitations.   A statute prescribing limitations to the right of action, generally running from the date of the consummation of the transaction, unless brought within a specified period of time.

Statutory redemption.   A mortgagor's right to redeem property after foreclosure; only some states offer this protection.

Subdivision.   The division of a parcel of land into smaller units for sale or development.

Subordination.   The process of making an interest in property that would otherwise be prior in time, and therefore superior, inferior to a later interest.

Subprime mortgage.   Loans made to borrowers not able to qualify for prime and Alt-A mortgages. These are borrowers with a credit score and history that would traditionally be considered weak and marginal.

Survey.   The process of evaluating real property in order to locate the physical limits of a particular parcel of land by the use of physical field evidence, written record evidence, and field measurements.

Swaps.   Interest rate swaps are part of the secondary mortgage market. They are derivatives wherein one party has a variable rate investment and enters an agreement to sell off, or swap the variable rate risk.

Taking.   The act of condemnation or the process of eminent domain used by a government to bypass the reluctance of some property owners to engage in a voluntary or consensual market exchange.

Three-party agreement.   The written agreement that binds together the developer, the construction lender, and the permanent lender, designed to spell out the conditions under which the various parties undertake to work with each other. It is sometimes called a "buy-sell agreement" when it calls for the permanent lender to buy the promissory note held by the construction lender.

Time-share development.   A development consisting of units with use rights, together with shared or common elements and expenses, sold with reference to blocks of time.

Title certificate.   A written reflection of an attorney's professional opinion about the status of title to real estate.

Title covenant.   A warranty of title contained in a deed or another instrument; the six widely recognized title covenants are (1) seisin, (2) right to convey, (3) covenant against encumbrances, (4) covenant of quiet enjoyment, (5) covenant of warranty, and (6) covenant for further assurances.

Title insurance.   A policy of insurance issued by a title insurance company that protects the insured against title risks.

Title opinion.   A written reflection of an attorney's or a title expert's professional opinion about the status of title to real estate.

Title registration.   See "Torrens system."

Title standards. The standards on which a title examiner relies for reviewing and then either approving or disapproving the quality of title as reflected by the records.

Torrens system. A system for registration of titles to land where, for each registered parcel of land, the government issues a certificate of title that is intended to be conclusive.

Toxic loans. Loans that are substantially degraded. The mortgaged property does not cover the outstanding loan amount, and the borrowers are unable to pay the amount owed. With the mortgage market collapse of 2007-2009, many mortgage-backed securities were greatly diminished in value because they were issued against toxic mortgages.

Transaction broker. A broker who has an arms'-length relationship with the seller and buyer, not acting as a fiduciary for either party.

Transactional misbehavior. When a party to a transaction tries to change the dynamics of the deal after the deal has been struck.

Transferable development right (TDR). A development and use right that can be used, bought, or sold to enhance the use of property located elsewhere.

Under water. A borrower is under water or upside down when the value of the mortgaged property is less than the outstanding debt.

Uniform Vendor and Purchaser Risk Act. A state statute governing contracts for the sale of real property that allocates the risk of loss between the vendor and the purchaser.

Upside down. A borrower is under water or upside down when the value of the mortgaged property is less than the outstanding debt.

Utility. The value or happiness one derives from a particular thing or activity, measured by the trade-off made between assorted choices.

Value. The measurement of the profit, equity appreciation, or cash flow realized from involvement in a real estate transaction.

Vested right. A right that a landowner can rely on in proceeding with a planned land use.

Warranty deed. A deed containing one or more title covenants; see "title covenants."

Wrap-around mortgage. A junior mortgage for which the principal includes the amount due on the senior mortgage.

Workout. A plan by the borrower and lender to complete a project and avoid the consequences of bankruptcy.

Zoning. Regulation of land use by local governmental authorities exercising the police power to protect the public health, safety, and welfare.

Table of Cases

Table of Statutes

Index